Upgrading And

Maintaining Your PC

www.abacuspub.com

Ulrich Schueller
Hans-Georg Veddeler

Quick Contents

Quick Contents

Table Of Contents

Table Of Contents

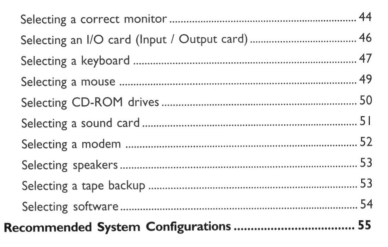

4 What Are Operating Systems 57

Table Of Contents

5   Ergonomics And Its Importance   91

Table Of Contents

Section 2

Components And Their Functions 95

Table Of Contents

7   Processing Data   131

Table Of Contents

8 **Storing And Saving Data** **161**

Table Of Contents

9   Communicating With Your PC   235

Table Of Contents

Section 3

Upgrading In Detail   317

10 Your PC Workshop   319

XV

Table Of Contents

11   Installing New Components   335

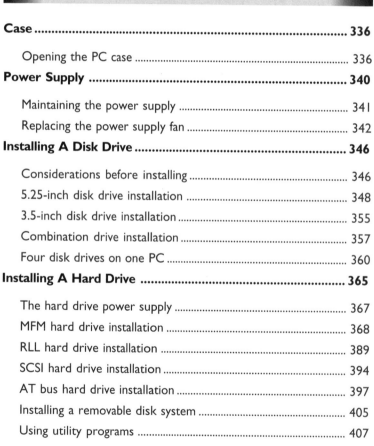

Table Of Contents

Table Of Contents

Table Of Contents

Table Of Contents

Section 4

Appendices   635

What's In This Edition

The one constant about the PC world is that it is always changing. Huge changes have occurred. Prices on components have dropped dramatically while PCs have become faster and more powerful. Users are clamoring for greater hard drive space, faster CD-ROM drives, faster modems and more RAM.

We'll explain the latest terms, hardware and components to you. Don't worry if you're not technically inclined or computer literate. You won't need to be technically inclined or computer literate to use the information in *Upgrading & Maintaining Your PC*. You probably already own the tools you'll need in your PC Workshop when it's time to upgrade your PC. The following summarizes what you'll find in this edition of Upgrading & Maintaining Your PC:

Section 1

Section 1 talks about general information, such as the components in your PC system and how they interact, the importance of ergonomics and tips on what to look for when buying a new PC. This includes tips for buying a new case, CPU, motherboard, hard drives, CD-ROM drives, expansion cards and much more.

Section 2

Section 2 talks about your entire PC system in detail. You'll learn about processors and what they do, including the 486 class of processors and today's super fast Pentium and Pentium class processors (including the Cyrix 6x86 and Advanced Micro Devices AMD-K5).

Section 3

Section 3 describes the steps of upgrading your PC in detail. These upgrades include installing new components (case, power supply, disk drive, hard drive, tape drive backup, CD-ROM drive, motherboard and expansion cards and more). Chapter 12 takes you through the steps involved in building a multimedia PC

Once you've upgraded your PC or bought a new PC, you'll want to know some maintenance tips and hints. Chapter 14 and Chapter 15 provide the necessary information to properly maintain your PC. Chapter 16 describes the companion CD-ROM in detail.

Section 4

Section 4 includes BIOS and hard drive parameters and a glossary of important terms you'll face when upgrading and maintaining your PC.

See Chapter 1 and Chapter 16 for information on installing and using the companion CD-ROM.

Section 1:
General Information

Contents

Introducing The Companion CD-ROM

1

You may not be sure what sort of equipment your computer contains. Perhaps a friend just bought a computer and has no idea what the new PC has "under the hood." This introduces you to the programs on the companion CD-ROM. See Chapter 16 for complete information on installing, loading and using the companion CD-ROM.

The companion CD-ROM contains several programs for checking system info, determining cache benchmarks, finding files and much more.

USING THE COMPANION CD-ROM

You must first load the MENU.EXE program located in the root directory before you can use the companion CD-ROM. When the program is loaded, you will have various buttons to select your utilities. Insert the CD-ROM into your CD-ROM drive. We're assuming in this chapter that the letter assigned to your CD-ROM drive is "D:". If this is not the case, simply substitute your CD-ROM drive letter instead of "D:"

See Chapter 16 for more information on installing and using the companion CD-ROM

Loading the MENU in Windows 3.x

Select the **File/Run...** command in the Windows Program Manager:

Introducing The Companion CD-ROM

Chapter 1

This opens the Run dialog box. Type the following in the "Command Line:":

```
d:\menu.exe
```

The Run dialog box should now look like the following:

Introducing The Companion CD-ROM

Then press the (Enter) key or click the (OK) button. The main MENU program will start. This MENU program is used to install or test various shareware utilities.

Loading the MENU in Windows 95

Select the Start menu and then the **Run...** command:

This opens the Run dialog box. Then type the following in the Run dialog box:

```
d:\menu.exe
```

The Run dialog box should now look like the following:

Chapter 1

Then press the Enter key or click the OK button. The main MENU program will start. This MENU program is used to install or test various shareware utilities.

Introducing The Companion CD-ROM

Installing Adobe's Acrobat Reader

Adobe's Acrobat Reader is a utility allowing you to view PDF files. Three PDF files are available on the companion CD-ROM:

Filename	Information
WRKSHEET.PDF	Printable work sheet form in the book
CATALOG.PDF	Current Abacus Book and Software catalog
MAINBOOK.PDF	Complete Upgrading... book in electronic form

If you already have Acrobat Reader, skip the next steps and go on to the CYRIX notes. Follow these steps to install Acrobat Reader on your hard drive (requires approximately 2 Meg on space on your hard drive). Insert the CD-ROM in your drive and load Windows. Select the **File/Run...** command from the Windows Program Manager. Then type D:\ACROREAD.EXE and press the Enter key.

Simply follow the instructions and prompts which appear on your screen. Double click the Acrobat Reader icon to load it. After Acrobat Reader is loaded, select the **File/Open...** command and select MAINFILE.PDF to view and read *Upgrading & Maintaining Your PC* directly on your PC screen.

Chapter 1 Section 1

Introducing The Companion CD-ROM

Chapter 1

Companion CD-ROM program notes

Many of the programs featured on the CD-ROM are fully functioning *shareware evaluation versions* of the best programs available today. Shareware benefits both the user and the author. By avoiding distribution, packaging, and advertising costs, prices of shareware remains low.

Keep in mind, however, that shareware programs are copyrighted programs (see the "Shareware, freeware and public domain software" information below). Therefore, the authors ask for payment if you use their program(s).

Special Cyrix Instructions

We've included the instructions for performing the Cyrix's upgrade test. This test will determine whether you can upgrade your older 386 PC to a 486 with a Cyrix chip. Please look it over carefully. The files required for this test are in the directory CYRIXTST. Please read the README.TXT in this directory for instructions.

Shareware, freeware and public domain software

Many of the programs included on the CD-ROM are fully functioning "shareware evaluation versions" of the best programs available today. Because shareware is copyrighted, the authors ask for payment if you use their program(s). You may try out the program for a limited time (typically 10 to 30 days) and then decide whether you want to keep it. If you continue to use it, you're requested to send the author a nominal fee.

Shareware benefits both the user and the author as it allows prices to remain low by avoiding distribution, packaging, and advertising costs. The shareware concept allows small software companies and program authors to introduce the application programs they have developed to a wider audience. The programs can be freely distributed and tested for a specific time period before you have to register them. Registration involves paying registration fees, which make you a licensed user of the program. Check the documentation or the program itself for the amount of registration fee and the address where you send the registration form.

Introducing The Companion CD-ROM

After registration you will frequently get the current full version of the program without restrictions and shareware notes as well as the option of purchasing upgraded versions later for a reduced price. As a rule, larger applications include a users manual. Shareware programs usually feature the complete performance range of the full versions. Some programs use special messages to indicate they're shareware versions. The message usually appears immediately after program startup or can be called from the Help menu.

The companion CD-ROM to *Upgrading & Maintaining Your PC* shows the variety of shareware available. To ensure that the program authors continue writing programs and offering them as shareware, we urge you to support the shareware concept by registering the programs that you plan to use permanently.

You'll find program instructions and notes on registration for the shareware programs in special text files located in the program directory of each program. These programs are usually called READ.ME, README.TXT or README.DOC. As a rule, the TXT, WRI or DOC extensions are used for text files, which you can view and print with Windows 95 editors.

Some of the programs on the companion CD-ROM are distributed as freeware or public domain. You can use these programs without paying a registration fee. Keep in mind that freely distributed programs cannot be used for commercial purposes and are sometimes subject to separate restrictions.

The MENU program is a component of the companion CD-ROM. It's neither shareware, freeware nor public domain. Please do not redistribute the MENU program from Abacus.

Chapter

1

Section

1

Introduction

A good starting point for anyone interested in "upgrading" and "maintaining" their PC system is to understand and define these terms.

What is "upgrading"

Upgrading a computer means increasing its performance level. This is normally done by adding hardware, replacing existing hardware with more advanced components or both. For example, you could add a larger hard drive to increase your PC's storage capacity.

You could also install a more powerful processor by replacing your computer's motherboard. This would enable your PC to perform tasks that the old processor couldn't handle, such as the following:

❖ Faster screen redraws which is usually important when you use graphic applications.

❖ Faster data calculation and processing.

❖ Faster loading and executing of applications, especially graphic applications.

❖ Running Windows (Windows 95) and Windows-based software faster.

So, by upgrading, your entire system becomes more powerful and efficient.

11

Introduction

However, upgrading also involves using compatible components, expanding your PC's hardware with specific applications and understanding how these components work.

Upgrading a system involves more than simply adding memory and a faster processor. The main reason for upgrading a PC is to increase the efficiency of the main application.

Obviously a computer used as a CAD workstation and a computer used for general office work have different hardware requirements. However, even two CAD based PCs can be configured quite differently. For example, one may use a different operating system instead of DOS, Windows for Workgroups or Windows 95.

Multiple operating systems have become more popular due to the increased capabilities of today's software and hardware. So, if you use OS/2 Warp, you can start your computer and run in either IBM PC DOS, Microsoft MS-DOS or OS/2 Warp. This ability is called *dual operating mode*. This is an advantage for many users. Other users require less capability and need to use one particular operating system.

Your experience level is another factor you should consider before upgrading a PC. The best hardware and software combination won't increase your efficiency unless you know how to operate the application properly. It's often useful to improve your computing skills before investing in new hardware.

What is "maintaining"

Maintaining your computer is a simple idea. It involves understanding the "insides" of your computer system. It's important to understand the components and how they operate. By understanding these components, you can keep them in good working condition. Often, maintaining your computer requires some troubleshooting when problems occur. With this book as your guide, you can perform simple maintenance or advanced upgrades. It's your choice.

Again, by understanding how the components work and relate to each other, you can isolate problems and find solutions. You can determine the best upgrading strategy for your PC by reading the information on PC systems in Chapter 3.

●●●

WHAT WE'LL TALK ABOUT

We've written this book for anyone interested in upgrading, maintaining and even repairing their PCs. This group of people probably consists of every PC user.

The areas on which we focus relating to upgrading and maintaining your PC include the following:

❖ The CPU and especially the Pentium (the brains of your PC)

❖ Memory installation and configuration

❖ Hard drives, hard drive installation and hard drive interfaces

❖ Video displays

❖ The latest storage devices (for example, 8x and 10x CD-ROM drives)

❖ Audio components (sound cards)

❖ Communication devices such as modems

❖ Software

❖ Plug and Play (PnP) installation

❖ Multimedia

●●●

WHAT'S IN THIS EDITION

The one constant about the PC world is that it is always changing. Huge changes have occurred. Prices on components have dropped dramatically while PCs have become faster and more powerful. Users are clamoring for greater hard drive space, faster CD-ROM drives, faster modems and more RAM.

Introduction

We'll explain the latest terms, hardware and components to you. Don't worry if you're not technically inclined or computer literate. You won't need to be technically inclined or computer literate to use the information in ***Upgrading & Maintaining Your PC***. You probably already own the tools you'll need in your PC Workshop when it's time to upgrade your PC. The following summarizes what you'll find in this edition of Upgrading & Maintaining Your PC:

Contents

We've divided the book into four sections. This section, Section 1, talks about general information, such as the importance of ergonomics...preventing eyestrain, neck strain and wrist strain. Chapter 3 talks about the components in your PC system and how they interact. Are you looking to buy a new PC? We have a special section in Chapter 3 that provides tips on what to look for when buying a new PC. This includes tips for buying a new case, CPU, motherboard, hard drives, CD-ROM drives, expansion cards and much more.

We also talk about the components to look for when you're upgrading. These include selecting the right operating system, CPU, motherboard, hard drive, expansion cards, CD-ROM drives and much more.

Chapter 4 talks about the different operating systems that you can use on your PC. Although you're probably using Windows 3.x or Windows 95, other operating systems are available, including OS/2's latest version called Merlin.

Section 2 talks about your entire PC system in detail. You'll learn about processors and what they do, including the 486 class of processors and today's super fast Pentium and Pentium class processors (including the Cyrix 6x86 and Advanced Micro Devices AMD-K5). Using one of these processors is virtually required for today's applications and for surfing the Internet.

You'll learn how to determine the performance levels of processors; clock speed isn't the only way to determine performance. You'll also need to understand the P-Rating and iCOMP index.

Section 2 also talks about the motherboard, system memory, bus, disk drives, hard drives and the CD-ROM drives and today's exciting removable storage systems such as the Zip drive and Jaz drive from Iomega or the SQ5200C and SQ3270 from SyQuest.

Did you ever wonder how you "talk" to your PC. Chapter 9 describes how we communicate with the PC through different peripherals.

Section 3 describes the steps of upgrading your PC in detail. These upgrades include installing new components (case, power supply, disk drive, hard drive, tape drive backup, CD-ROM drive, motherboard and expansion cards and more).

Ever want to build a PC? Chapter 12 takes you through the steps involved in building a multimedia PC

Once you've upgraded your PC or bought a new PC, you'll want to know some maintenance tips and hints. Chapter 14 and Chapter 15 provide the necessary information to properly maintain your PC. Chapter 16 describes the companion CD-ROM in detail.

Chapter

2

Section

1

Components In A PC System

3

Perhaps you've wondered why so many types of PCs are available with so many different combinations of components.

A PC is a versatile machine because it can perform many functions. However, it requires the right type of system configuration before it can be used effectively. In other words, you don't want to spend money on a 100 Meg hard drive if most of your work involves graphics or desktop publishing. On the other hand, a 200 MHz Pentium with a 1.2 Gigabyte hard drive probably is probably too much if most of your work involves simple word processing.

The five components of a PC you should consider when planning a system configuration include the following:

1. Processor

2. RAM

3. Video memory

4. Video card

5. Hard drive

We'll talk about these components in more detail in Section 2. The chapters in Section 2 describe the individual elements and capabilities of these components and methods to increase their performance.

Components In A PC System

In this chapter, we'll talk about specific examples of selecting components for a PC system. In the second part of this chapter, we'll present the configuration for a typical multimedia PC system. Chapter 11 describes how you can assemble a computer multimedia system.

HOW PC COMPONENTS INTERACT

The number and diversity of the products flooding the PC market can overwhelm any consumer. Even experienced users can have problems determining what are the best components to select for a PC system.

To help in selecting the correct components, you must understand the components involved in your system. You should also have some experience with the software products you plan to use. This is important to determine how changes to the configuration will affect these products.

All PC systems are different

One basic rule to remember is that all PC systems are different.

Your personal computer is a personalized system. A PC system that's perfectly suited to your needs and applications may not be powerful enough for another user. A "correct" configuration can be determined only by how you'll be using the system.

Your needs and demands on your PC are likely to change in the future. So, what you may consider to be an "ideal configuration" today may be very different from an "ideal configuration" in the future.

Keep in mind that each new upgrade or component may not be the last one you'll ever need. To believe otherwise is both unrealistic and costly. The best purchase is usually the one that satisfies today's needs and your needs for the next six months.

Third party PCs (usually called *clones*) normally combine several types of components and several component manufacturers. So, some computer stores may have Pentium 160 MHz systems with 16 Meg of RAM and a 1.2 Gigabyte hard drive. Other stores may have Pentium 160 MHz systems only in tower cases. It may seem these systems are sold only by looks and price. However, an effective configuration is the basis of every capable PC system. The configuration criterion is different for a custom built system than for an existing PC system that is upgraded by exchanging or adding components.

Since the prices for different PC components are becoming increasingly smaller, the more powerful component is usually affordable. For example, the difference in price between a Pentium 100 CPU and a Pentium 120 CPU is about $75. This is especially true with today's IDE hard drives. For example, the price difference between a 1 Gigabyte and a 2 Gigabyte hard drive is about $125.

Since today's Pentium motherboards will work with either a Pentium 100 MHz or Pentium 120 MHz CPU, the small price difference of many components can lead you to make configuration decisions based on saving only a few dollars. However, if you use good judgment and you plan your system with realistic expectations, you may save hundreds of dollars.

Chapter

3

Section

1

SELECTING COMPONENTS #1: WORD PROCESSING

Brandi is a graduate student. She wants to assemble a PC system that she can use for word processing. Her friend Barb operates a desktop publishing and graphics business. She's looking for a PC she can use for her work.

Although her system should be flexible enough for future upgrades, Brandi won't place many demands on her system. For this type of system, Brandi should use as a minimum a 486DX2/66 processor with a VGA color monitor. The size of the hard drive isn't important for saving files that are primarily word processing. Older files can either be backed up to diskettes or other backup devices or simply deleted. As long as it's possible to swap the motherboard, this would be the perfect system for Brandi. This system should cost between $600 and $800.

Barb's desktop publishing/graphics business, however, places different demands on a PC system. She requires not only a powerful and fast processor but also a large hard drive.

Chapter 3

Since Barb's work usually involves a lot of printing, she must be able to continue working while printing. So, she'll need a PC that can perform several tasks at once. Her PC must also have enough memory to print documents in the background. She'll probably want to consider using this computer in a network environment in her near future.

Based on these requirements, the minimum hardware requirement that Barb needs is a Pentium running at 120 MHz. The system should be equipped with at least 16 Meg of RAM to handle the software required for desktop publishing and graphics. The hard drive in this system shouldn't be smaller than 1.2 Gigabyte to store the large file sizes. A Super VGA color monitor is also needed. This system should cost about $1,400.

SELECTING COMPONENTS #2: PLAYING GAMES

Suppose that you want to configure a PC that will be used mainly for playing computer games. First, you must consider the types of games you'll be playing.

Simulation games (i.e., programs that use intensive graphics) place the most demands on a PC system. The following is a minimum system configuration for this example:

❖ 486DX2 running at 66 MHz

❖ 8 Meg of RAM

❖ Fast hard drive with at least 1.2 Gigabyte of hard drive space

❖ A VGA color monitor

❖ These games may also require that your PC use a math coprocessor (depending on the simulations).

This system should cost between $900 and $1,200. One note of caution: Several of the most popular entertainment programs are available only on CD-ROM. This requires you to include a CD-ROM drive. If this is the case, the CD-ROM drive should be a minimum 4x speed drive (about $60 to $75). A faster 6x CD-ROM drive costs about $100.

COMPONENTS TO LOOK FOR IN A NEW PC

If you're planning to buy a new PC, tailor a system to your specific needs and applications. Make certain this system is flexible. You may need to upgrade it to meet your future demands. Remember, each dollar you spend today on something you don't need until tomorrow is money wasted. This is because a component's price decreases the longer it's been on the market.

This section talks about what you should be looking for when buying a new PC. Because all personal computers consist of a few basic components, we'll use a "stripped down" computer in talking about these components. Most of these components are described in the "Components To Look For When Upgrading" section in this chapter and again in Section 2.

Cases

The box or shell in which all of the other components are assembled is called the *case*. The case is typically made of metal, plastic or a combination of the two.

Cases vary by size, profile and color. Deciding on a case usually depends on which of the two major styles of case you prefer. These two styles are *desktop* and *tower*.

Desktop computer case

A desktop computer cases rests horizontally on your desktop. The advantage of a desktop case is that it doesn't take up a lot of space on the desk. The tradeoff of using this more compact desktop case is that there usually isn't a lot of room inside the case to add a lot of peripherals.

Example of a desktop case

Components In A PC System

Tower cases

Tower cases (see picture on the right) are designed to stand upright either on the floor or on a shelf. They're available in different sizes and shapes according to the height of the unit (a full tower, a midi-tower and a mini-tower case). As you'd expect, the larger the case, the more space there is inside the case for adding components. Avoid buying a PC in a mini tower size if you plan on adding four hard drives, two floppies and several add-ons. These cases are usually too small and present problems when you upgrade or install standard-size replacement parts. If you're planning to build a PC with , you should probably buy a full tower case.

Example of a tower case

Power supplies

The case usually also includes the power supply. This is true whether you buy a desktop or a tower case. The power supply produces a regulated source of electricity so the voltage doesn't vary. Power supplies have electrical connectors that supply the motherboard and other devices with +5V, -5V and + 12V.

A power supply is rated by the number of watts of power which they can deliver to all connected devices. Older model PCs could easily use up to 200 watts of power. Fortunately, the components used by today's computers are much more energy efficient; we haven't seen a computer in a long time that's required more than 200 watts of power. Most power supplies are rated for at least 230 watts to provide a safety margin when you may need a little extra power.

Most tower cases and some desktop cases also include a cooling fan. This fan removes the heat from within the enclosed case. Excessive heat can cause premature failure of the components. Pentium CPUs generate considerably more heat than their 486 predecessors. While you may not like its continuous hum, it's a good idea to choose a case - desktop or tower - that has a cooling fan.

CPU "Central Processing Unit"

Selecting a CPU is the single most important factor in how powerful your new PC will be. Keep one important idea in mind when shopping for a new computer: Buy

See Chapter 7 for more information on the Central Processing Unit (CPU)

nothing less than a Pentium or Pentium-class processor to power your PC system. This is true regardless of the reason that you're planning to use your PC.

Motherboard

The motherboard is the large circuit board which "holds" most of the other components. The CPU, memory, video cards, hard, floppy and CD-ROM drives and other input/output cards fit into the motherboard. The

See Chapter 7 for more information on the motherboard

motherboard should have eight expansion slots to provide for future expansion. Older PCs had only three slots, which did not leave room for much expansion.

Main memory (RAM)

You'll often hear memory called SIMMs. A computer's main memory or RAM is built from small circuit boards called SIMMs (Single Inline Memory Module). Pentium motherboards are designed to use standard 72-pin

See Chapter 7 for more information on SIMMS, RAM and main memory

SIMMs. The term SIMM is simply a fancy name for the way in which the memory is packaged on small circuit boards. If you count the "fingers" on the bottom edge of a SIMM, you'll see why it is called a 72-pin module (see picture below).

A 72-pin SIMM

Components In A PC System

The amount of RAM in a new PC today should be at least 8 Meg; 16 Meg is usually recommended by most software publishers.

Video card

A small plug-in card containing specialized chips which generate the signals for displaying text and graphics on the video monitor. You'll probably hear a term like Super VGA card (SVGA or Super Video Graphics Array) when shopping for a new PC. These cards are capable of displaying more colors and better resolutions than earlier cards. An SVGA card is recommended with most of today's PCs.

See Chapter 7 for more information on video cards

Also, look for a color monitor that is compatible with the SVGA card.

I/O card

Another small plug-in card containing the electronics for controlling the hard drives, floppy drives, communication ports, printer port and game port.

See Chapter 7 for more information on I/O cards

The major types of I/O cards include the following:

❖ IDE (Integrated Drive Electronics)
   This is the least expensive way of connecting a hard drive to the PC. It supports two hard drives but neither drive can have a storage capacity exceeding 528 Meg.

❖ EIDE (Enhanced Integrated Drive Electronics)
   Most new PCs include the EIDE card. It's faster than the IDE card and can be connected to four hard drives with storage capacities exceeding 528 Meg or other devices such as CD-ROM and tape drives.

❖ SCSI (Small Computer System Interface)
   The fastest and most flexible means of connecting a hard drive and other components is to use a SCSI card. However, it's also the most expensive. SCSI cards can support up to seven devices including hard drives, removable devices, tape drives, printers, scanners, etc.

Hard drives

A device for holding megabytes (millions of bytes) or gigabytes (billions of bytes) of information. A hard drive not only has more capacity than a floppy drive, but reads and writes data dozens of times faster.

See Chapter 8 for more information on hard drives

A PC today, again regardless the reasons you're buying a new PC, should have at least one hard drive with a storage capacity of 1.2 Gigabytes. Many PCs include two hard drives. The smaller capacity hard drive is used to store applications and system information. The larger capacity hard drive is used to store data and other larger files.

Chapter

3

Section

1

CD-ROM drives

A CD-ROM drive is a device that reads CD-ROMs that are used to hold programs and information. CD-ROMs provide an economical and convenient way to distribute large programs and huge amounts of data.

See Chapter 8 for more information on CD-ROM drives

You'll hear terms like "4x" or "8x" or "10x". These numbers refer to the speed of a CD-ROM drive or, in other words, how fast the CD-ROM disc spins. Faster speeds obviously result in faster transfer times from CD-ROM to your PC. For example, an 8x CD-ROM drive transfers data at a rate of 1200K per second.

Sound card

A sound card is a plug-in card that can capture, digitize and playback sound. The sound may be music, voices or effects in either monaural or stereo.

See Chapter 9 for more information on sound cards

Two terms you'll often hear with sound cards are sampling size and sampling rate. They determine the quality of the sound produced by the card. For good sound quality, make certain the sound card in your PC has at least a 16-bit sampling size and a 44.1 KHz sampling rate.

Other terms you might hear concerning sound cards are full-duplex and half-duplex. If you want to talk to and listen to someone at the same time, as in a normal conversation, buy a full-duplex sound card. Then you'll be able to talk and listen to other users over the Internet at the same time. Although you can still do this with half-duplex cards, users must take turns talking and listening.

Make certain the sound card is either a Sound Blaster card or is Sound Blaster compatible. Then your PC will be able to use its full sound potential.

Modems

A modem is a plug-in card (called an internal modem) or a small box (called an external modem) that converts digital information into a form that can be sent back and forth over ordinary telephone lines. A modem is used to connect one computer to another computer in different locations.

See Chapter 9 for more information on modems

A modem lets you connect to the Internet and other online services such as CompuServe and AOL.

Modem speed is measured in kilobits per second (Kbps). This speed determines how fast it can send and receive data. Make certain the modem in your new PC operates at 28.8 Kbps or better. Although you can connect to the Internet with a modem operating at 14.4 Kbps, you'll soon become frustrated when you realize this is too slow. Faster modems, such as 31.2 Kbps and 33.6 Kbps, are also available but are more expensive.

WHEN TO UPGRADE YOUR CURRENT PC

If your system and software are running slowly but satisfactorily, then you should consider buying a CPU upgrade package. This is especially true if you're using graphic or CAD programs, graphic intense games, desktop publishing, multimedia or data oriented software.

If you have an 8086 or 8088 based PC, it's much better to upgrade your entire system. Even if you have an 80286 based PC, upgrading the processor to a 486 usually is recommended. The rest of the system is designed to work with the slower 286 processor.

Components In A PC System

You should have no problem upgrading if your system (mainly your motherboard inside your computer) follows industry standards. This involves swapping your old motherboard with a newer, more powerful one. If not, you'll need to determine your upgrading options such as Pentium OverDrive chips, SCSI II adapters, etc. To determine if your board can be upgraded on your system, check with the dealer or manufacturer from whom you bought the computer. You'll need to determine if a certain upgrade board will work with your system.

The most economical way to upgrade your system so it has multimedia capability is to buy a *multimedia upgrade kit*. These kits are available from companies such as Sony, Creative Labs, NEC, Toshiba and others. Each upgrade kit has features and prices that vary depending on the speed of the CD-ROM and the quality of the sound card/interface that is included. Therefore, make certain to know what you want before shopping. At the very least, buy an upgrade kit that has a CD-ROM drive and sound card. Other upgrade kits may include software, speakers, microphone and other equipment you may not need.

Even a 486 processor can be upgraded by using the OverDrive chip technology by Intel. See Chapter 6 for more information on the OverDrive and the 486DX processor. You'll probably have two choices:

❖ Plug the OverDrive chip into a special slot in your system designed for it.

❖ Remove the existing processor and replace it with the OverDrive chip.

Many OverDrive upgrades are available from Intel. For example, a 486SX or 486DX processor can be upgraded to a 486DX2 processor.

Many experts believe if you spend 25% to 35% of a new system's price on upgrading, it's better to buy a new system that will have the horsepower you'll need. This is a decision you'll need to make. If a new Pentium 200 system (including monitor) is $1995 and upgrading your old PC will cost less than $700, maybe you should consider upgrading.

Upgrading is a different ballgame

If you're upgrading your PC and are planning to exchange your motherboard, you'll need a different approach to selecting computer components.

Chapter 3

For example, suppose that you're exchanging your tired 386 motherboard for a 486/66MHz board. You should replace the very slow MFM hard drive system with an IDE drive. This is especially true if the capacity of the existing hard drive is too small for today's applications.

However, hard drive performance is less important if the motherboard is changed only to improve processor performance during extensive mathematical calculations. This is especially true if the system is only used for word processing purposes. In this case, the existing hard drive may be adequate.

If your system's video refresh rate is too slow, this doesn't necessarily mean that you should switch to a faster motherboard. A faster graphics card and more video RAM usually solves this problem.

Upgrading saves money

Upgrading a PC system requires different considerations than assembling a new system. Also, it's usually cheaper to upgrade if the existing system is based on a 286 or 386 motherboard and standard components than to trade your PC for a new one.

For example, to upgrade to a higher processor, simply install a new motherboard and, perhaps, a new hard drive system. You usually don't need to change the case, floppy drives, graphics card and keyboard of your existing PC. You would also have to buy all new components if you replace your entire system.

If you're upgrading your system, consider your specific needs. Selective upgrading involves considering tomorrow's step today, so your next upgrade will be as easy as possible. Upgrades will always be compromises between the technology and power you feel you need and the amount of money you're willing to spend.

The following section explains what to look for when selecting individual components.

COMPONENTS TO LOOK FOR WHEN UPGRADING

The previous sections showed examples of the different demands that are placed on a PC system. In this section we'll talk about what you need to look for in specific components if you're upgrading your PC system.

Components In A PC System

Selecting components is probably the single most confusing and time consuming part of upgrading your PC. Many factors must be considered when buying components. When you start shopping for components, you may be overwhelmed by all the choices available. Don't panic, we'll point you in the right direction. The following pages are some of the factors that you'll want to consider when you're upgrading your PC.

Selecting an operating system

Chapter 4 talks about the different operating systems from which you can choose to run on your PC. The system that you'll likely use is Microsoft Windows 95 for many reasons, including the following:

See Chapter 4 for more information on operating systems

- ❖ It includes the features and power required by today's applications.

- ❖ Its interface is easier to use than the unfriendly DOS command line prompt.

- ❖ Ability to run several applications simultaneously ("multitasking").

- ❖ Huge amount of software and applications available.

Your PC must include a 32-bit processor to use Windows 95. A minimum system requirement would include a 486/66 processor with an external cache of 128K. Keep in mind this is a *minimum system*; you'll likely discover this system to be impractical. Therefore, we recommend using nothing less than a Pentium 100MHz processor with Windows 95.

Selecting the right motherboard

The motherboard is a large circuit board that accepts the CPU, memory, plug-in peripheral cards, various connectors and the supporting circuitry for the system.

See Chapter 7 for more information on the motherboard

Selecting a motherboard is the most crucial component that you'll buy. You're likely to have more questions about selecting a motherboard than any other component. You must select from dozens of makes and models of motherboards. The upside to this is that since so many companies make motherboards, there's a lot of competition which means high quality and low prices.

Chapter 3

Section 1

Pentium motherboard

Follow these suggestions when selecting a motherboard. You'll see that your selection will be partially determined by which chipset is used on any particular motherboard.

The specific features provided by any motherboard are usually determined by which chipset is used on that motherboard. A chipset provides the supporting circuitry to control most of the other components on the motherboard. See "Selecting RAM and memory" for more information on chipsets.

The two main benefits of chipsets are:
1. The motherboards are less prone to problems
2. The motherboards are less expensive

Chapter 3 Section 1

Select a motherboard that will accommodate the type and speed of your CPU

Because we recommend the Pentium and Pentium class processors, we also recommend selecting a motherboard that supports the Pentium CPU. Some Pentium motherboards are built to handle CPU speeds up to 133 MHz. The latest motherboards can handle clock speeds of up to 200 MHz. Although a 180 MHz Pentium is not yet available from Intel and the 200 MHz Pentium is just starting to ship as we go to press. Since you're a wise shopper, buy a motherboard that will be able to work with these faster CPUs.

Select a motherboard that has the type of system bus that you prefer

You have two choices here:

- ❖ PCI bus

- ❖ VL-Bus

The one you select determines which type of add-in cards (such as the video card) you'll use in your computer. The VL-Bus (VESA Local bus) was originally designed to be used with the 486 processors. Plug-in cards for the VL-Bus are capable of transferring data to and from the CPU at much higher speeds than the original AT bus, a performance limitation left over from the 286 computers.

Components In A PC System

However, most of the new motherboards use the PCI bus. It can transfer data 64-bits at a time at rates up to 66MHz. Some motherboards, called combos, can simultaneously accommodate add-on cards for both the PCI bus and VL-Bus, so if you need to use both types of cards in your PC, choose one of these combo motherboards. In addition to PCI bus slots and VL-bus slots, all motherboards also have slots for older ISA or EISA plug-in cards. This lets you use the "legacy" 8-bit and 16-bit ISA cards and 32-bit EISA cards in your new PC.

A typical Pentium motherboard has three or four slots for PCI or VL-bus cards and three or four slots for ISA/EISA cards. The PCI bus is now a defacto standard for Pentium systems, so we recommend a PCI bus motherboard for simplicity, wide availability of other peripheral cards and future expansion capabilities.

Select a motherboard based on whether you want onboard I/O

A motherboard with onboard I/O has the built-in electronics for controlling fixed drives, floppy drives, communication ports, a parallel port and usually a game port. Buying a motherboard with onboard I/O, means that you won't have to buy a separate add-on board for handling the I/O. Onboard I/O also frees up one of the slots on the motherboard, a factor worth considering if your case is small or you are planning to add a lot of peripheral cards.

Make certain the onboard I/O has these characteristics: EIDE (Enhanced IDE) interface capable of handling 4 fixed drives and 2 floppy drives, one parallel and two high speed serial communications ports using 16550 UARTs for faster, more reliable data transfer.

Select a motherboard which supports pipeline burst cache

One means of improving access to main memory is called *caching*. Standard cache allows four bytes of data to be transferred from cache to the CPU in eight clock cycles. A special feature of the Pentium is its ability to access memory in burst mode where the same four bytes of data can be transferred in only five clock cycles. The cache is built-in on some motherboards and added separately on other motherboards. The more recent motherboards accept a type of cache called COAST memory (Cache On A STick). See "Selecting cache memory" for more information.

Select a motherboard which supports the type and amount of memory that you're likely to use

Most Pentium motherboards have four sockets which accept 72-pin SIMMs. Since a single 72-pin SIMMs vary in capacity from 4 Meg to 32 Meg, a motherboard with four sockets can have anywhere from 8 Meg (using two 4 Meg SIMMs) to 128 Meg (using four 32 Meg SIMMs). If you need more memory, look for a motherboard that has six or more 72-pin SIMM sockets.

Some motherboards also have sockets to accept the older 30-pin SIMMs. If you're on a tight budget and have a considerable amount of money invested in 30-pin SIMMs, then you can extend your investment in this older memory by selecting a motherboard that has sockets for both 30-pin memory and 72-pin memory. Otherwise, we recommend buying a motherboard that accommodates only 72-pin SIMMs.

Most of the Pentium motherboards are able to take advantage of the faster EDO memory. You should select one of these motherboards even if you aren't initially planning to use EDO memory. Many users prefer to buy non-parity memory. If you're one of those who like the security which parity memory offers, make sure that the motherboard supports parity checking.

Selecting a processor

The most important factor in the determining the performance of your PC is selecting the correct CPU, or processor. The processor of your PC determines the speed of executing instructions (programs). A minimum upgrade we recommend is to the Pentium class

See Chapter 7 for more information on the Central Processing Unit (CPU)

processor. However, wherever you shop for components, you'll be able to find bargain priced 486 CPUs. You should avoid buying a 486 processor for one simple reason: Why should you invest in yesterday's technology. A Pentium class processor will give your Windows 95 the horsepower it demands.

Chapter
3.
Section
1

Components In A PC System

Pentium class processors from Intel (left) and the Cyrix 6x86 processor (right)

The power rating of a processor is based on its *clock speed*. This is because the work that a CPU can perform is paced by the speed of its internal clock. The faster the clock runs, the more work that the CPU can get done; therefore a more powerful computer.

The clock speed of a CPU is measured in *megahertz* (MHz) which stands for millions of cycles per second. A Pentium CPU with a higher clock speed is more powerful than a CPU with a lower clock speed. As you would expect, the more powerful CPUs cost more than the less powerful ones.

The following tables lists the street prices of Pentium CPUs as of this printing. These prices will change, you can see that for a few additional dollars, you get an incremental increase in performance.

Street Prices Of Pentium Processors (as of December, 1996)				
Intel Pentium	Street price ($)		Intel Pentium	Street price ($)
75 Mhz	100		130 Mhz	250
90 Mhz	125		150 Mhz	350
100 Mhz	150		166 Mhz	400
120 Mhz	200		200 Mhz	550

Cyrix's C6x86 CPUs are targeted at users who want better performance at a better price. Cyrix has cleverly named their processors to complete with Intel's Pentium. As Table 2.3 shows, Cyrix's C6x86 P120+ runs at an internal clock speed of only 100MHz. However, benchmark tests show that the performance of this CPU exceeds that of a Pentium 120 CPU.

Similarly, the C6x86 P200+ runs at a clock speed of only 150 MHz yet performs better than a Pentium 200. While there may be some disagreement over which CPU is better, Cyrix does offer an alternative to Intel's Pentium. The C6x86 CPUs are plug compatible with the Pentium CPU, meaning that the ZIF socket on the motherboard will accommodate either manufacturer's processor.

Street Prices Of Cyrix C6x86 Processors (as of December, 1996)		
Cyrix C6x86	Clock speed (MHz)	Street price ($)
C6x86 P120+	100	125
C6x86 P133+	110	150
C6x86 P150+	120	175
C6x86 P166+	133	200

We've found that many Pentium motherboards will accept the C6x86 processors. These motherboards require special jumper settings to handle the different clock speeds and voltage requirements of the Cyrix CPUs. The Cyrix CPUs also include their own CPU cooling fans since they tend to run "hotter" than the Intel processors.

Chapter

3

Section

1

We recommend upgrading to a faster CPU for increased performance in your PC. However, if you can't afford one of the faster Pentiums today, you can always upgrade to a faster CPU tomorrow. When your checkbook is feeling healthier, you can replace yesterday's 75 MHz Pentium CPU with tomorrow's newer and faster 200 MHz by simply removing the slower one from the motherboard and inserting the faster CPU.

The prices of CPUs have been falling quite rapidly and most industry watchers predict that they'll continue to drop in price. However, waiting for the prices to fall means that you won't be able to use the computer today. We recommend that you do not delay the purchase. Although it's likely to be cheaper tomorrow, you'll be delaying the fun, pleasure and utility of using that new computer now.

Selecting a CPU cooling fan

A Pentium CPU has about 3 million transistors packed into a package about 2-inches x 2-inches in size. Therefore, these processors generate a lot of heat. Because a Pentium uses about 15 watts of energy, we strongly recommend that you use a cooling fan to remove or disperse the heat from the CPU.

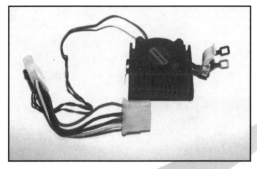

This CPU cooling fan will help keep a Pentium class processor running cool

A cooling fan consists of these two parts:

❖ Heat sink
A square metal plate that sits on top of the Pentium.

❖ Fan
The fan housing clips over the top of the metal plate and locks the assembly in place. The connectors on the fan are then connected to either a motherboard connector or a power supply connector.

NOTE

Although we mention the Pentium processor or a Pentium computer, the Cyrix 6x86 processors are plug compatible with the Pentiums. However, the 6x86 processor requires about 22 watts of power and, therefore, generate significantly more heat than a Pentium. If you install a Cyrix processor, make sure that you install a quality CPU cooling fan. See Chapter 6 for more information on the Cyrix 6x86 processor.

Selecting RAM and memory

A computer's main memory or RAM is built from small circuit boards called SIMMs. Pentium motherboards are designed to use standard 72-pin SIMMs. If you count the "fingers" on the bottom edge of a SIMM, you'll see why it is called a 72-pin module.

See Chapter 7 for more information on SIMMS, RAM and main memory

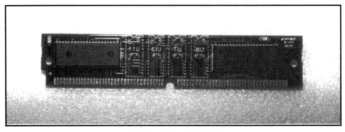

A 72-pin SIMM

Most Pentium motherboards have four 72-pin sockets. The four sockets are organized as two banks of two sockets each (called Bank 0 and Bank 1). Since both sockets in a bank must contain SIMMs, you must add SIMMs to the motherboard in pairs. In other words, you cannot add a single SIMM at a time. Bank 0 must be filled before Bank 1.

So, for example in a 16 Meg system, you can use two 8 Meg SIMMs in Bank 0 or four 4 Meg SIMMs in both Bank 0 and Bank 1.

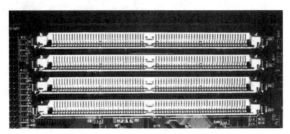

This motherboard has four 72-pin SIMM sockets

When you select RAM, you have to specify several characteristics:

❖ **Amount of memory on the SIMM**
   Represents the amount of RAM that the module adds to your computer. The amount is stated in megabytes (usually abbreviated as Meg or MB or Mb). This number represents millions of bytes of memory.

❖ **Arrangement of chips on the SIMM**
   Describes the way in which the individual chips are accessed on the SIMM. This can also be considered as another way to describe the amount of memory on the SIMM listed in the table on the right.

Arrangement	Capacity
1x32 or 1x36	4 Meg
2x32 or 2x36	8 Meg
4x32 or 4x36	16 Meg
8x32 or 8x36	32 Meg

❖ Time to access data
Represents the amount of time required to access any piece of data within the SIMM. The time is expressed in nanoseconds (represented in ns). This amount is one-billionth of a second. In the above examples, the 4 Meg SIMM has a speed of 70 nanoseconds and the 8 Meg SIMM has a 60 nanosecond speed. For Pentiums 120 MHz and above, use 60 nanosecond SIMMs or faster.

It is possible to "mix" two SIMMs of different speed. However, the access speed will be the slower of the pair. So, for example, if you mix for example 70 ns and 60 ns SIMMs, the speed will be 60 ns.

❖ Parity or non-parity
Determines whether a SIMM has parity checking. Parity checking is a way to make a computer's memory more reliable. A byte of RAM consists of 8 bits of memory without parity checking. However, with parity checking, a byte of RAM consists of 9 bits of memory.

The extra bit is a "check" bit that is used to make sure the data in the remaining 8 bits is valid. Designations of 1x36 or 2x36 or 4x36 or 8x36 indicate it's a SIMM with parity bits.

> **NOTE**
>
> Many Pentium motherboards sold today use non-parity SIMMs. Make certain the memory you buy matches the type of memory supported by the motherboard. Select a motherboard that use parity memory if you're building a PC or upgrading your PC and a require the utmost in uptime and data security.

❖ EDO or non-EDO
EDO represents Extended Data Out. It's a newer type of SIMM that is 10 to 15 percent faster than conventional SIMMs. An EDO SIMM fits in all motherboards that accept 72-pin SIMMs but the faster access time is available only if the motherboard is designed specifically to use EDO SIMMs.

One final suggestion when buying SIMMs: Always buy SIMMs in pairs. Most memory specialists recommend that both SIMMs in a pair are made by the same manufacturer. For the small difference in price between EDO and non-EDO SIMMs, we recommend buying the EDO type and enjoy the performance gain.

Also, we recommend a minimum 16 Meg system to take advantage of the Pentium's power, especially if you're running Windows 95. You can try to get away with 8 Meg, but we doubt you'll be happy with an under performing PC.

Selecting cache memory

Selecting cache memory is quite easy. You'll probably be asked if you also want to add cache memory when you're buying your motherboard. You'll want to add one of two types of cache memory: static RAM chips or COAST modules. The choice depends on the design of the motherboard. Some motherboards have onboard cache built-in but will also let you add more cache memory by adding a COAST module.

The figure on the right shows a single SRAM (Static RAM) chip. These chips come in different capacities. If your motherboard has 8 sockets totaling 256K, you'll want to buy eight 32K x 8 SRAM chips which costs roughly $40.

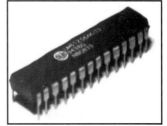

The following lists some approximate costs for SRAM:

Amount of SRAM	Street price
32K x 8 SRAM	$5.00 each
64K x 8 SRAM	$8.50 each
128K x 8 SRAM	$16.00 each

A second type of add-on cache is a COAST module. This module easily plugs into a special socket on the motherboard. If your motherboard has a slot for a COAST cache module, you'll be able to buy a 256K module for about $40.

A typical COAST module

Cache memory is very fast, with cycle times of about 15 nanoseconds. By adding cache to your system, you can enhance the performance of your computer system for a very nominal cost. In general, cache memory is a good investment for your computer.

39

Chapter 3

Selecting a hard drive

An old phrase for computer users is "you can never have too much hard drive space". It's still true today. You'll need a larger capacity hard drive if your PC has a hard drive smaller than 200 Meg (or a hard drive with less than 100 Meg free). Windows 95 requires approximately 60 Meg of hard drive space itself. The 32-bit programs written to take advantage of Windows 95 will demand more space than similar programs for Windows 3.x.

See Chapter 8 for more information on hard drives

Prices for IDE hard drives are so attractive that you shouldn't buy a hard drive with less than 1 GB capacity. In fact, the price difference between a 1 GB hard drive and a 1.6 GB or 2 GB drive is very small, so we recommend that you select one with a larger capacity for your system.

A typical IDE hard drive

The price of hard drives continues to drop dramatically. Although the prices vary across the country, we've found these to be typical or average prices:

Hard drive capacity	Street price
850 Meg	$170.00
1.2 Gigabyte	$200.00
1.6 Gigabyte	$240.00
2.1 Gigabyte	$290.00

Don't underestimate the importance of hard drive capacity. A typical hard drive today has a storage capacity of 1.2 Gigabytes. This amount continues to rise. Measure the hard drive capacity according to the size of the applications you plan to use. Remember that a hard drive becomes slower as its available space is filled. This is especially true as the files become more fragmented.

The four most common sizes we've seen are 540 Meg, 850 Meg, 1.2 Gigabytes and 1.6 Gigabytes. You'll want to get as large a hard drive as you can afford. Chapter 8 describes how to install hard drives.

Access time

You've probably heard of *access time* as a consideration when comparing hard drive performance However, most drives deliver an excellent track-to-track seek time of under 12 milliseconds. Don't worry too much about two or three millisecond difference.

Major manufacturers

The following table lists the major hard drive manufacturers and their Web sites. We suggest contacting one of these manufacturers for more information.

Hard Drive Manufacturers			
Manufacturer	Web site address	Manufacturer	Web site address
Conner	www.conner.com	Fujitsu	www.fujitsu.com
Microsoft	www.microsoft.com	NEC	www.nec.com
Seagate	www.seagate.com	Toshiba	www.toshiba.com
IBM	www.ibm.com	Western Digital	www.wdc.com
Quantum	www.quantum.com	Samsung	www.samsung.com

Selecting a video card

Yet another important decision in making your PC perform well is to select a good video card. Today's Pentiums are so powerful and the amount of data that these CPUs can process is considerable. Most of you will use either Windows 3.11 and Window 95. These graphical interfaces "draw" tremendous amounts of text to the screen by way of the video card. Thus a slow video card can *waste the speed of a fast Pentium CPU.*

See Chapter 9 for more information on video cards

Components In A PC System

Early PCs were designed around the classic 16-bit ISA (Industry Standard Association) bus or the later 32-bit EISA (Extended ISA) bus. This limited pathway to the video card was therefore a bottleneck to fast video performance. Don't even consider using an older ISA-bus video card. At the very least use today's newer VL-bus or even more superior PCI video cards. They offer a tremendous performance gain over the ISA video cards.

The VL-Bus (VESA Local bus) was designed to improve the video performance of ISA systems by moving data between the CPU and the video card at a much faster speed. Today, both the PCI and VLB system bus on a Pentium motherboard provides a wider, streamlined pathway for the video data which greatly improves the overall PC performance. Don't try to save money by buying an older generation video card. Instead, buy a PCI or VLB video card (matching the system bus of your motherboard).

A PCI video card

Since the PCI bus is now the defacto standard for Pentium class PCs, we recommend a PCI motherboard and video card.

In selecting a video card, you usually have to select the type and amount of memory for the card. These two factors determine the display speed and maximum display resolution of the card. Two types of memory are available: DRAM and VRAM.

DRAM (Dynamic Random Access Memory)

This is the same type of memory as the computer system's main memory. A card with DRAM is less expensive to buy than the same card with VRAM. It's acceptable for typical office tasks (word processing, accounting, etc.).

VRAM (Video Random Access Memory)

A video card with VRAM can generate the display faster than DRAM. VRAM is technically a form of DRAM but is designed specifically for video cards. It's "dual-ported", which means two paths are available to the same memory location. This second path lets the video circuitry access the VRAM at the same time as the CPU so that neither one has to wait for the other.

VRAM is faster and more expensive than DRAM but is perfect for working with and displaying intense and colorful graphics.

A video card with more memory can operate at a higher resolution. If you're planning to run mostly word processing or accounting applications on your PC, then 1 Meg of video memory is probably enough. However, more highly graphical applications such as CAD, games or desktop publishing, you may want to consider a card with 2 Meg of video memory.

> **NOTE**
>
> The maximum resolution of the card can be achieved only if your monitor is capable of displaying that resolution. At a later point in time, you can upgrade a 1 Meg DRAM video card for about $40-$50 to gain higher resolution and color depth.

Major manufacturers

The following table lists the major video card manufacturers and their Web site address. We suggest contacting one of these manufacturers for more information.

Video Card Manufacturers			
Manufacturer	Web site address	Manufacturer	Web site address
ATI	www.atitech.com	Cirrus Logic	www.cirrus.com
Diamond	www.diamondmm.com	Genoa	www.genoasys.com
Hercules	www.hercules.com	Matrox Graphics, Inc.	www.matrix.com
Number Nine	www.numbernine.com	Orchid	www.orchid.com
Trident	www.trid.com		

Components In A PC System

We mentioned VRAM and DRAM above because they're by far the most common types of video card memory. Two other types of video card memory include EDO DRAM (Extended Data Out DRAM) and WRAM (Window RAM).

Selecting a correct monitor

In selecting a monitor, remember that not all monitors are created equal. The major factors to consider are the screen size, dot pitch, refresh rate, interlace, maximum resolution and energy saving features.

See Chapter 9 for more information on monitors

The most economical monitors are 14-inch in size. If you spend a lot of time (two or more hours a day) using the computer, you should consider either a 15-inch or 17-inch monitor. Some users, such as graphic artists and CAD users, may even want to a consider 21-inch monitor. These monitors, as you would expect, are extremely expensive. You'll discover, however, a larger screen is much easier on the eyes.

Dot pitch

The characters and graphics on a color monitor are formed by a set of three color triads. The *dot pitch* is a measure of the spacing between adjacent triads. When this measure is smaller, The characters and graphics appear tighter or sharper to the eye with a smaller dot pitch. You'll find inexpensive monitors with a dot pitch of .35 or .38 mm . However, we recommend a monitor with a dot pitch of .28 mm or smaller. Some of the more expensive monitors have a dot pitch of .25 mm.

Refresh rate

The refresh rate is the frequency (measured in hertz (Hz) per second) at which the characters and graphics are redrawn on the screen. A monitor with a high refresh rate will show less flicker in the image. This will help reduce eye strain. The refresh rate should be about 72 Hz (72 times per second).

Most of today's monitors today are have a *multisync* feature. This means that they are able to adjust their refresh rate within a range of values to match the signals that the video card outputs to the monitor. In other words, you can adjust the resolution of a multisync monitor to suit your requirements. Other monitors are capable of displaying only one resolution.

Non-interlaced or interlaced monitor

A monitor redraws the screen by using an electron gun which shoots a beam at inside of the screen from the left side to the right in lines starting at the top to the bottom. A monitor is designed to operate in one of two ways. In either mode, the time to redraw the entire screen is identical.

❖ Interlaced
Monitors that operate in interlaced mode refresh the screen in two passes. The odd numbers are redrawn during the first pass. The even number lines are redrawn during the second pass.

Less expensive monitors use interlace mode since they can be designed to operate at lower refresh rates.

❖ Non-interlaced
Monitors that operate in non-interlaced mode refreshes all the lines sequentially from top to bottom. Non-interlaced monitors significantly reduce screen flicker which can help reduce eye strain.

Although they're slightly more expensive, we recommend buying a non-interlaced monitor for the highest quality display.

Maximum resolution

The maximum resolution is the number of individually addressable pixels that the monitor is capable of displaying. We recommend that you select a monitor that has a resolution of at least 1024 x 768 pixels. Many monitors can display up to 1280 x 1024 pixels, but they may cost more. Keep in mind that the a monitor's maximum resolution cannot be achieved unless the video card is capable of operating at that resolution as well.

A monitor is one of the heaviest consumers of electrical power. Newer energy saving monitors are capable of going to "sleep" when the computer is sitting idle for a length of time. A computer's video card must send and the monitor must be capable of responding to a DPMS (Display Power Management Signal). Selecting an energy saving monitor can save from $25 to $75 a year in electrical costs.

Major manufacturers

The following table lists the major monitor manufacturers and their Web site address. We suggest contacting one of these manufacturers for more information.

Monitor Manufacturers			
Manufacturer	Web site address	Manufacturer	Web site address
Acer	www.acer.com	Trident	www.trid.com
Hitachi	www.hitachi.com	Sony	www.sony.com
NEC	www.nec.com	Viewsonic	www.viewsonic.com
Princeton	www.prgr.com	Zenith	www.zenith.com

Selecting an I/O card (Input / Output card)

An I/O card provides the primary input and output connections for the CPU. If you selected a motherboard that doesn't have onboard I/O, then you'll have to buy a separate I/O card.

See Chapter 7 for more information on I/O cards

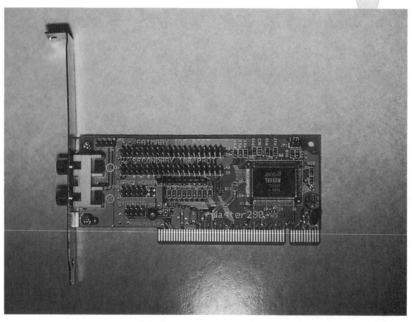

If your motherboard does not have built-in I/O, then you'll have to buy a separate I/O card similar to this one; it fits into a PCI slot

An I/O card is another small plug-in card containing the electronics for controlling the hard drives, floppy drives, communication ports, printer port and game port. We mentioned in this chapter the three types of I/O cards:

❖ IDE (Integrated Drive Electronics)
This is the least expensive way of connecting a hard drive to the PC. It supports two hard drives but neither drive can have a storage capacity exceeding 528 Meg.

❖ EIDE (Enhanced Integrated Drive Electronics)
Most new PCs include the EIDE card. It's faster than the IDE card and can be connected to four hard drives with storage capacities exceeding 528 Meg or other devices such as CD-ROM and tape drives.

❖ SCSI (Small Computer System Interface)
The fastest and most flexible means of connecting a hard drive and other components is to use a SCSI card. However, it's also the most expensive. SCSI cards can support up to seven devices including hard drives, removable devices, tape drives, printers, scanners, etc.

When shopping for an I/O card, select one which supports the EIDE standard so that the devices that you connect to it can take advantage of the higher data transfer rate. Most EIDE I/O cards will support up to four fixed drives (hard drives and CD-ROM drives).

The I/O card also has connections for other types of input and output devices. Almost all I/O cards will support the following:

❖ Two floppy disk drives

❖ Two serial (communication) ports

❖ One parallel port

❖ One game port

Be sure to select an I/O card whose serial port is 16550 UART compatible. This ensures that the serial port is capable of communicating at higher data transfer rates without "losing" data - in other words, making it more reliable.

Selecting a keyboard

Many different keyboards are available but they all fall into one of two categories:

Chapter 3

Standard design

The older style keyboard has 84-keys; under no circumstance should you use this type of keyboard. The extended AT-style keyboard has 101-keys including a numeric keypad and a second set of cursor keys. A new Windows 95 keyboard has two additional keys.

See Chapter 9 for more information on keyboards

Ergonomic design

Ergonomic keyboards are shaped differently. They are designed to fit the contour of your hands are be easier on your wrists and fingers (see the following illustration). Consider an ergonomic keyboard if most of your PC work involves typing. For example, the Microsoft Natural keyboard positions the hands slightly apart from one another. It takes a short time to get used to touch typing in this position, but it is quite comfortable to use.

Traditional keyboard (top) and the new ergonomically designed keyboard

Major manufacturers

The following table lists the major keyboard manufacturers and their Web site address. We suggest contacting one of these manufacturers for more information.

Keyboard Manufacturers				
Manufacturer	Web site address		Manufacturer	Web site address
Acer	www.acer.com		Fujitsu	www.fujitsu.com
Alps	www.alpsusa.com		Qtronix	www.qtronix.com
BTC	www.asiannet.com/behavior-tech		Microsoft	www.microsoft.com
Cherry	www.industry.net/cherry.electrical		Mitsumi	www.mitsumi.com
Chicony	www.chicony.com		Reveal	www.reveal.com
Focus	www.focuskey.com			

Selecting a mouse

We've combined three input devices into the mouse category. These devices (mice, trackballs and touchpads) are all used to move the mouse pointer around on the screen. One advantage of trackballs and touchpads over mice is that they don't require a large surface area in which to operate.

See Chapter 9 for more information on "mice"

The following illustration shows a few of the popular "mouse" devices:

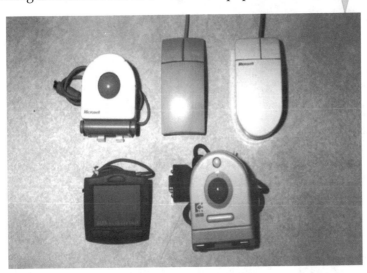

Mice and trackballs and touchpads let you move the mouse pointer around on the screen

Major manufacturers

The following table lists the major mouse manufacturers and their Web site address. We suggest contacting one of these manufacturers for more information.

Mouse Manufacturers			
Manufacturer	Web site address	Manufacturer	Web site address
Alps	www.alspusa.com	Microsoft	www.microsoft.com
Genius	www.genuis.on.theweb.net	Mitsumi	www.mitsumi.com
Logitech	www.logitech.com		

Selecting CD-ROM drives

Your PC system should include a CD-ROM drive. Too many applications and programs are available only on CD-ROM today (including operating systems like OS/2 Warp 4.0; Windows 95 is available on CD-ROM or diskettes). You'll soon discover that the benefits of a CD-ROM drive upgrade will outweigh the investment for increased performance and versatility.

See Chapter 8 for more information on CD-ROMs and CD-ROM drives

You'll be able to find great bargains on 4x and slower CD-ROM drives. Resist the temptation. A better choice is to upgrade to at least a 6x CD-ROM drive, however, consider the 8x speed drives for the best price to performance ratio. Since you're probably buying or upgrading to a Pentium computer system, you won't want to be slowed by an older CD-ROM drive.

CD-ROM drives with a 10x speed are available but the cost is quite high compared to the quad speed drives. The prices range from $189 for a 6x drive to $299 for a 10x drive. The CD-ROM drive technology is continually changing with something faster. Prices will continue to drop as new technology becomes available.

CD-ROM drives can be connected to your computer in one of three ways: through the IDE interface, through a SCSI interface or through a proprietary interface. To minimize complexity, choose an IDE CD-ROM drive. We selected an IDE CD-ROM drive for the computer illustrated in this book. This eliminates the need for a separate add-in card to support the CD-ROM drive.

Major manufacturers

The following table lists the major CD-ROM drive manufacturers and their Web site address. We suggest contacting one of these manufacturers for more information.

CD-ROM Drive Manufacturers			
Manufacturer	Web site address	Manufacturer	Web site address
Acer	www.acer.com	Reveal	www.reveal.com
Creative Labs	www.creativelabs.com	Samsung	www.samsung.com
Pioneer	www.pioneer.com	Sanyo	www.sanyo.com
Hitachi	www.hitachi.com	Sony	www.sony.com
Mitsumi	www.mitsumi.com	Teac	www.teac.com
NEC	www.nec.com	Toshiba	www.toshiba.com

Selecting a sound card

Although many varieties of sound cards are available, the vast majority are "Sound Blaster" compatible. This means that programs written to work with Sound Blaster cards will also work with these sound card.

See Chapter 9 for more information on sound cards

Even those who are not sound card experts can definitely hear the difference in quality between a conventional 8-bit sound card and a newer wave table sound card. If you're on a tight budget, buy a 16-bit "Sound Blaster compatible" sound card. Otherwise, for superior sound quality, buy one of the new 32-bit wave table sound cards. We recommend that you look for a sound card that is Plug 'n' Play compatible which greatly simplifies setup and configuration.

Major manufacturers

The following table lists the major sound card manufacturers and their Web site address. We suggest contacting one of these manufacturers for more information.

Sound Card Manufacturers				
Manufacturer	Web site address		Manufacturer	Web site address
Creative Labs	www.creativelabs.com		Reveal	www.reveal.com
Gravis	www.gravis.com		Turtle Beach	www.tbeach.com
Media Vision	www.mediavision.com			

Selecting a modem

If you plan to "surf" the Internet you'll need at minimum a 14.4 Kbps modem although we strongly recommend the much faster 28.8 Kbps modem. If you ever looked at a Web page using a slower modem (14.4 Kbps or less), you'll know why you shouldn't buy one of these slower modems. They'll keep you waiting and staring at the monitor much too long. In other words, select a modem that's at least 28.8 Kbps.

See Chapter 9 for more information on modems

Some metropolitan areas now provide ISDN service. By using ISDN, you can connect to many service providers at speeds to 128 Kbps. An ISDN modem is obviously more expensive than a conventional modem, but if you are working from home or are going to be transferring large amounts of data, an investment in the more expensive ISDN modem will make your work more practical. Some ISDN modems are "combos" - they are backward compatible with conventional analog modems and also provide the faster digital technology of ISDN lines.

Major manufacturers

The following table lists the major modem manufacturers and their Web site address. We suggest contacting one of these manufacturers for more information.

Modem Manufacturers				
Manufacturer	Web site address		Manufacturer	Web site address
Boca	www.boca.com		U.S. Robotics	www.usr.com
Cardinal	www.cardtech.com		Supra	www.supra.com
Hayes	www.hayes.com		Zoom	www.zoomtelcom
Motorola	www.mot.com/mim/isg			

Selecting speakers

If you're familiar with high fidelity ("hi fi") music speakers for your home stereo system, then you know that you can spend anywhere between $10 and $2000 for a speaker. It's almost the same for computer speakers. Computer speakers differ from conventional speakers in that they are self-amplified.

The inexpensive speakers are battery powered. We don't recommend them, since you'll surely spend a lot of money for batteries.

Most computer speakers are AC powered and have separate volume and tone controls.

You'll probably choose your speakers based on the maximum volume that you need from your multimedia programs and games.

Major manufacturers

The following table lists the major speaker manufacturers and their Web site address. We suggest contacting one of these manufacturers for more information.

Speaker Manufacturers				
Manufacturer	Web site address		Manufacturer	Web site address
Altec-Lansing	www.markivaudio.com/altec		Labtec	www.labtec.com
Bose	www.bose.com		Reveal	www.reveal.com
Yamaha	www.yamaha.com		Sony	www.sony.com
Koss	www.koss.com			

Selecting a tape backup

With today's large hard drive capacity, it's not practical to back up your valuable data to floppy diskette like it was a short time ago. Many of you don't acknowledge the need to back up your data. But there will come a time when you wish you had taken steps to safeguard all of the hours and energy that you spent to make your files, data and programs work perfectly on your system. One day - POOF - your hard drive will suddenly die and you'll be left with no way to recover your files.

See Chapter 8 for more information on tape backups

53

You can avoid this kind of disaster by investing about $200 to $250 for a tape backup drive and taking regularly scheduled backups.

Major manufacturers

The following table lists the major tape backup manufacturers and their Web site address. We suggest contacting one of these manufacturers for more information.

Tape Drive Backup Manufacturers				
Manufacturer	Web site address		Manufacturer	Web site address
Colorado	www.hp.com		SyQuest	www.syquest.com
Conner	www.seagate.com		Teac	www.teac.com
Iomega	www.iomega.com			

Selecting software

Keep one thing in mind when selecting software to use with Windows 95: Software written for Windows 3.x and DOS cannot take full advantage of the powerful features in Windows 95. Therefore, look only for programs written specifically for Windows 95

Most publishers have released Windows 95 versions of software originally available in Windows 3.x. Other major software firms have written new software to run under Windows 95.

These are a few of topics you need to consider as you set out to upgrade and maintain your PC. Computer technology is dynamic, which means that it is always changing. Tomorrow's upgrade concerns will quickly replace those of today. We trust you'll find *Upgrading & Maintaining Your PC* to be "The Smartest Way to Stretch Your PC Investment."

RECOMMENDED SYSTEM CONFIGURATIONS

Let's summarize different hardware configurations. This section lists the minimum configurations for Windows/Windows for Workgroups, Multimedia PC and Windows 95. Remember, these are *minimum* configurations. Your specific needs will likely require more powerful components, peripherals or both.

Windows 3.1/Windows for Workgroups 3.11

The minimum system configurations for a PC system using Windows 3.1 or Windows for Workgroups 3.11 include the following:

- ❖ 486/66 MHz motherboard

- ❖ At least 4 Meg of RAM

- ❖ 512K VGA card

- ❖ Fast IDE 120 Meg hard drive with integrated cache

- ❖ High transfer rate controller

Multimedia PC system

The following is the minimum requirement for a PC system to be considered a multimedia system.

- ❖ Pentium 60 MHz processor (faster is recommended)

- ❖ 8 Meg of RAM (16 Meg or more is recommended)

- ❖ 1.4 Meg 3.5-inch floppy drive

- ❖ At least 1 Gigabyte hard drive

- ❖ 4x CD-ROM drive with D/A output, volume control, a minimal data transmission rate of 300K/second at no more than 40% CPU use, and an average access time under one second.

- ❖ SVGA card

- ❖ MF2 keyboard

- ❖ Microsoft-compatible mouse

- ❖ MIDI interface

- ❖ Audio card with:

- ❖ 16-bit digital to analog converter with 22.05 and 11.025 KHz sampling rates, DMA capability, and its own hardware interrupt

- ❖ 1 or 2 Serial ports

- ❖ 1 or 2 Parallel ports

- ❖ Game port (optional)

The configuration we illustrated before exceeds these basic requirements for power and performance. This configuration would simply have to be enhanced with a sound card with multimedia capability, such as the Sound Blaster Pro by Creative Labs, and the CD-ROM drive described. This would result in a PC that far exceeds the minimal requirements for multimedia operation.

Refer to Chapter 12 for information on building a multimedia PC system.

Windows 95

The minimum system configurations for PC using Windows 95 PC includes the following:

- ❖ Pentium or Pentium class processor

- ❖ 16 Meg of RAM (32 Meg of RAM is recommended)

- ❖ 1.2 Gigabyte hard drive with at least 520 Meg of free space after installing Windows 95.

What Are Operating Systems

4

You're probably wondering why we're discussing operating systems in a book that is primarily about PC hardware. After all, isn't an operating system software?

Actually, an operating system is vital to the hardware of the PC system. In this chapter we'll discuss today's most popular operating systems:

An operating system is the master control software that runs your PC.

- ❖ Windows 95
- ❖ Windows 3.1
- ❖ Windows for Workgroups (WfWG)
- ❖ MS-DOS
- ❖ OS/2 (Version 4.0)
- ❖ Windows NT (Version 4)

The operation and especially the effectiveness of the hardware in any PC system depends on its operating system. The best and fastest microprocessor is useless if your operating system cannot use its functions. Also, certain limitations of the operating system might make expanding memory or adding a larger hard drive totally useless.

Chapter 4

The efficiency of a PC system also depends on the optimal configuration of its operating system. It's often possible to solve problems by changing the system configuration instead of spending money on new hardware components. We'll illustrate the connections between your system's hardware and its operating system by summarizing the functions this important software performs.

Operating system tasks

Perhaps you've already discovered how important the operating system is to how your PC system operates. You simply cannot use your computer if the operating system cannot load or cannot run. All computer functions won't execute and programs won't load.

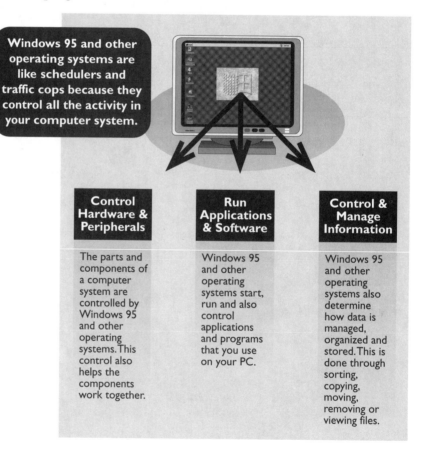

Windows 95 and other operating systems are like schedulers and traffic cops because they control all the activity in your computer system.

Control Hardware & Peripherals	Run Applications & Software	Control & Manage Information
The parts and components of a computer system are controlled by Windows 95 and other operating systems. This control also helps the components work together.	Windows 95 and other operating systems start, run and also control applications and programs that you use on your PC.	Windows 95 and other operating systems also determine how data is managed, organized and stored. This is done through sorting, copying, moving, removing or viewing files.

What Are Operating Systems

The operating system's main task is to provide the functions required to operate the PC system. In other words, the operating system is a connection between your system's hardware and its application programs. This makes it possible for different programs to access a uniform structure. This is especially important for hardware components. These components can vary significantly, depending on their manufacturer or processor architecture. Also, without an operating system, each application program must provide its file management system or disk drive routines besides its intended function.

All operating systems must also provide several utility programs supporting the general use of the PC system. For example, a program for formatting data carriers is essential; most operating systems have this standard function.

However, an extremely powerful and user-friendly file manager supporting common file management tasks, such as copying, moving or deleting files, is more difficult to find.

The standardization of hardware functions is the biggest problem in the development of different operating systems. As an operating system ages, it's more difficult for the system to accommodate updated hardware components, such as advanced processors, without discarding an established standard.

Obviously, manufacturers aren't eager to do this because existing or older applications will then no longer be compatible with the revised operating system. This is the main reason why little development has occurred in PC operating systems although hardware technology evolves constantly. Only recently has this situation changed.

Finally PC users can choose from a larger selection of operating systems. All these systems try to remain compatible with existing software, although they do this in various ways.

Don't be afraid to try some of the many features and advantages offered by your operating system. The owner's or user's manual which came with the operating system package will explain how you can get the optimal configuration for your system. Also check third party publishers or vendors for titles specific to your operating system.

Chapter

4

Section

1

MS-DOS 6.2 AND 6.22

Since MS-DOS 5.0 was clearly an important improvement over earlier versions of MS-DOS, you may have wondered why a new version of MS-DOS was needed, especially considering the popularity of Windows.

However, many experts believe updating DOS is important. A major reason Microsoft continues to develop MS-DOS is that it remains an important operating standard for the PC. So, when this standard is improved, millions of PC users benefit.

Furthermore, Windows 3.x and Windows for Workgroups are operating environments that require MS-DOS. So, increasing the performance of MS-DOS also increases the performance of Windows.

Summarizing DOS 6.2 and 6.22

Before talking about the new features of DOS 6.2 in detail, the following summarizes the features of DOS 6.2:

❖ MS-DOS works even more closely with Windows. Certain drivers have been optimized and important programs are included in both MS-DOS and Windows versions.

❖ MS-DOS 6.2 has a powerful help system that lets you search for and print out information.

❖ MS-DOS 6.2 offers improved data security, with programs for virus detection, backups and recovery of deleted files. Since these collaborate closely with the other MS-DOS functions and are available as Windows versions, they will quickly evolve into a standard.

❖ MS-DOS can effectively double your valuable hard drive space by automatically compressing data.

❖ MS-DOS 6.2 includes a defragmentation program to reorganize your hard drive, where files tend to become scattered and fragmented over time. Defragmenting can speed up hard drive access and allow larger permanent swap files for Windows.

❖ MS-DOS 6.2 can automatically optimize main memory with MEMMAKER. Better drivers for extended memory also make more memory available for MS-DOS and Windows.

❖ A new hard drive cache (SMARTDRV.EXE) offers improved performance with Windows and compressed hard drives.

❖ MS-DOS 6.2 offers flexibility in the AUTOEXEC.BAT and CONFIG.SYS files, as well as the option to ignore bad system files for "emergency" starting.

All improvements and extensions preserve maximum compatibility to existing versions of MS-DOS and DOS programs. MS-DOS 6 is 100% compatible with previous versions (according to Microsoft).

Better memory management

MS-DOS 6.2 improves upon the already impressive collaboration between MS-DOS 5.0 and Windows 3.1. In some respects, MS-DOS and Windows are so well dovetailed that using a "different" operating system or interface may severely impair performance.

MS-DOS 6.2 improves the allocation of available memory, leaving more memory free for application programs. These improvements are carefully tuned to Windows memory requirements, so both program packages profit from them with neither one encroaching on the other.

For many users who were formerly not managing options and parameters to the best advantage, the available memory will increase drastically with MS-DOS 6.2. The new version includes a powerful utility called MEMMAKER that handles memory optimization automatically.

Workgroup client

A network card that is installed in your computer can easily be connected to one or more Windows for Workgroups computers, Windows NT computers or a LAN Manager Server.

You then have easy access (controllable by passwords) to the hard drives and directories of Windows for Workgroups computers. Access control can also be exercised from other programs using a memory-resident pop-up program.

Chapter 4 Section 1

Using a network printer in a Windows for Workgroups network is equally easy. This not only solves many problems associated with printing to different printers, but also saves the cost of purchasing additional printers or complicated printer switches.

Data security features

MS-DOS 6.2 includes a robust assortment of programs for ensuring data security. Most have already proven their worth as popular products of well-known utilities developers.

One great advantage of the data security features is the same programs work in both DOS and Windows. This way, a hard drive backed up from Windows can be restored from within DOS. Program operations and interfaces are also the same when scanning for viruses and recovering deleted files.

The only difference is the Windows programs use the Windows display capabilities, while the DOS programs use the SAA interface.

Hard drive compression program

A hard drive compression program is of little value unless it is 100% safe and works well with Windows. The MS-DOS 6.2 "hard drive doubler" works with Microsoft's MRCI (Microsoft Realtime Compression Interface). This means the compression technique is thoroughly integrated and will not interfere with any DOS commands or Windows processing.

The SMARTDRV cache program is also designed for seamless integration with Windows. SMARTDRV can cache hard drives and diskette drives, including disk write accesses. As a result, drastic increases in access speed can be achieved.

SMARTDRV can also lend memory to Windows to help alleviate bottlenecks. A special Windows application called SMARTMON lets you monitor the caching process. You can use the information obtained to optimize cache settings.

Another useful feature for working with Windows is the ability to add menus and options to the AUTOEXEC.BAT and CONFIG.SYS system files. This is good news for users who previously had to get along with compromises in system file settings, or who used different variants for DOS and Windows and copied them over as needed. Now you can choose from multiple configurations in the MS-DOS start phase.

This makes it easy to use the optimal configuration for MS-DOS or Windows according to your needs.

Protecting valuable data is increasingly vital to PC users. MS-DOS 6 offers clear advances in data security, as seen in the following areas:

Anti-virus programs

MS-DOS 6.2 offers effective protection against computer viruses through an anti-virus program for MS-DOS and Windows. Besides checking both hard drives and diskettes for stored viruses, the program also scans memory to provide active protection against any viruses and their attempts at destruction.

Powerful backup

Backing up your hard drive is fast and easy with MS-DOS 6. The Windows variant of the backup program can even run as a background application. Users with little or no experience can expect to perform trouble-free backups with ease.

The use of special hardware capabilities makes the backup program very fast, and the number of diskettes required is considerably reduced by data compression techniques.

File recovery

A program called UNDELETE in MS-DOS 5.0 was available to recover deleted files. The program, however, required a good working knowledge of DOS and could not be run in Windows. UNDELETE in MS-DOS 6.2 is more powerful and easier to use. Files are temporarily stored in a hidden directory instead of being deleted immediately. This provides better protection against accidental data loss, especially with network drives. The Windows 3.x version of UNDELETE also lets you restore files from within Windows.

Hard drive improvements

Besides data security, great value is placed on the efficient use of hard drive space. MS-DOS 6.2 offers several aids for efficient disk usage:

DriveSpace (formerly DoubleSpace)

Despite constantly increasing hard drive capacities, program requirements for disk space seem to increase even faster. Therefore, finding enough disk space continues to be a concern for many users. MS-DOS 6 includes a special program that effectively doubles the storage capacity of an existing hard drive. In most cases, the compression technique that accomplishes this is barely noticeable to the user. Whether there is an impact on overall performance depends mostly on the speed of the drive itself. For slower disk drives, compression coupled with caching and defragmentation (see below) can actually improve access time.

Microsoft is likely to set a standard with its integrated compression software DriveSpace. The danger of compatibility problems or data loss is then drastically reduced compared to compression programs of other developers.

The compression program is very user friendly, requires no special procedures to use, and can also compress diskettes and removable hard drives. Installation is so safe that, if interrupted by a power loss, the procedure can simply be restarted and will continue without problems. The program can also recognize disks that have been compressed by Stacker. Optimal compatibility with Windows, the MS-DOS 6 defragmenter DEFRAG; and the cache program SMARTDRV is guaranteed.

DriveSpace (Windows 95)

Microsoft Windows 95 utility DriveSpace won't handle compressed drives larger than 512 Meg. Larger drives require that you use the new Microsoft Windows 95 Plus CD-ROM utility called DriveSpace 3. It compresses larger capacity hard drives, and, more importantly gives higher compression ratios with high-performance machines.

Other compression packages, such as the popular and flexible Stacker from Stac Electronics, are also available.

SMARTDRV

MS-DOS 5.0 included the cache program SMARTDRV to speed up access on slower hard drives. In MS-DOS 6.2, this program is considerably more powerful and user friendly. MS-DOS automatically sets up the program during installation and also enables caching for write accesses, clearly enhancing overall performance. When SMARTDRV is used in conjunction with DoubleSpace, the improvement is even greater, since compression permits greater quantities of data to be cached. Also, SMARTDRV works smartly with Windows. It can lend space to Windows, and a utility called SMARTMON can be used from within Windows to monitor and control SMARTDRV.

DEFRAG

A disk tends to become fragmented with repeated use. As files are created, changed and deleted, gaps develop in the data, so instead of covering a contiguous area it is scattered in disconnected pieces. This requires more frequent disk access and can slow performance considerably.

MS-DOS 6.2 includes a utility called DEFRAG that can restore order to your disk. Unlike similar utilities from other vendors, DEFRAG is integrated by MS-DOS 6 to work trouble-free with SMARTDRV and DoubleSpace. It can even support and enhance their performance.

Memory optimization

Version 5.0 of MS-DOS brought significant improvements in memory availability. Many computers that previously had 450K - 520K free for application programs could increase this to 580K - 610K under MS-DOS 6.

MEMMAKER

Unfortunately, taking advantage of these improvements was not always easy. Many users were reluctant to use the available techniques because of their intricate nature and the complicated control parameters required to implement them. Some mistakes could even hang the system and make it impossible to restart the computer.

MEMMAKER makes memory management safe and easy. You no longer have to worry about disabling your computer by choosing the wrong settings.

MS-DOS 6.2 uses more special resources for memory management and can be optimized explicitly for Windows. Complete compatibility with all MS-DOS programs that use high or extended memory can be expected.

Improved EMM386

The EMM386.EXE memory manager has been improved and expanded. It gives more high memory to TSR programs and device drivers and can manage both extended and expanded memory in a single pool, eliminating the need for prechecking of memory type. The result is more available memory for application programs.

Additional improvements

Memory management information

The user has better access to the details of memory management. MS-DOS 6.2 includes a special diagnostic program called MSD (Microsoft Diagnostic), that provides information about particular regions of memory and device drivers. The MS-DOS command MEM also has additional options that extend the amount of information available to the user.

Safer installation

Besides the many enhancements to the user interface and typical user tasks, DOS 6.2 offers notable improvements for the system manager and advanced DOS user as well. Installing DOS 6.2 is so safe that you can even restart your computer during installation and then continue the process or restore the system to its former status.

Variable boot options

The installation process addresses all the major system components. Optimal settings are generated for available memory. Disk compression and caching can be implemented with flexibility and ease.

MS-DOS 6.2 network extension, available from Microsoft, simplifies network (Windows for Workgroups, Windows NT, or LAN Manager) connection by automatically recognizing an existing network card and performing the appropriate setup. An installed OS/2 will also be recognized and considered.

MS-DOS 6.2 lets you include flexible configurations for booting in the system files AUTOEXEC.BAT and CONFIG.SYS. Then, depending on your particular purpose, you can specify which configuration should be used for startup.

Many users had major problems after modifying their systems because the AUTOEXEC.BAT or CONFIG.SYS files were improperly changed. Such problems could even prevent the computer from starting.

INTERLNK for desktops and laptops

MS-DOS 6 provides the ability to perform an "emergency" boot by ignoring both of these system files. Press the F5 key. Alternatively, you can request an interactive mode in which you confirm or skip the commands in the system files line by line.

Besides the help available for individual commands MS-DOS 6.2 includes a freestanding utility providing menu-controlled documentation on all MS-DOS commands including examples of how they're used. The documentation can also be printed.

Even without special network hardware, MS-DOS 6.2 allows easy data exchange between two PCs with a null-modem cable. This feature is useful to laptop or notebook users who frequently exchange or update data with a second computer.

MS-DOS 6.2 includes ScanDisk which is a utility for scanning disks for errors and making the errors so DOS avoids them.

Tips for installing DOS 6.2 and 6.22

An automatic installation procedure copies MS-DOS from the original diskettes to your hard drive. The installation procedure creates AUTOEXEC.BAT and CONFIG.SYS files with simple default settings that don't fully use the capabilities of the operating system, and can even lead to problems in its operation. Use the EDIT CONFIG.SYS command to improve these settings. A simple CONFIG.SYS file might look like this:

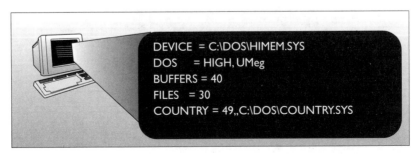

```
DEVICE = C:\DOS\HIMEM.SYS
DOS    = HIGH, UMeg
BUFFERS = 40
FILES  = 30
COUNTRY = 49,,C:\DOS\COUNTRY.SYS
```

We don't recommend changing any of the other settings made by the installation program. For example, using the MODE CON command to set certain code pages can lead to problems, especially with displaying the correct characters on your screen.

Refer to your DOS manual for more information about the best configuration for your system.

MICROSOFT WINDOWS 3.1

Windows 3.x is technically an extension of DOS and is not a true operating system. Therefore, it isn't loaded when the system is booted but is instead started with the WIN command from the DOS prompt. Windows is merely a "shell" that Microsoft designed to enhance the interface and operation of DOS, the actual operating system. So, in that sense, it's an *operating environment*.

Windows 3.11 desktop

Advantages of Windows 3.1

Windows 3.1 lets you have more than one program running at the same time. Furthermore, you can exchange information between those two programs. Windows 3.1 uses a common interface for all programs. This makes it a superior environment for programmers compared to DOS.

Tips on using Windows 3.1

If you want to use Windows 3.1 instead of upgrading to Windows 95, make certain your system meets the following *minimum* requirements:

❖ 486/66 MHz motherboard

❖ At least 4 Meg of RAM

❖ 512K VGA card

❖ Fast IDE 120 Meg hard drive with integrated cache

❖ High transfer rate controller

❖ High density disk drive

Note that this is the minimum for Windows 3.1. These requirements won't be enough for most practical purposes. You'll need more RAM, hard drive space and a faster processor to be productive with most of today's applications.

The 4 Meg RAM should be configured correctly. For example, make certain additional RAM isn't configured as expanded memory (e.g., through the EMM386.EXE driver). This is because Windows uses only extended memory. Also, verify the appropriate extended memory driver, HIMEM.SYS or HIMEM.EXE, is entered as a DEVICE statement in your CONFIG.SYS file.

Don't install any software that will remain resident in extended memory. For example, installing a virtual disk drive using RAMDRIVE or VDISK will make that segment of memory unavailable to Windows.

Allocate only a minimal amount of memory if you're using a hard drive cache program such as SMARTDRIVE. Although such programs help optimize hard drive access, their efficiency doesn't increase with the amount of memory they are given.

So, you shouldn't use more than 2 Meg of RAM for SMARTDRIVE. Additional memory won't increase the program's effectiveness and will only take valuable memory away from Windows. This may actually cause Windows to access the hard drive more frequently, so ultimately Windows operates less efficiently.

The Windows 3.1 version of SMARTDRIVE reserves 1 Meg of memory as cache space on a PC with 4 Meg of RAM.

Enhanced mode

Enhanced mode is the most powerful Windows 3.1 operating mode. By starting Windows 3.1 in enhanced mode, you can operate your PC in the virtual mode. This allows true hardware multitasking, which in turn, lets your PC can act like several separate DOS PCs, all working on their own applications. You can switch between these different DOS tasks as needed.

NOTE

Enhanced mode increases performance only if your system has a large amount of RAM. If you have less than 4 Meg of RAM and don't need the capabilities of Enhanced mode, you should use Standard mode.

To activate Enhanced mode, use the /3 switch when starting Windows. By starting Windows in this way, it's also possible to operate in Enhanced mode with only 1 Meg of RAM, although this isn't necessarily efficient or desirable.

To use Windows efficiently, many demands are placed on the system's hardware components. So the amount of memory your PC has, and the hard drive seek time, affect the overall performance of the Windows environment. So, you should consider several factors when configuring Windows. Occasionally, just a few simple changes can lead to noticeable increases in performance, without requiring expensive hardware upgrades or expansions.

Using a permanent swapfile

Using a permanent swapfile makes it much easier for Windows 3.1 to temporarily store information on your hard drive. This increases Windows' speed. Version 3.1 of Windows automatically creates a swapfile when it's installed on your hard drive.

Windows needs a contiguous segment of hard drive space to create a swapfile. So you should defragment your hard drive using a defrag utility before actually calling SWAPFILE. It's important to defragment your hard drive regularly to keep Windows running efficiently.

You should consider upgrading to Windows 95 if you're finding that your system is running much too slow. Windows 95 is a true operating system since it doesn't rely on DOS. Windows 95 is designed to take advantage of the power of today's powerful processors.

WINDOWS FOR WORKGROUPS

Windows for Workgroups (WfWG) is a more powerful version of Windows 3.1. WfWG, like Windows 3.1, is not a true operating system since it too depends on DOS to operate.

WfWG is a full network implementation of Windows 3.1. It allows you to share files and printers with other computers connected to a network. These computers can access files and applications and even send E-mail to one another. To take advantage of WfWG, make certain you have networking cards and cables properly installed.

WINDOWS NT 3.1

Microsoft released Version 3.1 of Windows NT (New Technology) in the summer of 1993. Like Windows 95, Windows NT is a true operating system. It can exchange programs with other computer platforms, such as Apple or NeXt systems.

System requirements

Installing Windows NT 3.1 requires at least 20 diskettes or a CD-ROM drive. It requires 12 Meg of RAM and 70 Meg of hard drive space. Unfortunately, NT is not compatible with any disk compression software although there are plans to release a DOS 6 compatible DoubleSpace in future versions.

If you've become familiar with the user interface of Windows, you'll quickly become familiar with the user interface of NT. However, this is also a disadvantage because the NT offers less object-orientation and task automation than you may need.

Chapter 4 Section 1

Network support

NT's built-in support for networking is compatible with Microsoft's LAN Manager networks. Both administrative and end-user functions are available through the Windows interface. Additional networking is possible with a limited set of command line-based TCP/IP tools for use with UNIX networking. NT also includes a single-user built-in version of Microsoft's RAS (Remote Access Services) that lets users dial into Windows NT from a remote Windows NT or Windows for Workgroups system.

Although NT does not yet include Novell NetWare support, there are plans to support over 100 network cards as well as additional NetWare support.

Because the hardware requirements for NT is restrictive, be very careful when upgrading to the NT. Be very specific when discussing your system and requirements with a dealer.

WINDOWS NT WORKSTATION 4.0

A more powerful version of Windows NT (see previous section) was released in late 1996. This new version is called Windows NT Workstation 4.0. It combines the ease of use Windows 95 with the reliability and security of Windows NT. This new interface improves your efficiency by helping you work easier and faster. You can enjoy the same user interface for all your Windows 32-bit desktops and servers.

Windows NT Workstation 4.0 will run on a system as low powered as a 486/25 processor with 12 Meg of RAM and only 110 Meg of space on your hard drive. However, Microsoft recommends using a Pentium or Pentium class processor, at least 16 Meg of RAM and at least 110 Meg available hard drive space.

Simplified installation

The new installation process simplifies the setup procedure when switching to Windows NT Workstation. Enhancements include a new easy-to-use interface, improved hardware detection, installation wizards and several tools that allow corporate customers to deploy Windows NT Workstation on multiple systems.

Installation tips

Although Windows NT 4.0 is easy to install, you may come across a few problems. The most likely problem involves hardware compatibility concerns. Make certain NT4 drivers for your hardware (sound card, video card, CD-ROM, network card, etc.) are available. Another common installation problem is caused by the fact that IDE CD-ROMs connected to a Sound Blaster IDE port are not supported. You will have to connect the IDE (Atapi) CD-ROM to the secondary IDE connector on your PC's motherboard to get it to work.

Windows NT cannot run older DOS-level device drivers. Also, no NT drivers can "talk" directly to the hardware. So, NT 4.0 currently has only a limited set of device drivers available. Use search engines like Infoseek or AltaVista to search Internet for information on updated drivers for your hardware.

Keep the following in mind about Windows NT before you install it:

1. Make certain to have plenty of free space on your hard drive. Windows NT 4.0 requires about 250 Meg of hard drive space for a "full" installation. Windows NT does not work with drive doubling software yet (i.e., Stacker, DoubleSpace, etc.). You'll need to decompress your data before installing NT if your current drive is doubled.

2. Windows NT will run with 16 Meg of RAM but more (at least 24 Meg) is recommended. (Select the "Compact" installation option during the Windows NT 4.0 setup process if you cannot upgrade above 16 Meg of RAM. This option installs none of the optional Windows NT 4.0 software components.)

3. Back up ALL your data before installing Windows 95. There is a chance the installation could fail and corrupt your hard drive.

Improvements in the Accessibility options

Several Accessibility options are now installed by default. This makes it easier for people with disabilities to use the system. These features include:

❖ Special key functions and support for alternative input devices that emulate the keyboard and mouse for users with limited dexterity.

Chapter 4 Section 1

73

❖ Scalable user interface elements, audible prompts during setup and high contrast color schemes for users with low vision.

❖ SoundSentry and ShowSounds functions that translate audible cues to visual cues for users who are hard-of-hearing.

These new features are the result of working with users that have disabilities, organizations that represent people with disabilities and software developers who create products for this market.

New Accessories

Many of the applications and utilities in Windows NT Workstation 4.0 first appeared in Windows 95. They've been designed to take advantage of new areas of the operating system, including the following:

❖ HyperTerminal
This new 32-bit communications application provides asynchronous connectivity to host computers such as online services. It's pre-configured to allow easy access to AT&T Mail, CompuServe, MCI Mail and other systems.

❖ WordPad
This 32-bit editor let you create simple documents and memos.

❖ Paint
This 32-bit graphics application lets you read PCX and BMP file formats.

❖ Quick Viewers
Lets you view files in the most popular file formats without opening the application that was used to create the file.

Selecting between Windows 95 and Windows NT 4.0

Both Windows 95 and Windows NT Workstation 4.0 are helping companies realize the benefits of a more reliable, more manageable operating system. Both run the latest versions of applications and take advantage of exciting new Internet technologies.

Selecting the right mix depends on the current needs and situation of your organization. Windows 95 is the easiest way to a 32-bit desktop with a reduced set of requirements, comprehensive compatibility and advanced mobile computing tools. Windows NT Workstation 4.0 is the most powerful 32-bit desktop with its high performance, and industrial-strength reliability and security.

Compatibility with DOS and Windows 3.x

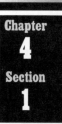

Windows NT Workstation 4.0 will run most MS-DOS and Windows 3.1 based applications. A few exceptions include some 16-bit games. More significantly Windows NT Workstation 4.0 does not support Adobe Type Manager fonts so some graphics applications will not work on Windows NT Workstation 4.0. Keep in mind that "most" of the applications written for Windows 95 will run on Windows NT Workstation 4.0. This doesn't mean "all" applications will work. Certain differences between Windows NT Workstation 4.0 and Windows 95 do not yet allow 100% compatibility of applications.

Microsoft plans to add support for support for Plug and Play (PnP) and Advanced Power Management in the next major release of Windows NT (late 1997/early 1998).

Windows NT Workstation 4.0 features

The main features of Windows NT Workstation 4.0 include the following:

- ❖ Uses the Windows 95 user interface

- ❖ Built-in access to the Internet and corporate intranets.

- ❖ Setup Manager utility to assist system administrators in creating installation scripts which reduce the time and effort required for deployment

- ❖ Improved version of the Windows NT Diagnostics Program to allow fast, remote desktop troubleshooting.

Microsoft Internet Explorer 2.0

Microsoft Internet Explorer 2.0 is Microsoft's easy-to-use Internet browser. Internet Explorer 2.0 embraces existing HTML standards, such as tables, while advancing HTML with new improvements like online video, background SSL support, and support for Internet shopping applications. Internet Explorer 2.0 also features performance enhancements that make it one of the fastest browsers available, on even the most complex Web pages.

Imaging for Windows NT

The Microsoft Imaging software for Microsoft Windows 95 is now available on Windows NT. This imaging software provides powerful imaging services that enable users to access and control information directly at their desktops.

Direct Draw and Direct Sound

Windows NT Workstation 4.0 now supports the multimedia APIs first introduced in Windows 95. Supporting these APIs allows developers to develop games and other applications that run on both Windows 95 and Windows NT Workstation 4.0 platforms.

Telephony APIs (TAPI)

Telephone API (TAPI) integrates the advanced telephone with the powerful capabilities of PCs. TAPI provides a level of abstraction for developing applications that are not bound to specific telephone hardware by supplying the means for applications to set up and control telephone calls.

Through the TAPI interface, communications applications can ask for access to the modem or telephone device, allowing the communications subsystem in Windows NT Workstation 4.0 to arbitrate device contention and negotiate with applications to share the communications device in a cooperative manner.

Unimodem (Universal Modem Driver) provides TAPI services for data/fax/voice modems so that users and application developers don't have to learn or maintain difficult modem "AT" commands to dial, answer and configure modems. Some of the new Windows NT Workstation 4.0 features that take advantage of TAPI/Unimodem support are Dial-Up Networking, HyperTerminal and PhoneDialer.

Performance tips

Disk defragmenting

The data on your hard drive will eventually become fragmented. To defrag the hard drive in Windows NT, select Disk Defragmenter (**Start/Programs/ Accessories/System Tools/Disk Defragmenter**). This will restore optimum disk performance.

If you install the Microsoft Plus! pack, an option called System Agent can schedule and run disk maintenance tasks automatically.

Checking for errors

An important part of keeping your system in good condition is to check your hard drive(s) for errors. To do this, use Scan Disk Defragmenter (**Start/Programs/ Accessories/System Tools/ScanDisk**) at least twice a month.

Virus checking

Windows NT doesn't include antivirus software. However, the Windows 3.x and Windows 95 antivirus software should still work. Buy a virus checker specifically designed for Windows NT 4.0 for the best protection.

●●

WINDOWS 95

Windows 95 is the successor to Windows 3.x and Windows for Workgroups. Windows 95 is a true operating system because it doesn't require MS-DOS to operate. It's also more graphical and user-friendly than either Windows 3.x and Windows for Workgroups. A complete discussion of Windows 95 would require a book in itself; so, our objective is to summarize the most important features. We've also included information throughout this book so you can upgrade your hardware and take advantage of the power and improved performance of Windows 95.

Chapter 4

The new Windows 95 user interface

System requirements

Installing Windows 95 requires 14 diskettes or a CD-ROM. Windows 95 will install over your current DOS and Windows operating systems. Additional add-ons from Microsoft for Windows 95 are available only on CD-ROMs. These include Microsoft Windows 95 Plus! and Windows 95 Tune-Up.

Minimum system configuration

Windows 95 works with a minimum system configuration of a 386/33 PC, 4 Meg of RAM and at least 60 Meg of hard drive space. However, this is not a practical system for running Windows 95.

Recommended system configuration

Our recommendation for a bare-bones Windows 95 system is a 486/66 PC with 8 Meg of RAM and at least 100 Meg of free hard drive space (for additional Windows 95 applications). If you're buying a new PC, don't buy anything less than a Pentium. Then you'll have the horsepower to use the full capabilities of Windows 95.

Different interface from Windows 3.x

Windows 95 uses a completely new user interface compared to Windows 3.x. You may need some time becoming acquainted with this new interface, especially if you're upgrading from Windows 3.x or Windows for Workgroups. Fortunately, you can adapt your software quickly with the advanced Windows 95 installation "wizards." They'll help you install Windows 95 and applications that are written for Windows 95.

A Windows 95 wizard at work

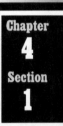

Features of Windows 95

Windows 95 is a true 32-bit operating system. It runs Windows and DOS programs faster because of its architecture. It's also multitasking so you can run more than one program at a time rather than relying on Windows 3.x ALT TAB fast-switching.

Your programs, if they follow Microsoft's guidelines, send data to each other. For example, you can have an Excel spreadsheet send its data directly to your Microsoft Word document.

What Are Operating Systems

Chapter 4

Depending on which version of the Windows 95 operating system you purchase (diskettes or CD-ROM), there are a few differences in features and applications included with each version.

The main features of Windows 95 are summarized below:

Wordpad and Paint

WordPad is a text editor for short documents. These documents can be formatted with different font and paragraph styles.

Use Paint to create, edit, and view pictures.

Plug and Play

Lets you add new features or components, such as processors, etc., to a computer without worrying about difficult and time-consuming installation steps.

Microsoft Exchange

This is an improved communications program. It lets you manage your E-mail and fax messages. It lets you view all your messages in one place regardless of whether they arrive by fax, E-mail or through The Microsoft Network.

Windows Explorer

Use Windows Explorer to see all the folders and files on your system. The right side of Windows Explorer shows the contents of the drive or folder you click on the left. Use Windows Explorer to move, open, print or delete documents and files.

Microsoft Network

This is Microsoft's online service that makes electronic information and communication easy for Windows 95 users. A small sampling of what you can access through the Microsoft Network includes the following:

❖ Electronic mail (including Internet mail)

❖ Bulletin boards

❖ Internet newsgroups and chat rooms to discuss and explore everything from movie reviews to PC technical issues.

❖ Latest headline news, sports and weather

❖ Reference information

Microsoft will also release two other products that integrate into Windows 95. One is Win95 Tune-up Pak which includes printer drivers, updated components and possible bug fixes. The second is Microsoft Plus, which will contain several utilities, games and communication software that Microsoft did not include with Windows 95.

Installing Windows 95

You can install Windows 95 over earlier installed versions of Windows (3.0, 3.1 or Windows for Workgroups 3.11). We recommend installing Windows 95 from "scratch". In other words, install Windows 95 in its own directory. By doing so, you'll improve the performance of Windows 95.

Remember to reinstall all your existing Windows programs if you install Windows 95 in its own directory. This is because the Windows programs that you installed put required files in your Windows directory (INI files, DLLs, etc.). So, when Windows 95 runs, it doesn't 'know' required files are in other directories.

Before installing Windows 95

1. Run a virus checking program (such as MSAV or Central Points Anti Virus software).

2. Make sure to free as much hard drive space as you can.

3. One extra precautionary step is to create a system boot diskette using the DOS Format /S command. Then copy your CONFIG.SYS and AUTOEXEC.BAT files to this boot disk. Use this diskette to boot to your old familiar DOS in an emergency.

Another point you must remember concerns system files. Windows 95 replaces many system files in DOS after it's installed. To make these replacement files available, add the following:

```
path = ...;C:\WINDOWS\COMMAND
```

subdirectory to your PATH statement (assuming that Windows 95 is installed on drive C:).

Windows 95 installation tips

Besides installing Windows 95, also do the "recommended" Windows 95 Startup diskette that is always selected for you. This will help eliminate later problems.

Another good protective measure is to choose the "Save System files" option when prompted. This will allow you to uninstall Windows 95 and restore your old DOS system files after you have installed Windows 95.

You will be able to install Windows 95 even if you have DoubleSpace, DriveSpace or STACKER installed. You will want to install Windows 95 on your uncompressed volume. You might have to change your uncompressed volume's size to complete the installation. Look at the documentation for your compression software's documentation to see how to do this.

Like OS/2 and WINDOWS NT, WINDOWS 95 gives you the capability to boot to an operating system of your choice. To set up a "Dual Boot" with DOS/Windows 3.1 and Windows 95 do the following. If you installed Windows 95 over an older version of Windows, you'll probably have to change your MSDOS.SYS file. Note: the MSDOS.SYS file is a Hidden and Read Only file by default. To change this file, you will have to change these attributes. You will have to add the line

```
BootMulti = 1
```

in the "Options" section.

This will allow you to start your previous version of DOS by pressing the function key F4 when you see the "Starting Windows 95" message on power up. You'll also have to reinstall your previous version of Windows. Make certain to put it in a directory other than the one in which Windows 95 resides. If you installed Windows 95 in its subdirectory you this should automatically be setup for you. So you will simply have to press the function key F4 to boot up your previous version of DOS. Switch to the subdirectory to start Windows 3.x that contains the previous version of the WIN.COM. Another option to boot your old DOS is to use a trusty old DOS boot disk.

TIP If you have a 4 Meg PC and Windows 95 seems sluggish, the best fix is to upgrade your memory. Some computer manufacturers buy back old memory chips so you may not have to discard your smaller capacity SIMMs or SIPPs.

For more in-depth information for beginners to expert users, you should check out our software package called **MegaPak for Windows 95**. It includes a CD-ROM of the best shareware available and a booklet of The Best Tips & Tricks for Windows 95.

OS/2 WARP

Many observers felt in 1987 that MS-DOS needed to be replaced by a more up-to-date system. IBM hoped that their new operating system called OS/2 would be the operating system to replace MS-DOS.

When IBM's new PS/2 personal computer series was introduced on the PC market, the new OS/2 operating system, which Microsoft helped develop, was also introduced. The many special features of this new operating system promised to solve all the problems inherent in DOS.

One such feature was the ability of OS/2 to run two separate programs simultaneously. Actually, multitasking doesn't happen simultaneously. Instead, the processor constantly switches from one program (task) to the other.

Another feature was the ability of OS/2 to use a fixed time frame. This is a capability not used by Windows. The operating system core has the ability to switch between active tasks. Therefore, a task that is stuck in an endless loop can be ended. This process prevents multitasking deadlock, which occurs when one of these tasks cannot be avoided.

Network support

OS/2, unlike MS-DOS, was designed to support PC networks. OS/2 3.0 uses its own server program called the LAN manager. It coordinates data transfers within the network. PCs operating under OS/2 can be configured as file servers as well as workstations, and can even be networked with MS-DOS computers.

Chapter 4

The Presentation Manager, which has been a part of OS/2 since Version 1.1, provides a user-friendly graphical user interface. This interface features a well-developed window operation, which is very similar to the Windows structure.

Actually, the Presentation Manager is an offspring of Windows 2.0, which was on the market during its development. However, unlike Windows, it isn't a separate part of the existing operating system. Instead, it represents the central operating system interface into which all standard functions of OS/2 have been integrated.

Compatibility

One of the concerns users have about purchasing a new operating system is that it won't be compatible with their existing programs. The developers of OS/2 have also considered this and have integrated a compatibility window into their Presentation Manager. This window ensures that all DOS programs can still be used and that some applications, which don't need to access hardware directly, can even be operated in the background. OS/2 also permits the user to switch to a DOS shell that's identical to the one found in MS-DOS 3.3.

Another feature lets you, while booting your system, select whether DOS or OS/2 should be loaded. This makes it possible to install both operating systems on the same hard drive.

You're probably wondering why, if OS/2 offers so many advantages, it isn't used by more PC users. We're not sure why this excellent system hasn't firmly established itself among PC users. Perhaps there isn't only one reason why it hasn't been able to replace MS-DOS on a larger scale. Several factors are responsible for this situation. For instance, the marketing strategy for OS/2 may not have been the best. Also, its relatively high price deterred many PC users from purchasing this otherwise excellent operating system.

Another reason for OS/2's limited use is that it's ahead of its time. The hardware requirements for this operating system were especially impractical. Since a good XT still costs several thousand dollars and an AT isn't attainable for many PC users, these requirements weren't feasible for most users.

As we mentioned, OS/2 required a 286 CPU or higher, as well as a minimum memory capacity of 1.5 to 2 Meg. When OS/2 was released, many 286 motherboards weren't even set up for memory expansions and an Intel Aboveboard with 1 Meg of RAM was extremely expensive.

Therefore, OS/2 was used primarily by professional computer users and was also successful in PS/2 systems. As hardware prices began to decrease, Microsoft released Version 3.0 of Windows.

OS/2 Version 3.0 ("Warp")

IBM released Version 3.0 of the OS/2 operating system in 1994. This version is more commonly called Warp. The most significant change from earlier versions of OS/2 is that Warp is a true 32-bit operating system. So, this system can be run only on 386, 486 and Pentium systems.

Warp is completely DOS compatible, including Version 6.2 of DOS. Warp lets you run a DOS program, a Windows application and an OS/2 application simultaneously in separate windows. DOS applications even run faster under OS/2 than under DOS alone because of OS/2's 32-bit structure.

Warp is a multitasking/multithreading operating system. This means that several programs can be executed simultaneously (multitasking) and that within these programs; independent program segments can also be executed simultaneously (multithreading). This capability is especially useful on multiprocessor systems. In these instances, the operating speed can be increased significantly.

With multitasking, the computer can execute several tasks simultaneously. For example, you could start a database application and start sorting a large database file. Then you could switch to the OS/2 command line and use the FORMAT command to format a new diskette. You then switch back to your word processing application to type a letter. All these tasks are executed side by side. You no longer have to wait until one task is completed before you can start another one.

Multithreading is a type of sub-multitasking. Programs can consist of smaller segments, or threads, that are in turn executed simultaneously. For example, a printing operation could occur along with other program operations. However, programs are simply threads themselves. Theoretically, each program or process is allotted up to 512 Meg of memory. Each process can contain up to 4095 separate threads.

Windows support

You can run Windows programs under OS/2. You can execute them either in full-screen mode, perhaps with a special Windows video card driver, or in a window in the WPS (Workplace Shell). Using a joint clipboard, you can easily exchange data between all Windows and OS/2 programs. Even DDE and OLE can be used.

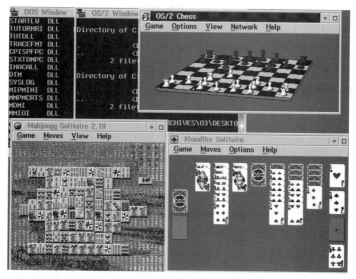

DOS, Windows and OS/2 software together

Older OS/2 programs still run under the current OS/2. Even most of the old drivers can still be used, although you should switch to the newer and more powerful 32-bit 2.1 drivers as soon as possible.

Advantages of Warp

Warp is a true operating system. It's not an environment system or DOS add-on like Windows 3.x. Another advantage of OS/2 is that its environment is familiar to DOS and Windows users. So, DOS and Windows users can easily use OS/2. OS/2 also enables users to run a large amount of existing software, such as existing DOS, Windows, and OS/2 programs.

You can easily upgrade your OS/2 system by adding networking or multimedia capabilities. You could also expand the system so it's a network server.

Conflicts with video adapters

OS/2 may encounter problems with a few special VGA cards that are equipped with a Turbo chip (e.g., for Windows). Cards using the Tseng ET4000 chip and a high-color mode may also encounter problems with OS/2. At certain times, the screen output may be lost unexpectedly.

However, the various hardware manufacturers most likely have adapted to this new operating system. If this happens, these quirks will probably be corrected within the near future.

OS/2 Warp 4.0 (code named Merlin)

IBM is planning a new version of OS/2 (code named Merlin) called OS/2 Warp 4.0 scheduled for release in the fourth quarter of 1996. As you would expect, OS/2 Warp 4.0 promises several new functions and improved features over OS/2 Warp.

Changes and improvements

Improved user interface

IBM has also improved the OS/2 Warp 4.0 user interface. The default desktop is much more attractive. A textured OS/2 Warp logo is the default desktop. However, several other bitmaps are included that you can use for the desktop. The icons have been improved with a more three-dimensional appearance.

OS/2 WarpCenter

The OS/2 WarpCenter is the most dramatic change. It's more useful than the OS/2 Warp LaunchPad. Clicking on the "Warp" logo displays a drop-down menu that shows an entry for each object on the desktop. The first-level menu changes automatically to include new objects as they're added to the desktop. Cascaded menus let you access the contents of these containers without having to open their windows.

Chapter 4

WarpGuide

Another improvement is the WarpGuide, which you can consider as a set of wizards

Universal client

This feature lets you connect to any network operating system. This includes NetWare, Windows NT Server and Novell's NetWare Directory Services (NDS) environment. IBM is establishing OS/2 Warp as a universal client that will connect to any server operating system similar to how OS/2 Warp Server is a universal server that will connect to any client operating system.

Also, Merlin will provide desktop access to all the world's most popular PC server platforms. They include OS/2 Warp Server, LAN Server, Microsoft Windows NT, Banyan Vines and Novell NetWare.

Merlin also will integrate IBM Personal Communications/ 3270 over TCP/IP. This features lets desktop users and mainframes communicate. This emulation capability increases productivity for the user by allowing access to information stored on a host computer.

Voice enabled and speech enabled

Merlin is the first major Intel-based operating system with built-in speech support. You can even navigate the Internet completely by voice, in any of six languages. Although this feature requires a minium 90 MHz Pentium and 24 Meg of RAM, using your mouse and keyboard is an option and not a requirement.

Internal Web browser

All your favorite Internet activities, including "surfing", are easy with OS/2 Warp 4. IBM also is placing heavy emphasis on integrated Internet capability. Merlin is to incorporate an internal World Wide Web browser (or use your provider). IBM plans to run native Java applications in OS/2 Warp for this browser in the future.

IBM includes WebExplorer 1.2 with Merlin. It not only links to the Internet but also has a link to the Workplace Shell.

Mobile File Synchronization (MFS)

You can access your network remotely through dial-up or ISDN connections. MFS (Mobile File Synchronization) allow users to take their work on the road or home yet still work on the network files from the office. This is an important feature for business executives, parents or anyone else who is away from the office yet must have access to the office network resources.

Also, they can disconnect from the network and know that their shared files will be updated when they log back on by using MFS. It will detect any conflict between the client and server files and automatically duplicate to the server any tasks performed at the client and vice versa, if the user so chooses. This ensures that users will be working with the most current version of their data.

Other changes

Merlin also supports TrueType fonts. Therefore, if you depend on TrueType fonts in your documents or applications, you can move them to Merlin.

Support has also been enhanced for Win32 APIs. This increases the number of Win32 applications that are compatible with merlin. (This excludes programs that specifically require Windows 95 or Windows NT to operate.)

Merlin makes life easier for developers because it allows using several programming interfaces. The network connectivity options are excellent, and the linkage with he Internet is unprecedented.

Merlin includes several backgrounds and color schemes. Also, Merlin includes different sound schemes, which let you not only see, but hear nature, (for example, the ocean). Listen to music and sounds, or record your own. OS/2 supports all popular multimedia formats. These formats include WAV files, GIF and JPEG graphics and many more.

System requirements and installation notes

The minimum system requirements for OS/2 Warp 4 include a 486/33 MHz processor, 12 Meg of RAM and 100 Meg of hard drive space for the operating system itself.

Importance Of Ergonomics

Many users have spent long sessions in front of their computer monitor. Therefore, different organizations have researched this aspect of computer use trying to determine if this leads to any negative side effects. In this chapter we'll discuss the various ways you can make your PC environment both comfortable and safe. These include video monitors and input devices

PREVENTING EYESTRAIN

We'll begin with your equipment setup. Position your monitor, keyboard, document holder, mouse, and perhaps your joystick, at equal distances from your eyes. (A distance of about 20 inches is ideal.) This way your eyes won't have to refocus constantly as you use these different devices. Use a copyholder to keep documents on which you're working at eye level. This will help prevent you from constantly looking up to the screen and down to the document. Adjustable "monitor arms" are available that let you position the monitor at the best height.

Importance Of Ergonomics

Chapter 5

Make certain the characters on your screen are large enough that you can still read them easily after long computing sessions. The ideal height for screen characters is about 0.1 inches (from 11-point to 14-point size). Their width should be no less than 50% of their height. The greatest chance of eye-damage results from working with higher resolution screens that are too small. This results in characters that are too small.

High resolution screens are excellent for graphics. However, use the standard VGA resolution of 640 x 480 pixels for long computing sessions. This resolution is particularly recommended for word processing.

The objects within your range of vision should be nonreflective and as light as possible. The characters on your screen and on your keyboard are most easily recognized when they're contrasted the background. For example, use black characters against a white or light gray background. This will place the least amount of strain on your eyes.

The sharpness of your picture is another important factor. So you should be particularly critical when selecting a monitor and graphics card. Avoid flickering monitors entirely.

The 'dot pitch' for VGA and Super VGA monitors is usually between .28 and .48 millimeters. We recommend the lowest dot pitch monitor that you can afford. Remember, you'll spend all your computer time looking a video monitor...be good to your eyes.

You can also reduce eye strain by occasionally exercising your eye muscles. Focus on a object in the distance and then focus on a object on your desk (do this a few times with different objects). Repeat this exercise several times per hour.

If you frequently spend long hours in front of your computer screen, you should get regular eye examinations. This way you can catch potential problems before they become too serious.

Lighting is important

Your work area should be brightly lit. Lighting designers specify an illumination level of approximately 700 lux for computer workstations. The light source should emit white light. However, it's impossible to determine the exact illumination level without a light meter.

Normally your work area should be about twice as bright as the average living space. Seventy percent of this light should fall directly onto your work surface. The remaining light should be reflected (indirect) light. It's important that the illumination of your desk surface doesn't produce any type of glare.

PREVENTING NECK STRAIN

Incorrect seating levels and poor positioning of your screen can result in permanent problems. Your seating level is extremely important. It should allow you to sit without becoming fatigued. You should be able to move your back without feeling restrained.

Your thighs should rest fully on the seat surface. The edge of the seat should not press into your legs. Your feet should always be able to touch the floor. Shorter people may need to use a footrest. In this sitting position, your hands should be freely movable about the desk surface. Make certain the keyboard and mouse remain within easy reach.

This may sound complicated, but it's easy to accomplish. Sit upright in your chair with your legs bent at a right angle. Your arms should rest on your desktop so they form right angles. Now adjust the height of your chair until it's in the proper position. Generally the best height for desk surfaces is around 28 inches.

By adding the average height of your keyboard (about an inch) to this measurement, the result is a height of about 29.5 inches. This is the height you'll want to attain.

For the best working environment, you should invest in a quality chair and desk. Also, the surface of your desk should match your equipment (i.e., ideally a bright, nonreflective surface).

Importance Of Ergonomics

PREVENTING WRIST STRAIN

The best way to avoid wrist strain is to keep your elbows level with the keyboard. Then keep your wrists straight and higher than your fingers.

To help prevent wrist strain, new keyboard designs and mouse designs have occurred recently. These new products are designed to eliminate Repetitive Stress Injury (RSI) conditions such as Carpel Tunnel Syndrome (CYS). The new Microsoft keyboard is an example of an ergonomically designed keyboard. Other manufacturers have also come to market similar keyboards.

You'll also find keyboards with built-in joysticks sometimes called 'joy buttons.' By using joy buttons you don't have to take your hands off the keyboard and reach for a mouse.

A mouse is not the only input device (peripheral) you can use with Windows or any graphic user interface. Other input devices include trackballs, touch pads, graphic tablets (with and without a pen) and joysticks. These devices feature dozens of designs for serious PC gamers.

The combinations of these devices mentioned above are endless. You only need to decide what is best for you now and the near future to use your PC comfortably.

Use a wrist rest with your keyboard. This will help raise your wrists and keep them straight at all times. Many mouse pads also now include wrist rests.

Section 2:
Components And
Their Functions

Contents

Processors And What They Do

6

Both the "heart" and "brains" of any PC system is the *processor*. All calculating and processing which your PC performs is executed through the processor.

Earlier generations of PCs had to divide the work between two or more processors. The additional processors perform more specialized functions such as calculation complex math formulas and graphics. Today's powerful Pentium processor performs all this work itself.

THE CENTRAL PROCESSING UNIT (CPU)

A computer *chip* or *processor* is a square or rectangular wafer of silicon. The size of a computer chip is about 1/16 to 5/8 of inch. The most important of all the chips on any PC motherboard is the *central processing unit*. As its name suggests, the central processing unit is central to the operation of your computer. Put simply, your PC system cannot operate without the central processing unit. (The terms microprocessor, central processing unit and CPU are used interchangeably.)

The CPU manages every step in the processing of data. It's where all the instructions are executed. This is also the part that controls all the other parts of your PC system.

Chapter 6

Microprocessors also control the logic of almost all digital devices, from clock radios to fuel-injection systems for automobiles.

The CPU is really the core of the computer system because it manages every step in the processing of data. This is where all the instructions are executed. This is also the part that controls all the others. It acts as the conductor and supervisor of the system's hardware components. Also, it's linked, directly or indirectly, with every other component on the motherboard. The CPU must do the following to execute an instruction:

- ❖ Fetch an instruction from memory

- ❖ Decode the instruction to determine which operation is to be performed

- ❖ Fetch the data from memory (if required)

- ❖ Perform the operation specified by the instruction

- ❖ Write the result back to memory, if required

Therefore, the CPU addresses and starts many component groups.

The processor uses address buses, data buses and control buses. These buses enable the processor to perform its tasks. These bus systems are configured differently, depending on the processor class of the PC, which we'll discuss later.

During the development of PCs, the architecture, or inner workings, of CPUs have evolved drastically. An increasing number of transistors and hardwiring have been integrated in extremely small spaces to meet the growing performance demands placed on PC processors.

For example, the Intel 80486 processor contains over 1.2 million transistors on a ceramic tile that's about three square inches and an eighth of an inch thick. This area contains the CPU, the math coprocessor and 8K of cache RAM.

The CPU can be considered as having two internal parts. One is the arithmetic and logic unit (called the ALU). This part controls and executes the basic instructions of the processor such as add, subtract, compare, logical AND and OR, etc.

The second part is the control unit. It's responsible for decoding the instructions, determining where the data will be found and determining where the next instruction in memory will be found.

Most CPUs also have a register file. This is a set of registers that can be loaded with data by certain instructions. The CPU can then reuse these instructions. Because data in the register file can be accessed without causing an external memory read, they can be used immediately.

Also note the interface between the CPU and the memory system is through two registers, the memory address register (MAR) which contains the address of the data or instruction referenced. The memory data register (MDR) contains either the instruction that has been fetched or the data word to be read from or written into memory.

The Intel Pentium processor is the most advanced PC processor available today. When Intel introduced the Pentium processor in 1993, it featured 100 MIPS (Million Instructions Per Second) at a clock speed of 66 MHz. This makes the Pentium almost twice as fast as a 486/66DX2 in integer performance. The differences are even more significant in floating-point performance. Depending on the instruction mix, the Pentium beats its predecessor by three to seven times. Also, it's completely binary compatible with all earlier Intel processors (the 486, 386, 286 and even the 8086).

An example of a CPU

Since so many components are located in a very small area, a special manufacturing technique is needed. This technique enables designers to construct elements as a small as a micrometer (one millionth of a meter). For a comparison, consider that a single human hair is wide enough to cover about 100 of these elements.

The 486 Class Of Processors

Most of today's PCs are shipped with a variation of either a 486 or Pentium processor. These processors are descendants of earlier processors developed by Intel since 1978. Intel is the leading manufacturer of microprocessors for IBM compatible computers. The 8086, 80286, 80386, 80486 and Pentium processors represent five generations and performance classes in the history of microprocessors.

The Intel 80486 processor

Most pre-Pentium class computers use a 80486 or a variation of the 486 processor. Intel introduced the 486 in 1989. The 486 was more than a simple processor; it was the first *integrated chip*. This chip consolidates four different function groups into one component:

Visit Intel on the World Wide Web for more information: www.intel.com

❖ Actual CPU

❖ Math coprocessor

❖ Cache controller

❖ Two 4K caches

The math coprocessor helped the 486 process both math and graphical functions much faster than previous processors. The 486 used a full 32-bit structure, both internally and externally. The clock speeds of a 486 are 66 MHz and 100 MHz.

The 486 was the first processor from Intel to include internal cache (two 4K caches for a total of 8K). The more powerful 486DX4 included a 16K cache controller.

Because of the internal cache controller, the 486 rarely had to wait for the PC's rather slow RAM. (The CPU operates at a higher frequency.) The cache acts as a type of intelligent buffer. Since this technique prevented long waiting periods, the 486 was the first processor to operate within a single clock cycle. This capability alone made the 486 far superior to the old 386.

The Intel 486DX CPU

The 486 included a complete command set (including those used by its predecessors). The 486 was downwardly compatible so it was able to run applications originally written for the earlier processors, including the original 8086.

The four types of 486 processors

Intel eventually released four types of 486 processors.

486SX processor

In 1991 Intel released a smaller "brother" of the 486 called the 486SX (shown on the right). This processor did not include a math coprocessor and it featured slower clock speeds (fastest was 33 MHz) .

486DX processor

The 486DX included a math coprocessor to speed the performance of complex math calculations.

486DX2 processor

In 1992 Intel released a new member of the 486 family called the 486DX2. The 486DX2 was designed to execute twice as fast as the "old" 486 because of *clock-doubling* technology. It could operate at clock speeds of 50 MHz and 66 MHz.

80486DX4 processor

In 1994 Intel released the 486DX4 processor which used clock-tripling technology (see picture on the right). This made its internal clock rate even faster than the 486DX2. The clock speeds of the 486DX4 reached rates of 75 MHz and 100 MHz.

Cyrix 486 class processors

Cyrix also manufactured 486 class processors.

Cx486DRx2 and Cx486SRx2 processors

If you're looking for a way to "instantly" turn your 386 computer into a 486 model, this chip will do it. The Cx486DRx2 and CX486SRx2 look like 386 processors to the motherboard and other components in your computer system, but it runs at twice the speed of the original 386 chip.

> Visit Cyrix on the World Wide Web for more information: www.cyrix.com

When you buy one of these clock-doubled upgrades, you get the processor, chip puller to remove your original 386, software to test you system and enable the 1K internal cache and installation instructions. You can upgrade your computer in about 30 minutes.

The companion CD-ROM includes a program called CYRXTEST.BAT that lets you determine if one of these upgrade processors is compatible with your 386 computer. You can call Cyrix for additional information at 1-800-46-CYRIX.

Processors And What They Do

The Cyrix Cx486 processor

Cx486DX2

Cyrix also made the Cx486DX2 processor. This processor has clock speeds of 50 MHz, 66 MHz and 80 MHz. Both 3-volt and 5-volt systems are available. The Cyrix integrated math coprocessor is 10% faster than the Intel 80486DX which means that complicated graphics and calculations can be performed much faster. An 8K internal cache speeds up access to RAM.

Advanced Micro Devices (AMD)

Advanced Micro Devices (AMD) also has versions of the 486 processor available. AMD's Am486DX is comparable to the Intel 486DX, with math coprocessor and 8K cache. It's available in clock speeds of 33, 40 and 25/50 MHz.

> Visit AMD on the World Wide Web for more information:
> www.amd.com

Although AMD's Am486SX has no math coprocessor, it does have an 8K cache. The Am486SX is currently available in 33 and 40 MHz clock speeds and in two volt versions: 3.3-volt, with power management features required by notebook PCs, and a 5-volt version.

Chapter 6

Another version AMD has available in the 486-class is the Am486DX2 which features a clock speed of 80 MHz. The Am486DX2 is designed for increased performance over other 486-class processors running at 40 MHz to 60 MHz.

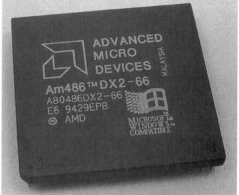

The Am486DX (shown on the right) is comparable to the Intel 486DX.

The Am486DXL2 includes a System Management Mode (SMM) and processor clock for more efficient power control. When the computer is not being used but is still switched on, system power can be reduced to less than 30 watts.

Feature oriented processors

The feature oriented processors were designed to be used in computer systems that use less electrical power. Not too long ago, these types of processors were the notebook, subnotebook and handheld computers.

These computer systems now include a new emerging generation of environmentally friendly desktop computers that consume less electrical power. The new performance oriented processors are designed to deliver more computing power to the user at far less cost.

SL processors

The SL processors were designed originally for use in mobile computers (laptops, notebooks and subnotebooks). These processors operate at 3.3 volts instead of the 5 volts required by their predecessors. Since these processors use less power, they extend the life of the batteries which run them.

In addition, an SL processor has a special System Management Mode (SMM) which can control the functions of a computer. For example, SMM can dim the LCD screen, switch off a hard drive or reduce the speed of the processor. All this helps extend the life of the batteries. The main function of SMM is power management. The SL processor complies with the Energy Star Program administered by the United States government.

SMM has two important features:

- ❖ A new interrupt called the SMI (System Management Interrupt)
- ❖ A new address space in which the SMM routines are executed

This separate address space is independent of the 486's main address space. Therefore, it doesn't interfere with operating system routines or application programs.

An SMI is issued to the 486 processor when the computer system requires a power management service from the SMM program. The processor begins running the SMM program in its address space. It then performs the requested service. A new RSM (Resume) instruction is used to exit the SMM program using. The computer system returns to its original condition. The system is unaware that it may have been suspended for a few minutes, hours or days by the SMM.

Most of the latest 486 processors incorporate the SL power management features. Except for operating at 5 volts, the 486SX, 486DX and 486DX2 processors contain the SL features. These chips called the SL Enhanced 486 processors. Some of the newer processors will even operate at 3.3 volts.

By using these new features, computer manufacturers can design computers that use less energy. The same processor used in a mobile computer can also be used in a desktop computer. This makes it easier for manufacturers to standardize their computer systems. It also helps them design "green" computers with an additional goal of saving the environment.

●●●

PENTIUM AND PENTIUM CLASS PROCESSORS

In late 1992, Intel announced the fifth generation of its compatible family of processors. Virtually everyone assumed that Intel would naturally call this new processor the 586. However, Intel realized they couldn't copyright or trademark a number designation. So, to prevent other companies from using the same name for the clone chips they were likely to develop, Intel called the new processor the Pentium.

Processors And What They Do

Pentium processors

It's easy to see why the Pentium is the most advanced processor yet developed; just look at a single statistic. The 486 chip contains the equivalent of 1.2 million transistors. A Pentium has more than 3 million transistors on board. This tells us that many more functions have been integrated into the Pentium processor.

Visit Intel on the World Wide Web for more information on the Pentium: www.intel.com

A computing rule of thumb holds the more integrated a chip, the faster it runs because the access time is reduced. Putting more functions on one chip means less time spent communicating with outside specialized chips, which would otherwise have to perform those functions.

The Pentium is powering most of today's PCs. It's responsible for creating a new generation of multimedia and applications based on communications. Although the Pentium processor adds new features and improvements, it's still fully software compatible with descendants of the Intel microprocessor family.

The Pentium processor can be used with several operating systems:

❖ Windows 95

❖ UNIX

❖ Windows-NT

❖ OS/2

❖ Windows 3.1/3.11

The Pentium has the horsepower to be used with calculation-intensive applications, including:

❖ 3-D modeling

❖ Computer-aided design/engineering

❖ High-throughput client/server

❖ Large-scale financial analysis

❖ Network applications

106

❖ Rich electronic mail

❖ Virtual reality

Intel points to five major areas that account for the Pentium's performance improvements.

Superscalar architecture

A 486 processor executes integer instructions through a single instruction pipeline in five discrete steps: prefetch, decode, address generate, execute and write back. When the 486 is executing an instruction, the pipeline is unavailable until that instruction passes to the decode step. Only at that time is the pipeline free to begin another operation on the next instruction.

The Pentium has two independent pipelines called the U-pipeline and the V-pipeline. This means that while one instruction is being operated on through one pipeline, the subsequent instruction can be handled by the second pipeline. Certain classes of instructions cannot be performed in parallel since a subsequent instruction may depend on the outcome of the first instruction's execution. Special circuitry on the Pentium insures these kind of dependent instructions are properly executed.

A processor having multiple instruction pipelines is termed superscaler architecture. For integer instructions, it's possible to execute two instructions in a single clock cycle. This is responsible for most of the performance gain of the Pentium processor.

Processor cache

The time to access main memory is multiple clock cycles longer than to access on-chip memory. To increase speed, the 486 processors all contain 8K of this on-chip cache memory. By keeping a copy of the data and instructions the processor needs in the cache memory, less cycles are used to access the much slower main memory.

The Pentium processor doubles the amount of on-chip memory by providing a separate 8K for data cache and 8K for instruction (sometimes called code) cache. Intel claims the data and instructions can be accessed immediately from the cache memory 95% of the time, speeding up performance enormously.

Chapter
6
Section
2

107

64-bit data bus

A 486 processor communicates with the outside world by using a 32-bit wide data bus. This means that 32 bits of information can be transferred from main memory to the processor with each clock cycle. The Pentium has a 64-bit wide data bus. This effectively doubles the amount of information the processor can transfer at once.

The Pentium also has a new burst transfer mode with built-in data integrity checking so information moves faster and more reliably over the data bus. These new features are capable of increasing the data transfer performance by 3 to 4 times over 486 systems.

Branch prediction

Any processor spends a large number of clock cycles performing branches. The Pentium uses a Branch Target Buffer (BTB) to speed up branch performance. Here's how it works:

The BTB is actually another small, high speed cache. When a branch instruction is encountered, the instruction and its branch address (the target) are saved in the BTB. In anticipation of a branch, the instruction code at the target address is preloaded into the instruction cache. If the prediction is right, the branch can be made immediately without having to wait for the instruction code at the target address to be loaded.

Intel claims the BTB can be used to predict the correct branch in more than 90% of the cases.

Floating point processing

Many of today's business applications are designed to use the built-in math coprocessor found in 486DX and 486SL systems and the 487SX coprocessor for 486SX systems. Spreadsheets, database managers, computer aided design, numerical analysis, and almost all graphic-intensive applications are speeded up by the floating point processing performed by a math coprocessor.

The math coprocessors in the Pentium has been redesigned to give much better performance. Many of the floating point operations can be performed in a single clock cycle. Overall floating point operations are improved by a factor of 3 to 5 times.

Here's a simplified block diagram of the Pentium processor:

Processors And What They Do

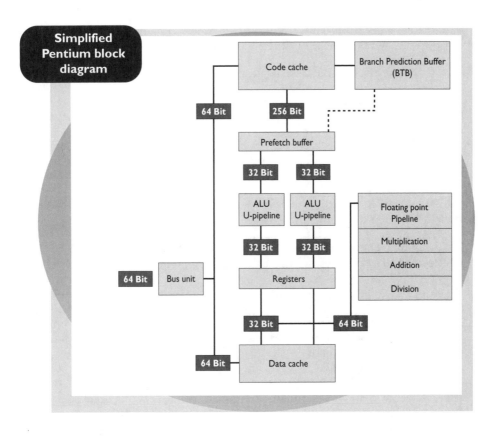

Simplified Pentium block diagram

Code cache

Branch Prediction Buffer (BTB)

64 Bit

256 Bit

Prefetch buffer

32 Bit

32 Bit

ALU U-pipeline

ALU U-pipeline

Floating point Pipeline

Multiplication

32 Bit

32 Bit

Addition

64 Bit

Bus unit

Registers

Division

32 Bit

64 Bit

64 Bit

Data cache

Comparisons

The following table lists the versions of the Pentium processor and their bus/clock speeds (in MHz) and the P-rating:

Pentium processor	Bus/clock speeds (in MHz)	P rating
Intel Pentium 100	66/100	100
Intel Pentium 120	60/120	120
Intel Pentium 133	66/133	133
Intel Pentium 150	60/150	150
Intel Pentium 166	66/166	166
Intel Pentium 200	66/200	200

Chapter 6

The original Pentium computers were shipped in June 1993. These computers used the 60 MHz processor and required extensive cooling features:

❖ Some used small cooling fans mounted directly to the processor.

❖ Others used an oversize heat sink (small ceramic or cast metal part mounted on top of the processor). A heat sink absorbs the heat the processor generates and ventilates it into the air inside the PC case.

❖ Others cool the processor by liquid chemicals which cool the chip by evaporation.

All use oversize cooling fans to exhaust the hot air generated by the Pentium processor from the computer case.

One notable characteristic of Pentium computers is they all use secondary caches. Many have 256K or 512K of secondary cache memory. Using a large, fast cache significantly reduces the time the Pentium must wait for external data thereby taking advantage of the Pentium's amazing processing speed.

Most of these earlier Pentium computers were designed as file servers. As such, they are equipped to accommodate huge amounts of main memory, fast secondary storage - mostly SCSI class hard drives and a high performance EISA or Micro Channel bus.

Intel is aiming to get Pentium computers on everyone's desktop and has aggressively reduced the prices of these processors. This has narrowed the price difference between a 100 MHz Pentium and DX2/100 system to under $100 in some cases.

Pentium Pro CPUs

The Pentium Pro processor is the next generation processor family from Intel. It's perfect for computers requiring powerful operating systems such as Windows NT or Unix. Pentium Pro processors are available with speeds of 150 MHz, 166 MHz, 180 MHz or 200 MHz.

> Visit Intel on the World Wide Web for more information on the "Pro": www.intel.com

The physical differences between a Pentium Pro and a Pentium include the Pros having built-in secondary cache and the ability of executing instructions in parallel.

The Pentium Pro processor is designed to deliver optimal performance with 32-bit software. However, it is possible to run your current software. (Early tests though showed that 150-MHz Pentium Pros ran 16-bit programs slower than existing Pentiums did.) The Pentium Pro processor schedules instructions at run time dependent upon data availability. This means that the Pentium Pro processor performs well on any code designed to run on previous generation 32-bit Intel processors. The Pentium Pro processor will also execute 286-targeted code, but the performance gain will not be as high.

If you're considering a Pentium Pro to run with Windows 95 (and can afford it), avoid the Pentium Pro 150-MHz version. This version of the Pentium Pro isn't much faster than P-166s yet costs much more. Instead, jump up to a Pentium Pro 200-MHz processor. They're about 14 percent faster than a typical Pentium-166 MHz processor. That's a significant performance boost when you consider that the average P-166 is 12 percent faster than the average P-133.

Since Pentium Pros excel when running 32-bit programs, dealers starting selling Pentium Pro systems with Windows NT (a true 32-bit operating system) instead of Windows 95. However, now many dealers and vendors are selling Pentium Pro systems with Windows 95 as well as with NT. They discovered that more 32-bit Windows 95 applications are now on the market. Furthermore, a Pentium Pro 200 is the fastest Windows 95 system you can buy.

Cyrix 6x86 CPUs

Cyrix manufacturers high performance processors that rival or exceed the Pentium processor class in many areas. The Cyrix 6x86 processor (called the M1 at one point) can run both 16-bit and 32-bit software. It's fully compatible with DOS, Windows 95, Windows NT, Windows and OS/2 operating systems. Furthermore, the 6x86 processor has been certified Windows 95 compatible by Microsoft.

Visit Cyrix on the World Wide Web for more information:
www.cyrix.com

Chapter 6

Instead of naming these chips for the clock speed at which they operate, Cyrix is using a name that suggests their performance capabilities compared to equivalent Intel Pentium processors. Notice the plus mark in each 6x86 processor names. This plus mark is used to indicate better performance. For example, a 6x86 processor with a P-rating of "P166+" (regardless of processor name and clock speed) indicates performance faster than a 166 MHz Pentium processor.

The plus mark indicates performance that consistently exceeds the same Pentium processor Megahertz level.

The table on the right explains these names. For example, while the P120+ operates at a clock speed of 100 MHz, its performance is better than that of an Intel Pentium 120.

Cyrix processor	Bus/clock speeds (in MHz)	P rating
6x86-P120+GP	50/100	P120+
6x86-P133+GP	55/110	P133+
6x86-P150+GP	60/120	P150+
6x86-P166+GP	66/133	P166+
6x86-P200+GP	75/150	P200+

The 6x86 is the first in a new series of high-performance, x86-compatible processors. This sixth-generation processor achieves optimum performance on existing and emerging software applications. The superscalar architecture of the Integer Unit allows multiple instructions to be processed simultaneously in two separate pipelines.

Through the use of innovative architectural techniques, the 6x86 eliminates many data dependencies and resource conflicts inherent in other microprocessor designs. The 6x86 consists of five major functional blocks:

An example of a C6x86 processor

❖ Integer Unit

❖ Cache Unit

❖ Memory Management Unit

❖ Floating Point Unit

❖ Bus Interface Unit

Instructions are executed in the X and Y pipelines within the Integer Unit and the Floating Point Unit. The Cache Unit stores the most recently used data and instructions allowing fast access to the information by the Integer Unit and FPU.

> **NOTE**
>
> The Cyrix 6x86 processor cannot be used as an upgrade processor for the 586 computer. Cyrix doesn't sell the 6x86 processor as an upgrade processor. However, some dealers or resellers may offer a 6x86 upgrade solution.

Physical addresses are calculated by the Memory Management Unit and passed to the Cache Unit and the Bus Interface Unit (BIU). The BIU provides the interface between the external system board and the processor's internal execution units.

Couple the performance with very attractive prices and you can upgrade to a Cyrix 6x86 CPU as easily as an Intel.

Advanced Micro Devices AMD-K5

Advanced Micro Devices (AMD) has manufactured microprocessors since 1982. AMD is the world's second-largest supplier of Windows-compatible processors. Most of AMD's business comes from Asia and Central and South America areas than in the U.S.

Visit AMD on the World Wide Web for more information: www.amd.com

Chapter
6
Section
2

The AMD-K5 (originally called AMD5k86TM) is AMD's alternative to the Pentium. It features an independently developed architecture that delivers the fifth-generation performance PC users need to run the latest Microsoft Windows 95 compatible software applications. The AMD-K5-PR75/PR90/PR100 processors and initial production of the AMD-K5 processor began in the second quarter of 1996.

The table on the right shows the AMD-K5 processors and their bus/clock speed.

Processor	Bus/clock speed
PR75	50/75
PR90	60/90
PR100	66/100
PR120	60/90
PR133	66/100
PR150	not available yet

Like Cyrix, AMD can compete head on with Intel because their chips are compatible with existing Pentium motherboards. In most cases you should be able to remove a slower Pentium processor (i.e., a Pentium 75 MHz) and insert a new, faster AMD K5 PR150 for a much noticeable increase in speed.

NOTE

The AMD-K5 requires a heatsink and fan. Several motherboard manufacturers support the AMD-K5 processors. However, older versions of motherboards may require a BIOS update from the manufacturer to properly recognize the AMD-K5 processors. Please contact your favorite dealer or motherboard manufacturer for more information.

Also, AMD designed the AMD-K5 line of processors to be pin compatible and socket compatible with the Pentium.

Furthermore, the AMD-K5 line of processors are fully compatible with Windows and Windows 95. This means that the AMD-K5 processor is compatible with the Windows operating systems but also with Novell NetWare, OS/2 Warp and tens of thousands of software packages.

The result is a true Pentium alternative for the PC industry. Although the AMD K5 line of processors doesn't include anything as fast as the 6x86 200+ from Cyrix, they tend to be less expensive than the Cyrix processors. The next entry into the AMD K5 line of processors is the K5-PR150 and soon thereafter the next generation of processors from AMD code-named the K6.

MMX

For the first time since 1985 (the release of Intel's 80386 processor) Intel has modified the base set of on-chip instructions, the lowest common denominator of DOS and Windows applications. A total of 57 instructions were added into Intel's MMX chip. The MMX chip, scheduled to start shipping in early 1997, is optimized for multimedia. It provides more complex gaming environments, better video playback and more powerful graphic features.

To achieve 10-20% enhancements over existing Pentiums' performance at the same speeds—and an estimated 60% gain with applications designed for MMX—Intel made three primary adjustments to the architecture of their chip.

1. 57 instructions specially designed for audio, video, and graphic data have been added. Many multimedia applications use parallel and repetitive sequences that these new commands streamline to improve overall performance.

2. Single Instruction Multiple Data (SIMD) has been incorporated into the new design. This allows one instruction to perform the same action on multiple pieces of data, which reduces compute-intensive loops common in multimedia programs.

    Intel uses the analogy of a drill sergeant having to command each individual soldier to come to attention versus the entire squad responding to a single command.

3. The on-chip memory cache has been doubled to 32k. This reduces the number of times the chip must access slower off-chip memory areas.

On-chip support is also incorporated for MPEG-2 and DVD.

This all provides vivid sound, rich colors, enhanced 3-D rendering and simultaneous, real-time activities, like multiple channels of audio, video and animation.

The MMX chips for desktop systems include 166MHz and 200MHz speeds and 150 and 166 speed chips are available for notebook computers. Overdrive enhancements should be available in the second part of 1997. The current price of a 200MHz MMX chip is about $500 but that price will continue to drop.

Many manufacturers already include the MMX chip in their PCs. MMX chips are fully compatible with existing resources. Only a few programs require MMX CPUs to run. Furthermore, programs that depend on MMX will probably be offered in both MMX and non-MMX varieties for a few years yet.

But is it worth it? The improvements you will see depend on how much an application relies on MMX enhancements and how aggressively it takes advantage of the technology. The real improvements will be seen primarily in multimedia (games, presentations, etc.) and graphic programs. It's really up to software developers to create programs that utilize the potential of MMX. Some MMX programs are available now and it won't be long before applications, particularly games and high-end graphics, make MMX a standard.

Chapter
6
Section
2

Cyrix 6x86MX CPUs

The 6x86MX is the latest series of processors from Cyrix. The 6x86MX, originally referred to as the M2 processor, this CPU is essentially a 6x86 processor with Intel MMX compatible instructions. Cyrix has added several enhancements which in turn boosts the performance of the 6x86MX. These include:

Visit Cyrix on the World Wide Web for more information: www.cyrix.com

❖ 64K Cache Unit - four times larger than 6x86 CPU

❖ TLB Size - three times larger than 6x86 CPU - enhances cache performance

❖ Voltage - 2.8V uses less power

❖ MMX - compatible with Intel MMX processors

❖ Socket 7 compatible

The table on the right lists the three 6x86MX CPUs that are available:

As with the 6x86 CPUs, these are cleverly name to indicate their relative performance compared to the Intel Pentium MMX CPUs.

Cyrix processor	Bus/Clock speeds (MHz)	P rating
6x86-PR166GP	60/150	P166+
6x86-PR200GP	66/166	P200+
6x86-PR233GP	75/188	P233+

AMD K6 CPUs

The K6 is the most recent series of processors made by AMD. Like the Cyrix 6x86MX, the K6 is another Intel MMX-compatible CPU.

Visit AMD on the World Wide Web for more information: www.amd.com

Although it is pin-compatible with the Intel Pentium MMX CPUs, AMD has claimed that the K6 CPU performs better than the Intel Pentium Pro CPUs. Independent tests have suggested that the AMD-K6 does deliver better performance than the Pentium Pro for some types of processing. And since the K6 is compatible with standard Pentium motherboards (Socket 7 compatible), the overall cost of a K6 computer system is less than a Pentium Pro system.

The table on the right lists the three K6 CPUs that are available.

The K6s are a very attractive alternative to the Intel and Cyrix processors. Some of the features which account for the K6 performance are the following:

AMD processor	Bus/Clock speeds (in MHz)	P rating
AMD-K6-166	66/166	P166+
AMD-K6-200	66/200	P200+
AMD-K6-233	66/233	P233+

❖ Integrated 64K Cache Unit

❖ Large TLB enhances cache performance

❖ Large branch prediction buffer

❖ MMX compatible with Intel MMX processors

❖ Socket 7 compatible

DETERMINING PROCESSOR PERFORMANCE

How well a processor performs in based on many factors. Although processing speed is probably the most familiar, you should consider other factors such as cache, power management and two rating systems.

Internal cache

Internal cache, also called *primary cache* or *L1*, is built-into 486 and later processors. It's a form of fast memory that retains a copy of frequently used data and instructions. Basic operations are faster because using this memory is faster than accessing the processor itself for an instruction.

You should use internal cache memory if it is available. A cache size of 128K is a sufficient for a PC in Windows 3.x or Windows 95. Processors with a large cache memory can hold more information and therefore run faster than processors with smaller cache memory. Make certain, however, that using internal cache memory doesn't conflict with any accessories you may need to use.

See Chapter 7 for more information on internal cache.

Chapter
6
Section
2

Chapter 6

External cache

External cache is located outside the CPU but still on the motherboard. External cache consists of a row of Static RAM chips (SRAM chips) of either 64K or 256K capacity, resulting in a cache of either 64 or 256K. External cache also increases the speed of frequently used data and instructions but is slower than internal cache. External cache memory sizes range from 64K to 1 Meg. The greatest improvement in system performance is probably the first 64K of external cache memory. The benefits diminish when you add more external cache.

External cache is also called *secondary cache* or *L2*. See Chapter 7 for more information on external cache.

Power management capabilities

A processor with power management capabilities such as System Management Mode (SMM) can put itself in a sleep mode if it isn't used for a certain length of time. It therefore requires minimum power to operate, however it has enough to sense a keystroke or mouse movement. It then returns to full power. Most notebook computers have this feature to prolong battery life.

Power management features also now extend to shutting down unused hard disks, modems, printers or other peripherals.

> **NOTE**
>
> Processors with power management features normally require BIOS firmware or other software to work effectively.

The strength of the electric current which the processor receives is its operating voltage. Processors are normally available with two operating voltages:

1. 3.3-volt processors are used when power consumption is a major consideration such as notebook computers.

2. 5-volt processors remain the standard for desktop computers.

A grid of small holes on the motherboard is where the processor is inserted. This grid is called the *processor socket*.

Clock speed

An important factor in determining the processor's performance is its *clock frequency* or *clock speed*. A crystal oscillator controls clock speeds using a sliver of quartz in a small tin container.

This quartz begins to oscillate (vibrate) when voltage is applied to it. This oscillation occurs at a harmonic rate that is determined by the shape and size of the crystal sliver. The oscillations originate from the crystal as a current that alternates at the harmonic rate of the crystals. This alternating current is the *clock signal*.

The clock frequency does not use minutes or even seconds but is measured in cycles per second and is specified by the unit "megahertz" (MHz). Today's fast Pentium class processors run millions of these cycles per second. Therefore, the speed is measured in megahertz (MHz)

One Megahertz (1 MHz) corresponds to 1 million cycles, or clock ticks, per second. A Pentium processor operating at a clock speed of 166 MHz, for example, can perform an operation 166 million times each second

The smallest element of time for the processor is one cycle. Any action the processor performs requires at least once cycle. It's not unusual that multiple cycles are required to complete an action. The clock speed has improved dramatically with each new generation of processor. For example, the old 8086 processor required four cycles plus wait states to transfer data to and from memory.

As its name suggests, a *wait state* is a clock tick in which nothing happens to prevent the processor from moving ahead of the system. Today's powerful Pentium class processors require only two cycles plus any wait states for the same transfer.

The time required to execute instructions also varies. The old 8086 and 8088 processors typically required 12 cycles to execute a single instruction. Compare that to today's Pentium class processor. It requires only one cycle to execute a single instruction.

Chapter
6
Section
2

119

Since PCs have different instruction execution times (in cycles), it can be difficult to compare systems based only on clock speed. Many other factors affect system performance. The following graphic shows this: One reason why the 486 processor is so fast is that it has an average instruction-execution time of 2 clock cycles. Therefore, a 100 MHz Pentium is about equal to a 200 MHz 486, which is about equal to a 400 MHz 386 that is about equal to a 1000 MHz 8088. As you can see, you must be careful in comparing systems based only on MHz.

The reason one processor can run "faster" than another processor even though both have the same clock rate run is efficiency. A better alternative is to use comparative performance tests called benchmarks. Two examples of this approach are the iCOMP Index and the P Rating.

External and internal clock speeds

The *external clock speed* is the speed at which the processor accesses information outside itself, in external cache memory or system RAM. The *internal clock speed* is the speed at which the processor obtains information within its own confines—in its registers or in its internal cache memory.

A processor with a higher clock speed normally run proportionally faster than an otherwise identical system and processor with a lower clock speed. For example, a 486DX with a clock speed of 50 MHz computes twice as fast as a 486DX with a clock speed of 25 MHz.

P Rating

We've mentioned how important clock speed (MHz) is in considering a processor. However, because of the technology used today in designing and creating processors, clock speed isn't necessarily the best way to measure a processor's power. In other words, although clock speed is still important, it's no longer an accurate or consistent measure of a processor's power. Instead, the "P-rating" is being used more often.

Major corporations such as Cyrix, IBM Microelectronics, SGS-Thomson Microelectronics and Advanced Micro Devices jointly developed the P-rating system. The P-rating system allows end-users to base purchases on relative PC performance levels rather than just the clock speed (MHz) of the processor. The new evaluation system relates the results of industry-standard benchmarks to what is achieved by an Intel Pentium processor of a given frequency.

Example of a P-rating

A Pentium 166 processor is inserted in a computer system with carefully documented configuration. A benchmark utility program called The Ziff-Davis Winstone 96 is run three times on the PC system powered by the Pentium processor. The benchmark results are averaged to provide a composite score.

Next, the Pentium processor is removed and replaced with another processor (for example the AMD-K5 processor). The Winstone 96 benchmarks are repeated. A Winstone score is obtained from the same system now running the AMD-K5 processor. The system configuration remains identical throughout all benchmark testing so any benchmark differences are the result of the processor itself. All peripherals are carefully documented.

If the benchmark tests second processor wins the same benchmark rating as the Pentium 90 but scores less than a Pentium 100, the processor is assigned a P-rating of 90. In other words, this number represents the quickest Pentium it can tie or beat. If the second processor scores slightly higher than the 90 MHz Pentium, the P-rating may be expressed as 90+.

The AMD-K5 processor is assigned the highest P-Rating at which it delivers average Winstone scores that equals the Pentium's. For example, if an AMD-K5 processor offers the equivalent performance of a 100 MHz Pentium, it receives a P-Rating of "PR100."

For example, a processor with a P150 rating would have performance comparable to a 150 MHz Pentium processor, regardless of its actual clock speed.

Whether the P-rating is the true measure of performance may be open to debate. Intel, naturally, claims that P-ratings are misleading. However, many feel the P-rating can be valuable as an aid when shopping for Pentium class processors. The rating can help end users understand true processor performance equivalences.

Chapter
6
Section
2

iCOMP Index

The iCOMP (Intel COmparative Microprocessor Performance) Index can provide a quick way to compare the performance levels of the Intel processors. Intel created this index to compare processors based on comparative power. The higher the iCOMP rating, the higher the relative performance of the processor.

iCOMP is a series of specific benchmarks that can be run against Intel processors to compare their relative performance.

Not surprising, the Pentium processors are the highest performing members of processors from Intel. The table on the right lists the different Pentium processors with their iCOMP rating.

Pentium processor	iCOMP Index 2.0 rating
75 MHz	67
100 MHz	90
120 MHz	100
133 MHz	111
150 MHz	114
166 MHz	127
200 MHz	142

INCREASING SYSTEM PERFORMANCE

System tuning

Although you cannot increase the performance of an existing processor, you can tune your system for optimum performance. System tuning includes deleting or reorganizing files and directories, defragmenting and caching your hard drive or maximizing the amount of unused RAM. Since several books and articles have been written on system tuning, we won't dwell on the subject here.

You have other ways of increasing your system's performance. For example, you can take your 286AT and convert it to a 486 or Pentium by replacing the motherboard. This lets you reuse the other components on your computer: the case, the power supply, the hard and floppy drives, the video card, etc.

Unfortunately, replacing a motherboard is a very expensive way to upgrade your computer, especially if your trying to increase performance. A computer only a few years old still uses a hard drive from a different era. This hard drive simply cannot have the performance characteristics offered by today's new class of hard drives.

Another way to boost performance is to upgrade your processor. The Cyrix line of upgrade processors let 386 computer users easily move up to 486 class performance. By simply replacing the 386 processor on most computers, an upgrade processor can increase a computer's internal performance significantly. The cost is a few minutes of work to replace the processor and few hundred dollars.

Adding a math coprocessor in a 486 system

A problem that a 486 processor has when working with binary numbers is the inability to work with fractions. When a computer is used to working with zeros and ones, it becomes difficult to work with a half of a number. So, computers use a technique called *floating point notation*.

Floating point notation is a method for storing and calculating numbers in which the decimal points don't line up as in fixed point numbers. The significant digits are stored as a unit called the *mantissa*. The location of the radix point (decimal point in base 10) is stored in a separate unit called the *exponent*.

Floating point methods are used for calculating a large range of numbers quickly. Floating point operations can be implemented in hardware (math coprocessor), or they can be done in software. They can also be performed in a separate floating point processor that is connected to the main processor through a channel

Pentium and Pentium class processors (and many 486 processors) have built-in floating point units and do not need a math coprocessor. However, if your 486 processor doesn't have a math coprocessor, then you can increase your performance by adding a *math coprocessor* to your system. Typical applications that do heavy number crunching are spreadsheets, computer aided design and other vector based graphic programs.

We'll use an example to illustrate the difference between using a coprocessor with vector graphics and pixel graphics. Suppose that you ask a friend to draw a circle of a specified size on a sheet of grid paper. One way to do this is to specify the coordinates of every point on the circle. Then your friend simply draws each of these points and the circle is completed. This is a *pixel-based graphic*. Each point is clearly and individually defined.

Chapter 6

Another way to construct the circle is to specify the coordinates of the circle's center and its radius. This is an example of a *vector-based graphic* since each point is defined only by its relation to the centerpoint and the circle's radius resulting in a formula (a vector).

Now we'll transfer this circle to the computer screen and try to move the graphic 3 inches (7.62 cm) to the left and 1 inch (2.5 cm) down. To move the pixel-based graphic, it's only necessary to shift information in video RAM. A coprocessor is not necessary since this is a task the CPU can perform easily.

However, to move the vector-based graphic, the coordinates to every point on the circle must be recalculated because its centerpoint is being moved. In this case, a coprocessor would be very useful because the task requires the CPU to perform several fractional operations.

As the number of floating point operations that are required increases, the more a math coprocessor will increase the performance of your system.

Most 286 and 386 based computers have a math coprocessor socket on the motherboard. By adding an appropriate model math coprocessor you can speed up these types of applications immediately. Math coprocessors are manufactured by Intel, AMD, Cyrix, ITT and USLI and are compatible with almost all CPUs.

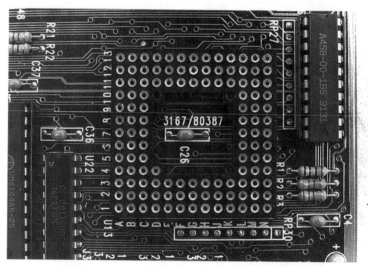

Math coprocessor socket on the motherboard

Processors And What They Do

The 387 is a math coprocessor manufactured by Intel

A math coprocessor on some 486 processors is already integrated into the chip. These 486es won't need a math coprocessor socket. However, other versions of the 486 processor, for example the 486SXes, do not have a built-in math coprocessor. So you can speed up math intensive applications by adding an appropriate math coprocessor to these systems.

One company that specializes in a high performance math coprocessor is Weiteck. Their coprocessor is designed to boost the performance of AutoCAD, a computer aided design application. The Weiteck coprocessor is significantly faster than standard math coprocessors.

Examples of math coprocessors

Chapter 6

OverDrive processors/486 upgrades

Your 486 may be too "young" to be simply discarded and yet is too slow to run today's newer software, hard drives or to surf the Internet. Perhaps the answer is to improve the performance of the system by upgrading the processor. This isn't always the best option but for some systems it may be the most cost-efficient option.

A CPU upgrade can be a quick, major boost to your system. They're usually easy to install and set up. However, some require changing CMOS settings or motherboard jumpers. In rare cases, installing a CPU upgrade in the wrong orientation or with the motherboard jumpers set incorrectly can damage the CPU, the motherboard or both.

The upgrades we talk about here all offer a noticeable boost in performance. They also replace the missing math coprocessor in the 486SX. Basically, each upgrade is a replacement processor with some special provisions to allow it to pop into and operate in an older PC's CPU socket.

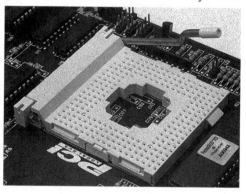

Installing one of these upgrades is simple. This is especially true if your PC has a ZIF socket. A ZIF (Zero Insertion Force) socket uses a simple lever which loosens or tightens its grip on the chip (see picture on the right). Total installation time is about minutes.

Intel

Intel OverDrive processors are a family of processor upgrades created for the 486 and Pentium class processors. If you're using a 486 processor, you'll discover that many of the applications you use daily, including word processors, desktop publishing, and even games, will run faster on an OverDrive processor.

Visit Intel on the World Wide Web for more information:
www.intel.com

Pentium OverDrive processors (for Pentium processors)

Pentium OverDrive Processors are available for the Pentium processors. Intel calls this "the ultimate PC upgrade." Pentium OverDrive processors help users improve the performance of virtually all PC software applications and become faster on the Internet.

The Pentium OverDrive processor has features similar to the Pentium:

* ❖ Advanced (.35 micron) Pentium processor technology

* ❖ Superscalar architecture

* ❖ 64-bit data bus

* ❖ Branch prediction

* ❖ High-performance floating point unit

* ❖ 16K on chip-cache

* ❖ Compatible pin-out for the 120/133 MHz Pentium OverDrive processor

OverDrive processors for PCs using a 486 processor

Intel offers two types of OverDrive processors for a PC using a 486 processor. You can probably upgrade your 486 processor to Pentium processor technology by installing the Pentium OverDrive processor, which has the following features:

* ❖ Pentium processor superscalar architecture

* ❖ 32K enhanced on-chip cache memory

* ❖ Super fast math coprocessor

* ❖ Integrated fan

The Pentium OverDrive processor is the recommended upgrade option for SX2 or DX2 processors. It also supports 486 SX and 486DX processors with either 237-pin sockets or 238-pin sockets.

Intel has two versions of the Pentium OverDrive processors:

Chapter

6

Section

2

127

1. 63-MHz Pentium OverDrive processors for 25/50-MHz systems

2. 83-MHz Pentium OverDrive processors for 33/66-MHz systems.

Intel DX4 OverDrive Processors

The DX4 OverDrive, like all Intel products, is a high quality processor. It's the recommended option for upgradeable Intel 486 processors. The features of this upgrade include the following:

- ❖ Intel's speed-tripling technology

- ❖ On-chip math coprocessor

- ❖ Enhanced 16K cache

- ❖ Heatsink

- ❖ On-package voltage regulation

Two versions of the DX4 OverDrive processor are available for 486 SX and 486DX processors:

1. 75-MHz IntelDX4 OverDrive processors for 20/25-MHz systems

2. 100-MHz IntelDX4 OverDrive processors for 33-MHz systems.

Future OverDrive processors

Future upgrades from Intel include higher speed Pentium OverDrive processors for today's Pentium processors. These include the following Pentium OverDrive processors:

- ❖ 180-MHz Pentium OverDrive processor upgrade for the 120-MHz Pentium processor

- ❖ 200-MHz Pentium OverDrive processor upgrade for the 133-MHz Pentium processor

- ❖ A future OverDrive processor upgrade for the Pentium Pro processor

These Pentium OverDrive processors will also upgrade 150 MHz and 166 MHz Pentium processors.

Kingston Technology

Kingston Technology Corporation was formed in 1987 during a severe shortage of memory chips. Kingston now designs and manufactures customized memory modules for over 2300 models of personal computers, servers, workstations and printers. Kingston is widely recognized as the original equipment manufacturer (OEM) of memory throughout the computer industry.

> Visit Kingston Technologies, Inc., on the World Wide Web for more information: www.kingston.com

TurboChip 133

Kingston Technology's TurboChip upgrades a 486 DX2, DX, SX2 or SX system to 5x86 clock-quadrupled processor technology. TurboChip 133 provides 5x86 power that is superior to Pentium-75 performance. So, installing a TurboChip 133 in a 486 system will give you the necessary power to run today's demanding operating systems (Windows 95, Windows NT and OS/2 Warp). Also, you'll have the power necessary to run today's powerful applications.

TurboChip 133 features 16K internal cache, cooling fan, built-in math coprocessor and up to 33MHz external bus speed processing. TurboChip 133 was designed with the Advanced Micro Device's Am5x86-P75 microprocessor and is compatible with all existing software and hardware. Therefore, you can still use your current software applications (except they'll run faster now).

Users do not need to worry about installation difficulties and physical restrictions when upgrading with TurboChip. TurboChip is the same physical footprint as the original 486. The cooling fan, however, makes it slightly higher. It's as easy as "Plug and Play"

The 168 pin layout allows TurboChip to upgrade systems with or without the OverDrive socket.

Evergreen Technologies, Inc.

Evergreen Technologies, Inc., is a world leader in the engineering of performance enhancement products for personal computers. Evergreen was founded in 1989 to design and manufacture processor upgrades for 286 computers.

> Visit Evergreen on the World Wide Web for more information: www.evergreen.com

Chapter 6

Evergreen uses the highest rated 133 MHz AMD 5x86 processors to upgrade 486 systems. AMD provides the best combined price/performance value among 5x86 processors, and the AMD 5x86 delivers a higher level of compatibility.

You can upgrade to an Evergreen 586 if your current CPU is a 486. Then you'll double, triple or even quadruple your clock speed (depending on the current CPU). The Evergreen 586 can be installed in a regular 486 socket or an OverDrive socket. Although it does not include a fan, the Evergreen 586 uses a heatsink.

The following lists a few of the Evergreen 586 features:

❖ Upgrades a 486 system to a 586/100, 120 or 133.

❖ Supports both 168 (169) and 237 (238)-pin CPU and OverDrive socket styles.

❖ Includes 16K of level one cache.

❖ Includes high-speed floating point math unit.

❖ Quadruples clock speed for 25, 33, DX2-50, and DX2-66 systems (DX2-50 and DX2-66 become 586/100 and 586/133 respectively).

❖ Triples clock speed for 33 and 40 MHz systems.

❖ Maintains PC investment and extends the life of 486 systems.

❖ Includes three year warranty.

Final notes on CPU upgrades

These upgrades will not give you the speed and advantages of replacing an ISA motherboard with even the least expensive new 486 PCI board that has a PCI video card. No 486 CPU upgrade can come close to the performance and features you would have from installing a new, low-end Pentium-class motherboard.

Processing Data 7

A personal computer is simply a machine that processes information (data). Like other machines, a computer does what it's told to do. We tend to forget this fact when we're facing a computer related problem. We may automatically blame the computer for the error although many times we are to blame.

For example, we assume that when a cup of coffee is too strong, either too much coffee or not enough water was used. In other words, we don't blame the coffee machine for the mistake. However, when a PC produces an undesired result, we usually blame the program or the computer system itself. However, we likely caused the error.

This coffee machine example follows the IPO (Input-Process-Output) principle. If the input is processed according to the same rules each time, the output depends on the input. This process is more complicated with an entire computer system consisting of hardware, software, and peripheral devices. The PC consists of several smaller systems, which operate according to the IPO principle.

The output of one system (for example, the output signal of the video card) is the input of another (in this case, the monitor). This system's output (the characters on the screen) is, in turn, the input for the "human information processing system" (i.e., yourself). Then you process what you see on the screen. Additional output (perhaps by entering a command line on your keyboard) is produced. This provides new input for your PC and the active application. All the systems involved in this process operate according to the IPO principle.

Processing Data

In this chapter we'll describe the individual elements of processing data. You'll discover how to increase your system's efficiency by improving how the components work with each other and with the application you want to run.

MOTHERBOARD

Components that are responsible for processing data are located on the PC's *motherboard*. Other terms for motherboard include *system board*, *main board* and *planar*. The term "motherboard" is used because it controls all other electrical components and peripheral devices. The motherboard in today's powerful Pentium and Pentium class computers should include eight slots or connectors so you can add additional plug-in boards. Hundreds of plug-in boards are available that you can use to do most anything imaginable.

Locating motherboards

The location of a motherboard depends on the style of PC case but it's quite easy to find. The motherboard in a PC system that is housed in a desktop case is attached to the bottom of the case. In upright cases, such as tower and mini-tower cases, the motherboard is attached vertically to one side of the case.

A motherboard's dimensions (i.e., its size, the location of its mounting holes, etc.) can vary depending on the manufacturer. Some motherboards are from brand name manufacturers and others are generic, or no-name, boards. Most generic motherboards have the same dimensions and, therefore, always fit into a generic case.

However, many brand name manufacturers have proprietary shaped systems so if the motherboard needs to be replaced or upgraded, they don't want users to swap their boards with boards from other manufacturers or with generic boards. So usually only boards and cases from the same manufacturer will fit together.

This is one of the reasons why you should buy PC clones. They allow you to swap components or add more powerful components. Appendix D lists generic dimensions and the available sizes for the boards.

This Pentium motherboard has a Triton II chipset and built-in I/O board

Today's motherboards usually consist of a nonconducting material. This material must be insensitive to heat (for example, Pertinax). You can imagine this type of construction as several layers of printed circuitry. A current flows through several fine conducting lines on each of these layers. These lines are easily visible on the motherboard. They're connected to the various chips and other components on the surface of the board.

As we mentioned, the motherboard contains all the electrical components needed to process a task. The CPU (such as a Pentium processor) and math coprocessor (a separate processor used in older PCs) form the PC's command headquarters. Other important components of the motherboard include the system and main memory, data buses and address buses.

We'll discuss these and other components in more detail in the following sections. Remember that you cannot swap all these components for others, sometimes not even for more powerful ones.

> **NOTE**
>
> If one of these conducting lines is broken, either by physical damage or an electrical short, your entire motherboard may be unusable. Because of the complex multilayer construction of modern boards, these components are almost impossible to repair. So you should always handle the motherboard carefully.

THE CHIPSET ON THE MOTHERBOARD

The motherboard's chipset consists of highly complex and coordinated ICs (integrated chips) that help the CPU manage and control the PC system. A chipset is typically a set of one to five chips that do the same work that over 100 components performed on the old IBM AT computers. They contain the local bus controller, cache controller main memory controller, DMA and Interrupt controllers and many others. Among other things, these chips help the CPU organize its access of RAM, as well as the data and address buses.

Several chipsets are available for PCs. They are usually soldered permanently to the various motherboards. Some well-known manufacturers of these chipsets include Chips & Technologies, Symphony, Opti, UMC and VLSI. Since so many companies introduce and improve chipsets, we cannot list all the differences between each of these chipsets.

Several chipsets are designed specifically for the Pentium class computers. If you're looking for chipsets for a Pentium class PC, make certain they can handle the following features:

EDO RAM (Extended Data Out RAM) support

Most of the Pentium motherboards are able to take advantage of the faster EDO memory. You should select one of these motherboards even if you aren't initially planning to use EDO memory.

Pipeline burst cache SRAM (Static RAM)

Caching is a way to speed up access to main memory. Using standard cache, four bytes of data can be transferred from cache to the CPU in eight clock cycles. A special feature of the Pentiums is its ability to access memory in burst mode where the same four bytes of data can be transferred in only five clock cycles. On some motherboards, the cache is already built-in. On other motherboards, the cache is added separately. The more recent motherboards accept a type of cache called COAST memory (Cache On A STick) This is a clever name for the small circuit boards which accommodate the pipeline burst cache memory.

PCI local bus

Most new motherboards use the PCI bus, which makes it the most popular bus today. The PCI bus is capable of transferring data 64-bit at a time at rates up to 66MHz. Some motherboards, called combos, can simultaneously accommodate add-on cards for both the PCI bus and VL-Bus, so if you need to use both types of cards in your PC, choose one of these combo motherboards.

A typical Pentium motherboard has three or four slots for PCI or VL-bus cards and three of four slots for ISA/EISA cards. The PCI bus is now a defacto standard for Pentium systems, so we recommend a PCI bus motherboard for simplicity, wide availability of other peripheral cards and future expansion capabilities.

Advanced Power Management (APM)

This Intel-Microsoft sponsored specification for battery-powered computers that allows software, system BIOS and hardware to communicate power measurements to slow down and speed up components.

Processing Data

Incompatibilities

Frequently incompatibilities between certain chipsets and other hardware components lead to problems within the system. So, if you're buying a new motherboard, check the documentation for the chipset you have in mind. It will explain any technical problems or incompatibilities; you'll then be able to change the chipset features and fine tune your motherboard. Keep in mind that incompatibilities between hardware components are often related to the chipsets used on a motherboard.

Examples of high performance chipsets

This section talks about the major chipsets used on Pentium motherboards. When you're selecting a motherboard, you can easily know which features the motherboard supports based on which chipset is used on that motherboard.

Acer Labs Aladdin chipset

- ❖ PCI bus only with ISA support

- ❖ I/O onboard

- ❖ Keyboard controller

- ❖ Up to 1 Meg of write-back pipeline burst cache

- ❖ Parity and non-parity memory up to 768 Meg; supports EDO memory

Intel Triton FX chipset

- ❖ PCI bus with ISA support

- ❖ I/O onboard for up to 4 IDE devices

- ❖ Pipeline burst cache

- ❖ Non-parity only memory up to 128 Meg; supports EDO memory

- ❖ Power management

Intel Triton II HX chipset

- ❖ PCI bus with ISA support

- ❖ I/O onboard for up to 4 IDE drives

- ❖ Pipeline burst cache

- ❖ Parity and non-parity memory up to 512 Meg; supports EDO memory

- ❖ Power management

- ❖ Universal Serial Bus support

Intel Triton III VX chipset

- ❖ PCI bus with ISA support

- ❖ I/O onboard for up to 4 IDE drives

- ❖ Pipeline burst cache

- ❖ Memory access about 10%-15% faster than Triton FX chipset

- ❖ Parity and non-parity memory up to 512 Meg; supports EDO memory; supports synchronous DRAM

- ❖ Power management

- ❖ Universal Serial Bus support

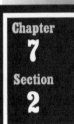

Chapter
7
Section
2

Opti Viper chipset

- ❖ PCI bus and VL bus with ISA support

- ❖ I/O onboard

- ❖ Up to 2 Meg of write-back pipeline burst cache

- ❖ Parity and non-parity memory up to 512 Meg; supports EDO memory

SIS chipset

- ❖ PCI bus and VL bus
- ❖ I/O onboard for up to 4 IDE devices
- ❖ Pipeline burst cache
- ❖ 2 Meg of write-back cache
- ❖ Parity and non-parity memory up to 512 Meg; supports EDO memory
- ❖ Power management

SYSTEM MEMORY

Most users were able to understand memory in the days before the PC was released. Home computers had between 1K and 64K of memory. The amount of memory jumped to 640K when the first PC became available.

Now, you'll hear terms like extended memory, EMS, expanded memory, XMS, LIM and many more. This section discusses these terms and how memory works.

Read Only Memory (ROM)

As we mentioned when IBM developed the PC, the memory segment between 640K and 1 Meg was reserved for system use. This address range has since been used as ROM (Read-Only Memory). So, unlike RAM, you can only read from ROM, and not write to it.

The term "ROM" actually no longer applies to every portion of system memory. However, the term still implies that this entire address range is controlled by the system. So, this memory is hardware controlled and cannot be used by external software under any circumstances.

This applies to the different BIOS systems that can be resident in a PC. Each motherboard is equipped with a main or system BIOS, also called ROM BIOS. The system BIOS is located in the upper portion of system memory. The uppermost 64K, below the 1 Meg boundary in every PC, are reserved for this purpose.

Address conflicts

A 192K address segment, which is reserved for adapter BIOS systems used in IBM compatible PCs, is located directly below the system BIOS segment. These can include EGA BIOS or VGA BIOS, as well as the BIOS for a SCSI hard drive controller. Network cards must also be addressable through a specific ROM address.

If several expansion cards in your system require their own BIOS, this reserved memory segment can quickly become too crowded, which leads to addressing conflicts. You should consider this possibility before purchasing such hardware. Many expansion cards feature user-selected BIOS addresses, so address conflicts can be avoided.

The memory segment reserved for video RAM, with a total size of 128K, is located below the address segment for the adapter BIOS systems. This memory segment uses the remainder of the entire 384K of memory reserved for the system. Remember that we're discussing only address ranges and not the information that's actually stored in these memory locations.

Instead of memory capacities, the memory sizes listed above represent addresses at which the CPU can access the corresponding memory locations. Except for the video RAM and the EMS window (see below), these memory addresses can be accessed with one read operation.

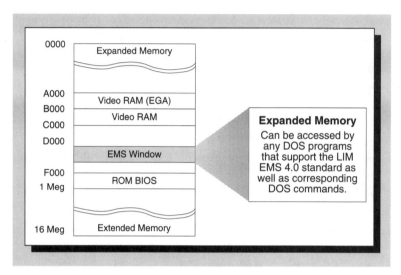

Expanded and extended memory

Physically, the memory contents represented by these address ranges are stored on, for example, the video adapter (video RAM and, where applicable, video BIOS).

As we mentioned, the system BIOS is located on the motherboard, while other BIOS systems are located on their respective expansion cards.

A BIOS is stored as a program routine on one or two EPROM chips.

EPROM chip containing the system BIOS

EPROM is an abbreviation for **E**rasable and **P**rogrammable **R**ead **O**nly **M**emory. EPROMs are reusable PROM chip that holds its content until erased under ultraviolet light. These PROM chips can be programmed using special equipment called a PROM programmer. A PROM programmer is a device that writes instructions and data into PROM and EPROM chips.

EMS Window

Depending on the number and size of adapter BIOSes and the potential presence of ROM BASIC, a contiguous memory segment of at least 64K will remain within the address range described above. According to the Expanded Memory Specification (EMS), which was created by Lotus, Intel, and Microsoft (LIM), this memory segment can be used by the operating system and its applications to access additional memory pages through the support of a special EMS driver.

Shadow RAM

As you can see, none of the memory bytes from the installed RAM chips are used by the PC's system memory. Physically, as well as in reference to its address range, system memory is completely segregated from the PC's main memory. Because of this, the capacity of the RAM chips installed on a motherboard can be fully allocated as main memory.

Shadow option

In today's PCs, CMOS SETUP often allows you to install a shadow RAM. This option allows the BIOS information usually found in system memory to be copied to RAM, or main memory. A shadow of the permanent BIOS is created in RAM. This enables the CPU to access BIOS information more quickly because RAM access is considerably faster than ROM access.

This shadow option for both the system and video BIOS is usually a default setting on most PC BIOS versions. The AMI BIOS provides the user with detailed shadow allocations for the entire address range of system memory, so adapter BIOSes can be copied to RAM in addition to the system and video BIOS.

To use such a shadow BIOS, you must reserve a corresponding memory segment within physical RAM and define it as a shadow memory segment. Remember that a physical portion of main memory must be reserved and specifically allocated to receive the BIOS information. This portion of memory will be used for this purpose only. So the available main memory is reduced by the size of the reserved shadow segment.

Shadow RAM reduces available RAM

The reallocation of main memory to shadow RAM isn't always performed the same way. You can do this many ways; each of these methods affects the remaining main memory differently.

With 286 BIOSes, usually an activated shadow option automatically subtracts 256K from the system's main memory. This is true regardless of how much memory is actually required for the RAM shadow. So, for example, at a total memory capacity of 1 Meg, the amount of available extended memory would decrease from 384 to a mere 128K.

Many 386 and 486 BIOS versions will reserve 384K of the RAM installed in the system, regardless of whether the shadow option is activated. So 4096K of installed memory, for example, would be reduced to 640K of conventional memory and 3072K of extended memory. However, other systems will reserve only the amount of memory from RAM that is actually required for the ROM shadow.

Shadow RAM increases speed

Activating the shadow option will increase system performance. This increase will be noticeable with 386 and 486 systems. However, particularly with 286 systems, the advantage of increased speed may not be worth the resulting decrease in main memory capacity.

NEAT chip groups permit remapping

In a few cases, primarily with boards using NEAT chip groups, expanded CMOS will offer the option of RAM relocation, which is also referred to as the relocate option or remapping. This option makes it possible to reallocate the memory, which has been reserved from RAM as shadow RAM, back to generally available main memory, if the shadow option isn't activated. Although this is an awkward procedure, it's quite useful for 286 systems with a limited amount of RAM.

Cache memory

Many of today's processors can operate at clock speeds of 25 to 133 MHz. As a result, PC main memories consisting of dynamic RAM chips are no longer able to keep up with the fast access times of these CPUs. At these clock frequencies, the processor is forced to spend half of its time waiting for RAM. This usually means the capabilities of the processor are not used effectively.

The two types of cache that are available are internal cache and external cache.

Internal cache

When your PC needs data, the computer first looks in the internal cache. Because internal cache is located on the CPU chip, it provides the fastest way for your PC to get data.

Since PCs execute their instructions sequentially, a program that is well-written will follow the "locality principle." This means that as many identical or neighboring memory locations will be accessed during program execution as possible. Programmers want to avoid program jumps to more distant memory locations (called "far jumps").

For a program loop that's executed several times, the same command must be retrieved from memory continually. When the CPU accesses a certain memory location, the contents of that address range, and at least the neighboring address range, are written to the internal cache and then passed to the CPU.

If an effective programming technique is used, the CPU's next memory access should occur in the same or the neighboring address range. So, in most cases, the required information can be obtained from the internal cache. Otherwise a much slower RAM access operation is performed.

This method optimizes the CPU's access to main memory. During operations that require information that's currently stored in the cache (cache hit), faster CPUs are used more efficiently. Only after cache misses is the CPU forced to access the comparably slower RAM.

Different manufacturers of PC motherboards use different caching strategies. These differences involve which data is stored and found, and how the cache contents are further used. The method by which information is copied from main memory to the cache may also differ. The size of the cache is another important factor.

The difference in the performance of two PCs with equally fast motherboards, one with an external cache and one without, will be dramatic. A cache size of 128K is a sufficient for a PC in Windows 3.x or Windows 95.

Internal cache is also called *primary cache* or *L1*.

**Chapter
7
Section
2**

143

Processing Data

External cache

To solve this problem, the entire main memory should be physically replaced by static RAM chips, which permit much shorter access times. However, this solution would be too expensive.

Therefore, a method, which had already been used in the 1960s on large-scale systems, has been applied in high-speed 386 and 486 PCs. This method involves installing an external RAM cache buffer. In this case, "external" means outside of the CPU, so the cache is connected with the processor through the bus system.

Static RAM chips of the external cache buffer

External cache is also called *secondary cache* or *L2*. It's located outside the CPU but still on the motherboard. External cache consists of a row of Static RAM chips (SRAM chips) of either 64K or 256K capacity. This results in a cache of either 64 or 256K, which is actually a small amount of memory when compared to main memory. The 82385 cache controller from Intel manages this cache.

External cache is slower than internal cache but nevertheless is much faster than RAM. If you're upgrading to a 486-based system, make certain to buy at least 256K of additional external cache.

Random Access Memory (RAM)

The motherboard contains another integral component of every PC system. The main memory, like the CPU, is essential to the operation of the PC system. Even the operating system, which is needed to execute a program, needs this memory to be loaded.

Main memory acts as a type of "short term memory" and is often referred to as RAM (Random Access Memory). The CPU uses this memory to perform its current tasks. The contents of main memory are changed and updated, as needed, while the processor is working.

Different program sections are frequently read from the hard drive and stored in memory while the program is running. Main memory consists of temporary memory, because all the information stored there is lost when the computer is switched off. However, mass storage devices, such as hard drives and diskettes, are capable of retaining information permanently.

Today's PCs have 4, 8, 16 or even 32 Meg of main memory, depending on their CPU class. Not long ago 640K was the standard size for the main memory of a PC. So, at that time, 1 Meg was considered an incredible amount of memory.

Memory chips

Approximately 12 different types of memory chips are used in today's personal computers. These chips are combined differently depending on the size and scope of the particular main memory.

The compatibility with a given motherboard is determined by the sockets on that board. The chips are simply plugged into these sockets. So, the soldering iron, which was used for memory expansions years ago, is no longer needed.

The different chips used for main memory can be divided into two groups: DRAM (Dynamic RAM) chips, and SIMM (Single In-line Memory Module) or SIP (Single In-line Packages) modules. The difference between these two groups is easy to explain.

While dynamic RAM chips consist of individual single-chip elements, several RAM chips are grouped into a single element in SIMM or SIP modules. So, SIMM or SIP modules are simply a group of RAM chips that have been soldered together to form a single component. We'll discuss these in detail later.

Processing Data

Before purchasing any RAM chips you will need to know the following:

- ❖ Speed of the chips

- ❖ Whether they are SIP or SIMM modules

- ❖ If you have 3 or 9 chip arrangements

- ❖ Number of pins (or prongs)

- ❖ Amount of RAM your PC will accommodate (4, 8, 16, 32, or 64 Meg) on the motherboard

For example, say your motherboard has 4 Meg installed. Four slots are full. No empty slots are available for additional memory modules. If this happens, you must pull the old 4 Meg modules and replace them with 8 Meg modules.

Dynamic RAM chips

Dynamic RAM chips are located in small black chip casings. Prongs protrude from the longer sides of DRAM chips. These prongs connect the chip to the rest of the system. Depending on the capacity of a chip, it will have 16, 18, or even 20 prongs.

Chips are available in capacities of 64K, 256K and even 1 Meg. They usually contain corresponding inscriptions (4164, 41256, and 411000 or 411024, respectively).

Recently a special version of RAM chips, which use a quadruple bit structure, is becoming more popular. These chips have four times the storage capacity of a normal 1-bit chip and are available as 464, 4256 and 4400 models.

However, you don't have to worry about the designations of RAM chips. With a little practice, you can determine a RAM chip's capacity by the number of prongs on the chip:

- ❖ 64 and 256 kilobit chips have 16 prongs

- ❖ 1000 kilobit chips have 18 prongs

- ❖ Quadruple bit chips have 20 prongs

This type of RAM chip is called *dynamic* because its memory contents must be refreshed continually. This means these chips constantly undergo a refresh rate. This is simply the nature of these components; the actual storage elements consist of only capacitors, which can either be charged or discharged.

Since such an element can take on one of two states, it corresponds to the value of one bit. So, one capacitor is needed for each bit.

For example, a megabit chip capable of storing precisely 1,048,576 bits of information contains over one million capacitors. However, such a capacitor loses its charge after a short time. It is possible to retain the information stored in the chip past this discharge time. To do this, it's necessary to read the status of the chip's capacitors and recharge them. This results in the refresh rate we talked about earlier.

The information stored in a chip cannot be accessed while the chip is being refreshed. Since the intervals between each refresh vary for different chips, you can select between "faster" and "slower" RAM chips. Access times for RAM chips are specified in nanoseconds (one-billionth of a second in duration). Access times usually range from 70 ns to 120 ns. You can recognize slower chips by their higher access times.

You can "mix" RAM chips of different access speeds. However, your PC will access all RAM chips at the speed of the slowest chip.

Bits and bytes

As we mentioned, these chips come in capacities from 64K to 1024K. However, a PC's main memory is assembled in kilobyte (K) segments. As you may know, eight bits make up one byte. Therefore, eight chips of 64 kilobits each is equal to 64K of memory. RAM chips are grouped in rows of nine elements each.

Eight of these elements are used for storing the actual data bits. So they can store between 64 and 1024K, depending on the type of chips used. The ninth chip acts as the control element and is responsible for performing the parity check.

The remaining chips during operation produce a continuous checksum. This is then checked against the parity bits stored in the ninth chip.

Processing Data

The three chip approach

You might initially think the quadruple chips mentioned above are an exception from the method of grouping nine chips together. However, it's easier to understand if you imagine the quadruple chip (the 4x256 kilobit chip is most often used in PCs) as simply four individual 256 kilobit chips.

At first the quadruple chips mentioned above, of which the 4x256 kilobit chip is most often used in PCs, may seem to be an exception from the method of grouping nine chips together. However, it's easier to understand if you imagine the quadruple chip as simply four individual 256 kilobit chips.

A row of 256 kilobit chips can consist of one of the following:

❖ Nine individual 256 kilobit chips

or

❖ Two quadruple 256 chips together with a single 256 kilobit chip (2x4+1=9), which is a total of three chips.

Because only three chip sockets are needed instead of nine, a complete row of chips occupies only one third of the space. This is true even if the quadruple chips have two more prongs on each side than the regular 256 kilobit chips.

SIP and SIMM modules

SIP and SIMM modules were developed as a result of computer applications continually requiring more memory. Each module corresponds to a complete row of memory chips. Since the amount of area occupied by such a module is considerably smaller than that used by the conventional DRAM sockets, significantly more memory can be installed on the motherboard.

These modules are available in 9-chip and 3-chip arrangements; the 3-chip arrangement seems to be the more popular arrangement. However, all motherboards aren't compatible with this technology.

It's possible that memory problems or even parity error messages will occur because the board isn't compatible with the 3-chip module. These memory modules are available in 256K, 1 Meg and 4 Meg capacities. If you determined your RAM chip configuration as we described in this chapter, you'll avoid these problems.

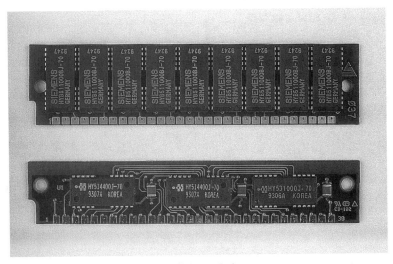

SIMM modules

SIP modules (Single In-line Packages) have a row of 30 small prongs which are inserted into a corresponding socket strip. SIMMs (Single In-line Memory Modules), however, do not have prongs. They use a type of contact strip similar to the ones used on expansion cards. So SIMMs are inserted into wrap or snap connectors.

Chapter

7

Section

2

SIP modules

SIMM expanders and "savers"

The Minden Group, Inc., and SimmSaver Technology, Inc., offer an excellent cost-effective solution to PC upgraders. They produce SIMM adapters that are designed to let you increase the amount of RAM memory modules without the need to discard yours . This can be a cost-saving option of upgrading your RAM without replacing all your RAM.

The Minden Group have three basic styles, depending on the configuration of your PC. Their SIMM expanders will do the following:

> Visit the Minden Group on the World Wide Web for more information: www.minden.com

❖ Adapt older 30-pin SIMM formats to 72-pin formats

❖ Expand 30-pin to multiple 30-pin formats, *or*

❖ Expand 72-pin formats to multiple 72-pin formats.

The plug and play (PnP) installation of these adapters lets you snap the modules into the SIMM slot(s).

SimmSaver Technology also offers several SIMM memory adapters. They provide many memory upgrade solutions designed to convert older memory modules into the new generations of PCs.

> Visit the SimmSaver Technology on the World Wide Web for more information: www2.dtc.net/~simmsave

SimmSaver Technology has adapters for the following:

❖ Double or quadruple your existing memory in your 30-pin, 72-pin and 168-pin systems.

❖ Convert older 30-pin SIMMs for use in the newer 72-pin SIMM systems, *or*

❖ Combine 30-pin SIMMs with 72-pin SIMMs in 72-pin systems

SimmSaver Technology also offers a product called Clockslider. It lets you, through software, tune the clock speed of your 386, 486 or Pentium class computer. This software manipulates the CPU speed with a single keystroke for performance increases of up to 40%.

Two memory banks

Regardless of which type of memory elements are actually used, the memory located on PC motherboards has been organized into two memory banks since the 286 PC . The first is designated as "Bank 0" and the second is designated as "Bank 1". Since it's usually possible to install several different types of memory chips, the size of a memory bank ultimately depends on the types of chips used. Older 286 boards can thereby be equipped with a maximum of either 1 or more Meg of RAM, depending on whether 256 kilobit chips or 1 megabit chips are used.

The motherboards of high speed 386, 486 and all Pentium PCs almost always contain SIMMs. When 4 Meg modules are used, memory capacities of 32 Meg "on board" can easily be attained. This is possible because a memory bank generally includes 4 sockets; so a total of 8 sockets can receive SIMM modules. Some boards even contain 16 such sockets, so a maximum of 64 Meg of on board RAM can be installed.

> **NOTE**
>
> Only memory chips of equal capacity can be used within the same memory bank. Although you can use chips from different manufacturers, we don't recommend this approach. Remember, memory access or speed is determined by the slowest chip in the RAM memory system. So, if your present system has 80 ns chips and you buy 60 ns chips when you upgrade, your memory access rate will still only be 80 ns. This obviously would be a waste of money buying the faster chips.
>
> Also, although chips from different manufacturers can be mixed within a memory bank, problems can occasionally occur.

Combining different memory chips

Two RAM memory characteristics need to be clarified at this point. Memory capacity refers to the size of the chip, that is 1 Meg, 2 Meg, 4 Meg, etc. Access time or access rate refers to the speed at which a particular chip will transmit data, such as 70 ns, 80 ns or 120 ns.

Using memory chips with different capacities between the two memory banks of a motherboard isn't always permitted. Therefore, you cannot necessarily mix chips in any given bank. For example, you cannot have a bank with 1 Meg SIMMs and 4 Meg SIMMs together. You could create a bank of all 1 Meg SIMMs and another of all 4 Meg SIMMs. Refer to the documentation with your motherboard for more information. It includes a section describing suitable RAM chips for the board.

Processing Data

Memory management

We mentioned the correlation between processor generations and addressable memory when we discussed the different PC processor generations earlier in this chapter. During the past several years the physical memory limit has been increased dramatically. As a result, the amount of memory that can be addressed by these processors has grown from 1 Meg to 4 Gigabytes.

We've mentioned that even today's Pentium processor is downwardly compatible with the original IBM PC from 1981 (based on the 8088 CPU). This means that all generations of PCs are still capable of operating in the same mode as the original PC. They are also using the same operating system.

Although this operating system is in its fifth generation, it still forces these modern PCs to work much below their potential. In addition to compatibility to the 8088 and the use of DOS, PC memory management is another problem of today's PCs.

The 8088 divided its addressable memory into a segment for the operating system and application programs (a maximum of 640K main memory) and another segment of system memory or controller memory. The latter portion contains address segments for the video adapter, the system BIOS, and other hardware components.

This system memory was set at a size of 384K, which results in a total of 1024K or 1 Meg of memory. This completely used the entire memory range addressable by the 8088 CPU.

MS-DOS 5 and higher and IBM's PC-DOS 6 and higher include several memory management utilities that may improve your system's performance. The arrival of Microsoft's Windows 95 operating system has new methods of managing your PC's memory. Although we cannot detail the information here, you should review the new information in Chapter 4. It's more detailed about memory and memory requirements for Windows 95.

Bus: The Electronic Pathway For Your Computer

You can consider the bus your computer's electronic pathway. The bus handles the delivery of information between the CPU and the other devices in your computer system.

The bus connects your CPU to the computer's main memory as well as with its expansion cards. Characters are sent through the bus to the screen. A scanner reads information which is then sent directly to RAM, bypassing the CPU.

For example, the bus supplies music data from RAM to a sound card so the CPU can perform other tasks. The processor is interrupted only when something is wrong. An example is when a memory address is no longer readable or when the printer is out of paper.

So, the bus is responsible for coordinating the operation of the individual system components. It's the central communication system of your PC.

Obviously, such an important and complex system can have a major impact on how a computer executes different operations. Therefore, the bus system's performance is a determining factor of the PC's overall performance. In this section we'll discuss the bus system in detail.

The bus consists of connections. You can picture these connections as a maze of wires. The majority of the CPU's connections are simply wires to the bus. Except for a few special functions, these conductors represent the processor's only connection with the outside world.

The CPU can, for example, access the PC's main memory and read the machine instructions of a program through these connections. It can also read, change, or move data stored in main memory. The connections used for transporting data are also called the *data bus*.

Chapter 7 Section 2

153

Processing Data

Address bus

Regardless of the type of data, the processor cannot simply send this data to the data bus. Instead, the processor specifies where to send this data by using another set of connections called the *address bus*. This is the internal channel from the processor to memory across which the addresses (but not the data) of data are transmitted.

The number of lines (wires) in the address bus determines the amount of memory that can be directly addressed as each line carries one bit of the address.

So, for example, today's Pentium class processors have 32 address lines and make up the address bus. You can use different swapping and switching techniques to your PC that allow a computer to use more memory than is directly addressable by its address bus.

System bus (or control bus)

The third addition to this group is the *system bus* (sometimes also called the *control bus*). This bus is necessary because several components are connected to the bus besides the CPU and the main memory banks. Without some controlling element, the bus would become a confusing combination of read, write or addressing operations by individual components. This is where the system bus is needed.

The system bus gives individual components access and determines whether the operation will be a read or write action. Like the address bus, the system bus also consists of a connection system (a maze of wires). How then is a component consisting of simple wires capable of executing a task as complex as controlling the bus?

Bus controller

This task is performed by the *bus controller*, which is the brain of the entire bus system. By using the system bus, the bus controller ensures bus operations don't collide, overlap, and that the operations are sent to the proper locations.

Increasing the bus speed

Obviously the performance of the bus system depends on the "intelligence" of the system bus. However, the speed and "width" of the bus (i.e., the number of parallel channels) have a more direct impact on the system's performance. We mentioned the 286 and 386SX systems use a 16-bit bus and the 386DX and 486 systems use a 32-bit bus. Pentium processors use a 64-bit bus.

Although you cannot change the data width of a CPU, it's possible to increase the operating frequency of the bus system. Various BIOS setups, such as AMI BIOS, offer the option of selecting between several bus frequencies. The original IBM AT bus ran at 8 MHz. Although this bus is still the standard today, many modern cards can surpass it.

If your system includes a BIOS with this option, increase your bus speed to either 10 MHz or 12 MHz. This can often increase the data transfer rate to your video card or your hard drive controller. However, on older models the hard drive controller may have problems handling the increased transfer rate.

Older MFM controllers, such as the WD 1003, frequently respond to this upgrade with occasional write errors. In these instances you must switch back to the original AT bus frequency.

Expansion slots

The *expansion slots* are the access sockets to the bus system. These slots allow the bus to connect with expansion cards such as video adapters and hard drive controllers. Expansion slots don't always have to include all connectors of the bus system. So you'll often find 8 or 16-bit expansion slots on a motherboard with a 32-bit CPU. You'll find these slots on the left and toward the rear of your PC's motherboard.

The 8-bit slots

Expansion slots are long, black plastic sockets. Some of these slots probably already contain expansion cards. The shorter one-piece sockets are the 8-bit slots, and the longer two-piece sockets are 16-bit slots. Sometimes you'll also see one particularly long or differently configured slot. Such slots are used for memory expansion cards, which are usually equipped with a 32-bit bus on 386 and 486 motherboards.

PCI bus

The PCI bus (Peripheral Component Interconnect) is currently the most sophisticated type of bus. Intel designed the PCI bus. It features a bus width of either 32 bits or 64 bits and speeds up to 66MHz. When the bus is used with 64-bit implementations, you can transfer data at speeds up to 264 Meg per second

One big boost for the PCI bus is that Intel has been able to push this new bus in parallel with its Pentium processors. A PCI bus runs at the same 60 MHz or 66 MHz as the processor itself. Also, it's capable of accessing the Pentium's full 64-bit width. Because of the success of the Pentium, all new PCs feature PCI bus architecture.

Also, the PCI bus supports the Plug and Play feature. This feature lets you add new components and devices without worrying about complex installation instructions.

The downside to the PCI bus is that adapter cards and peripherals must be redesigned to take advantage of the PCI local bus

The PCI local bus is now the defacto standard for all Pentium and Pentium Pro computers. If you're upgrading to a Pentium, you won't be able to ignore this bus.

Three board configurations are possible with the PCI bus. Each is designed for a specific type of system with specific power requirements.

5-volt specification

The 5-volt specification is designed for stationary PCs (desktops, etc.).

3.3 specification

The 3.3 specification is designed for portable PCs (notebooks, portables, etc.).

Universal

The universal specification works with either the 5-volt or 3.3-volt specification.

EISA bus

The MCA bus could not be manufactured by clone companies without paying huge royalties to IBM. So, a new standard was created by leading computer manufacturers (except IBM). The primary goal of this new standard was to meet the higher performance demands created by 32-bit processors. This group, called the Gang of Nine, developed the EISA bus.

Chapter 7

Illustration of 32-bit slots of an EISA board

The EISA bus (Enhanced Industry Standard Architecture) is an enhanced version of the old AT bus. Since the EISA bus is a true 32-bit bus, all 32 data bits of the CPU are present in the expansion slot.

The high data transfer rate attained through this expansion isn't the only advantage of the ISA bus. A more significant, but rarely used, advantage is the EISA expansion slots are capable of "multimastering." This means that several processors can access the same bus simultaneously. Therefore, by inserting a CPU expansion card into the EISA slot you can create a parallel-processor system easily.

Another advantage of the EISA system is that it's fully compatible with the ISA bus. This means that you can use any old expansion card in the new EISA slots. These cards won't run any faster on the new slot. However, this usually won't matter because many cards, such as printer interfaces or floppy controllers, don't need to run faster.

The increased performance of the EISA bus is most noticeable with graphic applications that use extremely fast EISA video adapters. These allow data transfer rates of up to 32 Meg per second, which is almost five times the rate attainable by the old AT bus.

Video Local Bus (VL-Bus)

One drawback of the ISA and EISA buses is that they typically run at a speed of 6 to 8.33 MHz. Furthermore, the ISA is limited to a 16-bit bus width. To transfer data to a peripheral, the CPU gets the data from system memory and places in on the bus. The CPU then notifies the peripheral that the data is ready. It then waits until the peripheral has retrieved the data. You can see there's many steps and overhead involved in I/O operations over the bus.

To transfer 32-bits of information over a 16-bit bus requires two accesses to the bus. A 486/33 MHz CPU with a 32-bit processing capability could overwhelm one of these buses.

The VL-Bus (also called VESA Local Bus) was designed to overcome the bottleneck created by the difference in processor speed compared to the difference in which data moves between the processor and a peripheral.

A system with VLB can access 32 bits of system memory directly at the speed of the processor. With a peripheral designed for the VLB, data transfer can occur without the intervention of the CPU at blazing speed.

The represents a tremendous improvement in throughput to any peripheral capable of handling the additional data.

The most common use of the VLB is accelerating the video display. A new generation of video cards are VLB compatible and can redraw at least 30 million pixels per second. This gain can make a remarkable difference in performance for the graphical user interfaces (GUIs) used in Windows and OS/2..

VL-Bus is used in 486 computers.

Chapter

7

Section

2

Storing And Saving Data

The amount of data that we process daily is constantly increasing. The demand for user-friendly programs has also increased the size of programs. As a result, the demand for high-capacity, high-reliability, and high-speed mass storage devices has also increased drastically.

These mass storage devices are included in a group of components called the *peripherals* of the PC system. Other peripherals, such as a printer, monitor, mouse, etc., are located outside the PC (see Chapter 9).

Mass storage devices such as hard drives are technically peripherals that are connected to the bus system through interfaces (usually expansion cards). The data exchange between the CPU and the storage device then takes place through this interface.

Chapter 8

A computer system uses a combination of mass storage devices to store applications, data, files and other information. So, a combination of CD-ROM drive and hard drive and disk drive is required part of today's powerful PC system. Information must be able to be both stored and retrieved fast. The speed at which data is retrieved depends on how data is organized on a particular data carrier and the data transfer rate of a particular storage medium. We'll talk about the types, limitations and new forms of modern storage devices in this chapter.

DISK DRIVES

The oldest storage device used in PC systems is the floppy disk drive (or simply, "disk drive"). This type of drive uses a removable data carrier. So, the drive and data carrier are separate components. This means that disk drives in one of today's formats (3.5-inch or 5.25-inch) are able to access different diskettes (of the same size).

Diskettes and diskette formats

Although CD-ROM drives and hard drives are the most popular storage devices used today, diskettes are still used in certain situations. Some manufacturers still use diskettes to distribute their software. Many users use diskettes to back up important data or files. Also, information is exchanged between two PCs by using diskettes.

The actual data carrier of a floppy diskette consists of a thin circular and pliable sheet of plastic that's been coated with a thin layer of magnetic material.

A 3.5-inch diskette with the protective cover removed

The thickness of this layer is about 0.00008 inches (0.002 mm) for different types of disks. Depending on the nature of this coating and the disk format used, formatting places a series of tracks and sectors on the magnetic material, so data can actually be stored on the disk.

Formats

Many sizes and formats have been used over the years (including an 8-inch floppy disk!). Today's powerful PCs use a 3.5-inch, 1.44 Meg high-density (HD) diskette. You can use other diskette formats such as a 3.5-inch super high density which have a smaller capacity than the 3.5-inch, 1.44 Meg high-density diskette. Some older PCs may be able to read a 5.25-inch, 1.2 Meg high-density (HD)

The 3.5-inch diskette has a hard plastic case with a small metal sliding cover on one edge. This cover protects the magnetic media from dust and other damage. The metal cover slides to one side when you insert the diskette in a drive which exposes the magnetic media.

On the opposite side, the plastic diskette case has two square holes, one of which can be covered with a small plastic slider that's built into the case. This slider allows the disk to be write-protected. The disk drive receives write access to the disk only when the write-protect hole is covered. The status of the write-protect tab is checked before each write operation. The second hole is an identification hole found only on high density diskettes.

Chapter 8 Section 2

The size and shape of 3.5-inch diskette vs. the older 5.25-inch diskette

Diskettes require formats that specify the exact qualities of a volume. Non-DOS diskettes cannot be read by DOS unless a special device driver is available.

The following table shows the formats available for 3.5-inch diskettes:

Type	Density	Capacity	Tracks	Sectors	DOS Version
DS DD	135 tpi	720K	80	9	3.2
DS DD	135 tpi	1.44 Meg	80	18	3.3
DS DD	270 tpi	2.88 Meg	80	36	3.3

The MFM (Modified Frequency Modulation) method is used in recording information on the magnetic coating of the diskette surface. The status of a data cell or data bit is determined by a magnetic flux change. If the center of such a data cell contains a flux change, then the cell's bit value is 1; if the flux change is absent, the cell carries the value 0.

Disk drives are usually reliable. Although disk drives are used frequently, they seem to work almost flawlessly under normal use. However, disk errors can still occur, due to wear and tear or poor handling.

Inside a disk drive

Disk drives consist of four basic components: The drive motor, two combined read/write heads, a stepper motor and the controller circuitry. The drive motor, which runs only during disk access, rotates the magnetic media of the diskette. This motor must maintain a constant speed of 300 revolutions per minute for 3.5-inch drives. A separate special control circuit is used to maintain this speed.

A combined read/write head is provided for each side of the diskette. The read/write heads are in constant contact with the carrier surface once the diskette is inserted in the drive. Obviously, the heads are subjected to a considerable amount of strain and wear. They are mounted on arms that move radially over the diskette's surface, so each track can be accessed.

These tracks are magnetically imprinted on the magnetic media, according to instructions from the operating system when the diskette is formatted.

The number of tracks on a diskette depend on the diskette format. For example, a 3.5-inch diskette will be divided into 40 or 80 tracks. In this case, each track will have a width of 0.01 inch (0.25 mm). The read/write heads are moved from track to track on demand by the stepper motor.

The disk drive's control circuitry coordinates the actions of the drive motor, the heads and the stepper motor, as well as the communication with the disk controller. The drive's circuitry is connected to the disk controller, which is located on one of the PC's expansion cards through a 34-line ribbon cable. This cable allows up to two drives to be operated alternately by the controller.

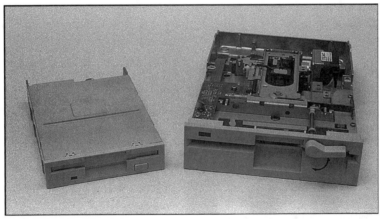

The size and shape of 3.5-inch disk drive vs. the older 5.25-inch disk drive

The high density drives used in today's PCs can format diskettes at 1.2 Meg (5.25-inch) and 1.44 Meg (3.5-inch) of data storage capacity. They're capable of reading high density as well as low density formats. Also, by using special parameters, they're capable of formatting diskettes at low density capacities.

Special types of disk drives

A drive arrangement that was popular is the *combination drive*. It consists of a very compact twin disk drive housed in a single case with only one cable connection. It has one 3.5-inch high-density drive and one 5.25-inch high-density drive.

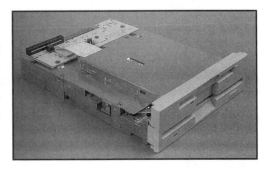

The advantage of a combination drive is that they create more space in a cramped PC housing. The case of the combination drive fits in the mounting bay for a single 5.25-inch drive. These drives don't limit the function or use of the storage medium in any way.

A 2.88 Meg disk drive was developed by Toshiba in the late 1980s. Other vendors then offered the drive as an upgrade. A 2.88 drive can read and write 1.44 Meg diskettes and 720K diskettes. These drives require DOS Version 5.0 or higher.

Although PCs are still shipped with a disk drive, their popularity has decreased because of the huge amounts of data and information that is exchanged today. Other mass storage devices, most notably the hard drive and CD-ROM drive, have replaced the disk drive as the primary storage device in a PC system.

HARD DRIVES

All PC systems today include at least one hard drive. Regardless of the reason(s) you use a PC, you'll need at least one hard drive. Most of today's applications require up to 20 Meg of disk space (just for the application itself). Operating systems like Windows 95 require even more disk space.

Physical characteristics

The physical appearance of today's hard drive is quite different from that of a hard drive a few years ago. The hard drive in your Pentium or 486 is only a few inches in length, about four inches wide and less than an inch high. The complete drive weighs about two pounds. Yet despite this small size, today's best hard drives can store over 1.2 Gigabyte of data. Compare this size and capacity to the first hard drives that were used in PCs. They had a storage capacity of only 10 Meg. They were four times higher, six inches wide, eight inches long and weighed close to ten pounds. Improvements in the recording methods and a more compact and efficient control circuitry have dramatically decreased the physical size of hard drives (see the following photograph).

The physical sizes of hard drives has decreased over the years

Hard drives are available in 3.5-inch and 5.25-inch formats. Hard drives with normal 3.5-inch dimensions (half-height drives) are available in capacities of up to 2 Gigabytes. PCs typically use 3.5-inch hard drives with a maximum height of 1.5 inches.

Inside a hard drive

Unlike disk drives and other storage devices, hard drives are sealed units from which the data carrier cannot be removed. Therefore, the commonly used term "hard drive" always refers to the drive unit as a whole.

Looking inside of a 3.5-inch hard drive (don't take apart your hard drive)

Storing And Saving Data

A hard drive consists of several disks that are arranged vertically and rotate around a common axis. These disks are made of aluminum and are covered with a synthetic coating that contains finely ground iron oxide, which allows the surface of the data carrier to be magnetized. Like floppy disk drives, hard drives consist of four component groups:

- ❖ The drive motor
- ❖ Read/write heads
- ❖ Stepper motor
- ❖ The control circuitry

The drive motor brings the disks to a rotational speed of 3600 RPM. Hard drives maintain this rotational speed until the power to the PC system is switched off. Otherwise, it would take too long to bring the disks up to this speed again before each hard drive operation.

It's important that the rotational speed doesn't vary by more than half of one percent. This is the responsibility of the hard drive's control circuitry. Laptops and notebooks frequently use a Power Management Controller to turn off the hard drive motor if the drive hasn't been accessed for a long time. This saves electricity and prolongs battery life. The hard drive must be brought back up to the correct rotational speed before the next disk access can occur.

The combined read/write heads reach between the disk surfaces. So each disk can be accessed both on the top and the bottom. The heads are always moved together, although only one writes or reads at a given time.

Hard drives are mounted on arms similar to those found on floppy drives. They're moved radially from track to track by the stepper motor. This particular action (i.e., the movement of the drive's heads from the disk's edge to its center), is one of the primary differences that can be found between different types of hard drives.

The read/write heads of a hard drive do not touch the data carrier surface. At such high rotational speeds this would inevitably lead to both a damaged disk and a damaged head. Instead, the heads float on a cushion of air caused by the high rotational speed. This is called the *Bernoulli effect*.

The distance between the disk surface and the head is so small that even a human hair is one hundred times thicker. Therefore, the hard drive is enclosed within a hermetically sealed case. The presence of even a single grain of dust could severely damage or ruin the hard drive. Therefore, never try to open the case of your hard drive.

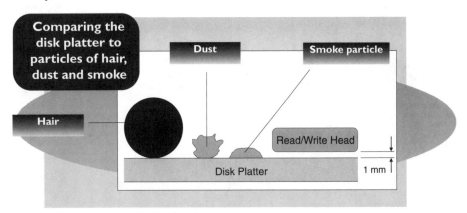

Tracks and sectors of a hard drive

Before the operating system imprints hard drives with a logical division, the hard drives are physically formatted. This process is called either *low-level formatting* or *hard formatting*.

When a hard drive undergoes a low-level format, each of the drive's disks is imprinted with a type of division system. This division on hard drives consists of *tracks* and *sectors*. Tracks are concentric circles on the disk's surface, similar to the rings of a tree trunk. These tracks are placed identically on each of the vertically stacked disks, so individual tracks line up vertically.

> **NOTE**
>
> Make certain to use the installation routine provided with the hard drive or the controller if you're performing a low-level format on either an MFM or ESDI hard drive. Read the appropriate information in the user's manual. Most manufacturers perform a low-level format on SCSI and all IDE drives at the factory.

Storing And Saving Data

To visualize this, imagine a track as extending through each separate disk in the shape of a hollow cylinder. The number of cylinders is simply the number of tracks on the hard drive.

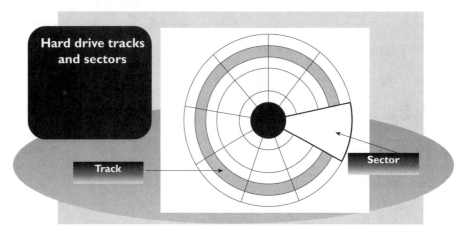

Hard drive tracks and sectors

Track

Sector

During a low-level format these tracks are further divided into a specific number of *sectors*. The low-level format records the sector header, trailer information and inter-sector and inter-track gaps. A dummy byte value or test pattern of values is placed in each the data area of the sector.

By dividing tracks into sectors, your hard drive can precisely specify a particular area on the disk's surface. For example, this type of address could be "cylinder 6, disk 2, bottom side, sector 8." This specifies a precise region on one of the disks in a hard drive.

The number of tracks, or cylinders, are determined by the hard drive manufacturer; the number of disks and, consequently, the number of read/write heads are also determined by the drive's construction. However, the number of sectors that are created when the disk is physically formatted essentially depends on the recording method and, therefore, the data density that's used. This factor in turn depends on the quality of the magnetic surface coating of the hard drive.

Storing And Saving Data

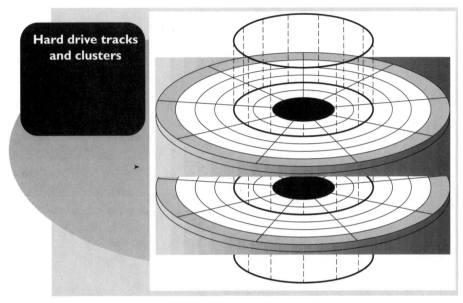

Hard drive tracks and clusters

This physical structure, which varies depending on the type of hard drive, determines the disk's data storage capacity. The smallest physical increment on a hard drive is the sector. A sector is capable of storing exactly 512 bytes of data per track.

To calculate the total number of these 512 byte segments in a hard drive, you must consider three other values:

1. Number of sectors

2. Number of heads

3. Number of cylinders

As we mentioned, the number of heads and cylinders are determined by the manufacturer. As an example, we'll use the ST-251 hard drive by Seagate. This drive is equipped with 820 cylinders, 6 heads, and 17 sectors.

Let's examine the surface of one of the coated disks more closely. After the physical divisioning, it's imprinted with 820 tracks. Since this hard drive uses the MFM method (see below), it's physically divided into 17 sectors. Therefore, each track contains 17 data segments of 512 bytes each. So the surface of this one disk is capable of storing 820 x 17 x 512 bytes, which results in a storage capacity of 7,137,280 bytes for that disk surface.

This particular hard drive model contains three rotating disks. So, it has six surfaces with this storage capacity, each of which is accessed by a separate read/write head. The total storage capacity of this hard drive is 7137280 bytes x 6, or exactly 42,823,680 bytes. Since one megabyte equals 1048576 bytes, this corresponds to a capacity of about 41 Meg.

The total data storage capacity of any hard drive can be calculated using the simple formula shown on the right.

> sectors x sector capacity x cylinders x heads = total capacity

Most hard drives use a sector capacity of 512 bytes. However, since the number of sectors varies with the recording method used for a particular hard drive, it's possible that some hard drives may have 26 or 34 sectors, even if the other parameters remain identical.

For example, the RLL method (see below) divides each cylinder into 26 sectors during physical formatting. If you replace the "sectors" value in the formula above with this number of sectors per cylinder, you'll receive a total storage capacity of 64 bytes.

This combination of parameters corresponds to the Seagate hard drive model ST-277R. Here we are referring to the drive's net capacity, which represents the amount of data that can be stored on the hard drive after it has been formatted under DOS.

The technical specifications provided with a hard drive usually lists the gross capacity of the hard drive. This amount seems larger than the final net capacity because a certain amount of disk space is needed for disk management. Don't underestimate the difference between gross and net storage capacities. This difference can reach 30 Meg on larger capacity hard drives.

For example, a 2 Gigabyte hard drive has a maximum net capacity of 1700 Meg (or 1.7 Gigabytes). Therefore, make certain you know a both the net capacity and the gross capacity of a hard drive.

FDISK and FORMAT

When the hard drive has been physically formatted as described above, MS-DOS places a logical division on the hard drive. First, the DOS program FDISK is used to divide the hard drive into separate logical drives or partitions. Since Version 4.01, DOS has been able to manage larger hard drives within single partitions (i.e., as a single logical drive (C:)).

However, it's still possible and, in some cases, even better, to divide the hard drive into several logical drives (C:, D:, E:, etc.).

Once the drive has been partitioned into logical DOS drives, a logical structure is created within each of these partitions using the DOS FORMAT command.

Clusters and the File Allocation Table

DOS divides each logical drive into allocation units that are called *clusters*. These are the smallest units in which DOS is able to access the hard drive. Each logical drive also contains a File Allocation Table (FAT). Each file that's stored on the hard drive is allocated at least one of these clusters.

A larger file, whose data blocks may be scattered throughout the disk, can be reassembled using the information stored in the FAT. The FAT records to which file each cluster belongs. It also records whether further clusters belong to that file and where these clusters are located.

DOS manages its logical drives with a 16-bit file allocation table. So, each FAT can contain a maximum of 2 to the 16th power (=65536) entries or clusters. So the size of a cluster depends on the storage capacity of its logical drive. The smallest allocation unit under DOS 5.0 covers 2048 bytes of storage space.

Starting at a hard drive size of 128 Meg, this cluster size becomes too small to allow the FAT to cover the entire drive. Therefore, hard drives of 128 Meg and up use clusters that cover 4096 bytes. Hard drives of 256 Meg and up even use allocation units of 8192 (double the previous amount).

This pattern is followed until the maximum size of a logical DOS drive is reached; this size equals 2048 Meg or 2 Gigabytes. DOS independently selects the appropriate cluster size during logical formatting.

Chapter 8 Section 2

173

Chapter 8

Encoding schemes

Throughout the development of hard drive technology, the demand for increased storage capacity and optimized access times have increased significantly. As a result, the system by which data is coded and recorded has also changed.

By refining this system, it's possible to achieve a higher density of data on the surface of a hard drive. This increases the drive's overall capacity. Although this increased density requires an extremely high degree of precision, it also requires the heads to move over smaller distances, which decreases access times.

Modified Frequency Modulation (MFM)

The basis of mass storage technology is Modified Frequency Modulation (MFM). This method has been the industry standard for disk drive systems for several years. Although MFM is still used on most floppy drives, most hard drives now use the more efficient RLL encoding.

In modified frequency modulation, electrical energy is transformed into a magnetic flux change within a data cell on the hard drive surface. This occurs through frequency modulation in the drive's read/write head.

Data bits are defined by the presence or absence of such a flux change within each individual data cell. During read access, these magnetic flux changes are transformed back into electrical impulses through the read/write head.

Data is transmitted serially so each flux change is followed by one impulse, bit for bit, one after the other.

This method has dominated the hard drive market, at least in "smaller" hard drives of up to approximately 120 Meg. The ST-506 hard drive controller is an excellent example of MFM hard drives.

This hard drive controller connects the hard drive with the PC's bus system. It consists of a rather complex expansion card that's connected to a maximum of two hard drives by a 34-pin conductor flat cable.

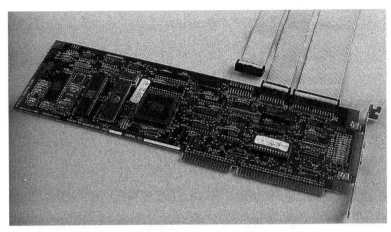

An MFM controller with controller and data cables

The data transmission to and from each hard drive takes place via a 20-pin conductor data cable. The MFM method requires the hard drive and controller to be a finely balanced, as well as a stable and completely synchronized operation sequence. So, installing a new controller can often lead to data transmission errors.

MFM hard drives are unable to provide information on their physical structure. Therefore, MFM drives must be "registered" with the operating system complete with all their parameters. Therefore, the hard drives found in BIOS hard drive selection lists are almost exclusively MFM drives.

Run Length Limited (RLL)

Because of improvements in hard drive construction, such as an improved surface coating and a special controller that further stabilizes the drive motor's rotational speed, slightly different coding systems can be used.

IBM developed the Run Length Limited (RLL) encoding method for their mainframe disk drives. In the late 1980s, disk drive manufacturers started using it to increase the storage capacity. Most hard drives now use a form of RLL encoding. The successors of the MFM method are called the RLL 2,7 method and the RLL 1,7 method. These types of hard drives have a structure that's identical to MFM drives.

RLL 2,7 method

The RLL 2,7 method was initially the most popular because of the improved magnetic coating of the hard drives and the special controller allow 26 sectors per track to be installed during physical formatting. This results in a storage capacity ("density ratio") that's 50% larger than the storage capacity of MFM drives. However, the RLL 2,7 method did not work well with high capacity hard drives.

Example of an RLL hard drive label

RLL 1,7 method

Most hard drives today use the RLL 1,7 method. These drives have a slightly poorer density ratio (1.27 of MFM) than the RLL 2,7 drives but are considered more reliable.

Identifying RLL drives

RLL hard drives are identified as such by the manufacturer. Although it's possible to format any MFM drive by using the RLL 2,7 format, this may cause data loss because the magnetic coating of MFM disks cannot handle the increased data density. Seagate, for example, designates its RLL capable drives with an uppercase letter "R" after its model number (ST-277R).

RLL hard drives also use the ST-506 interface format. The connection between the controller and the hard drive is identical to the one used in MFM drives. However, RLL controllers are often equipped with a special BIOS which must be informed of the hard drive being used.

Advanced Run Length Limited

An additional increase in storage capacity, or density ratio, was achieved by further development of the RLL method. The RLL 3,9 or the ARLL method (Advanced Run Length Limited) permits an even higher data storage density.

Controllers using this coding system place 34 sectors on each track. This results in double the data density and, therefore, double the storage capacity of an MFM drive.

However, these hard drives were unreliable and more expensive since they required higher quality components and construction. The few companies where were manufacturing ARLL drives have virtually disappeared.

Hard drives and I/O cards

You'll need an I/O card (Input/Output card) to connect the hard drive with the motherboard and CPU. This interface is a small plug-in card that contains the electronics for controlling the hard drives, floppy drives, communication ports, printer port and game port. The three types of I/O cards are the following:

❖ IDE (Integrated Drive Electronics)
   This is the least expensive way of connecting a hard drive to the PC. It supports two hard drives but neither of which can exceed a storage capacity of 528 Meg.

❖ EIDE (Enhanced Integrated Drive Electronics)
   Most new PCs include the EIDE card. It's faster than the IDE card and can be connected to four hard drives with storage capacities exceeding 528 Meg or other devices such as CD-ROM and tape drives.

❖ SCSI (Small Computer System Interface)
   The fastest and most flexible means of connecting a hard drive and other components is to use a SCSI card. However, it's also the most expensive. SCSI cards can support up to seven devices including hard drives, removable devices, tape drives, printers, scanners, etc.

Enhanced IDE

One of the most significant developments in interfaces is the Enhanced IDE (Integrated Drive Electronics) interface. IDE interface drives were standard with the 386 and 486 systems. Enhanced IDE is an open architecture based on the standard IDE hard drive interface. Enhanced IDE combines the low cost and ease-of-use of IDE with the SCSI-like features and functions in PCs. High capacity Enhanced IDE drives are less expensive than SCSI drives.

IDE combination controller

They also let you to connect a maximum of four internal devices. This capability eliminates the need for a second controller card (and its accompanying drivers and settings for interrupts and ports) for CD-ROMs or tape backup systems. IDE hard drives are the most popular drive interfaces today. Most 3.5-inch and 2.5-inch drives shipped today are for the IDE interface.

The IDE interface consists of a 40-pin conductor cable (see illustration on the following page). This cable passes data from the hard drive controller over a type of simple host adapter directly to the bus in 16-bit data width.

IDE hard drives use a coding system that's similar to the RLL and ARLL method. This means they also use high data storage densities. However, to the PC system, IDE drives will usually emulate a standard MFM or RLL hard drive.

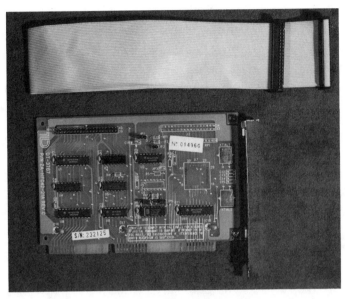

An IDE controller with a 40-pin conductor cable

An IDE hard drive must be "registered" with the processor since the drive is actually managed from there. However, the hard drive parameters that are specified usually correlate to the actual properties of the drive only in the case of lower-capacity drives.

The solution that's used is to store more data on a small disk surface. To clearly understand this solution, visualize how a hard drive is divided into individual sectors. Let's use an example. Imagine a pie that's decorated with concentric rings of cherries. If this pie is then divided into 17 equal slices, the result would represent the typical structure of an MFM drive with 17 sectors. On the pie you'll be able to see the outer cherry rings contain noticeably more cherries than the inner ones.

However, hard drives are not structured this way. Think of the calculation of net storage for a hard drive. Each sector always had a capacity of 512 bytes per track, regardless of whether that sector was located on an inner or outer track.

So, Conner Peripherals developed hard drives that are able to place more sectors on the disk's outer tracks. This special division is managed by a complex integrated control circuitry, which allows the system to address the drive like any "normal" hard drive.

The translation parameters are stored in the CMOS of the system BIOS, and the integrated on-drive controller then translates disk operations into the logical division of the hard drive. So the hard drive operates in translation mode.

This is also why IDE hard drives shouldn't be physically formatted when they're used for the first time. A low-level format would destroy the manufacturer's logical structure. This would make the hard drive only partially usable, if at all. IDE hard drives simply need to be imprinted with a DOS structure, which consists of the logical drives and allocation units described above.

Under normal circumstances, it's possible to operate two IDE hard drives with one interface. However, you must ensure the two integrated controllers don't compete with one another for the leading position within the system. To do this, one of the drives is declared the master drive and the second is declared the slave drive. This creates a clear hierarchy for disk operations.

Another special characteristic of IDE hard drives is their integrated error correction. With the other hard drive types that we've discussed, unusable spots on the disk's surface are marked as "bad tracks" during physical formatting. This ensures that this track won't be used for data storage in subsequent disk operations.

However, IDE hard drives set aside one reserve sector for each data track. If errors are discovered on a particular track, this spot is automatically replaced by the reserve sector. Since the track remains unchanged externally, an IDE hard drive always appears error-free.

SCSI

The SCSI hard drive system offers a completely different approach than the systems described. The SCSI (Small Computer System Interface) is the only controller that allows more than two consecutive hard drives to be driven. This is possible because the SCSI system isn't only a hard drive system.

SCSI primarily consists of a standardized interface, through which intelligent subsystems can be connected to the PC's bus system. Connecting one of these intelligent subsystems to a computer requires only a simple host adapter.

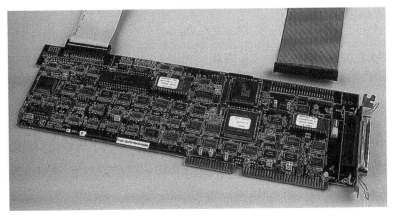

A SCSI controller with a 50-pin conductor cable

These host adapters are used with various types of SCSI devices (tape streamers, printers, scanners, etc.). The "brains" of the SCSI system are always found on the actual device or peripheral.

However, an SCSI controller is more than a host adapter. It's capable of managing eight SCSI devices, including itself, in one PC system. It doesn't matter whether these eight devices are tape streamers, hard drives, scanners, printers, or simply several separate hard drives. So an SCSI controller shouldn't be confused with a hard drive controller.

On an SCSI drive, the hard drive controller is always built into the hard drive's on-board control circuitry. Unlike the hard drive systems we discussed earlier, hard drives with SCSI interfaces transmit data in parallel, so eight data bits are transferred simultaneously.

Hard drive performance considerations

If you compare the performances of various hard drive types, you'll discover some very drastic differences. We'll discuss these differences in the next few pages.

Storing And Saving Data

Average seek time

The average amount of time required for the read/write head assembly to move from one track to another track is called the *average seek time* . It's measured in milliseconds (ms). Many buyers are influenced into buying a hard drive based on its average seek time. However, don't rely only on the average seek time. A drive with an access time of 10 ms won't necessarily outperform a hard drive with an average seek time of 15 ms.

A much more reliable method of determining hard drive performance is comparing the average access time.

Average access time

The *average access time* is an important factor because this value determines how much data the drive can read or write in a specific time. Like the average seek time, the average access time is specified in milliseconds (ms). One millisecond equals 1/1000th of a second.

Most hard drives available today have average access times ranging from 9 to 14ms. A lower access time for a hard drive means that it's capable of accessing data faster. Some of the specialized operations that a hard drive performs, such searching for a specific record in a large database, are helped by a hard drive with a fast access time.

Capacity

The amount of data and information your hard drive can store is measured in megabytes or in gigabytes. The size of your hard drive should be at least 850 Meg although 1.2 Gigabyte is usually recommended. The applications that are written for Windows 95 and Pentium class processors will require enormous amounts of hard drive space. Windows 95 requires 40 Meg of hard drive space. Some applications designed to work with Windows 95 require even more hard drive space.

Interleave ratio

When a hard drive is physically formatted, each of its tracks is divided into a specific number of sectors. Before this division can occur, the drive's *interleave ratio* or setting must be determined. This setting determines the logical sequence in which the sectors of a track are accessed during the disk rotation. The controller uses these sectors as a read/write address.

To understand the difficulty of this task, imagine the disk is a dart board. The outer track is marked and divided into 17 equally large sectors. The disk begins rotating at a constant speed. Your task is to throw darts at the disk until all 17 sectors are full of darts. Since you're an excellent shot, you always hit the top sector. An assistant hands you the darts at a constant speed. Your task is complete when the entire track (all 17 sectors) is full of darts.

If your assistant can hand you the darts at a proper speed, you'll complete the task after one revolution of the dart board. However, if your assistant is a little slower, you'll need more than one revolution to fill the dart board with darts. The same thing happens even if your assistant is fast enough, but the darts are handed to him or her too slowly.

The dart board with its sectors represents an MFM hard drive, you represent the read/write head, and the darts represent data. Your assistant is the hard drive controller and his or her dart supplier is the PC's data bus.

The number of sectors that move underneath the head, before it receives the next instruction from the controller, corresponds to the number of disk revolutions it requires to write on or read a complete track with all of its sectors.

A fast controller with a fast data bus can pass data so quickly the sectors can be read continuously in their physical sequence. So after one revolution of the hard drive, the head can read the entire track and the data are already on their way to the processor.

However, if one of the components in this chain is too slow for this pace, the logical sequence of sectors must be organized differently than the physical sequence. Therefore, this sequence will be inherently different from the physical sequence in which the sectors are actually found on the disk.

This is exactly what the interleave setting determines. For example, if you specify an interleave setting of 3, the read/write head will access only every third sector. So, three complete revolutions are needed to access the entire track.

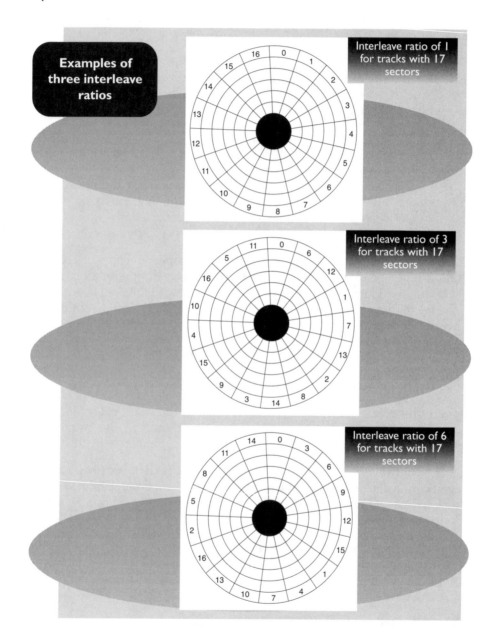

Examples of three interleave ratios

Interleave ratio of 1 for tracks with 17 sectors

Interleave ratio of 3 for tracks with 17 sectors

Interleave ratio of 6 for tracks with 17 sectors

An incorrect interleave setting can produce drastic consequences for the data throughput between the hard drive and the PC's memory. For example, an experiment with different interleave factors showed that a fairly slow MFM hard drive in a 25 MHz 386 system with an interleave ratio of 3 achieved a transfer rate of 182K/sec. Changing the interleave setting to 1 increased the transfer rate by 40%, which raised the rate to 297K/sec.

Although this still isn't the best data transfer rate, the increase obtained by correcting the interleave is impressive. In a test with a 10 MHz 286 system, the same hard drive with the same controller operated at a disappointing throughput of 33K/sec.

In this case, returning the interleave setting to 3 was preferable. This brought the transfer rate up to 182K/sec, which resulted in more than a fivefold increase.

The optimal interleave setting for a PC system can be determined only through experimentation. Unfortunately special software is needed to change the interleave factor without losing data.

Otherwise the hard drive will have to be low-level formatted with different interleave settings. Then a test program must be used to determine the transfer rate for each interleave.

Disk cache

Many SCSI and IDE drives today have cache memory built directly into the drive. The disk cache is an area of memory where the computer stores recently used data. The amount of cache depends on the manufacturer but can be as high as 1 Meg.

The disk cache can help both the PC and hard drive by storing data the computer has recently used. The PC looks first in the disk cache when it needs data before it accesses the hard drive. The advantage is that the disk cache can supply data thousands of times faster then the hard drive.

As you can see, using a disk cache can greatly improve the performance of the hard drive.

Storing And Saving Data

Optimizing a hard drive

When you first start working with your hard drive, files are distributed sequentially over the clusters of the hard drive. However, over time, these files are become larger or smaller as you add or delete data. Also, entire regions of the hard drive may be deleted. So subsequent file operations can cause larger files to be scattered over the hard drive in several fragments.

This condition, which is a natural result of hard drive use, is called *file fragmentation*. As a result of fragmentation, the hard drive must access many different tracks to find all the scattered portions of a single file. Since this is a time-consuming process, the data transfer rate decreases. As you can see in the following illustration, the image is located split in four locations on the hard drive. This requires more time for the hard drive to find each fragment of the image:

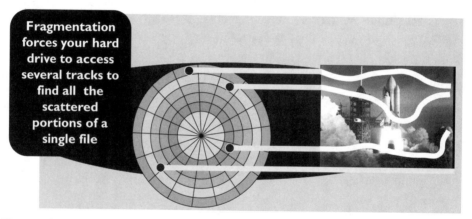

Fragmentation forces your hard drive to access several tracks to find all the scattered portions of a single file

To avoid the problems caused by fragmentation, you should defragment your hard drive at least once a month. This will place all parts of a file in one location or at least closer together. This reduces the time required for the hard drive to "piece together" the single file.

Windows 95 includes a program called Disk Defragmenter. You can even continue using your PC for other tasks as Windows 95 defragments your hard drive. Your PC will, however, work slower.

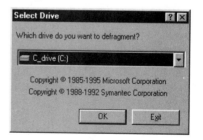

After you defragment your hard drive, the file is back into one contiguous location on the hard drive:

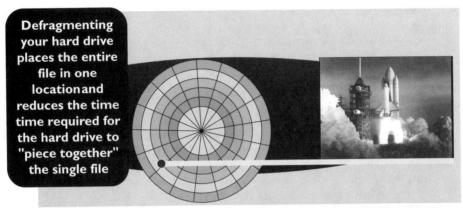

Defragmenting your hard drive places the entire file in one location and reduces the time time required for the hard drive to "piece together" the single file

Searching and repair disk errors

You can improve the performance of your hard drive by using a disk repair program to search for and repair errors. You should check a hard drive for errors at least once a month.

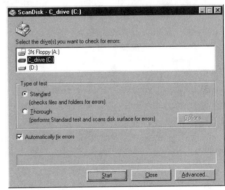

ScanDisk in Windows 95 verifies both the file structure and disk sector integrity. ScanDisk can repair the File Allocation Table (FAT) and the directory if it finds any problems. If ScanDisk detects bad sectors in the middle of a file, the clusters containing the bad sectors are marked bad in the FAT. ScanDisk then attempts to read the file and bypass the affected area of the hard drive.

Increasing bus frequency

Another way to increase hard drive performance applies to motherboards with NEAT chip sets or motherboards with 386DX or higher processors. The bus system usually operates at the original AT speed (frequency) of 8 MHz.

With these particular motherboards, it's possible to change the bus system frequency in the CMOS setup. However this change may cause problems with some PC components, especially expansion cards.

So, you should try to raise the bus frequency only in smaller increments. In Chapter 13 we'll describe these steps.

If you follow these steps but the data transfer rate of your system still isn't increased enough, you may have to install different hardware components. The correct interleave setting is extremely important if you have an MFM or RLL hard drive. In this case, you should ensure that your hard drive controller is capable of operating at the ideal interleave ratio, particularly if this ratio is 1:1. Older MFM and RLL controllers are usually designed for interleave ratios of only 1:3 or 1:2.

However, in this case, installing a new controller is useful only if you're absolutely sure the optimal interleave for your system is 1:1.

If you own a fast hard drive system (EIDE, SCSI), you may also want to consider installing a hard drive controller with up to 2 Meg of cache. This can increase hard drive performance significantly.

If you've tried to increase your hard drive's performance with all the non-hardware options but you're still not satisfied with the results, you may want to purchase a new drive. One option is to swap your current hard drive for a drive with a lower average seek time. Although this will improve the system's performance slightly, a significant improvement can be achieved only if the new drive is at least 10 ms faster.

You can achieve the largest increase in performance by installing an entirely new hard drive system. You should also remember that several other factors affect the data transfer rate between your hard drive and your PC's memory. Often these are indications that your entire system lacks the necessary performance.

This problem can usually be solved only through radical upgrades, such as exchanging your motherboard while also installing a new hard drive system and additional RAM. This is especially true if you're switching from a text-oriented user interface, perhaps on a 286 PC with 40 Meg of disk space and 1 Meg of RAM, to a graphical user interface, such as Windows for Workgroups 3.11 or Windows 95.

In this case, the installation of a more powerful hard drive causes a slight improvement in performance. However, without an improved overall system, you'll never be able to use the capabilities of a more powerful drive.

Another choice to increase the capacity of your hard drive is using software that doubles the capacity of your hard drive without the hardware expense. Companies such as Stacker, Microsoft and others produce disk doubling software. MS-DOS 6.2 and 6.22 include the new disk doubler DriveSpace (formerly DiskDoubler).

CD-ROMs And CD-ROM Drives

You probably own or at least have heard audio CDs. Audio CDs have virtually replaced the familiar "album" or "LP" as the main source of music and sound. CDs have also made a huge impact in the computer world as well. Their popularity has increased to where they're as common as a hard drive in a PC system.

The basic technology for using CD-ROM on your computer is borrowed from the audio CD world. One part includes the term "compact disc" or its abbreviation CD. The ROM part of the name is an acronym for Read Only Memory. In its basic version, a CD-ROM for a computer is strictly a read-only medium. Therefore, you cannot write to a CD like you can a floppy diskette or your hard drive.

A CD-ROM drive with a caddy

Advantages of using a CD-ROM

Why is there so much excitement concerning CD-ROMs? A hard drive, after all, can store more information than a CD-ROM. A user can also access that information on a hard drive much faster than a CD-ROM. The reason that CD-ROMs have become so popular is their low cost, they can be mass produced and can contain huge amounts (650 Meg) of data.

For example, not only are entire encyclopedias stored on one CD-ROM, but they include video clips, sound clips and animation. Large databases, such as the entire phone listing for the US, is available on a CD-ROM.

Besides using WAV files and MIDI files, a CD-ROM drive also lets you play audio CDs and store the audio tracks in appropriate formats. You must have a sound card with the appropriate software installed on your computer before you can use sound with your CD-ROM.

The following table lists some of the advantages you'll enjoy by using a CD-ROM:

Advantage	Explanation
High storage capacity	650 Meg of data on a plastic disc about 5 inches in diameter
Portability	Portable and replaceable medium
Standardization	Industry-wide recording formats
Data cannot be changed	Strictly read-only
Sturdiness	Durability much greater than that of other magnetic media such as 5.25-inch and 3.5-inch floppy diskettes.
Reasonably priced	Low manufacturing costs
Additional options	Audio capable, special compression of audio, image and video data

The following illustration shows the tremendous storage capacity of just one CD-ROM:

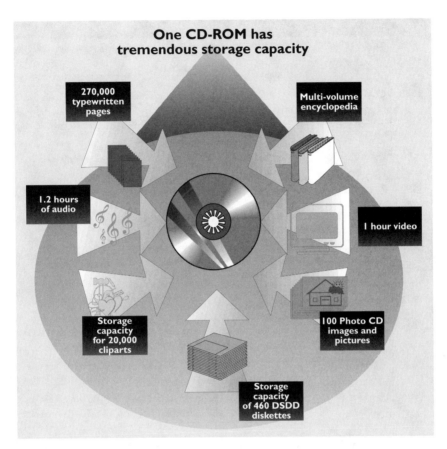

CD-ROM history and development

The following table highlights the history of the CD-ROM technology:

Chapter 8

Year	Product	Explanation
1979 - 1982	Audio CD	The audio CD is released. It becomes such a large competitor to the record album that today few "record" companies actually release albums ("LPs") but instead use audio CDs.
1985	CD ROM	The CD is adapted to the computer world and called a CD ROM. However, initial interest is slow; software developers are slow to release applications on CD ROM because the hardware is too expensive for general use.
1989 - 1991	CD ROM/XA	The CD ROM standard is enhanced. Multimedia requirements for hardware are specified.
1992	Photo CD	The Kodak Photo CD lets users store conventional photo images on CDs. Meanwhile, the photo CD, which is somewhat different from the XA standard, has developed into a world-wide recognized standard.
	CD-I	The CD-I (CD Interactive) is aimed at the entertainment branch of users. By means of a CD-I player, which can be directly connected to a television set, you can read playback CDs.
1993	3DO, CD32, Sega MegaDrive	3DO and CD~32 are two platforms from the home electronics world. 3DO was designed for games and presentations; CD~32 and Sega MegaDrive are strictly game consoles. In the years to come you can expect about three new game platforms per year.
	Video-CDs	A new standard is established, enabling users to achieve quality video playback on the PC for the first time.
1994	Hardware	Prices for CD-ROM drives fall below $200 which makes them affordable for all PC users. Thousands of CD-ROM software titles are available.
1995	2x, 4x and 6x speed drives	2x speed drive prices fall below $70. 4x speed drive prices fall below $150.
		6x speed drives begin shipping 85% of new PCs are shipped with CD-ROM drives installed at the factory
1996	8x, 10x and 12x speed drives	2x speed drives considered old technology. 4x speed drives considered old technology. 8x to 12x speed drives start shipping.

Technology behind a CD-ROM

Data on a CD-ROM is stored as a series of zeros and ones much like a typical diskette. However, unlike your hard drive and disk drive, CD-ROMs rely entirely on laser technology. Because the CD-ROM uses laser technology, no physical contact or damage occurs to the CD surface. Also, CD-ROMs feature a very high recording density. The diameter of the laser beam can be focused so precisely that information can be stored on tracks that are very close together.

The following illustration shows how optical scanning works on a CD-ROM drive.

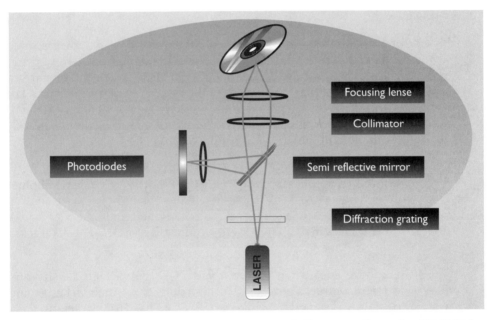

Semi reflective mirrors align the laser beams before it strikes the CD-ROM. When the laser beams are directed onto the CD-ROM they penetrate the semi-reflective mirror. A collimator is used to direct the laser into parallel beams. When the beam strikes the surface it shrinks to an astounding 0.6 micrometers in diameter. The beams pick up the information on the surface of the CD-ROM and are then reflected. The semipermeable mirror redirects the beams to the photodiodes. From there, the electronic processing takes place.

Physical makeup of a CD-ROM

A CD-ROM consists of a reflective layer of aluminum applied to the synthetic base. A layer of transparent polycarbonate covers the base. A final protective coating of lacquer is applied to protect the disk from dust, dirt, and scratches.

A circular hole 15 millimeters in diameter appears in the middle of the disc. Like phonograph records, CD-ROMs are imprinted with only one spiral data track. You may be surprised that, unlike a record groove, this track is read from the center of the disk outward. In other words, a CD-ROM drive always reads the data from the bottom of the disc and not from the top where you see the label.

Pits and lands

If you examined the surface of the CD-ROM carefully with a microscope, you would see that it has several small depressions or indentations. The depressions in the surface of the disc are called *pits*. The areas between the pits are called *lands*. A land is the normal, flat surface of the disc. The transition from a land to a pit or the transition from a pit to a land is used to represent binary 1. Land and pits are used to represent binary 0. The length of a land or the length of a pit determines how many binary 0s are represented.

Approximately 4-5 million pits per CD are arranged in a single, outward running spiral. This spiral is referred to as a track and is 3.75 miles (6 kilometers) long. The elements of the track are so dense there is only 1.6 thousandths of a millimeter between each element. If you imagined that the CD had been enlarged to 12 meters in diameter, there would still be more than six tracks next to each other within one millimeter.

One striking difference when you compare a CD with a high density 3.5-inch diskette is the tpi, or tracks per inch. The high density 3.5-inch diskette manages to store 96 tpi (tracks per inch), while the CD-ROM has 16,000 tracks in the same space!

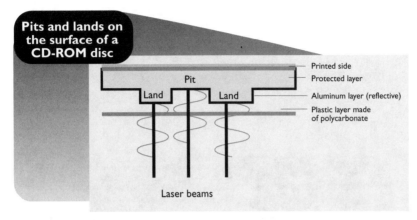

Pits and lands on the surface of a CD-ROM disc

Pit

Land

Land

Printed side
Protected layer
Aluminum layer (reflective)
Plastic layer made of polycarbonate

Laser beams

The incoming laser light is reflected both by the pits and the lands. A small time difference of the reflected light from the laser results since the pits are deeper than the lands. The depth of the pits is designed to be exactly half a wavelength deep. As a result, the adjacent reflected laser beams in the transitions between the pits and the lands erase each other. The light of the laser that hits the pits and lands is reflected in its entirety, while almost nothing is reflected from the laser beams in the transitions between them. This makes it easy for the photodiode circuitry to decode the data.

Arranging information on the CD-ROM

Neither the pits nor the lands represent information on the CD. Instead, it's the transitions between pits and lands that carry the information.

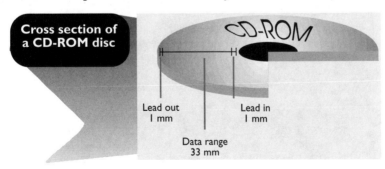

Cross section of a CD-ROM disc

CD-ROM

Lead out
1 mm

Lead in
1 mm

Data range
33 mm

Chapter 8

Channel bits and frames

The smallest unit of information on a CD-ROM is called a *channel bit* . The logical value of 1 is represented by a transition between land and pit. Those are precisely the places on which nothing is being reflected. A land or a pit represents a 0. A byte is made up of fourteen of these channel bits (not 8).

A CD-ROM drive reads a collection of channel bits as a *frame*. A frame consists of the following:

Number of bits	Explanation
27	Synchronzing the laser
17	Subcode byte (1 byte of 17 bits)
136	Error detection and error correction (8 bytes of 17 bits each)
408	Usable data area (24 bytes of 17 bit data bytes)
588	Total bits

This table shows 17 bit data bytes account for only part of the data that is recorded on the disc (408 bits). Also, 180 other bits of information are in each frame.

Data areas, sessions and sectors

By comparison, a hard drive uses only 192 bits (24 bytes X 8-bits) to represent this same amount of data. Every CD-ROM contains at least three data areas collectively called a *session*.

❖ Lead-In
The first area, on the innermost tracks of the disc, is called the Lead-In. It contains the table of contents, sometimes called the CD TOC .

❖ Data area
After the Lead In comes the actual data

❖ Lead-Out
Appears at the end of the CD comes the Lead-Out.

A CD-ROM with more than one session is called a *multiple session CD-ROM*.

The smallest logical data block that can be read from the CD is a *sector*. That is, a complete sector must always be transferred. Sectors are not exclusive to CD-ROMs; you'll also find sectors on hard drives. The sector size varies on hard drives (depending on the total capacity of the drive). For example, a hard drive with 1 Gigabyte storage capacity has a sector size of 16K. However, a sector always contains 3,234 bytes on a CD-ROM. This figure includes 784 bytes for error detection and correction.

A sector consists of 98 consecutive frames. Combining these 98 frames, we see that a sector has the following attributes:

1 byte/frame x 98 frames/sector =	98 bytes for control information
24 bytes/frame x 98 frames/sector =	2,352 bytes for usable data area
8 bytes/frame x 98 frames/sector =	784 bytes for error detection and error correction
	3,234 bytes total per sector

It's possible to store 2,352 bytes of usable data (98 frames containing 24 bytes of data). Of the 2,352 bytes, 12 are used for synchronization to identify the sector and 4 are used for the header to identify the address and mode. This leaves 2,336 bytes for user data.

Audio CD's use the entire 2,336 bytes. However, CD-ROMs use 288 of these bytes for additional Error Correction Code (ECC) leaving 2048 bytes for user data. The following shows how the data is organized within a sector:

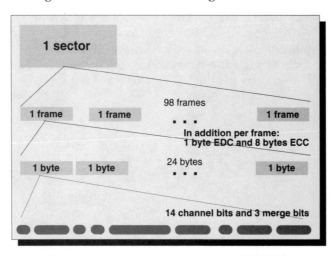

How sectors are organized on a CD-ROM

Chapter 8

The following shows how the basic layout of a sector on the CD disc:

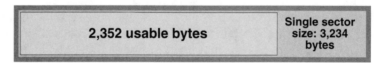

Varying rotation speed

Each sector of a CD has the same length. This is where a sector on a CD-ROM is different from the sectors of a hard drive. No matter where the track is located on the disc, the sectors will always be of equal length. More sectors appear within a revolution at the end of the track, or the outside of the CD, than on the inside, closer to the center.

To scan the surface, the laser has to maintain the same speed over each sector. It has exactly 1/75 of a second to pass over a sector. That means the rotation speed must vary. When outer areas are being read, the rotation speed is very high, when the drive accesses the inner areas, the speed decreases.

The speed of the read head above the CD-ROM surface is always 1.3 meters per second. When the head is over the outer edge of the disc, the CD turns at 500 revolutions per second, while the head turns at 200 revolutions per second when it is over the inside of the disc.

CLV mode and CAV mode

When information is stored in sectors of equal length within a track, as is the case with a CD, we refer to it as *CLV mode* (Constant Linear Velocity). Hard drives don't store information this way. Hard drives have many tracks arranged in a concentric circle around the center. Each track contains the same number of sectors. This procedure is called *CAV mode* (Constant Angular Velocity).

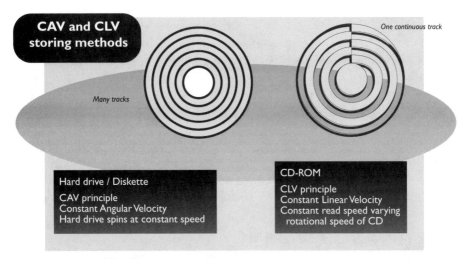

CAV and CLV storing methods

One continuous track

Many tracks

Hard drive / Diskette

CAV principle
Constant Angular Velocity
Hard drive spins at constant speed

CD-ROM

CLV principle
Constant Linear Velocity
Constant read speed varying
  rotational speed of CD

Connecting a CD-ROM drive

A CD-ROM drive is a peripheral device that must be connected to the bus of the PC through a controller. The following illustration shows the four types of controllers you can use.

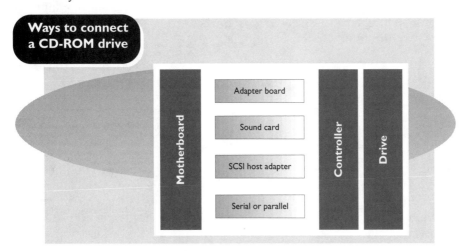

Ways to connect a CD-ROM drive

Motherboard

Adapter board

Sound card

SCSI host adapter

Serial or parallel

Controller

Drive

Chapter
8
Section
2

Adapter boards

Some CD-ROM controllers are located on an adapter card that is plugged into one of the PC's expansion slots. These adapter cards are specifically designed for a particular CD-ROM drive and are sold with the CD-ROM drive. In most cases, proprietary adapter boards are not interchangeable.

Sound cards with an integrated CD-ROM interface

Some sound cards have built-in CD-ROM controllers. Certain models of the Sound Blaster or Audio Blaster Pro are examples. Panasonic, a large CD-ROM drive manufacturer, has tried to standardize the sound board CD-ROM connection called MICE. Other CD-ROM drive manufacturers use a proprietary Mitsumi interface.

Some of the newer sound cards have a SCSI interface (Small Computers System Interface). The SCSI interface lets you connect several peripheral devices simultaneously. This standard originated with Macintosh computers and was later adopted in the PC world, where it has become the most efficient option for connecting drives.

SCSI host adapter

The SCSI card, which you can install in your PC, is called a host adapter. In fact, a host adapter really is a kind of host for many types of peripheral devices. There are two different SCSI host adapters:

1. A small 8-bit SCSI host adapter lets you connect a maximum of two SCSI devices. The devices could be CD-ROM drives, hard drives, tape drives, flopticals etc.

2. A larger 16-bit SCSI host adapters can manage up to seven additional devices.

The SCSI interface operates at a higher processing speed than other interfaces. That's why most doublespeed or quadspeed drives are manufactured with the SCSI interface. Another advantage of SCSI is its flexibility with future operating systems. This interface is required for the Windows NT, OS/2, and UNIX operating systems, since other CD-ROM connections are not supported.

Connection options

Serial ports for CD-ROM drives are quite rare. We only know of a few drives that work with the RS-422 interface. Two of these drives include the Philips CM 205 and CDD 462, both of which have been around for a while. Since we're dealing with a type of Philips standard here, the selection of controllers is very small. Only the Philips 8 bit controller and a version of the Pro Audio Spectrum designed specially for Philips have RS-422 adapters.

Parallel ports are more common, and are preferred for use with notebooks, which usually don't have internal connection options for a controller. While connecting external devices does not pose a problem, the data transfer rates are quite low.

You can also purchase a SCSI adapter which can be connected to the parallel port. In this case, any SCSI CD-ROM drive can be attached to the notebook.

Buying a CD-ROM drive

As we mentioned in Chapter 3, too many applications and programs are available only on CD-ROM today (including operating systems like OS/2 Warp 4.0). Therefore, your PC system should include a CD-ROM drive. You'll hear terms like "4x" or "8x" or "10x". These numbers refer to the speed of a CD-ROM drive or, in other words, how fast the CD-ROM disc spins. Faster speeds obviously result in faster transfer times from CD-ROM to your PC. For example, an 8x CD-ROM drive transfers data at a rate of 1200K per second.

You'll find great bargains on 4x and slower CD-ROM drives. There's a reason for these bargain prices; don't even consider these drives. At the minimum, upgrade to a 6x CD-ROM drive. We recommend the 8x speed drives for the best price to performance ratio. Since you're probably buying or upgrading to a Pentium class computer system, you won't want to be slowed by an older CD-ROM drive.

Interface

CD-ROM drives can be connected to your computer in one of three ways: through the IDE interface, through a SCSI interface or through a proprietary interface. Most CD-ROM drives use a SCSI interface. These interfaces are identical to the SCSI interface used in hard drives.

The second type is a proprietary interface. These interfaces are normally designed for a specific purpose. Since these interfaces are designed for a specific purpose, they may be incompatible with your system. You'll find these interfaces most often in multimedia upgrade kits or as a special deal in a closeout sale.

Stick with a relatively standard interface such as the SCSI. In this way you can almost guarantee that your system will be compatible with future upgrades and improvements.

Internal vs external drive

Internal drives are usually cheaper but they require you to take apart your computer to install them. External drives do not require you to take apart your computer if you have a SCSI interface installed. Otherwise, you must still take apart your computer to install the SCSI interface. Internal drives also require a free drive bay; this could be a problem on certain PC models.

External models are usually more expensive because of the casing and external power supply. Special advantages of external drives are they're portable, have durable cases and most can be powered by batteries. External models are considered portable because you can plug one directly into a SCSI port on the back of your computer or share it among several computers (providing each has a compatible interface).

Two factors determine if you'll use an external drive. The first is whether you'll use the drive with more than one computer. The second is if there's enough room for the CD-ROM drive and controller in your PC.

We recommend buying an external or portable CD-ROM drive only if there's no other solution for your computer. You'll have to determine if their higher cost and poorer performance will satisfy your requirements.

Should you buy an upgrade kit?

Often CD-ROM drives are bundled with sound cards as an upgrade or multimedia kit. To determine whether you should consider such multimedia packages, consider the example of stereo equipment. When you want to buy stereo equipment, you're faced with a choice of buying either complete stereo system or individual components. If you choose the first option, you won't need to assemble the components. You also have a system that is guaranteed to work immediately. However, the best way to maximize technical performance and personal preference is to build your system from individual components.

You can transfer these experiences to the combination of CD-ROM drive, controller and sound card. We recommend buying a multimedia kit if you're looking for a reasonably priced solution with a minimum amount of configuration problems. If you want maximum performance, build your system with individual components: 32-bit sound card, SCSI controller and a at least a 6x CD-ROM drive.

The load and drive mechanism

Users often underestimate the importance of the CD-ROM drive mechanism. The CD ROM in some drives is inserted in a special plastic cartridge called a *caddy* before you can insert the CD into the drive.

This extra case for the CD is a very practical idea. You can damage a CD-ROM with frequent or careless use despite their sturdiness. Read errors on the CD can lead to catastrophic consequences. A caddy helps protect and extend the life of the CD-ROM. Since the number of CD-ROMs being used is dramatically increasing, store your most valuable CD-ROMS in a separate caddy. Examples of the most valuable CD-ROMs would include the most expensive and those you use most frequently.

Some CD-ROM drives have a motorized drive tray like those on an audio CD player. Although it's more convenient to work with such drives, the CD-ROMs are much less protected as they are in a caddy.

One small, but convenient part of a CD-ROM drive is the eject button. Higher end models usually have motorized ejection. While this option is quite convenient and enables users to eject CDs through software, there is one disadvantage. You cannot press the eject button when there is no power for the drive. For such cases, the drive should also have an emergency eject mechanism or button. Usually there is a small opening into which you can insert a paper clip to remove the CD-ROM.

Another point to consider is whether your drive bay is covered by a door. The optical mechanism and drive motor components are extremely sensitive to dust. A door will protect those parts from dust. It should close whenever you insert or remove the caddy. High quality drives also have an automatic cleaning mechanism. These drives have a built in brush that removes dust and foreign particles from the mechanism at regular intervals.

Audio capability

Most CD-ROM drives are capable of playing audio CDs. The necessary electronic circuitry is included on a single chip to convert digital audio data back to sounds. Most drives have a headphone jack and some have one or two audio jacks to connect to a stereo system.

Your drive should be able to read a conventional CD-ROM that meets the Yellow Book standards. An example is the ability to play back an audio CD. The only requirement is that the drive support the ISO9660 and High Sierra standards for the file system of the CD-ROM. Only very old drives (before 1989) may meet the High Sierra standard, but not the ISO9660. Make certain the drive you select has audio capability.

Access time

CD-ROM drives are notoriously slow. Therefore, you should study two values carefully when buying a CD-ROM drive. The first is the *data transfer rate*. This is the speed at which the drive can transfer data to the computer. A data transfer rate of 150K/s was the standard for a long time.

Doublespeed drives, as its name suggests, doubled the rotation speed. A double speed drive rotates twice the speed of earlier CD-ROM drives. For computer data, the term doublespeed means that twice as many sectors can be read per time unit. As a result, the data transfer rate increases to 300K/s. The drive can be switched back to normal speed to read audio data.

Recent advancements now include drives with 6x or 8x or 10x or even 12x speeds. The data transfer rate of 600K/s that can be achieved with a quadspeed drive approaches the speed of some hard drives. So, you can imagine how much faster a 12x speed CD-ROM drive is over the old 2x and quadspeed drives.

Hard drives of the top performance class attain a data transfer rate between 800KB/sec and 1.8 Meg per second. At this speed they're up to ten times faster.

The second value you should look for in a CD-ROM drive is *mean access time*. Before data can be transferred, the desired sector must be selected. If the desired sector is on the outer edge of the CD-ROM, but the laser is positioned on the inside, access will take longer than if the laser is switching between two adjacent sectors. So, different values are used to specify the access time.

Mean access time is the amount of time required for the head to move over half the tracks. Specifications for mean access time vary between drives Most drives list values from 200 to 400 ms. Although CD-ROM drives are gradually matching data transfer rates for hard drives, only slight improvement in access time is expected. A mean access time of under 10 ms is common for hard drives. CD-ROM drives have access times 20 times higher (even under the most favorable circumstances). Besides mean access time, look for maximum access time for a CD-ROM drive. This represents the time for the head to move from the innermost to the outermost track.

Use the CDCHECK program on the companion CD-ROM to check the values for data transfer rate and mean access time. CDCHECK measures an access time resulting from moving to randomly selected sectors besides the mean access time. You can also display the maximum access time using CDCHECK. See Chapter 1 and Chapter 15 for more information on the companion CD-ROM.

Multispeed CD-ROM drives

The latest wave of CD-ROM drives are 8x (8 times), 10x (10 times) and even 12x (12 times). In the past year, both doublespeed (2x speed) and quad speed (4x) drives have been replaced by faster CD-ROM drives (starting with 6x). Resist the temptation to buy either a doublespeed or even quad speed CD-ROM drive. Although with a little searching you can find "great" prices for these drives, their technology is too old for today's requirements (not to mention requirements for the future).

Many of today's fastest CD-ROM drives are available in upgrade kits that are available from several companies (see below). If you decide to buy a CD-ROM drive separately, we recommend nothing less than a 6x CD-ROM drive. Keep one thing in mind concerning the "x" when referring to the speed. The x-factor is intended to indicate the drive's speed compared to original 150K-per-second, or 1x, CD-ROM drives. However, if you look carefully at the different drives you'll find huge discrepancies between the drives' theoretical throughput (and some manufacturer's claims) and the actual performance you can expect on your own system.

Chapter 8

In other words, an 8x or 10x drive doesn't necessarily mean that it runs 8 or 10 times faster than the original 150K-per-second, or 1x, CD-ROM drives. Normally, when a manufacturer says their drive operates at speeds of up to 12x, they're usually referring to sequential reads. This is when you're copying files from a CD-ROM or when installing software.

Why you may need a faster CD-ROM drive

The need for high-capacity storage, and fast access to the data, is becoming more important for everyone. Consider today's computer games as an example. Most graphics-intensive games now require 8 Megabytes or more of RAM. These games are also requiring more hard drive space with each new release. Although, news about developments in mass storage seldom makes the headlines, they're just as much key parts of any computer system as RAM or the CPU.

8x speed drives

Although 4x and 6x CD-ROM drives are still adequate for most of today's applications, low prices make 8x drives a good value. You can find 8x drives in the $350 to $450 range from NEC, Diamond and other manufacturers.

12x speed drives

CD-ROM drive speeds have reached 12x (and will undoubtedly go higher). Examples of 12x drives are from Plextor, Diamond, Hitachi and other manufacturers.

Several PC manufacturers such as Gateway 2000, Dell Computer Corp, Cannon Computer Systems and MidWest Micro offers 12x CD-ROM drives as standard equipment on some of their PCs.

Upgrade kits

Most users have found the most cost effective way to buy a CD-ROM is to buy an upgrade kit. These kits usually include several software titles, a sound card, microphones, speakers and joysticks. Although the accessories are seldom high quality, you at least have everything you need at one time.

Prices of CD-ROM drives

The following table lists some typical prices for CD-ROM drives (January, 1997). The prices in your area may be higher or lower.

Drive speeds	Access time	Transfer rate	Average price
4x	220ms	614,400 K/sec	$99 or less
6x	145ms	921,600 K/sec	$105 or less
8x	100ms	1,228,800 K/sec	$125
10x	100ms	1,536,000 K/sec	$135
12x	90ms	>1,800,000 K/sec	$160

KODAK PHOTO CD

The Photo CD, developed by Eastman Kodak and Philips, was introduced in the United States in 1992. The idea of the Kodak Photo CD is simple. It allows you to have films "developed" onto a CD (compact disc) instead of normal photographic paper. Then you can view the images on your computer, television screen or transferred to videotape. The Photo CD also plays audio CDs through headphones or your stereo system.

Visit Kodak on the World Wide Web for more information:
www.kodak.com

The Kodak Photo CD system in a sense combines the technologies of photography and digital imaging. It combines the convenience, low cost and image quality of traditional photography with the benefits of digital technology. Since its introduction, Photo CD has become a defacto standard for high-quality, low-cost storage of digital images for the desktop.

Who uses the Photo CD technology

The Kodak Photo CD system provided a new way for photographers to enjoy their pictures. You can take standard 35 mm photographs to a photofinisher and have the photos scanned onto special compact discs. Then you can easily transfer the photographs to your PC. Use an image editor to edit, retouch, enhance and export the images to other computer applications.

Chapter
8
Section
2

Storing And Saving Data

Chapter 8

Printing and publishing

Photo CD scans offer printing and publishing professionals a low-cost, high-quality alternative. Photo CD technology is a very cost-effective method of scanning, storing and using color images in a standard format for use on all computer platforms.

Presentations and training

Professionals who support the creation of presentations — along with those who deliver large numbers of presentations — can use Photo CD images to communicate more effectively. Photo CD technology provides a more interactive presentation than possible with either videotape or slides, and presentations that are faster, easier and cheaper to produce than with high-end multimedia authoring packages.

Archiving large collections

Owners of large-scale collections, containing 500,000 images or more, can convert their current film images and photography to digital form using Photo CD technology. After you convert these images, they can be used, managed, archived and distributed in an on-line database (such as the Internet). On a smaller scale, individual photographers can distribute on-disc portfolios, making it easy to show images to customers while controlling the use of their high-resolution images through Photo CD features such as encryption or watermarking.

Desktop publishing applications

Photo CD technology lets you place quality photographs quickly, easily and inexpensively into newsletters, brochures, flyers, etc.

Other examples

The format developed for storing 35 mm photographs at full resolution can be extended to other types of images for other applications. These applications include professional photography, catalogs and medicine. For example, the scientific and medical community is using this technology for documentation and training.

Consumers can use Photo CD Master discs for commercial applications. For example, a real estate agent in Philadelphia with a hot prospect moving from Boston can send the client a disc containing photographs of available housing.

Advantages

The Photo CD is durable. The National Bureau of Standards states the Kodak Photo CD will last at least 100 years.

Other advantages would include the following:

Low-cost scans

It usually costs less to have a 24-exposure roll of 35 mm film scanned onto a Kodak Digital Science Photo CD Master disc than it is to use scanning services (or buying a desktop scanner).

High-quality images

On a Photo CD Master disc, the highest resolution level (2048 x 3072 pixels) captures all the image data 35 mm film has to offer. Other disc formats offer higher resolutions for applications such as professional photography and color prepress operations.

Consistent colors

Photo CD Master disc images are produced using Kodak scanning algorithms and color management software, ensuring consistent, high-quality color .

Multiple resolutions

The Kodak Digital Science Photo CD Image Pac File format on Photo CD discs stores each image at multiple levels of resolution. This lets you work with the smaller, lower-resolution images on-screen and then use the highest resolution version for output.

Convenient storage

Each Photo CD Master disc provides long-term, low-cost storage of approximately 100 images. The Photo CD Portfolio II disc format can store more images at lower resolution.

Multi-platform support

The Kodak Photo CD will run on Mac, PC, UNIX or DOS system.

Chapter 8

DIGITAL VERSATILE DISK (DVD)

DVD, or Digital Versatile Disk (also called Digital Video Disc), is a new type of CD-ROM that is designed to hold 4.7 Gigabytes (enough for a full-length movie) and possibly as much as 17 Gigabytes. The first DVD discs are expected to be available to consumers in early 1997. Many experts believe that DVD disks will eventually replace CD-ROMs, VHS video cassettes and laser discs.

The idea of DVD is to include products and software that follow specifications developed by the largest computer, consumer electronics and entertainment companies (see below). They intend to create a range of compatible products based on a new generation of the Compact Disc format that provides increased storage capacity and performance, especially for video and computer applications.

NOTE

We mentioned that "DVD" is sometimes called Digital Video Disc. It was originally intended for video playback. However, with its immense storage capabilities, it offers potential applications well beyond only video. So the term Digital Versatile Disk is being used more frequently.

These discs will work either with DVD-Video players, similar to conventional videodisk machines or with DVD-ROM drives, similar to the CD-ROM drive in your PC.

Many experts also believe that DVD will be a boom for the CD-ROM industry. The popularity of the Internet and the World Wide Web has dramatically affected sales of many products that were available on CD-ROM (encyclopedias, maps, medical and science titles, etc.). CD-ROM publishers hope the larger storage capacity and better performance of DVD will let them develop titles that are not available on the Internet or WWW.

The good news is that great effort has gone into making the DVD-ROM drives backward compatible. Backward-compatibility means you won't have to throw away your old CD player if you replace it with DVD. Then you can at least use your current CD format if new DVD-ROMs aren't available in large numbers soon.

Tremendous storage capabilities

One DVD disk holds 4.7 Gigabytes on one side of a disk. This is enough room for 133 minutes of MPEG-2 compressed video and Dolby AC-3 Surround Sound (enough to include 94% of all movies produced). The format also allows for double-sided discs of both single layered and double layered construction.

A DVD disc looks similar to a CD-ROM. However, one DVD disc will store the following:

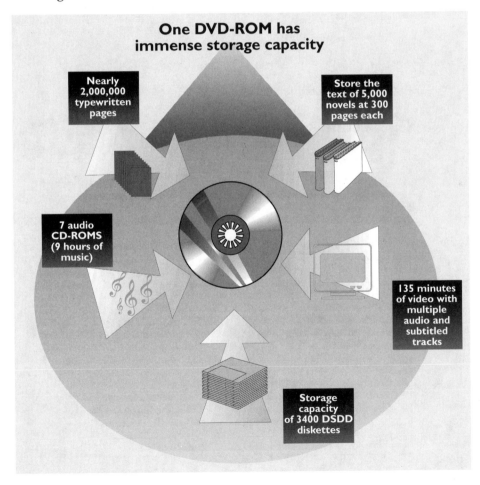

One DVD-ROM has immense storage capacity

Nearly 2,000,000 typewritten pages

Store the text of 5,000 novels at 300 pages each

7 audio CD-ROMS (9 hours of music)

135 minutes of video with multiple audio and subtitled tracks

Storage capacity of 3400 DSDD diskettes

The capacity of just one 17 Gigabyte DVD disc is even more overwhelming. It has the potential to hold the following information:

- ❖ Godfather I and Godfather II and Godfather III movies

- ❖ All the original Beatles albums plus the solo efforts of John Lennon

NOTE

Conceived by the Moving Picture Experts Group, MPEG-2 conserves storage space by scanning successive frames and pixels within a frame for repetitious information. Only information that changes from pixel-to-pixel or frame-to-frame is re-encoded digitally. Static scenes, such as two people talking against an unmoving blue sky, require far less memory than fast- moving action scenes. Even scenes with a lot of movement but a redundant background, such as a space battle, use less storage space.

- ❖ A pile of books taller than the Empire State Building

The following table lists the physical specifications of a DVD-ROM:

DVD-ROM Physical Specifications	
Disc diameter	120 mm (4.75 inches)
Disc thickness	1.2 mm
Disc structure	2 bonded 0.6 mm substrates (1 per side)
Laser wavelength	650 nm / 635 nm (red)
Track pitch	0.74m
Shortest pit length	0.4 m
Disc capacity	Single layer - 4.7 Gigabytes Dual layer - 8.5 Gigabytes Two sided - 17.0 Gigabytes
Data transfer rate	10.08 megabits/second
Audio/Video Specifications	
Video compression	MPEG-2
Audio	2-channel linear PCM 5.1-channel Dolby Surround AC-3 Maximum eight audio tracks
Running time, one-sided, single-layer	135 minutes of video 9 hours of audio
Subtitles	Up to 32 languages

The Consortium

As we mentioned, ten companies called the *Consortium* control specifications for DVD. They're the biggest consumer electronics, computer and entertainment companies in the world. Each member of the Consortium does the following:

- ❖ Contribute patents and other technology to the design and implementation of DVD

- ❖ Agree to conform to the standard

- ❖ Receive a share of the licensing revenue that will be collected by an administrative entity to be designated by the consortium.

The Consortium includes the following companies:

- ❖ Sony Corporation and Philips Electronics have been the leaders and were responsible for licensing the Red Book Audio CD format.

- ❖ Matsushita Electrical Industrial Co. joined Philips and Sony in developing the White Book Video CD format.

- ❖ Toshiba and Time Warner Video concentrated on the movie and home video market.

- ❖ Pioneer Electronic Corp. is the main manufacturer of existing analog laserdisc technology

- ❖ Hitachi, JVC and Mitsubishi are also included

Thompson/RCA/GE is also a member now, and has already made over 2 million MPEG-2 decoders for its DSS receivers.

Apple, IBM and Compaq have considered systems with built-in DVD-ROM drives. None have officially said when the computers will reach the market. Experts also predict that IBM will offer at least one Aptiva desktop model with a DVD-ROM drive. Toshiba America plans to release stand-alone DVD-Video and DVD-ROM drives by early 1997.

Computer industry giants Microsoft, Intel, IBM and Apple are not a direct part of the Consortium. They do, however, sponsor a technical interchange committee that works with the Consortium.

Chapter 8 Section 2

Problems with DVD

The success of DVD may depend on whether, or when, the software providers jump on board. DVD is currently more promise than reality. Few, if any, DVD devices are available. The Consortium members are still developing long term solutions to copyright concerns and the standards for compressing and copy protecting data.

Copy protection

Copy protection primarily concerns bootleg movies and not necessarily pirated software. The computer industry favors a lenient copyright policy. However, the music and movie industries want strict copyright protection built into the DVD specification. Most industry watchers were optimistic the members would reach a settlement as we went to press with this book.

Compatibility

Many consider compatibility and not security as the larger problem. We mentioned that DVD-ROM drives will read current CD-ROM titles. However, DVD-Video players will not work with existing audio CDs or videodisks. Also, many multimedia developers and corporate users who have adopted CD-Recordable (CD-R) technology will want to upgrade to DVD. Unfortunately, they'll soon discover that DVD systems cannot play CD-R discs.

Other problems

The quality, availability or selection of early DVD titles may disappoint some users. Most of the first releases on DVD will likely be titles converted from CD-ROM. However, the CD-ROMs available now already play on the DVD-ROM drives. Furthermore, any software or other titles released on DVD-ROM would probably also be available on CD-ROM. This may be necessary for the publisher to reach a much larger market. However, why not save time and money and not even release a DVD-ROM version; the CD-ROM will work on the DVD-ROM drive anyway. The main reason to use a DVD-ROM is if the size of the title exceeds the capacity of a CD-ROM disc. It would also have to be cheaper or easier to use one DVD disc than several CD-ROMs.

Another factor with DVD's debut concerns the high price. Most first-generation players, including those from Toshiba and Sony, are expected to cost more than $600. If so, DVD will be a tough sell to cost-conscious consumers. The street price for a 8x CD-ROM drive is less than $200.

A more technical question concerns what level of performance DVD-ROM drives will have playing a CD-ROM. The playback performance of a DVD Video disc is already defined. However, the speed it plays a CD-ROM is not. In other words, does it play the CD-ROM at 6x or 8x or 10x or even 2x? The spin rate required for DVD purposes is only about 3x, because of the higher pit density, so high speed CD-ROM playback may be an extra cost.

Comparing the DVD with a CD-ROM

Like CD-ROMs, nothing touches the DVD-ROM. Therefore, picture and sound quality won't degenerate with repeated use. Also, data stored on a DVD-ROM is similar to how data is stored on a CD-ROM. Microscopic pits are embedded in the disc during its production. Data is stored in these pits. Then when the DVD-ROM is played, a laser beam reflects light from the surface, detecting pitted areas and converting the information to an electrical signal.

We mentioned in this chapter that an infrared laser is used to read CD-ROMs. However, DVD uses a laser that emits light in the shorter red wavelength. This thinner beam can read smaller pits, which means 4.7 Gigabytes of data can be packed on a disc.

Furthermore, DVD uses two layers of encoded information (optical discs use a single layer). The area separating these layers is half the width of a human hair. The laser can read the first layer of pits, then pass through a semi-transparent coating to seamlessly play back the second layer. This dual-layer design boosts storage capacity to 8.5 Gigabytes.

Storage potential is doubled again because each disc can be double-sided thanks to a process developed by Matsushita Electric Industrial Co., Ltd. (MEI). This process seals two 0.6 mm discs back-to-back with a form of a photo-resin that hardens when exposed to ultraviolet light. This brings total capacity for a DVD disc to an overwhelming 17 Gigabytes.

Video quality is actually designed to be better on a DVD disc than on a laserdisc. Picture quality is marked by nearly 500 lines of horizontal resolution, which is twice the resolution of a conventional videotape and almost 20 percent better than a laserdisc.

Final notes

Within a few months the copyright issues will be solved and DVD will hit the stores. Playing music, watching movies, and accessing data may never be the same.

REMOVABLE STORAGE SYSTEMS

Various types of removable storage systems are becoming more popular. These systems are used for backing up data. One example of removable storage device is pictured on the right. The purpose of removable storage systems is to combine the flexibility and portability of a disk drive with the capacity and access time of a hard drive. It also requires the data carrier be enclosed in a hermetically sealed protective housing to protect the system from dust and other particles.

Different manufacturers are offering increasingly more powerful, portable and flexible removable storage systems. We'll talk about two companies in particular (Iomega and SyQuest). Storage capacities have already reached one Gigabyte. Average seek times range from 12 to 60 milliseconds.

It's even possible to use some models of removable hard drives instead of your fixed hard drive without an appreciable loss in performance. However, most removable storage systems are used primarily for backing up data since they can easily be installed alongside several other hard drive systems. Such a setup allows extremely fast data transfer between a hard drive and a removable disk. This is probably the quickest way of backing up large amounts of data.

Tape backups

Have you tried backing up the contents of even a small capacity hard drive to floppy diskettes? You'll need dozens of diskettes and a lot of time. A much alternative is to back up your hard drive using a tape drive. These devices are ideal data backup systems because of their unlimited storage capacity and the high level of data security ensured by their thorough error correction methods.

QIC drives

The tape drive industry formed the Quarter Inch Committee (QIC) in the early 1980s to standardize the tape industry. The current standard specifies two cartridge sizes. A two letter code at the end of the QIC standard designates whether the tape standard is based on the full-sized cartridge ("DC") or a mini cartridge ("MC"). You can either install QIC drives internally or attach them externally to the case. Many drives operate through the floppy disk controller in your PC.

They are available in storage capacities of up to 250 Meg, but rarely exceed data transfer rates of over 100K/sec. The floppy disk controller simply isn't capable of transferring data at a higher rate. However, floppy QIC drives are quite affordable.

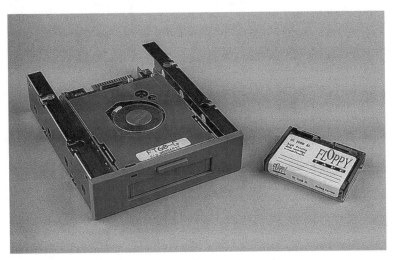

A floppy QIC drive with cartridge

Chapter
8
Section
2

Higher capacity QIC drives

Some QIC drives require a special adapter, such as a SCSI host adapter. The advantage of these QIC drives is that they easily have much larger capacities (500 Meg). External drives are usually connected to the PC through the parallel port. This type of QIC drive isn't "registered" with the system and, therefore, isn't assigned a logical drive letter.

To access the drive, the data backup software simply locates the device at a predetermined port address and accesses it at this location. The drive is useless without this special software. The data transfer rate of these drives using SCSI interfaces depends primarily on the particular SCSI controller. You're usually able to install special software drivers that can increase the transfer rate even further. This allows data throughput of approximately 11 Meg per minute. The data transfer rate of these drives using a parallel interface is about 4 Meg per minute.

Makeup of the tapes

The tapes used by QIC drives consist of specially designed cartridges similar to audio tapes. By using software-based compression techniques, it's possible to store information on these cartridges at double capacity. Like diskettes, these cartridges also must be formatted before they can be used to store information. Since this process is time-consuming, you may want to purchase preformatted cartridges. Cartridges are also available in different sizes, similar to floppy diskettes. The most common sizes are the 3.5-inch and the 5.25-inch formats.

Backup options

The most important advantage of a tape drive is its ability to back up an entire large hard drive in one operation. However, the backup software usually features various backup options. It's possible, for example, to back up only selected files, or you may want to backup files depending on their time and date labels. By using a tape drive along with a good data backup program, you can easily perform hard drive backups.

Great strides have been made in the development of large and super large capacity tape backup units. By far, tape backup of your data is the most popular and the most cost-effective method. The largest manufacturer of tape backup systems is Colorado Memory Systems (now a part of Hewlett-Packard). These drives have enjoyed a history of proven reliability. Mass storage devices (or tape backups) are manufactured by several companies.

Types of backup systems

You can buy two types of tape backup systems:

1. Internal (include SCSI and IDE)

2. Two external (parallel or serial ports)

If you're upgrading your system and have the space (or open bay) inside your PC case, install an internal tape backup system. However, if you prefer the flexibility and convenience of a portable unit that can attach to any PC, an external parallel or serial tape system is recommended.

Today, all tape backup units include the following:

- ❖ Tape drive unit
- ❖ Software
- ❖ Interface card
- ❖ At least one cartridge

Several tape backups will not include the interface card. That is because they plug into your internal SCSI or IDE drive board. Before buying a backup system, check your connectors and meet card. You can save money by not having to buy a tape drive with an interface card.

Buying a tape drive

You'll obviously need to buy a tape drive that has a capacity matching the amount of data you want to backup from your hard drive. However, don't forget about future upgrades, applications, etc., that will require additional hard drive space.

Another point to remember is to consider the cost of both the tape drive and the tapes.

Major manufacturers

The following table lists the major manufacturers of tape backup systems and their Web site address. We suggest contacting one of these manufacturers for more information.

Manufacturer	Web site address	Details
Colorado Tape Backup Systems	www.hpcom	New 'Jumbo' line includes backup capacities from 350 Meg to 1.4 Gigabytes.
Conner	www.conner.com	Tape Stor tapes hold between 400 and 800 Meg of compressed data.
Pacific Micro Data	www.pmicro.com	Uses D.A.T. tapes from 4 Gigabytes to 48 Gigabytes.
Iomega	www.iomega.com	Produces 'Ditto' external tape backup systems. Iomega also produces the very popular 'Zip drive'. This new storage device stores information on 100 Meg disks that are removable.
Additional tape backup systems are available, for example from Mountain (408.438.6650 or fax 408.438.7625). We recommend contacting these manufacturers for their specification sheets on their systems.		

The following pages talks about more specific information on some popular tape drives available today.

Zip drive from Iomega

The Iomega Zip drive similar to an oversize floppy. It combines two technologies: Standard hard drive heads and the magnetic media used in diskettes. The main advantage for the Zip drive is its portability. It weighs about a pound and you can put in your pocket to carry it to another location. Its other advantage is its low cost ($199).

Interfaces

The Zip drive connects to your computer through a parallel port or SCSI controller

Media

The Zip drive is similar to a hard drive in performance. The 100 Meg capacity floppy size disks have enough room for small hardware backups, run applications, or store dozens of high quality photographs. When one disk is full, insert a new disk. A 100 Meg disk is about $15-$20.

Simply insert a cartridge to open the protective door. This in turn exposes the media and engages the motor.

220

Writing data

The media disk, rotating at 3000 rpm creates a cushion of air. To write data, the magnetic head emits a charge that changes the polarity of a spot of the magnetic media

Reading data

The Zip drive features a 29 ms seek time so you run software right from the drive. When the magnetic head passes under the disk, it detects changes in the polarity of the magnetic coating created during the write process.

Zip drive includes "Zip Tools" software to help store, share, back up, organize and manage all your files and data.

Jaz drive from Iomega

The Jaz drive from Iomega is a portable drive with a removable 1 Gigabyte cartridge. You'll find that it runs faster than most hard drives. The Jaz drive can be used with today's Pentium class computers or PCs with a 386 or 486 processor. Other computer systems with a SCSI interface may also be compatible.

> Visit Iomega on the World Wide Web for more information:
> www.iomega.com

The 1 Gigabyte cartridges cost as little as $159.95 (a 540 megabyte disk is available for $84.95). The Jaz drive weighs only 2 pounds, which adds to its portability. Because of this small size, you can share hem, mail them, collect a whole pile of them, and never run out of storage. Since these cartridges can hold 1 Gigabyte, one cartridge can hold 8 hours of jazz tunes, a 2-hour movie, 150 color photographs, or huge amounts of Internet material.

The Jaz drive is ideal for multimedia applications. It's also provides an inexpensive backup solution for small networks and large files. The Jaz drive is compatible with Windows 3.x or Windows 95 or OS/2 Version 2.x or greater (Iomega supplies the drivers). Other operating systems such as Windows NT, UNIX and NetWare are also compatible.

You can use the Jaz drive as a network shared device but the proper network drivers must be used. The drive can also be used to backup the server when connected to a workstation on the network. No special drivers are needed to do this.

Zip drive includes "Zip Tools" software to help store, share, back up, organize and manage all your files and data. Also Jaz Guest is included. The included SCSI software driver lets you access the Jaz drive without installing permanent software drivers.

When Jaz was introduced, it was the largest and fastest removable drive system available. The following lists a few of its features:

- ❖ 1 Gigabyte storage

- ❖ 3.5- inch by 1 inch form factor

- ❖ External drive weighs 2 pounds with automatic termination

- ❖ Sophisticated 256K read/write cache

- ❖ Sustained transfer rate of up to 6.73 Meg per second

- ❖ Average seek time is 10ms (read) and 12ms (write)

- ❖ Rotational speed of 5394 rpm

Different models

Insider

The Insider (SCSI model retail price is $599.95) is a 3-1/2 inch drive that you can mount in any standard 3.5-inch bay. The package includes a 5.25-inch mounting kit, 50-pin ribbon cable, Jaz Tools disk, floppy disks for DOS/Windows/ Windows 95 systems and Macintosh systems

Portable

The Portable (SCSI model retail price is $749.95) is a small, dark green, external drive that has two 50-pin high-density Fast SCSI-II connectors, SCSI ID select switch (0-7), on/off switch, and an external power supply (brick). It also includes a SCSI cable, 25-50HD converter, Jaz Tools disk, and floppy disks for both DOS/Windows/Windows 95 systems and Macintosh systems.

SyQuest

Several manufacturers offer other removable disk systems, which, in view of their capacity and transfer rate, are much more powerful. The most popular systems are manufactured by SyQuest.

Visit SyQuest on the World Wide Web for more information: www.syquest.com

SyQuest has manufactured removable cartridge hard drives since 1982. Since that time, they've become a world leader in removable cartridge hard drives. The capacities of the current line of removable cartridge hard drives range from 200 Meg to the very high performance double-platter, 3.5-inch drive system, SyJet, with a storage capacity of 1.3 Gigabytes.

Examples of removable hard drives manufactured by SyQuest include the following:

EZFlyer

The EZFlyer is the latest addition to SyQuest's 3.5-inch EZ family. Its excellent for storing files for data intensive applications such as desktop publishing, multimedia, graphics, etc. The EZFlyer can also be used if you frequently download files from the Internet.

It has an access time of 13.5 ms and a maximum sustained data transfer rate of 2.4 Meg per second. The EZFlyer provides endless storage capacity with additional cartridges (230 Meg). EZFlyer reads, writes and formats 230 Meg and 135 Meg cartridges and is available in external SCSI and Parallel Port configurations for Macs and PCs.

The EZFlyer removable hard drive has a suggested retail price of $299. The data cartridges (230 Meg) have a suggested retail price of $29.95. Multiple cartridge packs are also available.

SyJet

The SyJet is SyQuest's highest capacity (1.3 Gigabyte) removable cartridge hard drive they're produced. SyJet reads, writes and formats to 3.5-inch, double platter, 1.3 Gigabyte cartridges.

SyJet features a sustained transfer rate of 3 Meg per second and an average seek time under 12ms. SyJet supports extreme data intensive applications such as full motion video. You may want to consider this system if you work in video editing and storage, desktop publishing, imaging, audio, high resolution, photography and multimedia. Configurations include an internal enhanced IDE, an internal SCSI, an external SCSI, and an external parallel port.

SyJet's performance matches that of hard drives installed as primary system storage.

SyJet's suggested retail pricing of $499 for an external SCSI subsystem including the drive, cables, software and one cartridge. The cost of additional cartridges is $99.95 each.

The SyQuest EZ135

The EZ135 can be used as a secondary storage device for the small office or home office user. The EZ135 has a 13.5 milliseconds access time, and a maximum sustained data transfer rate of 2.4 Meg per second. EZ135 configurations include external SCSI and Parallel Port versions.

The SyQuest SQ5200C

First shipped in 1994, the SQ5200C was first shipped in 1994. It has a capacity of 200 Meg, 18ms average seek time, 64K buffer, and sustained transfer rates of up to 1.9 Meg per second (5 Meg per second burst). The SQ5200C reads and writes SyQuest 44 Meg, 88 Meg and 200 Meg hard disk cartridges, protecting the investment of SyQuest's customers who have purchased more than a million SQ555 and SQ5110/SQ5110C series hard disk drives and several million 44 and 88 Meg hard disk cartridges.

The SyQuest SQ3270

Ideal for the laptop and desktop market, the SQ3270 is a high capacity, high performance removable cartridge hard drive. The capacity of each cartridge is 270 Meg. The average seek time of 13.5 ms matches many current hard drives.

Bernoulli box

Bernoulli drives are often associated with the 20 Meg removable cartridges manufactured by Iomega Corporation. This system uses a principle that was discovered in the 18th century by the Swiss physicist Jean-Baptiste Bernoulli and is still used everyday, such as in aviation. For example, the wings of the airplane are made so the speed of the airflow above the wing is greater than the speed below it. This results in greater pressure below the wing than the pressure above the wing. This produces "lift" that helps the plane take off.

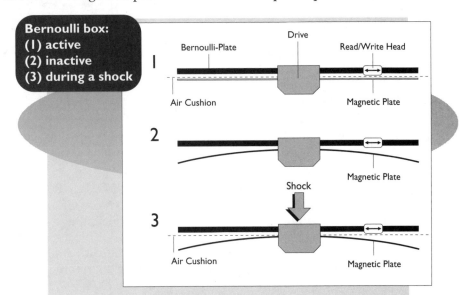

Bernoulli box:
(1) active
(2) inactive
(3) during a shock

Iomega used this principle in the Bernoulli Box. In this form of backup device, a flexible magnetic disk, similar to a floppy disk, rotates very closely to a circular plate that contains the magnetic read/write heads. The circular plate draws in and manipulates air flow as the disk is spinning. This lifts the disk up towards the plate close enough that the head-to-disk spacing is very small (50 microns for the Bernoulli Box). It otherwise "sags" when at rest.

When it achieves a rotational speed of 2000 RPM, the disk is completely flat and even. It is separated from the surface of the read/write head by a stable layer of air. So physical contact between the disk surface and the head is impossible under normal operating conditions, like in normal hard drive systems.

225

In all other respects, a Bernoulli box operates like any other hard drive. Also, because the magnetic head does not touch the disk, head crashes are virtually impossible. Furthermore, since the disk is closely and securely aligned with the magnetic head, more data can be stored and accessed. This is because the head can accurately read/write from more tracks than otherwise possible. The relatively high rotation speed helps achieve access times that are comparable to those of slower hard drives.

The drive is controlled by a simple host adapter. If there are many other expansion cards, this adapter frequently encounters addressing conflicts. However, the adapter's address can be selected manually.

Visit Iomega on the World
Wide Web for more
information:
www.iomega.com

Iomega has Bernoulli Box drives in internal and external 150 Meg and 230 Meg models. The street prices for these range from about $350 to $600 depending on the interface. The 5.25-inch Bernoulli cartridges are available for approximately $95 for a single 130 Meg cartridge or $430 for a five-pack, with 230 Meg media roughly another $5 per cartridge.

WORM drives

A special development that is somewhat related to CD-ROM drive technology is the WORM (Write Once Read Many) system. Unlike the CD-ROM drive, however, you can write information to a WORM disk. The limitation is that you can write information to these disks only once (the "Write Once" part of WORM). This data is then permanently stored on the disk and cannot be changed, deleted or overwritten. It's possible to read the data stored on the disk as often as necessary (the "Read Many" part of the name).

Since the permanence and irreversibility of the information stored using WORM technology is inherent in the physical nature of the data carrier, it is often used to archive legal, judicial, accounting and other business data.

A WORM CD is constructed slightly differently than conventional CD-ROMs. The media layer appears between two plastic layers. The WORM drive, much like a CD-ROM drive, uses a laser. A WORM drive uses the laser to write to the disk by burning very small areas into the pigment layer of the media. This vaporizes a small portion of the layer. This creates a vapor bubble that expands into the base layer, forming a pit. These areas contain the data.

WORM drives have two major disadvantages. The first is the high cost for both the drive and the cartridges. Some WORM drives can cost thousands of dollars and the cost of a cartridge can be close to $200.

The second disadvantage concerns incompatibilities. Drive manufacturers use proprietary data format. So, a WORM disk from one company may not work with a drive from another company. Also, a standard disk size doesn't exist for WORM drives.

These disadvantages are the reasons many experts recommend staying away from WORM drives unless you have massive amounts of data to backup which you never want to be changed or deleted.

MO drives (Magneto-Optical)

Ideally, you should be able to write to a storage device repeatedly. This storage device should combine an exchangeable data carrier, high storage capacity and fast data access.

We've mentioned (and you've probably discovered long ago) that storage techniques like the disk drive cannot handle extremely large amounts of data required by today's Pentium class computers.

The maximum possible data density is predetermined by the method used to read the information stored on the medium. The use of a laser beam in scanning the data carrier allows for an exceptionally high data density and therefore also for large amounts of data to be stored on a minimal surface area.

However, this storage technique is based on permanent physical imprints in the storage medium. The combination of these procedures has resulted in a system that uses a magnetic data write procedure and an optical read method. This means that instead of a combined read/write head, two separate heads perform write and read access.

Magneto-optical drives (MO drives) successfully combine these techniques. MO drives store vast volumes of data on removable, random-access discs. They use a combination of a laser beam and magnetic field to change the molecular alignment of a disc's data-substrate layer.

Chapter 8

MO drives have capacities of 128 Meg and 230 Meg. The 3.5-inch formats are most common. Also, 600 Meg and 1.2 Gigabyte, 5.25-inch MO drives are available.

Advantages

MO technology is an exceptionally stable method for long-term storage. They're also an easy way of transferring large graphic files or other files that can't fit onto standard floppies.

Disadvantages

The disadvantage of using an MO drive is three passes are needed to rewrite a disc. The first pass erases the old data, the second pass performs the actual write and the third pass verifies the data. This results in a very slow performance level.

Also, MO drives suffer with a slow access rate (typically, 60 milliseconds). The price/performance level of MO drives put them out of reach for many users. However, as the MO technology expands, perhaps its price/performance level will become more affordable to more users.

Structure of MO disks

The structure of a MO disk is somewhat similar to CD-ROMs. Between the base layer of polycarbonate and the reflective coating, a layer of rare-earth alloy is applied. This material reacts to both optical and magnetic forces.

To write data to the disk, first the drive applies a magnetic field to the disk. This field is oriented to write the binary digit 0 on the disk. The "write head" of an MO drive consists of a powerful laser that heats tiny portions of the disk's surface to 160 degrees Celsius. This is the Curie point, or the temperature at which the crystals in the mirror layer change their polarity to match that of the magnetic field. This makes all binary data in the sector consist of 0s. While these particles cool to lower temperatures, a magnetic field is used to align them in a such a way that a magnetic spot is created.

To read data onto the disk, the drive first removes the magnetic field.. This information is read by a weaker laser. When it uses the laser to aim a beam of light at the mirror layer, a phenomenon known as the Kerr effect causes the crystal alignment to alter the polarization of the reflected beam. The amount of beam polarization determines its intensity, and a polarizing filter in the read head then determines whether a 0 or a 1 was read on the disk by the level of beam intensity. A special technique is used to determine the alignment of the magnetic spot through the beam's reflection and its polarization angle.

The level of precision required by this read/write technique requires that an exact data track be present, which is imprinted on the MOD by the manufacturer.

Several companies manufacture MO drives. They include the following:

M-O Drive Manufacturers	
Manufacturer	Web site address
Maxoptix Corp	www.maxoptix.com
Hitachi America	www.hitachi.com
Sony Electronics Inc.	www.sony.com

Flash RAM

An entirely different type of storage medium is currently being developed. This device consists of RAM chips that can retain information permanently without using electricity to sustain their information.

An example of flash memory miniature card is from Intel. Despite being smaller and thinner than a matchbook, this card handles 2 Meg of removable storage for digital cameras, voice recorders, Personal Digital Assistants and other hand-held electronics. You can use an adapter to insert the Miniature Cards into the PCMCIA slot of your laptop PC. Intel has plans for an 4 Meg version and future plans for an 8 Meg and 64 Meg versions in 1997.

A flash memory card specification war may be brewing, however. The Compact Flash Association, led by flash memory manufacturer SanDisk, is promoting its CF specification. SanDisk's CF card can already be found in the IBM PalmTop 110. CompactFlash Association members include NEC, Apple, Motorola and Polaroid.

SHOPPING TIPS

Keep one thing in mind when shopping for or upgrading your current backup hardware. Your should be able to back up all your data files (preferably your entire hard drive) onto three or fewer cartridges. Also, try to make the process simple and quick.

Note on assessing storage needs. Never consider the size of your data as compressed capacity. Instead, consider the original size of the files (called *native capacity*). Most manufacturers and retailers use a 2:1 compression ratio when advertising backup devices.

Below we'll review the some of the methods that we've talked about in this chapter.

QIC tape

QIC (Quart Inch Committee) tape is the most cost-effective desktop backup solution and currently the most popular. However, it also is usually plagued with cryptic standards and proprietary formats.

Because of proprietary systems, make certain you understand the write and read compatibilities of the QIC drive. In other words, the tape system of one manufacturer may not work with another manufacturer's drives or products. This is especially true if you use data compression.

An enhanced successor to QIC is called Travan. It features larger capacities than the competing QIC-Wide standard:

❖ 400 Megabyte (uncompressed) for QIC-80

❖ 800 Megabyte for QIC-3010

❖ 1.6 Gigabyte for QIC-3020

Travan drives and media are, of course, more expensive than QIC products. They are, however, backward-read-compatible with current QIC tapes.

Other companies have extended the life of an existing QIC-80 tape drive. Gigatek and Verbatim, for example, carry EC-1000 cartridges. By installing a software upgrade, these cartridges can hold 400 Meg of uncompressed data. This saves you from buying new hardware. Gigatek also plans to market similar 1,000 foot cartridges for QIC-3010 and -3020 drives.

If your system has 2 Gigabyte or larger hard drives, helical-scan tape-backup solutions provide even more capacity and faster speeds. These solutions range from 4mm DAT to more specialized 8mm drives. Half-inch digital linear tape (DLT) drives are the fastest and highest-capacity (10 Gigabyte) tape products, but are beyond most budgets.

Removable hard drives

We've mentioned that tape backup is ideal for offline archiving. Removable cartridge media are best for online storage. They also let you take files home or exchange files with coworkers or service bureaus. Iomega's Bernoulli Boxes and SyQuest's removable hard drives have comparable drive costs, though SyQuest cartridges cost less and are somewhat faster.

Cartridge drives like the Zip and Jaz combine tape-like affordability, floppy disk-style convenience and near hard drive speed. Iomega's 100 Meg Zip drive and SyQuest's quicker, 135 Meg EZ135 each sell for about $200, plus $20 per cartridge.

Magneto-optical (MO) drives

Magneto-optical (MO) drives are good for long term data storage but are relatively expensive. Although CD-R drives were not originally intended as backup devices, , they're becoming more popular to "burn", or master, important data. Make certain the mastering software of the CD-R drive supports the formats you need.

CD-ROMs

To get the best of optical and CD-ROM technology in one, consider a phase-change drive. For about $1,000, you'll get a quadspeed CD-ROM player, plus support for 650 Meg phase-change optical discs—which are rewriteable, although not readable by regular CD-ROM drives, as are discs created by CD-R burners.

Many backup products use floppy disk drive and parallel-port connections. A faster alternative is to use SCSI and the newer, more cost-effective Enhanced IDE interfaces. For example, ATAPI Enhanced IDE tape drives combine DAT-like speeds with the pricing of a QIC drive.

External tape and cartridge drives that plug into parallel ports are relatively slow, especially with systems that lack enhanced parallel ports. They are, however, convenient solutions for notebook owners or offices planning to share a backup solution among several PCs. Make certain the drive has a pass-through connector so you can still use your parallel printer.

Network backup solutions

Network backup solutions suggest another set of criteria. For a reliable network backup solution, look for the following:

❖ Bulletproof reliability

❖ Unattended automatic operation,

❖ Comprehensive supporting software

Popular solutions include the following:

- ❖ Multitape jukebox

- ❖ Autoloader units

- ❖ Hierarchical Storage Management (HSM) systems that intelligently manage online and backup storage.

Chapter
8
Section
2

233

Communicating With Your PC

9

Communicating with your PC uses other components and devices than those we've discussed so far in Section 2. Because the devices belonging to this group are usually located outside the PC's case, they're called *peripherals*. Although most of these devices are outside the PC's case, they're essential to the operation of a PC system.

Peripherals let you communicate with your PC and let it communicate with you. You use peripherals to send information to your PC, to direct the processing of this information and to receive the processed or recorded data.

Therefore, these devices are designed to translate human forms of communication into information that can be processed by the computer, and vice versa. This process is possible only within a specific framework or structure.

Although there are exceptions, verbal speech generally cannot be used to send data to the computer. The most commonly used method of sending data to the computer is by using the keyboard. This is a character-oriented method that's based on written human communication.

Not long ago, users communicated with computers on a binary basis, using only values of 0 and 1 (off and on). Obviously, this method would make it impossible to use many of today's applications, such as word processing programs.

Chapter 9

The effectiveness of input and output devices depends on the skill of the person using them. For example, the fastest keyboard isn't very helpful if you're a two-finger typist, and whether you like or dislike using a mouse may depend on personal preferences as much as on the size of your hand.

SENDING DATA TO YOUR PC

You'll need a means of inputting, or sending, data to your PC. Your PC is virtually useless without an input device of some sort. Although the keyboard is the most widely used device, other devices can also be used to input data. We'll discuss these peripherals in this section.

Keyboard

The keyboard is the most important input device of your PC. Because Microsoft Windows and Windows 95 have become the dominant operating systems in the PC market, the mouse has also become a necessary input device. However, the keyboard is still the primary way to enter data.

The keyboard is the most important input device of your PC. It lets you send instructions and commands to your PC

Several varieties of keyboards are available today. These range from color-coded keyboards for beginning typists to "fun" custom color designed "theme" keyboards to the new sleek ergonomically correct keyboards. You can improve your proficiency and comfort by choosing the right keyboard. Except for graphical applications such as AutoCAD, the information or data of almost every application is character-oriented. For example, word processors, databases, spreadsheets, and desktop publishing (DTP) programs process letters, numbers, and other characters.

Keyboards are specifically designed for entering these characters and are still the fastest way to perform this task. Acoustic character entry, or speech recognition, is still in its infancy. Even text entry using OCR (Optical Character Recognition) programs, which basically "read" by recognizing certain shapes as specific characters, first require a written or typed text. This original copy is usually created with a keyboard.

236

How keyboards work

A PC keyboard consists of a series of keys or switches that are mounted in a case. Each of these switches doesn't have to be connected to the PC with a separate wire because a special electronic circuitry is also located in this case. This circuitry enables the information entered on these keys to be sent to the PC through a serial cable.

Make codes and code pages

For this purpose, each key is assigned two codes. The *make code* is triggered when a key is pressed down and the break code is triggered when the same key is released again. This also enables the operating system to work with keyboards of different languages or arrangements, since a specific character is triggered only when the key code is received by the operating system.

The character assignments are stored in tables called *code pages*, which specify a particular character for each key code.

This is also how foreign keyboard drivers are used. The KEYB command simply loads the specified table, which is then used to assign the appropriate character to each code sent from the keyboard.

If you briefly hold down a specific key, the character that's assigned to that key will be printed repeatedly on your screen. This process is triggered by the keyboard processor. If this processor receives a key's make code but doesn't receive the corresponding break code within a certain time period, it outputs this key code repeatedly.

The number of key codes that are sent per second is also referred to as the *typematic rate*. Several utilities and applications allow you to change this rate.

Keyboards today

Today most PC keyboards have 101 keys that are grouped into different areas.

Function keys

Above the main group of character keys, you'll find twelve function keys arranged in three clusters of four keys each. These function keys let you specific tasks (depending on the software or application). For example, many applications use the F1 key to display online help information.

Communicating With Your PC

Chapter 9

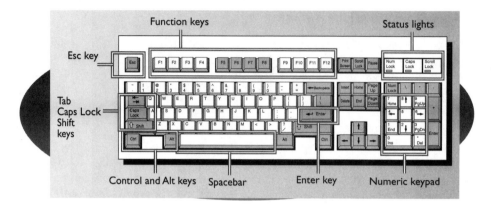

Numeric keypad

A numeric keypad appears on the right side of the keyboard. Use these keys to enter numbers 0 through 9 when the NumLock light is turned on by pressing the (Num Lock) key. The numeric keypad can also move the cursor when the NumLock light is turned off.

Cursor keys (arrow keys)

Moving the cursor is usually done by the special cursor keys located next to the numeric keypad.

Status lights

The current keyboard status is indicated by a row of three LEDs. These LEDs let you determine whether the Num Lock, Caps Lock, or Scroll Lock functions are active.

Other keys

Press the (Spacebar) to move the cursor. Many programs will say "Press any key to continue". When you see this message, the program is usually referring to the (Spacebar). The (Ctrl) and (Alt) keys are used with other keys to perform a specific function. Press (Esc) to quit a current task.

238

Since this keyboard has been so popular, it now represents the industry standard. However, it's neither particularly ergonomic or efficient. Some manufacturers have introduced a more ergonomic layout. The keys on these keyboards are easier to reach, which helps reduce wrist strain (see Chapter 5). The new Microsoft keyboard is an example of an ergonomically designed keyboard. Other manufacturers have also come to market similar keyboards.

Traditional keyboard (top) and the new ergonomically designed keyboard

You'll also find keyboards with built-in joysticks or even a small ball sometimes called "joy buttons" or "built-in pointing devices." The advantage of these keyboards is that you don't have to take your hands off the keyboard to reach for a mouse.

Several keyboard manufacturers have followed Microsoft's lead and include two special keys use the specific features of the Windows 95 operating system. You can program these special keys to include software macros.

Difference between various keyboards

The biggest difference between various keyboards is the way they are constructed. The construction of the key contacts, in particular, varies depending on the manufacturer.

239

Chapter 9

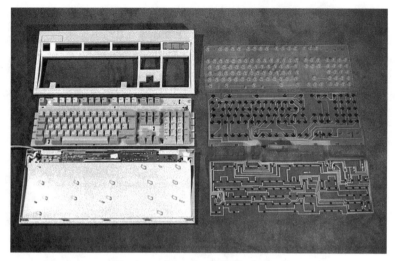

The interior of a foil keyboard

Foil contacts

Since keyboards that use foil contacts can be produced easily and inexpensively, they are found in several PC systems. With this technique, two sheets of foil are imprinted with the actual contacts and their connections. These sheets of foil are laminated on either side of a layer of insulating material so the contact surfaces of the two sheets are separated slightly. Keys are mounted just above these contacts, and when one of these is pushed, the contacts below are pressed together, closing a circuit. A small spiral spring or a flexible plastic element is used to raise the key again after it's released.

This foil technology is so advanced the reliability and life span of these types of keyboards can be compared to those of more expensive systems.

Metal contacts

Although keyboards with "real" metal contacts are more expensive to produce, they are found in almost as many systems as the foil keyboards. This technique uses individual switches for each key; metal tabs are pushed together when a key is pressed. These tabs usually will be plated with gold or another noncorrosive conductor to prevent the contacts from becoming fouled. As with the foil system, metal or plastic springs are used to push the key back up once it's released.

240

Touchless keyboards

The most elaborate and, consequently, the most expensive technology is found in touchless keyboards. Three different methods are used for these systems. The piezoelectric method uses the piezoelectric effect, by which crystal tiles produce an electrical voltage when pressure is exerted on their surfaces. This type of keyboard has a small piezo-crystal under each key. So each time a key is pressed, a small electrical voltage is produced by the crystal below.

This voltage can then be registered and processed by the keyboard circuitry. The optoelectrical method uses light-gates mounted below each key to detect keystrokes. Pressing a key blocks the light gate below. Since this method is both expensive and fairly unreliable, it's used only in certain industrial applications.

The magneto-mechanical method, using the HALL effect, is used much more frequently. In these systems, a small permanent magnet is mounted on the underside of each key. When a key is pressed, its magnet is brought near a HALL sensor. The magnet produces a change in the electrical state of the sensor that's then detected and processed by the keyboard circuitry.

Tips on using a keyboard

You should be able to tell whether a character has been activated. The keys on a good keyboard should either have a distinct pressure point or a very clear stop. Furthermore, the characters should be triggered at exactly that moment. This doesn't happen on many keyboards. In these instances, simply touching a key lightly may trigger the character, even if the pressure point hasn't been reached.

Your keyboard shouldn't move when you're typing. This usually happens with inexpensive keyboards. To ensure that this doesn't happen, the keyboard should be fairly heavy, or should have a nonskid underside. Also, your keyboard should be adjustable so its position is comfortable for typing. Many keyboards have two feet that raise the back of the keyboard so it tilts toward you.

> See Chapter 3 for information on selecting a keyboard.

Chapter 9 Section 2

Chapter 9

Use the "feet" to raise the back of your keyboard so it tilts toward you

Keyboard cables that are too short can also be an annoying problem. However, this problem can easily be solved by purchasing a special extension cable. We've also found that spiraled cables have no important advantages over straight cables.

Check your keyboard to see if it has small bumps on either the D and K keys or the F and J keys. Use these "bumps" to position your fingers better and more accurately on the keyboard.

"Bumps" on the F / J keys or D / K keys help position your fingers

Since each user has different needs and preferences, a single keyboard won't meet everyone's needs. So when you're looking for a keyboard, consider its overall quality and then try it out thoroughly.

Windows 95 keyboard

The Windows 95 keyboard features three additional keys (two logo keys and one application key). These keys are designed to add more compatibility and functionality to Windows 95. Tactile feel with step sculptured keycaps for improved typing ergonomics. This keyboard features an oversized Enter key for greater typing comfort and accuracy.

One example of a Windows 95 keyboard is the Alps Enhanced Windows 95 Keyboard. Alps Electric has been manufacturing keyboards for many of the largest computer companies for over 20 years. This keyboard features a full 105-key layout in a trim, compact space-saving package.

The three unique Windows 95 keys give you complete command over your applications. Its special Windows 95 keys provide instant command over applications to save you time and effort. The first two Windows keys open the Start menu so you look at the list of all active applications. The third key is the Applications key. When you press this key, a pop-up menu opens the same menu as clicking the right mouse button in many Windows applications.

One good feature is the Erase-Eaze backspace key. The Backspace key is usually difficult for many users to reach on most keyboards because it's placed so high on the keyboard. However, the Erase-Eaze key is ergonomically located next to the Spacebar. So, all you need to do is use your thumb to select it. The result is faster, more accurate, and more comfortable typing.

Although this keyboard is designed for Windows 95, it's also compatible with Windows 3.1. Simply download a free driver from Alps On-line services and the special Windows keys will work with Windows 95 and Windows 3.1. This is good news if you're using Windows 3.1 now but plan to upgrade to Windows 95.

Chapter 9

Mouse

As we mentioned, the mouse is a close second to the keyboard as the most important input device in your PC system. Today's powerful operating systems like Windows 3.11 and Windows 95 virtually require that you use a mouse. Also, most software designed to run on those operating systems, especially graphic and desktop publishing software, require the use of a mouse.

The mouse is a handheld device that is used primarily to move the cursor or pointer on the screen. Most applications and operating systems virtually require that you use a mouse.

The mouse is a handheld device that is used primarily to move the cursor or pointer on the screen. It's also used to select and move items. It basically consists of a small box that can be moved in any direction on either the surface of your desk or on a special mouse pad. This movement is registered by the PC system, evaluated by a special program called the *mouse driver* and passed on to the application program. Most applications indicate the relative position of the mouse on the screen with a small arrow known as the *mouse pointer*.

The majority of mice have two buttons located on top of the mouse but some mice have three buttons. However, few applications use the middle button.

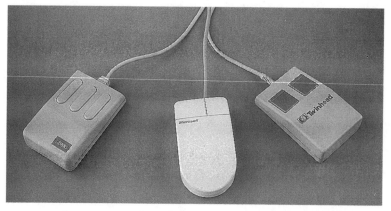

A mouse can have two or three buttons depending on the manufacturer

Mouse actions

Working with a mouse is called a "mouse action". The following describes the different mouse actions:

Click and double-click

Move the mouse on a flat surface to move the mouse pointer to any location on the screen. For example, you would do this to select a particular menu or command. This command can then be selected by pressing the left mouse button (called *clicking*).

Clicking twice in rapid succession, called *double-clicking*, is often used to open a document or start a program.

Right-click

To display a list of commands in Windows 95 and applications written specifically for Windows 95, click the right mouse button.

Drag and drop

Move the mouse pointer over the desired item on the screen. Then press and hold down the left mouse button. Keep holding the mouse button pressed down but move the mouse pointer to where you want to move the item. Then release the mouse button. This is how items are moved, deleted, copied, etc., in Windows 95.

Connecting a mouse

The mouse is usually connected to the COM1 port or other serial port. When purchasing a new mouse, make certain it has the correct plug since there are two different standards. Most systems use a 9-pin sub-D connector. This is the connector that's used for the first serial port in most PC systems.

A 25 to 9-pin adapter

However, 25-pin mice are also available. You'll need an adapter for the 9-pin plug to use these mice. This adapter, which is usually attached to your PC's jack with screws, can protrude from the back of your PC.

Chapter 9

So, if you're planning on or are forced to place your PC directly against a wall, you should either purchase a different mouse or plug your mouse into a port with the proper connector, perhaps COM2.

It's also possible that a 9-pin mouse plug must be connected to a 25-pin jack. Remember that some PCs aren't equipped with a 9-pin serial port; often COM1 is also found in the form of a 25-pin jack. Appropriate adapters can be used in this case also. Sometimes these adapters are even supplied with the new mouse.

Bus mouse

Some mice, also called *bus mice*, aren't connected to the PC through a serial port. Instead, they are plugged into the PC's bus system directly using a special expansion card. Often you'll find an appropriate mouse connector on other types of expansion cards, such as graphics cards or combination controllers.

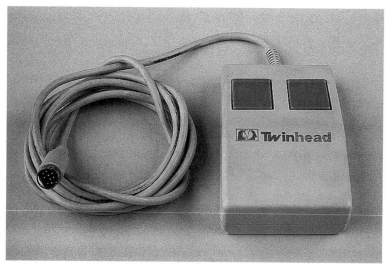

A bus mouse with its jack

Two different versions of this system are available. Among other things, these versions differ in the type of connector used for the mouse. So, if you want to install a bus mouse and are already using a certain type of connector, make certain your new connector will be compatible with your existing jacks.

In both instances, the mouse must be registered with the system through a special mouse driver. This device driver should be included on the diskette that's shipped with a mouse. You must either add this driver as a DEVICE entry in your CONFIG.SYS file or, if it's an EXE or COM file, load it from the operating system environment. In the latter case, it's easier to perform this task in your AUTOEXEC.BAT file. By doing this, you don't have to remember to load the driver each time you use an application that requires the mouse.

Two different types of data formats are used in mouse systems: Mouse systems mode and the Microsoft mode. These systems have different hardware and driver software.

Most mice will allow you to switch between the two modes. However, you may also need to install a different mouse driver, depending on the mode used.

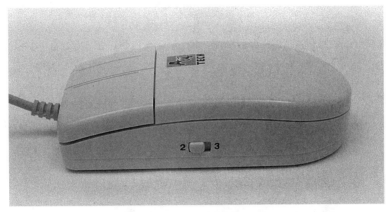

Most mice allow you to switch between two modes

Your application must also be configured for the mouse mode that you're using, which can be a complicated process. Over the past few years the Microsoft mode has become the standard; most applications can be driven with a Microsoft-compatible mouse. So, you shouldn't encounter any problems if your mouse isn't able to operate in Mouse Systems mode.

How a mouse works

When you move a mouse across a flat surface, a rubber or plastic-coated steel ball, which is recessed in the underside of the mouse, registers this movement. This ball then transfers this movement to two rollers that divide the movement into separate vertical and horizontal components.

Chapter
9
Section
2

The rotation of these rollers is registered electronically and is transformed into impulses that can be evaluated by the PC. The roller movement is generally captured by using a *mechanical method* or an *optoelectronic method*.

Mechanical method

The mechanical method uses a gear to constantly open and close an electrical contact while the mouse is being moved. The frequency of the impulses created in this way depends on the rate at which the mouse is being moved. This value is then evaluated electronically and processed further.

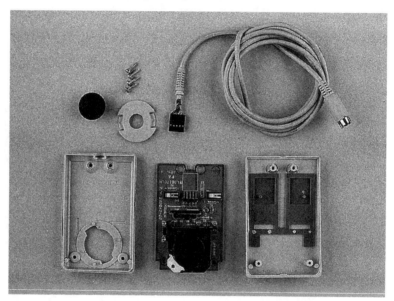

The internal components of a mechanical mouse

Optoelectronic method

The optoelectrical method, which actually uses a very similar technique, is both more reliable and more durable. This method also alternately opens and closes a switch. However, the switch used in this process consists of a light gate that registers the motion of a small wheel lined with holes. This method is almost entirely free of wear and tear, has a higher resolution, and is protected from dust and dirt.

Although quite expensive, another type of mouse, which is constructed without any moving parts, is also available. This type of mouse uses an optical method to register movement.

See Chapter 3 for information on selecting a mouse.

The bottom of this mouse contains two or more photo transistors as well as at least one light source (usually a light emitting diode (LED)). With this type of mouse, you must use a special mouse pad, which is imprinted with a fine grid of lines or matrix of dots.

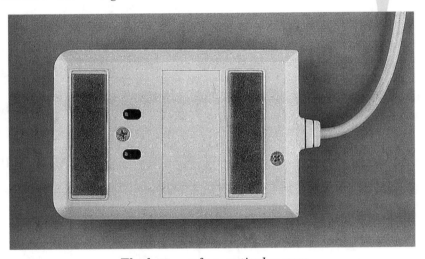

The bottom of an optical mouse

Chapter

9

Section

2

The pattern on the mouse pad is scanned by the photo transistors and is transformed into a standard mouse signal. This technique protects the mouse against wear and tear and dirt particles. Also, it offers very precise positioning.

The mouse wire that connects the mouse to the keyboard bothers many users. Therefore, some manufacturers offer wireless mice. These mice transmit the mouse data either through radio waves or, more commonly, through an infrared signal. A receiver is connected to the PC, similar to a normal mouse, at one of the computer's serial ports.

The wireless mouse contains both the transmitter of this signal and a battery to provide power for this transmitter. This battery must be changed regularly, which is a disadvantage of this system.

Chapter 9

Usually the system includes a special fitting that's integrated into the transmitter and supplies the mouse battery with electricity.

Unfortunately this charging unit operates only when the PC is switched on. So the mouse cannot be used during much of a computing session. Some manufacturers avoid this problem by supplying several exchangeable batteries that can be charged separately.

Trackball

A trackball operates like a mouse on its back. Because the trackball is stationary, it's very useful if you don't have much room on your desktop to use a mouse. Instead of moving the trackball across a surface, you use the palm of your hand or your finger tips to roll the trackball within its housing.

A trackball is basically an upside-down mouse. It remains stationary while you use your fingers to roll the ball and move the pointer on the screen.

When selecting a trackball, the location of the mouse buttons is important. You should be able to operate these buttons without removing your hand from the ball. Otherwise, it would be very easy to accidentally move the ball. So, you should always thoroughly test a trackball before buying one.

A few trackball keyboards have been available in the past. These keyboards combine the two primary input devices (mouse and keyboard) into one unit. However, you can remove some of the keys to control the size of the keyboard. The cursor keys are usually removed or moved to another location.

Manufacturers of trackballs

Several companies make trackballs for the PC or Mac or both. These include the following:

Trackball Manufacturers	
Manufacturer	**Web site address**
Compaq	www.compaq.com
Genius	www.genuis.on.theweb.net
Kensington Microware Ltd	www.kensington.com
Logitech	www.logitech.com
MicroSpeed	www.microspeed.com

Perhaps a trackball is the nifty peripheral that you've wanted to add to your PC system. As more sophisticated products such as Logitech's TrackMan Vista become available, the trackball pointer may be worth considering for some users.

Logitech TrackMan Vista

> **NOTE**
>
> Becoming familiar with the "quirks" of using a trackball may take some time. This is especially true if you've been a mouse user for a long time. One tip that we've found might help. Start by taking your finger off the trackball after you move the cursor where you want it. Then click a button. Otherwise, the cursor position may change and you'll be clicking on items you don't want.

We'll single out the Logitech TrackMan Vista trackball as an example of some features that you should look for when buying a trackball. Logitech did a good job of designing TrackMan Vista to fit your hand. Most users will be able to rest their entire hand comfortably on the unit without unintentionally moving the cursor or clicking a button. It requires that you use only one finger to rotate the trackball. The Vista uses three buttons (similar to other Logitech trackballs). Your fingers are free to use the top two buttons and the primary side thumb button. This will give you a natural feeling when clicking.

To take advantage of the real power behind the buttons, install MouseWare Enhanced. It lets you assign several commands and keyboard actions to the middle and right buttons. These commands let you assign draglock, double-click and other commands you often use. Customize your cursor attributes and click speeds. The Smart Movr feature automatically places the cursor on default selection boxes.

Joystick

Joysticks and mice perform basically the same function. However, they operate very differently and are used with different applications. Joysticks are used mainly with computer games. Many of today's computer games, especially simulators, either require a joystick or are significantly improved by using a joystick.

A joystick is used in computer games. It allows you move objects and people quickly and accurately in any direction.

Your PC has a port that is specifically designed for connecting a joystick. This is called a *game port*. Game ports let your PC read the location of a joystick handle and the status of each joystick button.

Most game ports can support two joysticks at once, although some PCs are equipped with only a single 15-pin sub-D connector. These game ports are usually on multi-I/O boards that come built into computers. So, if you want to connect two joysticks to this type of game port, you'll need to use a Y-connector, which you can find in most computer stores.

If your PC doesn't have a game port, you can easily add an appropriate game port expansion card. This card usually includes two connectors that allow you to use two joysticks. However, first you should determine whether a game port is hidden somewhere in your PC system. This port must sometimes be activated by changing a jumper setting on the port expansion card. If your system has a sound card, it's possible the game port is included with this card. If so, the game port simply must be activated.

NOTE

Never try to connect two game cards to your PC at the same time...it simply won't work. Even more important, you could damage or destroy the cards or other components of your system. Two joysticks, however, can be used with a single game port.

A game port card for two joysticks

What if your PC is too fast

Many systems, particularly those with external caches, may encounter problems when a joystick is used. This happens when the port addresses are read so quickly the game card can't keep up. In these instances you must use a special high-speed game card, such as the ones produced by Gravis. This company also produces special joysticks which should, when used with their game card, solve any potential speed problems.

The presence of a joystick doesn't need to be registered with the system; the joystick is simply plugged in. Certain test programs should be able to detect the presence of a game port. However, if you're using such a program, its test results may not match your system's actual configuration. We've found that all game ports aren't recognized by these programs, and that not every game port that's reported actually exists.

A joystick consists of a small lever that's mounted on two rotational axes and placed in a plastic case. This case also contains two buttons, called fire buttons. The lever is moved forward and backward as well as side to side. This is similar to the control column of an airplane, which was used as a model for the joystick.

Chapter 9

A potentiometer, or variable resistor, similar to the one used in the volume knob of a radio, is mounted along each rotational axes. When the lever is moved, the change in position results in a different electrical resistance in the corresponding potentiometer, which is registered by a small electronic circuit. This circuit produces a signal in accordance with the measured resistances and sends this signal to the PC.

This technique distinguishes PC joysticks from most of the inexpensive joysticks that are used in many video games and home computers. The joysticks used in these instances are generally digital joysticks that register the joystick position with simple micro switches or electrical contacts. This means these joysticks don't permit gradiated settings. So it would be impossible to control a flight simulation program with this type of joystick.

> **NOTE**
>
> PC users who have disabilities that prevent them from using a mouse or a trackball can use the SAM-Joystick. It moves the cursor at a rate proportional to the extent the stick is moved. The cursor stays at its current location when you let go of the stick. A drag-lock button lets you perform drag operations. For more informaiton contact: R. J. Cooper & Associates, Dana Point, CA, (800) 752-6673

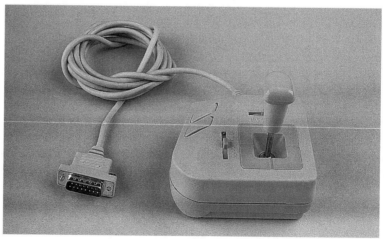

A joystick with fire buttons and adjustment sliders

Useful features when buying

You can select from several controllers that are available today. Therefore, you'll probably have no problems finding one that will improve your score. This is fortunate because no single game controller can be the best choice for all gamers.

The CH Products F-16 Combat Stick, Microsoft Sidewinder 3D or QuickShot Skyhawk appeal to users requiring a joystick with a light touch. At the same time, other users may need joysticks with a heavier action. They should look at the IBM Flight Controller Joystick or Logitech Wingman Extreme.

Most joysticks include very useful features. Trim adjustments are particularly helpful because they enable you to adjust your joystick's central or zero setting. To do this, most joysticks use sliders or knobs besides the standard joystick lever and fire buttons.

NOTE

Calibrate your joystick often...consider it part of the game. The speed and performance level of the joystick won't help if you're off center. Remember, you can never be too rich, too thin, or too calibrated. Hardware calibration is a process used to adjust the mechanical and electrical alignment of the joystick itself. The joystick calibration that you run at the start of many games is a software calibration. It's used to calibrate or align the software with the joystick. This process affects the software but has no effect on the joystick.

However, these adjusters shouldn't be accidentally bumped while the joystick is being used. Another useful feature allows the joystick spring to be deactivated. Then the joystick maintains its position instead of returning to the center setting each time it's released.

Flightstick-style controllers provide a hat-switch. It lets you change directions or views quickly (depending on the game). Most of these controllers also provide a built-in throttle control.

An unusual type of joystick is the Microsoft's Sidewinder 3D Pro. What separates it from other joysticks is that it is digital. In other words, it generates digital signals instead of using potentiometers. However, a digital joystick requires that you use software that is written expressly for digital joysticks. Otherwise, you won't get the performance improvements of a digital joystick. It is however compatible with games that don't support digital joysticks.

Chapter
9
Section
2

255

Manufacturers of joysticks

The following lists several manufacturers of today's popular joysticks and controllers.

Joystick Manufacturers			
Manufacturer	Web site address	Manufacturer	Web site address
Gravis	www.gravis.com	QuickShot	www.quickshot.com
CH Products	www.chproducts.com	SpaceTec	www.spacetec.com
Microsoft	www.microsoft.com	ThrustMaster	www.thrustmaster.com

Digitizing tablet

A digitizing tablet, also called a graphics tablet, is a precision drawing tool. It's mainly used to digitize vector oriented drawings or pictures. Digitizing tablets normally consist of a hard plastic electromagnetic tablet and a penlike stylus. Engineers and graphic artists have relied on graphics tablets for many years. However, several manufacturers have introduced scaled-down versions directed at the family PC market.

A digitizing tablet or graphics tablet is a special input device used to digitize vector-oriented drawings or pictures.

Because of conflicts with existing software and hardware, installing a digitizing tablet can create problems. We hope this situation changes when tablet manufacturers publish Windows 95 drivers with Plug-and-Play capabilities.

Designers, architects or technical draftspersons use digitizing tablets in professional graphics applications. Unlike a mouse, a digitizing tablet provides a higher level of precision with which the pen or pointer can be positioned. However, this isn't important to most PC users.

Using a digitizing tablet

The original image is simply traced with a special pen or a device similar to a mouse that's equipped with a magnifying glass and a pair of cross-hairs. The most versatile tablets and pens have software that lets you "map" a small portion of the tablet (for example, 1 square inch). This will let you move across your entire screen with only tiny movements of your wrist.

The position of the pen or the cross-hairs is registered by the digitizing tablet, which is placed below the original drawing. This is usually done by charging the pen or pointer with electricity. This causes a change within a constant electromagnetic field. This flux is then evaluated and transformed into usable data.

A professional digitizing tablet

This technique is similar to that used with a light pen, except that this is a collection of hundreds of these systems. A fairly complex electronic circuit is used to collect the information from these individual systems. The information is then changed into a serial signal that can then be sent to the PC through a normal COM port.

Chapter 9

When it comes to artistic work, using a pen feels as if you're drawing with a pencil or painting with a brush. A tablet that features pressure sensitivity means that lines are drawn and color applied according to how much pressure you apply.

Buying a digitizing tablet

Before buying a digitizing tablet, thoroughly it under the conditions in which it will be used. A good idea is to test it with the software that you'll be using. If you're planning to use a digitizing tablet instead of your mouse, you'll need to find a mouse driver that's designed for that specific tablet. Keep in mind that not all tablets are completely Microsoft-compatible.

Most experts agree that a digitizing tablet is not a good substitute for a mouse for opening and closing files and navigating around a program. The pen's fine movements are a disadvantage and it's not as easy to control as a mouse. So you probably won't be using a digitizing tablet in your average or normal tasks on your PC. However, a digitizing tablet can be very useful if you're artistically inclined.

The more expensive digitizing tablets offer several useful features that increase its effectiveness in professional applications. One of these features allows the original drawing to be secured or fastened in various ways. Some systems use a simple clamp but others use more elaborate methods. These methods include electrostatic technology or a perforated surface combined with a vacuum system that holds the paper securely on the tablet.

Although an expensive option, using a cordless pen may increase productivity by providing more mobility. This is especially important with large images.

Manufacturers of digitizing tablets

Popular digitizing tablets would include those from the following manufacturers:

Digitizing Tablet Manufacturers	
Manufacturer	Web site address
Acecad, Inc.	www.acecad.com
Calcomp	www.calcomp.com
Mutoh	www.mutoh.com
Wacom	www.wacom.com

Communicating With Your PC

Wacom ArtPad II

We'll single out Wacom as an example of the features of a specific digitizing tablet. They've been a leader in digitizing tablets for many years. Wacom's leadership is in large part because due to its patented technology that lets its UltraPens work without batteries and operate more smoothly compared to other products. Therefore, you don't have to worry about replacing batteries.

> Visit Wacom Technology Corp on the World Wide Web for more information: www.wacom.com

The UltraPen works quite well with most paint and drawing programs, particularly those specially configured to take advantage of its pressure sensitivity. By using a pressure-sensitive pen, press gently to get thin lines or lighter color or press firmly to draw thick lines or denser color. This is just like pressing hard with a nondigital tool such as a paintbrush (the drawing program must supports pressure sensitivity).

The Wacom pressure-sensitive pen also has the ability to erase. It works like an eraser on a pencil. Whatever you draw you can undo with the eraser (including erasing text in a word-processing document). The eraser is also pressure-sensitive so you can use it to create special effects like shading and feathering. You can even set it to perform other functions, such as Undo, Cut or Copy.

Installing the ArtPad II is easier than installing other digitizing tablets. ArtPad II is Plug-and-Play compliant. This means that Windows 95 automatically detects a new hardware device and prompts you for a driver disk.

The ArtPad II's comprehensive manual contains information on pointing, clicking, dragging, erasing and adjusting pressure sensitivity. It also talks about troubleshooting problems.

The ArtPad II includes a pen holder so the UltraPen doesn't get misplaced.

Chapter 9

Section 2

Chapter 9

Scanners

A scanner lets you digitize pictures or graphics, such as photographs, line art (i.e., clipart) and magazine or newspaper clippings. In other words, it's a device that reads graphics and text into your PC. Scanners are the most popular and cost effective method of importing these images into your PC. The picture or graphic is scanned by light-sensitive semiconductor elements. The signal from these elements is transformed into a sequence of bytes that's read into RAM. Then you can send the sequence to the screen or save it in a file.

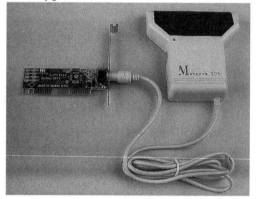

A scanner is a device that reads graphics and text into your PC. It digitizes pictures, photographs or other graphics and text so you use your PC to edit these images.

Types of scanners

Hand-held scanners

A hand-held scanner is the least expensive type of scanner. It looks like an oversized computer mouse. A hand-held scanner has a scanning width of approximately four inches and is ideal for copying small images, such as signatures, logos and small photographs. You simply roll the handheld scanner over an image.

The advantage of handheld scanners is that they take up a lot less room on your computer table. They're useful for their portability and low price. Because they usually connect through the parallel port of your PC, hand scanners can be easily shared from workstation to

Handheld scanner and accompanying interface card

workstation. Many people find them ideal for use with a notebook or laptop.

Hand scanners were also good inexpensive alternatives when desktop scanners cost thousands of dollars. However, since flatbed and sheetfed scanners have come down in price, the appeal of handscanners has diminished.

260

Although less expensive than ever before, handheld scanners will have the same limitations as before. Most users have problems dragging the scanner in a straight line because hand scanners require a very steady hand and a very smooth surface. (To overcome these problems, many hand scanners now have alignment templates to help guide you when scanning. Also, one manufacturer ships a motorized "self-propelled" unit to help stabilize its scanner).

Scanning in color images can be a difficult process. Hand scanners can scan only a four inch wide photo or part of a document in a single pass. You can, however, use software to scan large photos by "stitching" together several scans to create larger images. Hand-held scanners are slower than flatbeds and photo scanners. Also, the weaker light sources of hand scanners make them less accurate than a flatbed scanner.

Nonetheless, hand scanners are very popular and are capable of high-quality, quick and easy, low-cost scans. If you use a hand scanner keep a simple tip in mind: roll 'em easy: The trick with handheld scanners is to roll them slowly and steadily. It's not too hard to do, but don't be in a rush.

We recommend, however, using a hand scanner only if your budget is very tight or if you want to do a one time job of scanning a small number of images and don't have access to a flatbed scanner.

Sheetfed scanner (or Personal sheetfed scanners)

A sheet-feed scanner produces more reliable scans than a handheld scanner. They're also typically less expensive than flatbed scanners. A sheet fed scanner can only scan single sheets of paper. So, you'll have to remove the page from a book or manual to scan it.

These scanners have recently become more popular. They're more like a fax machine than a copier; they move the page being scanned past the scanning head, rather than the other way around.

This limits sheetfed scanners to scanning a single sheet of paper at a time. This is why sheet fed scanners are usually used for low volume scanning. However, some units come with built in document feeders that can scan multi-page documents unattended.

Chapter 9

Sheetfed scanners tend to be less exact than flatbed scanners. This is due to the problems of moving a sheet of paper without introducing distortions. Still, a sheetfed scanner is a good choice for handling paperwork without giving up much desk space. The resulting quality is ideal for easy filing or sharing E-mail or PC-fax information.

Flatbed scanner

The most popular desktop scanner and most practical type of scanner today the flatbed scanner. Flatbed scanners, as the name implies, have a flat glass surface (also called platen or bed) on which you place the object to be scanned. Flatbed scanners look and work like a photocopier. After you place the object you want to scan on the glass surface and close the cover, the scan head or light bar moves underneath your document to scan the image or object. Flatbed scanners are used to scan flat originals of various sizes, such as photographs or prints or even small three-dimensional objects like coins, keys, hands, etc.

The ScanMaker E3 and E6 scanners are examples of flatbed scanners (photo courtesy of Microtek)

A flatbed scanner is ideal when you want to scan pages from a book without removing the pages.

Although flatbed scanners tend to be a lot more versatile, they can cost as much as $300 more than a handheld model.

Photoscanners

Photo scanners are small and relatively inexpensive motorized scanners that work with photograph size images. These types of scanners are very easy to use. Their speciality is capturing images from family photos. The size of the image they can scan is limited to a photograph. On the plus side, they are easy to use and don't take up nearly as much desk space as a flatbed scanner does.

An example of this type of scanner is the EasyPhoto Reader from Storm Software.

It's designed specifically to scan photos (resolution of 400 dpi). The scanner plugs into the back of your printer port. The scanner automatically feeds the image through so you do not have to worry about uneven and jagged scans of your pictures (a common problem with handheld scanners). It can be used like a handscanner for images that are too large to be fed through the scanner

Scanners and bundled software

Similar to other peripherals in your PC system, a scanner also includes utilities and bundled software. These programs are designed to help control the scanner and to make them easier to use.

Utilities

Scanner utility programs offer several features that can enhance the capabilities of a specific scanner. They also let you define the exact part of an image you wish to scan or to emphasize. Some utilities can even turn a combination of scanner and printer into a copy machine (even a color copy machine). This is done by redirecting the data from the scanner directly to the printer for output. Then you can print the image immediately without saving the scan as a file. Likewise, a scanner and a fax modem can displace a traditional fax machine with the help of a fax utility that redirects the scanned data straight to the fax modem driver software.

Software used by the scanner

The most useful scanning software lets you resize, zoom, and edit previews quickly and easily. You should also be able to control the brightness as well as the shadows and highlights (called white point, midpoint and black point) of the image. Make certain any scanner that you're considering buying can save images in a standard format such as TIFF or PICT.

Bundled image editor

Also, most scanner manufacturers bundle an image editor with their scanners. Unfortunately, the quality of the image editors bundled with a scanner varies widely. Some scanners include the "full" version of an image editor. Other scanners may include low-priced, limited edition (LE) versions of popular image editors.

Although LE versions lack the important advanced features, they're usually enough to get you started. Then, as you become more experienced, you'll probably need a more powerful image editor. Since you'll want to upgrade eventually, consider buying a full version of the image editor when you buy a scanner. You might get a good package price for the scanner and the image editor. Keep in mind too that an upgrade offer might be included with the LE version bundled with the scanner. This upgrade offer lets you buy the full version of the software but at a special price.

Drivers

Every scanner, regardless of its features and type, depends on the computer to which it's connected for instructions on what and how to scan. These signals are supplied by driver software that runs on your computer and translates instructions into commands the scanner understands.

OCR (Optical Character Recognition) software

A scanner can, of course, scan text on a page. However, you cannot edit the text because your PC considers it as a graphics file and not a text file. By using OCR software, your PC can read the image as a text file. An image is scanned onto a page, the text is read into the computer and then translated to a data file. You can then use a word processor to edit the text.

If you're planning to do OCR scanning, we recommend testing scanners and OCR packages using a sample of documents before buying. You're looking for accuracy greater than 90% or better. If the accuracy is less than 90%, you're probably better off typing the text in yourself (might be a good idea first to see if the text is already available in digital form). Also, make certain the OCR package is compatible with the scanner in which you're interested.

Even the best OCR package available today can achieve little better than 99% accuracy. So, even with the best OCR software, you'll have to correct one out of every 100 characters

TWAIN drivers

TWAIN is an acronym for Technology Without An Interesting Name. It allows applications to send their scanning instructions in a standard format that any compatible driver software can understand. The advantage of using a TWAIN driver is that you can scan images directly into an image editor or other application such as a word processor. So, virtually all TWAIN programs can work with any TWAIN-compatible scanner (if both hardware and software meet the TWAIN standard). Most applications even use the same menu command for scanning (the **Acquire...** command in the **File** menu) which makes scanning from different applications even easier.

> **NOTE**
> Make certain that whatever brand of scanner you buy includes TWAIN drivers. The most popular photo and image software is designed to interact with these new scanners.

Hardware requirements and considerations

You need a special interface card before you can use a scanner. This card transmits the information read by the scanner to the PC. Because different scanner manufacturers use different data transmission methods it's usually not possible to operate a scanner on an interface card from a different manufacturer.

All scanners use one of three interfaces normally used by your printer (SCSI, serial or parallel ports) to connect to your PC. Most scanner interface cards use the DMA system (Direct Memory Access). This means the card places information, sent by the scanner, in a reserved memory area. The active software can then access this data from this area. Although most interface cards let you select the DMA channel through a jumper setting, the default setting usually doesn't have to be changed.

Most cards are configured by the manufacturer. However, if your system meets with a DMA conflict once you've installed your scanner, select a different DMA channel with the settings on your scanner card. Unfortunately this procedure depends on the scanner. So, if you need to change the default configuration, see the documentation included with the scanner. Experiment with different settings if you're not sure how to configure the card. However, make certain to write down the initial settings before making any changes.

A second jumper setting usually also allows a port address to be selected for the scanner card. Again, the default settings are usually correct. You must change the default port address setting on one of the conflicting cards only if your system includes other expansion cards that use the same address. These would include a network or sound card.

Often, an available hardware interrupt (IRQ) is needed to use older scanner systems. In this case, you'll come across a problem with 8-bit adapter cards. This is the same problem that occurs when installing additional ports. Only the first 8 IRQs are available on an 8-bit slot and these are often already used.

Conflicts usually occur with the printer interface that uses either IRQ7, as it should, or in other cases IRQ5. So, you should set your scanner card to the interrupt that isn't being used by the printer interface. If you don't have a test program that can tell you that interrupt is being used by the printer interface, you may want to try IRQ5 first.

Also, your scanner card may be able to share the interrupt of the second serial port (COM2), interrupt IRQ3.

Once you change a card's port address, DMA channel, or an IRQ, you may need to reinstall or reconfigure all the software for that card to activate the new settings. Changes in the settings of network cards are especially complicated. In this case, you may need to reinstall the entire network. So, you should make these changes only if you cannot correct the conflict by changing the setting on the other card, which in this case is the scanner card.

Selecting a scanner

Before selecting a scanner, you should understand a few of the terms and words you're likely to hear.

Bit-depth

The amount of information a scanner records is measured by its *bit-depth*. Different scanners record different amounts of information about each pixel. The most basic type of scanner is called a 1-bit scanner. It only records black and white; each bit can express two values (on and off). However, to see the several tones in between black and white, a scanner must be at least 4-bit (for up to 16 tones) or 8-bit (for up to 256 tones).

A scanner with a higher bit-depth can record what it sees more accurately when it looks at a given pixel. This, in turn, results in a higher quality scan. Most color scanners today are at least 24-bit. These scanners are called 24-bit scanners because they collect 8 bits of information about each of the three primary scanning colors (red, blue and green). A 24-bit scanner can theoretically capture 16.7 million different colors. However, the number is often much smaller. Because this is near-photographic quality, these scanners are also called *true color* scanners.

You may also see 30-bit or even 36-bit scanners becoming more popular in 1997. These scanners can capture billions of colors (at least in theory).

NOTE

Keep in mind that not all monitors can display a 24-bit, true color image. Many older monitors display only 8-bit images (256 colors). If a scanned image looks patchy, distorted or just "bad" on your monitor, it may be due to your monitor and not the scanner or the image.

Single pass or three pass

Most color scanners today are *single pass* scanners. These scanners read the red, blue and green light in the same scan. This is obviously much faster than the three pass scanner. The first generation of scanners required three passes of the scanhead (the lighted bar that holds the scanning circuitry) to scan an image. In other words, one pass would be made with a red filter, the second pass made with a blue filter and the third pass with a green filter. The scanner then had to combine the colors into a finished scan.

The problem with these scanners was their slow speed. Since three separate scans were required, scanning time was tripled. Also, combining three separate scans occasionally resulted in one scan being misaligned (called *registration problems*) and other image quality problems.

Three-pass scanners are now usually considered old technology. So be careful: When a scanner is available in a discount catalog for an unbelievably low price, check to see if it's a three-pass scanner.

Resolution

The most important term to understand refers to the *resolution* of the scanner. We could describe resolution simply as a measurement of how many pixels a scanner can read in a given image. Let's use a grid, like that of a chessboard, for an example of measuring scanner resolution.

Chapter
9
Section
2

Chapter 9

If a chessboard has eight squares along each side, the resolution of that chessboard would be 8 x 8. If the chessboard had 300 squares along each side, its resolution would be 300 x 300.

A scanner has two types of resolution called optical and interpolated resolution. The more important of the two is *optical resolution*. Typical optical resolutions are measured in dots per inch (dpi). You'll see scanners with resolutions of "300 x 300 dpi" or "300 x 600 dpi" or "400 x 400 dpi" and so on. It's safe to assume that a scanner can capture more detail if it has a higher dpi. In other words, say a scanner samples a grid of 300 x 300 pixels for every square inch of the image. It sends a total of 90,000 readings per square inch back to the computer (300 x 300 =90,000). A higher resolution produces more readings while a lower resolution produces less readings. Although higher resolution scanners normally cost more, they produce much better results than lower resolution scanners.

The second type of resolution is called *interpolated resolution* or *enhanced resolution*. Many scanners use software in an attempt to improve optical resolution. This new measurement is the interpolated resolution. You might see maximum interpolated resolutions of 2,400 x 2,400 dpi or better.

Interpolation works fine, in theory. It's supposed to sharpen your scan by telling the scanner to, for example, turn a 300 x 300 dpi scan into a 600 x 600 dpi scan. It does this by collecting data from two adjacent points of the image. Then the readings are averaged and a new pixel is created to fit between those two points. Unfortunately, interpolation usually always diminishes the quality of the scan. At the very best, interpolation doesn't greatly improve the overall quality of the image.

Optical resolution is often indicated using two numbers. The first number describes how many sensors are on the bar that collects the data for the scan. The second number refers to the number of dots the bar can scan as it moves from the top to the bottom of the page. The slower the bar moves, the higher the number.)

The scanhead on some scanners will stop more frequently as it moves down the page. These scanners have resolutions of 300 x 600 dpi or 300x1200 dpi. Don't be fooled; keep in mind that the smallest number in the grid is the more important. You won't get more detail by scanning more frequently in only one direction.

Select a scanner that will most closely satisfy your needs. If you want to scan just clipart, line art or black and white images, a black and white/grayscale scanner is enough. Use a color scanner if you plan to scan color images (you can also scan black and white images with color scanners).

Major manufacturers

The scanner market is benefiting from the growing interest in digital processing and imaging for both small businesses and home users. About 1.3 million scanners were sold in North America in 1995. Industry watchers expect that number to jump to 4 million units by the end of the decade.

Manufacturers are helping this situation by releasing scanners that are easy-to-use (in many cases, reducing the task to a single mouse click) and that are very affordable.

The following table lists the major hard drive manufacturers and their Web site address. We suggest contacting one of these manufacturers for more information. The following pages include information on specific scanners offered by these manufacturers.

Scanner Manufacturers			
Manufacturer	Web site address	Manufacturer	Web site address
Hewlett-Packard	www.hp.com	Sharp	www.sharp-usa.com
Mustek	www.mustek.com	Umax	www.umax.com
Epson	www.epson.com	Nikon	wwwklt.co.jp/nikon
Microtek	www.mtecklab.com	Canon	www.canon.com
Logitech	www.logitech.com	Envisions	www.envisions.com
A.I.M. Inc./Relisys	www.relisys.com	Storm Software	www.easyphoto.com

Final notes on scanners

Finally, through software and the appropriate hardware available today, you can even attach your fax machine to your PC. You can attach a cable and use appropriate software to transform your fax machine into a 100+ DPI scanner.

Even experienced users occasionally need help when using a scanner. So, you may be able to avoid some common scanning problems by following these simple tips:

Chapter

9

Section

2

1. Use, good clean photographs in your scan.

2. Try to match the resolution of your scanner with that of your printer.

3. Don't be afraid to experiment...you may be surprised by what you learn!

4. Use a slow and steady motion when rolling a hand scanner.

5. Use image editing software to tweak the scanned image if necessary.

SEEING AND HEARING

Now that you have a means of inputting data into your PC, you need to make certain your PC can communicate back to you. One way the PC communicates to you is by displaying data on a monitor. The PC uses video Cathode Ray Tube (CRT) technology to display data, i.e., to communicate with the user.

Monitors

The monitor is an important interface between you and your PC. Your PC can communicate with you by displaying messages and information that it has processed. The status of an application is indicated through the monitor and you, in turn, make your entries based on the displayed information.

The monitor is an important interface between you and your PC. It displays text, graphics and images generated by the video card.

So, the monitor, along with the keyboard, enables you and the PC to exchange data. In this section we'll take a closer look at how a monitor actually creates its picture. We'll also discuss the differences between various PC monitors. The picture quality of any monitor depends not only on the technical characteristics of the monitor, but also whether the proper video card is being used.

Monochrome and color monitors

As its name suggests, monochrome monitors produced only one color for all images. The most popular monochrome monitors were amber, green and white. The color of the phosphors on the screen determined the color of the images.

Today, however, monochrome monitors are rarely used. Operating systems like Windows 3.x and Windows 95 require a color monitor. Color monitors naturally use a more sophisticated technology than the old monochrome monitors. Color monitors use separate video signals for red, green and blue (the three primary colors).

These three primary colors can be mixed to produce most of the other colors, depending on the software and video card that is used in your PC. Because the picture signal consists of three components for the primary colors, three separate electron beams are used (one for each of these colors).

The phosphorous layer on the inside of the screen is also constructed differently in color monitors.

Coating the screen with three different phosphorous layers called triads. They consist of the primary colors: one red phosphor, one green phosphor and one blue phosphor (RGB). These triads are organized in the same configuration as the electron guns. They're designed so the electron beam for the red pixels will hit only the red phosphorous layer, and the beams for the layer hit only the blue phosphor. The holes in the mask have a diameter of less than 0.4 millimeters.

The center to center distance between these individual holes (dot pitch) determines the number of colored dots that will fit into one screen row. If a monitor displays a resolution of 1024 x 1024 colored pixels, which today's VGA and SVGA color monitors generally do, each row must contain 1024 of these pixels or holes.

The physical length of a screen row is determined by the size of the monitor. A 14-inch diagonal monitor has a horizontal screen width of about 11 inches (28 cm). Most 14-inch monitors are sold with a 0.28 mm dot pitch. This means that a resolution of 1024 x 768 pixels cannot be displayed clearly. However, most monitors supposedly display this resolution.

If you line up 1024 holes 0.28 mm apart, you'll get a row that is 28.67 cm long. However, the screen is only 28 cm wide. Also, monitors don't use the entire height and width of their screen. So, a 14-inch monitor couldn't display this resolution at 0.28 dot pitch. This would be difficult even with a 0.26 dot pitch mask.

However, these monitors usually produce a picture even if the graphics card specifies this resolution. The monitor simply converts the specified resolution to one that it can actually display. In most instances, this doesn't significantly affect the quality of the picture. However, this method won't produce suitable pictures with applications that depend on the precision of your monitor's resolution. A higher resolution simply requires a larger monitor because a larger area is needed to display more information.

Selecting a monitor

In selecting a monitor, remember that not all monitors are created equal. The major factors to consider are the screen size, dot pitch, refresh rate, interlace, maximum resolution and energy saving features.

Screen size

The screen size of a monitor is measured diagonally across the screen. Common monitor sizes are 14-inches, 15-inches, 17-inches and 21-inches.

The most economical monitors are 14-inches. If you spend a lot of time (two or more hours a day) using the computer, you'll appreciate a 15-inch or 17-inch monitor. Some users such as graphic artists and CAD users might consider 21-inch monitor although this size monitor is quite expensive.

NOTE

When you see an advertisement for a monitor, keep in mind that manufacturers usually advertise the diagonal measurement of the picture tube inside the monitor. This measurement is larger than the true viewing area of the monitor. So, make certain you ask for the size of the viewing area when shopping for a monitor.

Dot pitch

The dot pitch is the distance between tiny dots on a screen. The characters and graphics on a color monitor are formed by a set of three color triads. The dot pitch is a measure of the spacing between adjacent triads. The characters and graphics appear sharper when this measurement is smaller. We recommend a monitor with a dot pitch of .28 mm or smaller. Expensive monitors feature a dot pitch of .25 mm; less expensive monitors have a dot pitch of .35 or .38 mm.

Refresh rate

The refresh rate is the frequency at which the characters and graphics are redrawn on the screen. The higher the frequency, the less the image appears to flicker. For flicker-free viewing, the refresh rate should be about 70 Hz or 70 times a second.

Almost all monitors today have a multisync feature. This means that they are able to adjust their refresh rate within a range of values to match the signals that the video card outputs to the monitor (see information below).

Interlaced or non-interlaced

A monitor redraws the screen by using an electron gun which shoots a beam at inside of the screen from the left side to the right in lines starting at the top to the bottom. The screen is drawn from top to bottom by an electron beam in a single pass in noninterlaced monitors. Interlaced monitors refresh the screen in two passes. The odd number lines are redrawn during the first pass and the even numbers are redrawn during the second pass. The time to redraw the entire screen is identical in either mode. However, less expensive monitors are interlaced since they can be designed to operate at lower refresh rates. Non-interlaced monitors appear to have a more stable image, but may cost a bit more. For highest quality, select a non-interlaced monitor.

The maximum resolution is the number of individually addressable pixels that the monitor is capable of displaying. We recommend that you select a monitor that has a resolution of at least 1024 x 768 pixels. Many monitors can display up to 1280 x 1024 pixels, but they may cost more. Keep in mind that the a monitor's maximum resolution cannot be achieved unless the video card is capable of operating at that resolution as well.

Chapter 9 Section 2

273

In other words, you cannot connect any SVGA video card with just any SVGA monitor. In this case, you must carefully consider the different types of cards and monitors if you want to avoid subsequent problems. Generally, anything that isn't standardized, such as higher SVGA resolutions and SVGA monitors, can cause problems. Unfortunately, all the manufacturers are following their own standards.

A monitor is one of the heaviest consumers of electrical power. Newer energy saving monitors are capable of going to "sleep" when the computer is sitting idle for a length of time. A computer's video card must send and the monitor must be capable of responding to a DPMS (Display Power Management Signal). Selecting an energy saving monitor can save from $25 to $75 a year in electrical costs.

Multisync monitors

Multisync monitors let you adjust the resolution to suit your specific requirements. These monitors can synchronize any video signal within a predetermined range of horizontal scanning frequencies. These monitors are flexible enough to operate on all PC graphics adapters, from the

> **NOTE**
>
> Since NEC reserved the rights to the multisync name, other manufacturers are forced to call their multisync monitors "multiscan" monitors. This term always refers to monitors that are able to synchronize a range of horizontal scanning frequencies that covers several different graphics standards.

Hercules to the VGA card. This applies if the particular monitor can use horizontal frequencies from 15.6 to 31.5 KHz.

Multisync monitors are usually equipped with an analog/digital switch that allows the monitor to be adapted to both digital and analog graphics cards. Although the designation "Multisync" may be used only by the NEC company, it was still misused. The "NEC 2A" monitor was designated a multisync monitor by NEC, although it's simply an analog multifrequency monitor.

Unlike fixed-frequency monitors, multifrequency monitors can synchronize several different horizontal scanning frequencies. Today most SVGA color monitors are built as multifrequency monitors, which enables them to synchronize higher resolutions. Usually these monitors accommodate horizontal frequencies of 31.5 to 35.5 KHz. So the term "analog multifrequency monitor" refers to monitors that are designed for several different horizontal scanning frequencies and use an analog signal. The only graphics card that uses this type of signal is the SVGA.

Usually the different frequencies are recognized by the monitor, which then automatically sets the proper synchronization. Because of this capability, these monitors are also called "autoscan monitors".

Major manufacturers

The following table lists the major monitor manufacturers and their Web site address. We suggest contacting one of these manufacturers for more information.

Monitor Manufacturers			
Manufacturer	Web site address	Manufacturer	Web site address
Acer	www.acer.com	Samtron	
Hitachi	www.hitachi.com	Sony	www.sony.com
NEC	www.nec.com	Viewsonic	www.viewsonic.com
Princeton	www.prgr.com	Zenith	www.zenith.com
Trident	www.trid.com		

Video cards

Before your PC can display data on a monitor, however, it must use a device called a video card. A video card (sometimes called a graphics card, video board, graphics adapter, etc.) is a small plug-in card containing specialized chips which generate the signals for displaying text and graphics on the video monitor. The video card acts as an interface between the processor and your monitor.

A video card translates instructions and commands from your PC to a signal the monitor can understand. Video cards are also called graphics cards, video display cards, video boards, graphics adapters, etc.

Since it is an expansion card, the video card is simply plugged into one of the expansion slots on the motherboard of your PC. This connects it to the computer's bus system. The card sends the information, received through the bus system, to the monitor as a video signal.

Chapter 9

The specialized chips on a video card include the video controller, the screen memory, or video RAM and the character generator. The video card continually sends a video signal to the monitor. The video controller reads the information stored in video RAM at regular intervals and sends this information to the monitor as a video signal.

See Chapter 3 for information on selecting a video card.

Major manufacturers

The following table lists the major video card manufacturers and their Web site address. We suggest contacting one of these manufacturers for more information.

Video Card Manufacturers			
Manufacturer	Web site address	Manufacturer	Web site address
ATI	www.atitech.com	Cirrus Logic	www.cirrus.com
Diamond	www.diamondmm.com	Genoa	www.genoasys.com
Hercules	www.hercules.com	Matrox Graphics, Inc.	www.matrix.com
Number Nine	www.numbernine.com	Orchid	www.orchid.com
Trident	www.trid.com		

Sound cards

When you boot your system, you hear a simple beep that's emitted from the computer's internal speaker. Unfortunately this was all the PC sound system was designed to do.

A sound card gives your PC the ability to play and record high-quality sound and music. It's a circuit board that plugs into an expansion slot.

As the PC evolved, many programmers tried to produce more interesting sounds from this speaker. These programmers managed to produce multi-voiced music under certain conditions. However, the sound quality was very poor. Even at this simple level, sound output required a lot of processing time and data. So using background sound for enhancing programs such as games was very limited.

Many sound cards still include a game adapter interface, a carry over from the days when sound cards were originally designed for games. By using a sound card, you'll experience an entirely new level of enjoyment playing today's games. Besides realistic sounds and effects, today's games feature digitized human voices and dialog and impressive musical scores.

A sound card with various accessories

The sound card is designed to replace the modest single-voice sound of the internal PC speaker with a multi-voice system that's capable of producing various sounds. Today's sound cards can produce from 9 to 256 different voices. The sound of each of these voices can be controlled individually and can then be played back simultaneously. Theoretically, the more voices a card is capable of producing, the greater sonic or tonal richness it will achieve.

What to look for in a sound card

The most popular sound cards and generally regarded as the best are those manufactured by Creative Labs, Media Vision, and Turtle Beach Systems. The sound cards from Creative Labs, in particular, have dominated the market for many years and are considered the standard by which other sound cards are compared.

See Chapter 3 for information on selecting a keyboard.

By adding one of the many available sound cards to your PC system, you can increase its sound capabilities. These capabilities include the following:

Chapter 9 Section 2

277

MIDI (Musical Instrument Device Interface)

MIDI is a programming language developed in the 1980s that allow computers and musical devices (normally a keyboard synthesizer) to exchange data. This allows you to play, record and edit music. Many musicians use MIDI to compose music on a computer.

MIDI makes a musical note sound as if it comes from several types of instruments. A sound card must have two serial connections to connect a MIDI device to your PC (a MIDI input port and a MIDI output port). You'll also need a keyboard and sequencing software. This software is used to modify the tempo, sound and volume of your MIDI files. It's also used to cut and paste different prerecorded music sequences.

The big advantage of MIDI files is that they require very little hard drive space. An hour of stereo music saved as a MIDI file requires less than 500K (a comparable WAV file would be 1000 times larger). This is the reason most games use MIDI sounds.

The sound quality using MIDI files can vary greatly depending on the card you select. The most important consideration is whether your card uses FM syntheses or wavetable synthesis for MIDI reproduction. FM synthesis merely imitates the sounds of musical instruments and speech. This results in inferior and less realistic sound. FM synthesis is found on low to mid-range sound cards.

Wavetable synthesis, however, uses actual recordings of musical instruments and speech. The result is a far superior realistic sound. The vast majority of sound cards use wavetable syntheses. High quality sound cards, such as the Sound Blaster AWE-32, use wavetable syntheses.

Sampling rates/capabilities

If a sound card has sampling capabilities, it's able to play back and, in some cases, record digitized sounds or sound samples. This feature is particularly useful with certain sounds, such as a snare drum, which are almost impossible to create through pure sound synthesis. Using a DAC (Digital to Analog Converter) solves this problem.

Several cards also include ADCs (Analog to Digital Converter), which transform analog signals to digital samples. These cards are equipped with microphone inputs so sounds can be sampled directly.

The sampling rate determines the quality of a sound sample. This factor determines how many analog values are digitized each second in a sound sample. The highest frequency that can be played back by a sample is exactly half of the sampling rate used.

For example, to reproduce a frequency range up to 6 KHz, a sampling rate of at least 12 KHz is needed. The other factor that affects the quality of a given sample is its sampling depth, which determines how many bits are used by the converter in encoding the analog signal.

Although 16-bit and even 24-bit converters are available, usually 8-bit DACs are used. However, none of these converters can turn an existing 8-bit sample into a 16-bit signal. So, a larger converter is useful only when the samples are made by the same sample width that's used to record the samples.

Unfortunately, the amount of data required for a sample increases with the sampling rate and the sampling depth of the sample. So, a sample file of 11025 x 60, or 661500 bytes, is needed to play back a minute of spoken text at the realistic sampling rate of 11.025 KHz on an 8-bit DAC. Because of this, several sound cards contain a compression device that reduces the size of these files.

Stereo sound

Although stereo sound is an excellent expansion of the capability of any sound card, most sound cards are strictly mono cards. Only a few of the cards on the market are sold as stereo cards. Other cards can obtain stereo capability through upgrades. You'll find that a stereo amplifier is included in some cards but the actual sound card can produce only mono sound. Later we'll discuss the limitations involved in using stereo sound.

Available accessaries

The accessories available for a sound card vary depending on the manufacturer. Not every card includes a high-quality audio amplifier, so you must connect the card to your home stereo amplifier if you want to play the sound over a stereo speaker. Several manufacturers even supply one or two external speakers and occasionally a microphone with their sound cards.

Although you shouldn't expect too much from these accessories, you may be pleasantly surprised by the sound quality that can be achieved with today's sound cards. Even the sound produced by connecting a stereo speaker to a sound card amplifier produces convincing results.

Chapter 9

To obtain the best results, you should connect the card to your stereo system. Unfortunately, none of the cards we've used includes a cord that's long enough to reach from your PC to your stereo. So if you want to set up your sound system in this way, you'll probably need an audio extension cord.

One accessory that's been overlooked by sound card manufacturers is an external volume knob, which would solve the problem of reaching behind the PC to adjust the card's volume setting.

The application is the deciding factor

Before you rush out to buy a sound card with several voices, a high sampling rate, stereo sound, and many other features, there are some criteria you should consider. The application you'll be using is the most important factor in determining which sound card is best for you.

NOTE

Microsoft's Windows 95 has made sound cards more user-friendly. If you're upgrading to Windows 95, look for the latest sound cards that are plug-n-play compatible with Windows 95. Using a sound cards that are plug-n-play will make installing a sound card much easier and faster.

Although sound cards are mainly used with computer games, it is with these applications that sound cards are most limited. This is because the majority of computer game manufacturers don't completely use the large selection of cards or their capabilities. Many games support only the few sound cards that are considered standards.

Since the AdLib card is the oldest sound card, it's supported by the most programs. However, since this card has only 11 voices and no sampling capabilities, it isn't exactly versatile or powerful. The most popular AdLib compatible sound card is the Sound Blaster card. Besides AdLib emulation, this card includes a sampling channel that's capable of sampling rates up to 44 KHz.

The Sound Blaster card contains two 4 watt amplifiers. Most software manufacturers support the Sound Blaster card. Because of its universality, the Sound Blaster card is today's standard for PC sound cards. So, many new cards are Sound Blaster compatible.

Multimedia demands more

The new set of MPC (Multimedia Personal Computer) standards created by Microsoft has set a new direction for the world of PC sound cards. These standards establish specific formats for sound output. However, none of the available sound cards meet all the requirements of the MPC standards.

We'll discuss these specifications in more detail when we discuss multimedia system configuration. However, Creative Labs has taken the lead in the realm of MPC compatible sound cards with its new Sound Blaster 16 ASP (Advanced Signal Processing).

Problems installing sound cards

Finally, we'll briefly discuss some of the problems that may occur when you add a sound card to your system. For several types of sound cards to operate properly, an IRQ must be available. To avoid conflicts with other expansion cards in your system, select an interrupt that's not already being used by your printer port.

If, like Sound Blaster, your new sound card has its own game port but your system already includes a game port, you must deactivate one of these ports. Usually it's easier to disconnect the game port on the new sound card because the documentation for the card is readily available.

Occasionally the port address of your new sound card may cause address conflicts. Usually the manufacturer sets this address to 220 hex. If one of the expansion cards in your system is already using the same port address, you must configure one of the cards differently. When you do this, usually you'll have to reinstall the software for that card. So it's best to reconfigure the card that requires the fewest software changes.

Major manufacturers

If you're seeking the highest quality of sound and music synthesis (instead of sound generation) several companies are producing 64-bit sound cards. The following pages include information on selected sound cards. Professional musicians and avid music enthusiasts have helped pave the way for higher sound reproduction boards. These 64-bit sound card companies include the following:

Sound Card Manufacturers			
Manufacturer	Web site address	Manufacturer	Web site address
Creative Labs	www.creativelabs.com	Reveal	www.reveal.com
Gravis	www.gravis.com	Turtle Beach	www.tbeach.com
Media Vision	www.mediavision.com		

Sound Blaster 32

The standard for sound card reproduction was 8-bit several years ago. Then PC sound technology improved dramatically with 16-bit sound. Now, the most common configuration includes 32-bit sound recording and playback. One card with this capability is the Sound Blaster 32 from Creative Labs. Sound Blaster 32

Visit Creative Labs on the World Wide Web for more information: www.soundblaster.com

is a high-end sound card. The Sound Blaster 32 offers a low-cost option for high quality PC sound.

The following lists a few features of the Sound Blaster 32:

❖ 32-bit sound capability

❖ Synthesizer chip for audio compression and decompression (requires no CPU time)

❖ 20-voice FM synthesis

❖ Downward compatibility with other Sound Blaster sound cards

Sound Blaster AWE32 PnP

The next generation wavetable synthesis sound card from Creative Labs is the Sound Blaster AWE32 PnP (full Plug-and-Play capability). This card features real instruments, sounds and digital effects processing. You can even add new instruments and sounds to the Sound Blaster AWE32 PnP. The following is a short list of its features:

❖ Fully Plug-and-Play compatible for easy installation and use

❖ Includes software and utilities for Windows 95 and DOS/Windows 3.1 systems

❖ Real sounds and CD-quality instruments for games and multimedia applications

- ❖ Sound Blaster products enjoy more software support than any other sound card

- ❖ Real instrument samples and real-time digital effects processing

- ❖ Real-time control of wavetable sounds and digital effects

- ❖ Add new instrument samples and sounds to the card

- ❖ Add up to 28 Meg of standard memory SIMMs to hold SoundFonts

- ❖ EMU8000 wavetable synthesizer with programmable effects engine for reverb & chorus

Contact your dealer or Sound Blaster for more information on which sound card would be ideal for your upgrade. If possible, visit Creative Labs award winning Web site on the Internet for more information (www.soundblaster.com).

Speakers: What your PC has to say

You've probably discovered that your PC can no longer remain silent or simply play the default system sounds. Although you've upgraded just about everything on your PC, you're still using the same original tinny speakers.

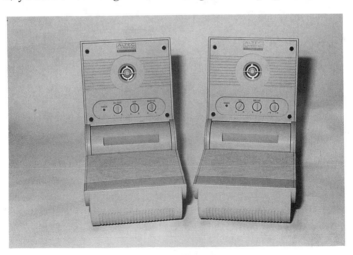

Examples of PC speakers

Chapter 9

This is what most price-sensitive computer buyers will do. All too often, the first budgetary victim is their system's external speakers. This may stem from a time when speakers were overlooked or treated with little respect. No one, from manufacturer to user, cared if the speakers sounded flat and tinny.

Today's PCs do more than just play default system sounds. This is due to today's sophisticated 32-voice, 16-bit sound cards and CD-ROM drives doubling as audio CD players. Speakers have assumed a more important role in the makeup of the PC system. They'll announce E-mail or play music while you surf the Internet or provide the realistic sounds for games like DOOM and Quake.

In other words, you may want to replace your system's tired bundled speakers with a set of multimedia speakers. The quality of sound generated by a PC is almost as good as what you get from audio CDs. The clear digital sound can rival many expensive audio components. PC speakers

> **NOTE**
>
> Several companies now manufacture monitors with built-in stereo speakers. However, the audio quality of these "multimedia monitors" usually is only slightly better than the speakers bundled with your PC. It's possible the magnets of these speakers can distort the images displayed on the monitor.

have become more sophisticated in design, power, quality of sound and effects. Recently, three-piece speaker system giants delivering 100-watts of peak music power or more have overshadowed mid-range speaker systems capable of delivering more than 20-watts of power.

How speakers work

PC speaker systems lack most of the features that you'll find on audio equipment. For example, they rely on external input. In other words, no tuner, no internal audio CD player or other signal sources are available. Even considering that, there is little difference between the speakers made for your stereo and those designed specifically for multimedia PCs.

Regardless of their cost and size, all speakers use magnets as part of their design. This is important point to remember: Since hard drives and floppy diskettes are magnetic media, the magnets in nearby speakers can cause data loss on disks. So, speakers designed for the PCs have magnetic shielding built into their cases to prevent damaging data or interfering with the monitor.

You don't need to use speakers designed expressly for a PC. Providing you can keep speakers at least a foot from your PC system, you can use your stereo speakers. If circumstances require more private listening, such as in your office, you can also use headphones. Virtually any headphone on the market is appropriate for computer use since they're typically used at a safe distance from the PC.

Getting the best sound

The best way typically to get the best sound out of small speaker components is with a three-piece design. These systems include two smaller satellite speakers that you can place on your desktop. They're designed to handle midrange and high frequencies (from 150 Hz to 20 KHz). The third piece is the subwoofer, a lunchbox-size component that handles notes below 150 Hz. This combination of speakers usually delivers better overall frequency response. Be warned that setting up a three-piece system involves connecting more cables, though, and may not be convenient in tight quarters.

What to look for when buying a speaker

Look for a few basics when purchasing speakers. They should be magnetically shielded; otherwise they may interfere with the hard disk or monitor. They should deliver the best sound when placed a few feet apart; look for easy setup because you're probably upgrading for enhancement purposes and you won't want a tangle of wires crowding your desktop.

For those who are serious about sound, some units come complete with subwoofers or equalizers. Those willing to pay more can fill an entire boardroom with sound or annoy their neighbors. Whatever your needs may be, your ears should ultimately make the decision.

Similar to buying any component for your PC, buying PC speaker systems requires more than simply checking specifications. Everyone has different levels of hearing ability. So, determining the sound qualities of speakers is very subjective. Also, most speakers emphasize one area of the audible spectrum over another. Therefore, the best way to determine a system is to test it yourself. A good dealer will let you "test drive" a speaker with your favorite games.

Chapter 9

When considering your multimedia speaker options, keep in mind what you'll be using them for and where, and how much you've already invested in your multimedia PC. If you are just going to be playing video clips and the occasional narration, you don't need to spend more than $100. Those who work in an open office setting, on the other hand, shouldn't worry about how many watts of power the speakers have and should look for models with up-front headphone jacks instead.

The following are a few buying tips to keep in mind when you're shopping for speakers:

❖ Look only for AC-powered speakers (battery-powered speakers are limited in their output).

❖ Good speakers can carry the load at high volumes so turn up the volume. Mediocre or inferior speakers may frequently create distortion and/or cracking at high volumes.

❖ The speaker should have a convenient front-panel volume control as well as a headphone port. Then if you need to use headphones (such as in the office), you won't need to use the often hard-to-reach sound card connection on the back of your PC. Make sure headphones adjust snugly without pressing against your ears. Continual pressure causes discomfort after a while.

❖ Three-piece systems usually have volume and power controls on the subwoofer. This makes it awkward for you to turn down the volume if the boss were to suddenly appear. This problem can be avoided if you plan to use software (i.e., a mixer program) to control the volume.

❖ Buy shielded speakers if possible. Speakers should be magnetically shielded to prevent interference with your monitor or possibly damaging data on the hard drive or floppy drive. (Subwoofers are designed to be hidden under users' desks and often are not completely shielded.)

❖ Multimedia speakers usually need to contain their own amplifiers. This is because even the best sound cards offer only 4 watts of amplification per channel. A built-in amplifier with 10 watts per channel is enough for an average office environment. More expensive speakers can deliver 30 watts per channel, with enough volume to rattle the windows.

❖ Check the service and warranty information carefully.

Manufacturer of speakers

The following table lists the major video card manufacturers and their Web site address. We suggest contacting one of these manufacturers for more information.

Speaker Manufacturers			
Manufacturer	Web site address	Manufacturer	Web site address
Yamaha	www.yamahacom	Aiwa	www.aiwa.com
Roland	www.roland.com	Altec Lansing	www.markivaudio.com/altec
AppleDesign	www.appledesigns.com	Atlantic Technology	www.artec.com/atlanctic/atlantic
Audio-Technic	www.asiannet.com/behavior-tech	Bose	www.bose.com
Cambridge SoundWorks	www.hifi.com	Sony	www.sony.com
Koss	www.koss.com	Labtec	www.labtec.com
NEC	www.nec.com	Recoton	www.recoton
Reveal	www.reveal.com	NuReality	www.nureality.com

Next we'll talk about specific speakers. Keep in mind that this is only sampling of available speakers; we're including the information to give you an idea of the speakers that are available and their capabilities. We're not necessarily recommending only these speakers or only these manufacturers.

NEC AudioTower Speaker System

This is a good system if you have a more modest need or budget. Sound is solid and consistent. Setup is very low-maintenance.

Altec Lansing ACS500

The tall (18 inches) Altec Lansing ACS500 includes two 3-inch midbass drivers, one 1.3- by 2.5-inch midrange and a 0.5-inch dome tweeter. The 6.5-inch subwoofer has a 40-watt amplifier rated at 0.8 percent THD. The satellite speakers feature an impressive 22.5 watts. One of the satellites contains controls for volume, center ("presence"), surround, and subwoofer. Also, the under desk unit has an additional volume control.

Chapter 9

To help balance the output, the ACS500 uses a push button that turns on a pink-noise signal to automatically cycle through the drivers in sequence. An additional pushbutton switches between regular stereo and a built-in Dolby Pro-Logic decoder. When playing appropriately recorded sound tracks, this decoder produces cinema-like surround sound without requiring rear-mounted speakers. To hear the full surround effect, try to sit within the "near field" (about 2 feet) of the desktop units.

Bose Acoustimass

Much smaller than the ACS500, the tiny (3 by 3 by 4.8 inches) desktop cubes of the Bose Acoustimass system contain 2.5-inch wide-range drivers that are driven by 20-watt amplifiers; the 5.3-inch driver inside the bass module has a 50-watt equalized amplifier. The unit has overall volume, treble and bass controls and an additional pair of input jacks. Unfortunately, you cannot control the balance between the satellites and the bass unit. Bose recommends placing the cubes at least 4 feet apart. Otherwise, the sound may seem to shrill.

Yamaha

One unit of the Yamaha satellites contains a volume and presence control (+- 7 dB above 10 kHz) and a power on/off button; the subwoofer has an additional volume control, a hi/low cut filter, and a power switch. The subwoofer amplifier is rated at 25 watts, with 10-watt-per-channel amplifiers in the desktop units. The speakers use pure spruce pulp rather than plain paper cones to emphasize the sound.

Multimedia Labs PC Amp-TC-1490-7SUB

If you're looking for true home-stereo-quality audio in the workplace, consider the Multimedia Labs PC Amp-TC-1490-7SUB speaker system.

The four-piece system includes a separate slimline amplifier with a five-band equalizer, a variable subwoofer slide control and gold-plated jacks for an external microphone and headphones. With all these extras, plus great sound, the street price of $270 is very affordable.

Advent Powered Partners AV622

For unobtrusive yet high-powered speakers for an office or desk area, also consider the Advent Powered Partners AV622. This is a three-piece system and produces excellent and clear highs and full bass sounds.

Final note

Your needs, preferences and budget will determine which speakers you'll buy. However, whichever speaker system you buy, you'll add quality sound that the original designers of the PC could not imagine.

PRINTERS AND PRINTING DATA

Besides the monitor and the keyboard, which are essential when using your PC, the peripherals for outputting data are also important. A printer is the most significant and most widely used of these peripheral devices. Often, a printer is the first major purchase after you buy a computer. It can used to print letters, invoices, newsletters, checks, books, transparencies and countless number of other items.

However, printers are not the only peripheral you can use to output or print data. We'll discuss these peripherals in this section.

When to use a printer

The printer enables you to obtain a "hardcopy" or paper printout of your data or information. It's difficult to provide an overview of all the available printers because of the various printing methods and the different accessories that are included with printers.

However, all these products have the same purpose: They are designed to print something, that you've created with your PC, on a piece of paper.

Chapter 9

Section 2

Communicating With Your PC

Chapter 9

Connecting a printer

The easiest way to connect a printer to any PC is through its parallel port or interface. Some printers are made to connect to the PC through a serial port. A printer must use the same type of interface that's used by your PC.

Most printers connect to the computer through the parallel port. The parallel interface is less expensive and faster than using the serial port. We don't recommend purchasing a serial printer. If you want to print graphics, the comparatively low serial data transfer rate will result in long printing times. We also don't recommend adding a serial interface to your existing printer. Instead, you should add a parallel port to your PC.

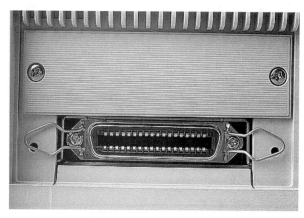

The parallel interface is usually located in the back of your printer

Not only does the parallel interface provide higher data transfer rates, it's also more affordable than an additional serial interface for your printer. Usually this interface must be ordered from the manufacturer.

The differences between interfaces are barely noticeable. So, almost all the interfaces will work with your PC. However, there are many differences between printing methods and other printer features.

As you can see, many factors determine the overall quality of a printer. Printers use various printing methods; each technique has its own advantages and disadvantages. In the following sections we'll provide an overview of the different printing methods.

290

Dot-matrix printers

Dot-matrix printers have been used for many years. This is the least expensive type of printer and can be used with almost all PC applications. All dot-matrix printers use the same printing method. These printers have a head (called a *printhead*) that has several wires or pins. These pins are driven in different patterns against an inked ribbon. This action makes the dot-matrix quite loud. A character is formed when the ribbon strikes a sheet of paper.

> **Dot matrix printers are impact printers. They're the least expensive type of printer and can be used with almost all PC applications.**

The printhead is moved horizontally by a stepper motor, either by using a geared belt or another method. This allows the printhead to be moved to any desired horizontal position. In the vertical direction, the paper is moved instead of the printhead.

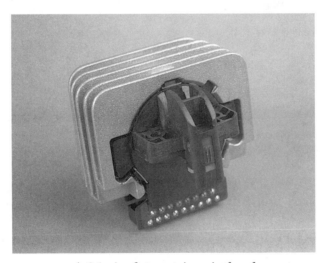

A 24-pin dot-matrix printhead

Paper

A dot-matrix printer uses a tractor system and perforated continuous form paper. This type of paper has holes punched along both sides that fit into the tractor system.

291

Chapter 9

Resolution

The print quality, called resolution, depends on the number of pins in the printhead. Dot-matrix printers are either 9-pin or 24-pin printers. A 9-pin printer is normally used for draft quality printouts and 24-pin printers are used for high quality printouts.

Some 9-pin printers have an NLQ (Near Letter Quality) mode. Each character is printed a second time but slightly to the right of the first character. So, the final character actually consists of twice as many dots. The NLQ can result in a comparable printout to that of 24-pin printers.

Print speed

Dot-matrix printers have respectable text printing rates. The print speeds range from 25 cps (characters per second, about 1 page per minute) to 450 cps or about 18 pages per minute). However, remember that you cannot rely on printing rates; high print quality is usually more important than a high printing rate.

Color dot-matrix printers

Only a few manufacturers offer devices that enable their dot-matrix printers to print color. This is surprising considering that such upgrade packages would be inexpensive. With the few printers that do offer this option, you simply must change the ink ribbon and install a special expansion card. This produces high quality color printouts.

Ink jet printers

Ink jet printers are also dot-matrix printers. However, these printers don't use a ribbon. They use a non-impact method to create the printed image. The printhead doesn't even touch the paper. Instead, it sprays a jet of ink in a fine mist onto the paper.

Ink jet printers are non-impact printers. The printhead sprays a jet of ink in a fine mist onto the paper. Ink jet printers are ideal for routine business and personal documents.

These printers are becoming more popular because of their printing method and falling prices. Another reason why this printer is popular is because it's one of the quietest printers available.

The print method used in ink jet printers is similar to the technique used in dot-matrix printers. The printhead (pictured on the left) is moved horizontally across the paper by a stepper motor, and the paper is moved vertically either by rollers or a tractor drive. The ink isn't applied through an ink ribbon but by the printhead itself. It contains several vertically arranged jet openings through which a special ink is sprayed onto the paper in tiny dots. Two different methods are used to propel the ink from the printhead: The thermal bubble jet method and the piezoelectric method.

The thermal technique uses a small heating element within the jet opening to heat the ink abruptly. A portion of the ink is vaporized, and this bubble of gas then forces the remaining ink out of the jet opening and onto the paper. Today this technique is so highly refined, this process can occur several thousand times in a single second.

Instead of heating the ink, the piezoelectric method contracts the entire jet opening to blow the ink out of the jet. Because of the piezoelectric effect, certain crystals will contract when subjected to an electrical voltage.

So a piezoelectric crystal is built into each jet opening, which makes it easy to control the expulsion of ink through an electrical ink. Since this method also allows ink jets to be sprayed several thousand times a second, fairly high printing speeds are possible.

Ink jet printers can print from 180 to 720 dots per inch. The quality of an ink jet printer at 300 dpi is superior to a 360 dpi dot matrix printer. This is because the ink jet prints characters formed by smaller dots.

As the amount of dots per inch (resolution) increases, and colors are used, a short delay occurs before actual printing can begin. It takes time for the printer to calculate all the "dots." Ink jet models are ideal when you will print less than 50 pages a day. Check the printer documentation for any manufacturer-recommended special papers or restrictions on envelope size.

A major advantage of this printing method is that it's fairly easy to use different color ink. Since color ink jet printers are more affordable, high quality multi-color printing is now possible even for the average PC user.

Chapter 9

Several new ink jet printers from Hewlett-Packard (the most popular laser and ink jet printer producer) are redefining the printer world. HP's DeskJet series include models 650C, 660C and the newest 855C. The 855C has a print resolution of 600 x 600 dpi (dots per inch) in black and 600 x 300 dpi in color and prints on plain paper. They're a long way from the now old OkiData color printers of the mid-80's. The prices for the popular HP ink jet printers range from $199 to $599 at most computer outlets.

Laser printers

Laser printers are ideal when you need extremely sharp images at excellent resolutions and with high printing speeds. Many PC users are buying laser printers since their prices continue to drop.

Laser printers are high speed printers for business and personal documents (especially graphics). The resolution ranges from 300 dpi to 120 dpi.

How laser printers work

The printing method used in laser printers is similar to the technology used in photocopiers. Instead of printing line for line, laser printers print page by page. Often laser printer manufacturers will actually use printing mechanisms from photo copiers. For example, Hewlett Packard laser printers are built exclusively with printing mechanisms that are used in Canon copiers. If you own such a laser printer, you can replace the toner cartridge with one used in a Canon copier.

To print a page at a time, the laser printer requires a large amount of memory. The ROM in laser printers creates a full page bitmap of the document. A bitmap is a dot-by-dot representation of each letter or character. The pulses of the laser copy the bitmap.

This laser light is then reflected by a series of mirrors onto a rotating negatively charged photosensitive drum. The laser light scans the drum and changes the printed areas to a neutral charge. The negatively charged plastic toner powder bond to the neutral areas but not the negative areas. Heat from the rollers fuse the dots of the characters onto the paper.

So the laser printer also uses a matrix printing system. This system generally achieves a resolution of 300 dpi, and, because of the fineness of the actual printed dots, this resolution is maintained in the final print. However, graphics printouts reveal the weaknesses of the laser printer system. Before a laser printout is produced, the entire page image must be transmitted to the laser printer (more than a Meg).

A Hewlett-Packard laser printer

Speed

Most laser printers print at a rate of 4 to 20 pages per minute.

Resolution

The print quality, called resolution, for laser printers is excellent. The minimum is 300 dpi and the maximum is 1200 dpi.

Paper

Laser printers use standard 8.5 x 11 inch paper or envelopes, labels and transparencies. However, make certain these items are designed for laser printers before you buy them or use them.

Chapter 9

Toner cartridges

Another similarity with photocopiers is that laser printers also use toner (a fine powdered ink). This toner is stored inside a cartridge.

Laser printer languages

A laser printer must understand how to print a document. To do this it uses one of two laser printer languages (Postscript or PCL).

Postscript

These printers are able to handle more complex documents. These documents can include difference colors, graphics and fonts. The big advantage of postscript printers is that any document created for one postscript printer will print identical on another postscript printer. Postscript is popular with graphic artists and publishers. This book was created with a Postscript printer.

PCL (Printer Control Language)

Most laser printers come with the PCL. Although it's less expensive than a Postscript printer, a PCL printer doesn't have the graphics capabilities or flexibilities of a Postscript printer. This type of printer is popular in normal business applications (accounting, record keeping, etc.)

Buying a laser printer

If you're shopping for a laser printer, you should consider the following:

❖ Reduce costs of supplies by checking if "economy" modes are available

❖ See whether additional printer memory is available (also the cost)

❖ Print quality (resolution)

❖ Is the printer compatible with major software publishers

❖ Are toner cartridges locally available

❖ Technical support and is online support available (Internet, CompuServe or America Online)

❖ Time required to print a page (compare the ppm - pages per minute)

❖ Length and conditions of the warranty

Color laser printers

Color laser printers are becoming more popular. Several companies now manufacture color laser printers. Examples of color laser printers include Apple's Color LaserWriter, Hewlett-Packard's Color LaserJet II, Lexmark's Optra C and QMS's Magicolor CX.

The standard resolution is 600 dpi for color lasers. Print speeds are typically about 3 ppm (pages per minute) for color documents and 12 ppm for monochrome. Standard printer memory is 8 Meg to 12 Meg. Paper capacities typically range from 250 to 500 sheets.

The first generation of color laser printers definitely were not plug'n'play compatible. In other words, using one of these early color laser printers involved more than adding color toner to the standard black toner. The newer color laser printers have eliminated or at least reduced many of those early problems.

Advantages of color laser printers

Since color laser printers use plain paper, the price per page for output is relatively low compared to other color printers.. Cost per page is an important consideration. This is especially true if you'll be producing large amounts of color documents. However, don't base buying decisions entirely on any cost per page claims. No standard for computing the price is available so can be different according to each vendor.

Also, since color lasers use plain copier paper, you can mix color and monochrome in the same print job. This can even be done on the same page. Best of all, it can all be done easily and inexpensively. This ability makes such color laser printers ideal for color presentations or for newsletters. You can use a color laser printer for virtually any job that requires both color and laser-quality text.

The print speed of color laser printers matches those of monochrome laser printers. They're also faster than some thermal-wax printers. This is even more impressive considering that a color laser printer must transfer toner four times (once for each color).

Although the price for a color laser printer has recently fallen, most start at about $6,000 today. However, unlike the prices for most computer components, the price of color laser printers may not fall as fast. This is due to their complexities and other costs (four color toner for example).

Printer problems

DIP switches

Printers are usually configured through DIP switches or through a configuration menu that can be accessed through switches located on the printer's front panel.

DIP switches on a printer

Character sets

Most printer problems are caused by incorrect printer configurations or incorrectly installed printer software. The most common mistake is an incorrectly set country code.

NOTE

Make certain to use a quality printer cable. Using bad printer cables is a leading source of printer problems. We recommend using a 6-foot parallel interface cable that feels *heavy*. Frequently, light weight cables don't use as much copper or conductors.

Unfortunately, printer configuration differs depending on your printer. Normally you must refer to your printer manual. Remember that most systems are shipped with the correct settings. So, try to use the printer before making any changes. If you must change a default setting, for example because a function isn't working properly, be sure to write down the original setting.

Plotters

The plotter is a special output device that's normally used for printing graphics and other drawings created on the screen. Plotters draw lines, circles, and other shapes, usually by moving a pen across a large piece of paper.

Plotters are a special type of printer used for very precise drawings of lines, circles, and other shapes. They move a pen across a large piece of paper to create the hardcopy.

Plotters create very accurate drawings. Therefore, they are frequently used with CAD (Computer Aided Design) applications. These applications are generally used to create technical and architectural drawings, as well as other vector-oriented (consisting of lines and curves) graphics.

Most plotters include a feature that enables you to switch pens so you can create color graphics and drawings.

Plotters aren't suitable for text output because each character must be drawn individually, which is time-consuming. Also, the characters always look mechanical because it's impossible to vary the line thickness without actually changing plotting pens.

However, in larger formats, where pen thickness isn't as important, plotters can create fairly good pixel graphics by simply drawing numerous individual dots. Actually, plotters can easily handle large format drawings.

As we mentioned, plotters are designed to draw lines. Straight lines can be precisely defined through their starting and ending points. So the plotter must move its pen, which is usually a wear-resistant felt-tip pen, to the starting position.

Then it lowers the pen to the paper, moves it to the ending position, and then raises the pen again. The plotter can access any specified point on the paper and either lower or raise its pen.

Chapter
9
Section
2

Circles drawn similarly

Circles can actually be drawn in the same way, by repeatedly moving to the ending points that lie on the circle. However, most plotters already have built-in procedures that produce perfect circles, ellipses, and arcs. In this case, the PC simply must inform the plotter of the circle's center point coordinates and its radius. The plotter does the rest.

The two popular types are the flat base and drum plotters. Each uses different methods to move the pen over the paper.

Flat-base plotters

With flat base plotters, the paper is placed completely flat on the plotter's surface. The pen is controlled by a mechanism that's mounted on a type of movable bridge that spans across the paper. Two stepper motors are used to move this bridge across the paper and to move the pen along the length of the bridge. This enables the plotter pen to access any desired set of X/Y coordinates on the paper.

A disadvantage of this setup is the flat plotter surface takes up a large amount of space, particularly with plotters designed for larger paper formats. So these types of plotters are usually mounted vertically either on a freestanding support or on a wall.

Drum plotters

With drum plotters, the drawing pen is moved only along a single axis, and the bridge that it travels along is attached to the plotter. To produce movement along the other axis, the paper is moved back and forth beneath the pen.

This is done quickly and as accurately as with flat base plotters. Even when the paper is moved back and forth several hundred times, for example when certain areas of a drawing must be crosshatched, the image usually doesn't become misaligned, although large distances can be covered by the paper in this process.

Drum plotters are available in various sizes, from standard letter size to legal size. It's easier to use larger formats with drum plotters because the entire sheet of paper doesn't have to lay flat.

As we mentioned, most plotters can use different pens. This allows the plotter to create plots using different line thicknesses and/or different colors. Like the actual drawing procedure, the pen selection is controlled through control sequences that are sent by a program (e.g., a CAD program).

So you don't have to insert the pens manually. A plotter should be able to choose from a selection of at least four pens; most models are equipped with six. However, there are also plotters with eight or even twelve different pens.

In most instances the plotter is connected to the PC through a serial port. Due to the relatively slow output speed of plotters and the vector-oriented command set, this transmission method is sufficient. As with other serial devices, it's important to verify the sending and receiving components are using the same protocol and the same data transmission rate.

For example, consider a Hewlett Packard plotter, such as the 7475A, with a 9600 baud data transmission rate, 8 data bits, 1 stop bit, no parity control, and which must be connected to the second serial port. In this case, you must enter the "MODE COM2 9600,n,8,1,p" DOS command.

The last parameter "p" is important because data transmission is often delayed during a plot while the plotter is executing a complex command. Without this parameter, the data transmission would be halted at such a pause.

As we mentioned, most plotters have a command set that allows complex operations to be accessed through single commands. The Hewlett Packard Graphics Language (HPGL) is the most widely used command set.

Various applications indicate that, with a few exceptions, a program written for the Hewlett Packard plotter usually works with other plotters. So it's important to look for HPGL emulation capability when purchasing a plotter.

Plotting without a plotter

If you have an application program that can produce HPGL files or you have an HPGL file you want to reproduce on paper, but don't own a plotter, you can use a plotter emulator.

These are small programs that can read HPGL files and convert them into pixel-oriented graphics that can then be printed with your dot-matrix printer. These types of programs are also available as shareware and public domain products.

Chapter 9

Section 2

301

For example, we've used Print GI, which is a shareware program that's available through many sources, such as Computer Solutions. Several graphics programs can also read and process HPGL files. If you have such a program, such as Designer by Micrografix, you may not even need a plotter emulator.

OTHER METHODS OF COMMUNICATION

Ports

The PC's ports aren't actually input or output devices. However, we're including them here because they are the only link between the PC and input or output devices, and, therefore, to the "outside world." Ports transfer information between the PC and its peripherals.

Serial and parallel ports transfer information between your PC and the peripherals connected to it.

Ports use either *parallel* or *serial* data transmission. In parallel data transmission, several bits of information (usually eight, which form a byte) are transmitted simultaneously over eight separate conductors.

Serial transmission, however, uses only a single channel, so all bits of information must be sent one after the other, or serially.

Obviously parallel data transmission is the faster method. For example, an 8-bit parallel port's transfer rate is ten times faster than a serial port's transfer rate. This is partly because serial transmission uses several control bits, which slow down data transmission.

However, an advantage of serial ports is that only a few conductors are needed. This results in thinner, more affordable, and more durable cables. Because of this, longer connections are easier to achieve with serial conductors than with parallel conductors.

A PC system can have a maximum of three parallel ports (LPT1 through LPT3) and four serial ports (COM1 through COM4). Also, PC systems usually have a serial keyboard port and a game port, which provides a special connection for two analog joysticks. Most PCs are shipped with one parallel port, two serial ports, and usually a game port that's located on a separate expansion card instead of on the combination controller.

The system assigns individual port addresses and specific hardware interrupts to these ports. Data input and output is then conducted through the corresponding port address. Interrupts play a slightly more complicated role.

It's possible through these special channels of the system bus to interrupt the CPU while it's performing its current task and to demand its attention elsewhere. This type of interrupt is used, for example, when you move your mouse pointer across the screen. The pointer must move when you move your mouse, instead of when the processor has completed its current task.

The distribution of port addresses and interrupts is predetermined. However, everyone doesn't follow this predetermined arrangement. The reason for this is the division of the AT bus.

The two interrupt channels IRQ10 and IRQ11, which are assigned to the serial ports COM3 and COM4, are located on the 16-bit segment of the bus (i.e., on the shorter portion of the expansion slot). However, since most port expansion cards are designed for 8-bit slots, they cannot use these IRQ channels. Therefore, other IRQs are used, although these may already be assigned to other ports. So, the addition of further ports on an 8-bit bus can easily lead to a shortage of available hardware interrupts.

The resulting problems can be solved in one of two ways. It's possible, under the right conditions, for two ports to share the same hardware interrupt. However, it's also possible that some ports don't need interrupts. The deciding factor in both instances is the type of device attached to the appropriate port. Many devices don't need an interrupt to operate. For example, parallel printers can operate without a hardware interrupt.

The mouse, however, must use an IRQ. If the mouse port, which is usually COM1, is forced to share an interrupt with another port (for example, COM3), the device attached to this second port cannot use the interrupt because the system will crash. Therefore, you cannot operate a modem and a mouse on the same IRQ.

Communicating With Your PC

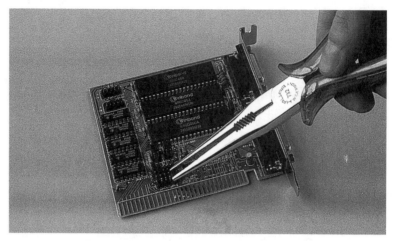

Port expansion card with configuration jumpers

Generally these port expansion cards will be equipped with several jumpers or one or more DIP switches that allow you to configure the card. You should refer to the documentation supplied with the card or a suitable test program, such as CHECKIT, to determine the exact correlation of IRQs and ports.

Most cards allow you to define the port addresses and interrupts for the ports built into the card. For example, if you want to add a third serial port to your PC, you'd be able to define it as COM4 and assign either IRQ3 or IRQ4 to this new port. This configuration isn't unrealistic. For example, if your system is equipped with an internal modem, COM3 might be occupied already.

When installing a multi I/O card, a card with two serial ports, and one game port, you must consider the game port. If your system already has a game port, you must disconnect it before installing the card. This is necessary because a second joystick is accommodated by a Y-splitter, which uses a single game port, instead of by a second game port. You cannot install a second game port on your system.

Modems

A modem lets two or more computers use telephone lines to transfer data. Because of this, most PC users are using modems to connect to the Internet and online services such as CompuServe and AOL (America OnLine). This ability allows users to contact thousands of other users and access huge amounts of information.

> **A modem lets two or more computers use telephone lines to transfer data. You need a modem to connect your PC to the Internet and online services (i.e., CompuServe and AOL).**

No special or separate telephone lines are needed to use a modem. You can use the same phone line for telephone and modem calls (although not at the same time). Also, make certain to disable the call waiting feature if you have it. Otherwise, it could disrupt your modem connection.

Modems can be used while you're traveling or when you're at home. You can send and receive E-mail messages (electronic mail) with thousands of other users. You can work at home and access files from the office and then send the completed work back to the office network.

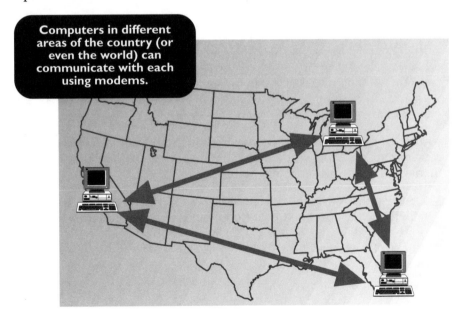

Computers in different areas of the country (or even the world) can communicate with each using modems.

Chapter 9

Another use for a modem in today's PC is to send and receive faxes. These modems, called fax modems, let you create a document on your computer and then fax the document to another computer or fax machine.

When a computer receives a fax, the document appears on the screen. You can review and print the document but you cannot edit the document unless you have Optical Character Recognition (OCR) software.

Modem types

When selecting a modem, you must decide between an external and an internal model.

External modem

An external modem is a small box that is connected to your PC using a serial cable (also called a *modem cable*). This modem is then connected to a telephone outlet using another cable. Some models permit you to run a telephone through the modem. The advantage of external modems is that you can connect them with more than one computer. External modems, however, do require valuable space on your desktop. They also require a free serial port.

Internal modem

Internal modems are cards that plug into an expansion slot within the PC case. Although less expensive than external modems, internal modems are more difficult to configure correctly. This configuration is necessary because internal modems have an integrated serial interface through which they communicate with the PC system. So the installation of an internal modem is similar to installing an additional serial port

As usual, how the interrupts are distributed is important. This is especially true considering that you'll be using a mouse. Make certain the mouse and the modem use different hardware interrupts.

Most newer modem cards can be configured for any of the four COM ports, and generally the interrupt (IRQ3 or IRQ4) can also be freely selected. Your system is probably using IRQ4 if it has only one serial port. If so, you should set your modem to COM2 and IRQ3.

However, if your system already has two serial ports, you can configure your modem to either COM3 or COM4, although IRQ3 should be used in either case. Since this interrupt is usually intended for the fourth serial port, it should be used for COM4.

Unfortunately this can lead to problems with older PC systems. In this case, it's possible that only two serial ports can be recognized. Because of this, the only alternative to sacrificing your second serial port is to swap your entire motherboard for a new one. This enables your modem to operate.

Some internal modems have a jumper on the surface of the card labeled "Pulse/Tone". This jumper allows you to select either pulse or tone dialing. Most modems are set to tone dialing by the manufacturer. Unless your phone line is set up for pulse dialing exclusively, use the tone setting.

Modem speed

The speed of a modem determines how fast it can send and receive information through telephone lines.

Modem speed is measured in bits per second (bps). You should not buy a modem with a speed less than 28.8 Kbps (28,800 bits per second). You still may find some modems with a speed of 14.4 Kbps. However, these modems are usually much too slow, especially when you're "surfing" the Internet.

Modems are also available in higher speeds such as 31.2 Kbps and 33.6 Kbps but these are more expensive than the 28.8 Kbps modems.

How modems work

The term "modem" is an abbreviation for modulator/demodulator. A modem converts your PC's digital pulses into analog signals and converts them back into pulses at the receiving side. The modem handles the dialing and answering of the call and controls the transmission speed. Several complex steps are involved in describing how two modems communicate with each other. However, since it's not important to understand <u>how</u> a modem works, only that it <u>does</u> work, we'll summarize these steps.

Chapter 9

Data compression

The ability to compress, or squeeze, data allows a modem to send more information faster. Data can be compressed several times smaller than its original size depending on the type of file. For example, a text file will compress much faster than a graphics file.

The receiving modem then decompresses the file when the information reaches it.

Error correction

Error correction is the ability that today's modems have to identify errors during transmission. In other words, error correction makes certain that the information being sent reaches its destination correctly. Information that is sent over a modem is broken down into smaller pieces called *packets*. The receiving modem examines the incoming data for damaged packets. If it detects a damaged packet, the receiving modem asks the transmitting modem to send a new copy to replace the damaged packet.

Modem problems

The most common problems that occur with modems involve interrupt conflicts, incorrect installation, or incorrect use of the communications software. Usually this software must be set to your type of modem.

If your modem isn't included in the selection offered by the program, you should try all other configuration settings before concluding that something is wrong with your modem.

ISDN cards are alternatives to modems

ISDN (Integrated Service Digital Network) is a worldwide high speed digital communications network phone line that is available in most areas of the US. At this time, ISDN is the best choice for a high speed connection to the Internet.

ISDN (Integrated Service Digital Network) can transfer information between an Internet Service Provider (ISP) and your PC about four times faster than a modem.

Because of its digital data transmission technique, ISDN transfers information between the Internet Service Provider (ISP) and your home about four times faster than a modem. Therefore, no modem using an analog line can match the speed of an ISDN connection.

To access an ISDN line, simply install an appropriate ISDN expansion card in your PC. This makes all the integrated services of the ISDN system (i.e., telephone, BTX, FAX and Teletex functions) available to your PC.

If you use the services listed above regularly, you may save a considerable amount of money by installing an ISDN. This is basically because the vastly increased transmission rate will cut phone times drastically.

Most ISDN cards include special software that's designed to operate with the card and provide these services. Since these programs are usually tailored to specific cards, they usually cannot be expanded or modified. Since not all cards have universal software, some options won't be available. So, you should examine thoroughly any ISDN package before buying it. Also, with some functions, such as mode emulations, which permit communication with a mailbox or another PC, for example, you must use a special program. You cannot use a normal terminal or telecommunication program with ISDN systems, because they cannot recognize the ISDN card.

Most ISDN cards include a fairly complete set of installation instructions. We haven't heard of or used any card that had to be configured. They are simply inserted into an available expansion slot. The rest of the installation was performed using the software provided with the package, according to the accompanying instructions.

The price of ISDN cards seems disproportionately high when compared with the simple electronics that can be used to operate these cards. Although several high-tech cards are available, their extensive capabilities won't be fully used in most situations. However, as ISDN systems become more popular, they may become more affordable.

Keep in mind that, like with modems, the slowest link in the chain is still the transmission line. The slower transmission line may make it impossible to run these cards at their full speeds. Also, if you're considering ISDN, make certain that ISDN service is available in your area (check with your local phone company). This type of communication does require additional telephone wiring and service from the telephone company.

Chapter
9
Section
2

309

Chapter 9

Network interface cards

One of the most important features of IBM compatible PCs is the ability to create networks among different systems.

PC networks, which consist of only PCs or PCs linked to a mainframe, are becoming more popular. This is happening because of the ever increasing amount of data that must be accessed by various users.

A network interface card connects every PC to a network so information and data can be exchanged.

A network card with BNC coupling

It's possible to use a network when several personal computers are located within close proximity of each other. These computers can perform different tasks while using the same software, data files, and perhaps the same printer.

Centralized data storage and decentralized use summarizes the idea behind PC networks. Usually networks consist of a main computer that manages the network and stores programs and data files.

These programs, data files, and any peripherals are used by the entire network. The main PC, also known as the file server, supplies the individual workstations with the needed information and resources on demand. It sends and receives data packages to and from individual workstations via the network connections.

To connect several individual PCs into a network, you must use a special software package that acts as the operating system of the network. Also, a network card must be installed in each PC that's on the network. This card transfers the data packages transmitted over the network connections to the PC's data bus.

These cards are available for all different PC bus widths, from 8, 16, and 32 bits. Various network cards are available. Selecting the proper card depends on the structure of the particular network. Unfortunately we don't have enough space to describe the different types of network cards on the market.

Network card configuration can be complicated

Network cards use a specific address range within the PC's system memory, as well as an interrupt request and a specific port address. With most cards, these settings can be selected through a set of switches or jumpers on the card's surface.

Depending on the other adapters and expansion cards in your system, it can be difficult to configure the network card correctly. Memory address, port address, and interrupt conflicts can cause problems.

Besides these basic considerations, there really isn't anything you can do to increase the performance of a network card. If the connections between the PCs in the network are working flawlessly, you've done everything possible.

Windows 95 and networks

The Microsoft Windows 95 Network Neighborhood has features designed for office LANs in mind. It has built-in network connections and administrative software to make connecting to an existing network or installing one much easier.

Windows 95 includes two types of network clients and two types of servers. The clients include Novell's NetWare and Microsoft networks. You can also create peer to peer networks between other Microsoft's versions of Windows on the network.

Windows 95 includes several 32-bit network client drivers for different networks. You can install as many network clients as you need. You can use Network Neighborhood to browse and connect to the servers on your LAN. It also includes a utility called System Monitor. System Monitor is used to monitor your network usage.

Microsoft Windows 95 incorporates all the necessary tools you need to connect your computer to an existing network. It also allows you to setup your own peer to peer network, which is important when working with groups of people on a particular project on a network.

Setting up a peer-to-peer network is advantageous in a small office if you have more than one computer. You will be able to share most of your machine's resources with the other machines. That is, you can share your printer, hard disk, floppy disk, CD-ROM, or your Folders on different drives with others.

To use the peer-to-peer network options you will need: a network card for each computer, the necessary cable to connect the machines and the software included with Microsoft Windows 95. We advise using the On-Line Help built into Windows 95 as well as following along with the Windows 95 manual to instructing how to use the Network Neighborhood.

LANtastic

LANtastic is the peer-to-peer operating system that proved itself against Novell (NetWare Lite and Personal NetWare) and Microsoft (Windows for Workgroups). It was, therefore, able to attain a small but significant segment of the market. LANtastic achieved this success because of several reasons:

- ❖ Its performance (functionality)

- ❖ Open architecture (available for all significant platforms, setting it apart from all other networks)

- ❖ Security (significantly better compared to, for example, Windows for Workgroups).

LANtastic has been running under (or rather, *with*) Windows starting with Version 3.x. If you've implemented this type of a network (Version 5.x or 6.x), you probably won't want to transfer it to a Windows 95 network for at least two reasons:

1. Very few advantages transferring to a Windows 95 network.

2. Any advantages are cancelled when you switch to the Windows 95 user interface.

Adaptation is relatively simple. All you need to do is select the appropriate LANtastic Client (LANT5) during the installation. One disadvantage is that the installation needs to be performed separately on each workstation. An exception to this is if the LANtastic net is server-oriented (this type of add-on is available from Artisoft). In that case you can perform the installation from or on the server, like with NetWare.

The advantage of installing Windows 95 over an existing LANtastic network, besides the security features we've mentioned, is in the large number of possible connections.

Although Windows 95 already works with several possible connections, LANtastic adds

NOTE

Before installing Windows 95 on a LANtastic network, request the *.INF files for configuring the network under Windows 95 from the manufacturer (Artisoft). Also, the LANtastic network can only be accommodated during Windows 95 installation. It's not possible to set up this client up at a later time.

even more. Connection to pure DOS PCs is no longer possible under Windows 95 (although it still was under Windows for Workgroups 3.1x). This is still possible with LANtastic, however.

Even OS/2 computers can be easily added to the network since LANtastic is also available in an OS/2 version. In an environment that includes many systems, it's an advantage to use Windows 95 and LANtastic together. However, LANtastic will have to implemented as the primary network. Since it is a 16-bit real-mode network client, it won't be possible to operate a second (32-bit protected-mode) network.

NetWare

The most widely-used server-oriented network is probably Novell's NetWare. Although many versions have been released (including 2.x, 3.x and 4.x), only Versions 3.x and 4.x are supported by Windows 95. Although it's possible that NetWare 2.15 and higher will work together, such networks probably won't meet the hardware requirements for running Windows 95.

Although it has always been possible to run Windows in Novell networks many problems have occurred. The combination between NetWare and Windows for Workgroups 3.1x has been a particularly difficult one. For example, Microsoft refused to provide hotline and service support when Windows for Workgroups was running on NetWare networks with diskless workstations.

Windows 95 contains 32-bit protected-mode software for working with NetWare. This software includes the network client (Redirector or Requester), an IPX/SPX compatible protocol and network management utilities.

The installation, setup and integration have been significantly improved with Windows 95. It's now even possible to set up remote-boot workstations (i.e., workstations without disk drives). Windows 95 automatically detects whether a Novell NetWare network is present and will modify the installation accordingly.

Windows NT and networks

Because Windows NT was available before Windows 95, many features of Windows NT were incorporated into Windows 95. Windows NT, on the other hand, still doesn't include the new interface found in Windows 95. Industry experts expect Windows NT Version 4.0 will have an interface very similar to Windows 95. Experts are also speculating about a possible combination of the two systems sometime in the future. Perhaps the reason they weren't combined before now is because of the huge hardware requirements demanded by Windows NT.

Windows NT is a client-server operating system (although the original version of NT was also intended to support peer-to-peer networking). Windows 95 can also be integrated as a client into an NT network. Since both systems are from Microsoft, this integration is no problem at all. Here again, the Client for Microsoft Networks is used. However, under Properties you'll need to enable the option Log Onto Windows NT Domain.

The Client for Microsoft Networks is also used when connecting to an NT network

The domain concept of Windows NT may already be familiar to you from the LAN Manager. A domain is a user group consisting of a definition of individual workstations. This domain can be logged on to a server. Only the members of this domain then have access rights. Such a domain can also be assigned to a second server, for example, so that this server can be accessed by the whole group (domain) without any further modifications of configuration.

Windows 95 displays workgroups and NT domains identically, both in the Network Neighborhood and in Explorer. It does not distinguish between the two, at least in the way in which it displays them. So, it may be desirable to differentiate between them by giving them corresponding names. This is especially true if the NT network is used for security reasons.

The advantage of integrating Windows 95, besides the added security functions, is that you can implement peer-to-peer functionality within a client-server network, allowing you to work effectively and easily in workgroups. The interface of Windows 95, which at the time is still better, is an added bonus.

Section 3:
Upgrading In Detail

Contents

Your PC Workshop

In the first two sections you learned about the components of your computer system and their functions. Now you can determine which types of upgrades are necessary for your PC.

Section 3 shows you how to make the necessary hardware changes in your system. You'll even learn how to build your own multimedia PC.

In this chapter, we'll discuss the basic requirements for such an undertaking. Please read the information presented in this chapter very carefully. This is true even if you're already familiar with working on your PC. You probably won't need to follow each instruction. However, you may find new information that may prove very useful in critical situations.

We don't want to discourage those of you who haven't performed any type of maintenance on a PC system. Not every point is crucial. You'll be able to complete the most important tasks correctly with a basic understanding of any given procedure.

Chapter 10

RULES AND DANGERS

You may be afraid to modify your PC, especially if you never worked inside a microcomputer system before. A computer is a highly specialized electronic device. Its complex maze of conductors and components can be extremely confusing.

Don't panic

However, you shouldn't worry about working with your computer. Let's compare this situation with using a complicated software package, for example the operating system. After using this software for a certain time, you'll be able to work comfortably with this program. You'll soon even manipulate its configuration.

However, you don't have to understand the program's source code to do this. Similarly, you don't have to completely understand the maze of components in your PC system to modify the program.

Although a basic understanding of how the individual components in this system interact is important, you won't need the technical knowledge involved in designing and building this hardware. Here again, the open architecture of the industry standard simplifies things by allowing major component groups to be exchanged.

Modifying your PC system also doesn't require as many manual skills as you might think. Certain repairs, particularly replacing defective components, may require using a soldering iron or multimeter. However, these situations rarely occur.

For most of the operations we'll discuss, you'll need only a screwdriver. You'll see that installing, removing, or exchanging most components doesn't require any special skills.

Tips and guidelines

If you can assemble a simple modular bookshelf, you can install a second floppy disk drive in your PC. Also, if you follow these tips and guidelines, you probably won't meet with any problems.

Take your time

Your biggest enemy is haste. Often, small mistakes will emerge later as problems which are extremely difficult to trace. Take your time and go over each step twice. If you're ever in doubt about something, it's better to go back and reread the appropriate chapter.

 Always read everything first

You should never start modifying your system before reading the appropriate chapter in this book completely. Begin your work only when you're familiar with all the details and understand the entire operation.

After you've answered all the questions that you may have about the operation, you can begin. Otherwise, you may suddenly realize, after you've disassembled your PC, that you're missing a part or that the planned modification isn't feasible on your particular system.

 Never use force

All socket and screw connections in your PC should fit together and come apart easily and without using force. Most connectors are one-way connectors that are designed to hook up in only one direction. This prevents polarity reversals.

However, with enough force, these connectors can also be connected incorrectly. The resulting reversal in polarity can cause serious damage to your system's hardware.

Therefore, you should immediately become suspicious if any step in your operation seems to require an excessive amount of strength or force. Double-check the procedure and proceed only when you're absolutely certain this is the correct way.

Chapter
10
Section
3

Ground yourself: Static electricity is dangerous

Electrostatic charges can easily reach 2000 volts or more. Although the small amount of current released in the discharge of this voltage may be harmless to humans, it can be fatal for computer components. CMOS components are particularly susceptible to this type of damage.

Sometimes even a charge of just over 5 volts is enough to ruin such a component, which may ultimately result in a ruined motherboard. Therefore, you should always discharge any static electricity that may have built up on your body before touching any electronic component.

The most reliable way to do this is to wear an anti-static wristband that's connected directly to an electrical ground. However, frequently touching a grounded object, such as the PC's chassis or a plumbing fixture, will achieve the same result. Remember, always touch your PC's chassis before handling any other component.

 Never open your monitor

You should never open your monitor under any circumstances.

Various components within the monitor store electrical charges that could violently discharge this energy even days after the

> **NOTE**
> The internal components in your monitor contain voltages high enough to pose a serious risk of injury or even death. This is true even when you've switched off your monitor and disconnected the power cord.

monitor was last used. Also, there is very little you can do with a defective monitor. Instead, you should consult a qualified technician.

 Turn everything off before continuing

Do not try to repair a running PC. This is especially true when installing an expansion card. This can quickly lead to a damaged motherboard or expansion card. Also, if you do this, you may harm yourself.

Unplug the power cord

Always unplug the power cords of every device in the system on which you'll be working. This way you'll not only prevent yourself from being electrocuted on poorly insulated power plugs, you'll also prevent the device from being accidentally switched on while you're working.

NOTE

The high and low voltages aren't positively separated in the power supplies used in your PC. So, it's possible to encounter 120 volts anywhere within the power supply.

Even a disconnected AC cord is no guarantee when working with your power supply. Certain components within the power supply can retain an electrical charge until long after you switch off the system.

You'll only need to open the power supply unit to install a new ventilation fan. Leave any power supply repairs to a qualified technician.

 Position the components carefully

Make certain your keyboard is stored in a safe place. Users often move the keyboard aside if it isn't being used. Consequently, it can fall off the desktop.

Also, remember the cables and power cords found behind your PC include your monitor cable. Therefore, placing your monitor too close to the edge of the monitor stand or table may lead to disaster.

 Be careful with power cords

Try to keep your floor as free of cords and cables as possible. You may want to place your power strip on your table or desktop. Make certain your cords are long enough so they have some slack. Especially when you're still trying out new components before installing them permanently, a slight tug on a cord that jars the PC housing could be detrimental.

 Keep food, liquids and cigarettes away from your PC system

Avoid spilling any liquids on the motherboard. Cigarette smoke also damages your PC.

Use correct screws

Unfortunately, not all screws in your PC are standardized. Screws differ not so much in diameter as in thread pitch. By forcing the wrong screw into a mounting hole, you can, for example, ruin the threads of your new floppy drive.

If a screw is difficult to tighten, check whether its thread matches that of the nut or mounting hole. The length of screws is also important. Various hard drives, for example, must be mounted with extremely short screws. Longer screws may penetrate too far into the housing and permanently damage electronic components on the interior.

 Keep small parts together

Frequently screws can fall into the power supply unit through the fan opening. Place all small screws and parts in an appropriate container, such as a paper cup.

If you drop something, immediately stop whatever you're doing until you've located it. Screws that fall into the power supply through the ventilation slot could eventually cause serious damage to the power supply of the computer long after you've forgotten the screw.

 Keep tools on the worktable

Never place tools in your PC. It's very easy to forget something that subsequently may lead to serious problems. It is best to reserve a certain area on your worktable solely for your tools. Then the tools are always handy and easily found.

 Maintain a log of all your work

You should always write down settings before you make changes. For example, when changing DIP switch or jumper settings, write down or draw the original configuration BEFORE changing that configuration.

When you must experiment with different settings, it's important to write down which combinations you've already tried, along with their results.

324

Test everything before reassembling

Don't reassemble your PC until you're absolutely certain that everything runs and your PC is working properly.

This can be particularly helpful when adding floppy or hard drives to your system. Ensure that you did not forget anything. Are the circuit boards screwed down tight? Are the cables correctly reattached? Are there any remaining screws?

PROPER TOOLS IN YOUR UPGRADING TOOL BOX

Your PC is a complex maze of conductors and chips. So, you probably think that you need a large collection of tools in order to modify your PC system.

However, this isn't true. For the most part, the components of your PC are assembled in standardized modular component groups. These modules are usually connected through a simple plug, a socket, or through rail connectors. Although certain repairs will actually require using specialized equipment, even with the required skill and knowledge, these repairs are generally not worth the time or money.

Therefore you don't need to run out and buy yourself an oscilloscope. Most of the operations which we'll talk about can be performed using tools which you probably have at home.

Essential equipment

The following tools and equipment are essential for effective maintenance of your system's hardware.

Chapter
10
Section
3

325

Your PC Workshop

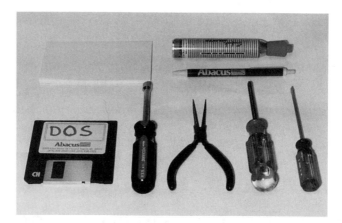

Essential tools and equipment

Screwdrivers

A small standard (flat-headed) screwdriver is needed for removing and tightening screws. Small screwdrivers also work extremely well for setting DIP switches.

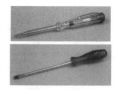

Your primary computer maintenance tool is likely to be small Phillips head screwdriver. This screwdriver is used for virtually all the screws holding your PC together. It should be high quality; good Phillips head screwdrivers have a snubbed tip, so the flanges engage deeply enough with the slots of the screw. These flanges should also have relatively sharp edges so the screwdriver is less likely to slip out of the screw head.

A medium Phillips head screwdriver is used primarily for removing your computer's housing. Ensure that it's good quality. Don't purchase a screwdriver with an extremely pointy tip.

Usually any small flat-headed screwdriver is sufficient. Models equipped with electrical test lamps in their handles are also perfectly usable.

Use a medium standard screwdriver to open, for example, the housing of your PC. You may not even need this screwdriver if

NOTE

Do not use magnetized screwdrivers. Also, don't hesitate to spend money for a good screwdriver. It will more than pay for itself by preventing stripped screw heads.

the housing of your PC is mounted with Phillips head screws. This screwdriver is a necessity for owners of brand-name PCs, such as IBM or Compaq.

Formatted floppy diskettes

We recommend using at least two 3.5-inch diskettes because one diskette may be destroyed when you try to get your system running correctly. Therefore, never use original diskettes for this purpose. Also, make certain to use diskettes that are write-protected.

Tweezers

Tweezers are needed to set jumpers and pick up various small parts that may have fallen into inaccessible areas of your PC. Plastic tweezers are ideal for this purpose, since they are nonconducting.

Needle-nose pliers

You'll probably use needle-nose pliers quite often in your upgrading work. This is especially true when changing jumpers. Needle-nose pliers are also used to pull off connectors that are difficult to reach and to loosen hex nuts, like the ones sometimes found on interface cards.

Paper and pencil

You'll need these to write down important information for later use. Write down everything you remove and their proper connections. This is the log that we mentioned in the first section of this chapter. This can eliminate guesswork and problems later.

Small container

Use a small container (e.g., a small cardboard or plastic box, or paper cup) to store small parts and screws. You can even use a clean and empty coffee mug. However, be sure that whatever you use doesn't tip over easily.

Chapter 10

Other tools

You may find additional tools to be a useful additions to your PC workshop. The following photograph shows tools which you may want to add:

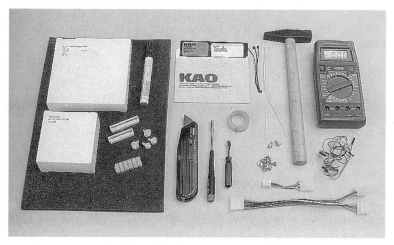

Useful additions to your toolbox

Permanent marker

A dark color marker will allow you to highlight parts and connections in your system. This can help you, for example, identify pin 1 of your floppy drive even after you've installed it.

An anti-static wristband

Using an anti-static wristband is the most reliable way to prevent electrostatic damage to your hardware components. You can keep the grounding wire out of your way while you're working by simply running it through the sleeve of your shirt.

Some anti-static wristbands have grounding wires that are much too short. In these cases, it's best to lengthen the wire by either soldering or clamping additional wire to the end of the grounding wire.

A diskette containing a hardware diagnostics program

If you own a program, such as CHECKIT! or DIAGS, make a working copy on a separate diskette and keep it in your PC workshop. These programs can be extremely helpful in finding errors or configuring an I/O port.

Several blank formatted diskettes

Use these diskettes to check the operation of your floppy drives. You also need to keep empty diskettes handy for eventual data backups.

An extra short screwdriver

Use this screwdriver to reach screws in tight places. Sometimes you'll even need to pull out expansion cards to maneuver a longer screwdriver within your PC. A short Phillips head screwdriver can provide a much easier solution in these instances.

NOTE

Special short screwdrivers with exchangeable bits are particularly helpful. They allow both standard and Phillips heads to be used with the same screwdriver. You'll find these screwdrivers in automotive supply stores.

A hex wrench

Hex wrenches are available as open end, box end, and screwdriver-type wrenches. They are also available as socket sets that are used with ratchet drivers. This type of wrench simplifies the installation of hex nuts on interface cards or your motherboard.

A small file

Occasionally a small file is needed to remove small imprecisions so that parts can fit together correctly. Often plastic castings will still have small burrs which can interfere with the operation of your PC's power switch. These burrs can easily be removed with a small file.

NOTE

Never use a file to shape metal components of your PC's hardware. You'll never be able to completely remove the metal shavings from the interior of your PC!

Chapter 10

IC insertion/extraction kit

These kits, available from an electronics supply store, are used for removing RAM chips and other ICs without damaging their sensitive contacts.

If you don't want to purchase this kit or you can't find one, you can also use the metal cover from one of your PC's expansion slots. Simply use the short perpendicular end to gently pry up the chip that must be removed.

A sharp flat knife

A simple kitchen knife with a flat blade is also useful. You'll need this knife for trimming oversized spacers and custom made ribbon cables.

Nonconducting foam

This can also be any sheet of nonconducting material on which you can place your motherboard while you're working on your system. It also serves as a perfect support for your hard drive while it's out of your system.

Extra jumpers (various sizes)

You may need to add extra jumpers rather than removing jumpers to achieve the correct configuration. So you may want to keep several extra jumpers available in your PC toolbox. You'll find jumpers of all sizes at your local electronics supply store.

Different standard size screws

These can be extremely helpful if you misplace or lose a screw from your PC.

Several spacers

These are needed when you remove or reinstall your motherboard. Since it's fairly easy to damage these spacers when you remove them, it's a good idea to have extras available.

A roll of electrical tape

Ideally the tape should be fabric-reinforced. We've found that this type of insulating tape is more durable and also adheres better.

Several wire connectors

These connectors are inexpensive and are available in any electronics supply store. Don't select particularly long connectors, because you'll probably have to trim them anyway.

A Y-power splitter

Often users begin to install a new hard drive and then discover that the power supply doesn't provide an extra power connection. If you're not sure whether your PC is equipped with extra voltage supply connections, you should include one of these power splitters in your PC tool box. These are also available in your local computer or electronics store.

Post and card connectors, ribbon cable

These are all the items you'll need to assemble your own floppy or hard drive cable. Perhaps you'll need such a cable when installing a 3.5-inch drive in your system, or you may need a cable extension for a particularly tall tower case.

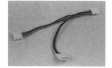

A hammer

A hammer may be needed to help mount the crimp connectors on the ribbon cable mentioned above. Any normal household or woodworking hammer will work.

Braided cable and connectors

Use only stranded or braided cable for your wire connections instead of single-conductor wire. If you use single-conductor wire, future problems through broken wires will occur.

Chapter
10
Section
3

A continuity tester

This specialized device is used only to trace problems in suspect wire connections, or in testing the polarity of the power switch on a new PC housing. Since you probably won't need a continuity tester, don't purchase one until it's necessary.

A soldering iron and rosin-core solder

As we mentioned, we won't discuss repairs that require a soldering iron. However, if you're familiar with the correct use of this tool, you may find it quite useful in repairing faulty cable connections. A properly soldered connection is generally much more reliable than a crimp connector.

A multimeter

If you don't already own a multimeter, you won't need to purchase one for your PC workshop.

NOTE

Be careful not to melt adjacent cable insulators. Also, never solder over your PC or any other exposed component. Doing this will most likely result in permanently damaging a component.

However, if you're familiar with a multimeter, it may provide valuable information in tracing problems, for example, with your power supply.

TIPS FOR YOUR PC WORKSHOP

The tools that you'll use when upgrading your PC should meet certain requirements. This is also true of where you'll be working on your PC.

Remember, mistakes are less likely to occur if your work environment is organized. Therefore, you should select a place where you can work without distractions.

Select a place where you won't be interrupted. Also, make certain enough counter or table space for the different hardware components and tools. A large table that you can walk around is ideal. This will allow you to access your PC from all sides; you won't constantly need to rotate or move it.

Don't underestimate the amount of space you'll need. Remember, a PC (even when it's assembled and operating) and its peripherals can easily take up a desktop.

There should also be ample, glare-free lighting. You must be able to recognize details, such as black type on dark brown components.

You should also have enough electrical outlets. Multiple-outlet power strips are ideal because they remove the hazardous maze of power cords on your floor. Such power strips usually include a main switch. This switch lets you switch off power at one time to all the components connected to the strip.

Your workspace should also include a chair. You can perform many operations while sitting. You'll frequently need to read various manuals and documentation.

So, to summarize, work in a well-lit room that's free of distractions. Use a free standing and sturdy table that you can reach from all sides without tripping over cables or wires. Keep everything within easy reach that you may need to use.

This is the ideal setting; sometimes all of these conditions aren't possible. However, remember the time you spend setting up your workspace also depends on how comfortable and confident you are about working with your PC.

Installing New Components

11

In this chapter we'll talk about the practical aspects of expanding and upgrading your PC system. Follow the instructions in this chapter closely. Don't panic if something doesn't work right away; don't give up after the first try. Remain calm and concentrate on what you're doing. That's the only way to get reliable, effective results. Take advantage of our experience and trust us. We have good reasons for telling you to do something a particular way.

The first time you used your PC, like most of us, you probably were hardly able to run "the thing." You eventually learned how to communicate with your PC and how it reacted to your instructions. You probably used software and applications when you worked with your PC. This chapter will help you learn about your hardware by *looking inside* it. You'll become familiar with your PC by taking it apart.

Most of the instructions have a similar structure. First, we'll summarize the necessary steps. This will give you an idea of the time and effort involved in a specific upgrading procedure. After the summary, we'll describe the steps needed to complete the upgrade.

We discuss all the components that you will probably want to upgrade or install with your project. Keep in mind that we have kept this information

NOTE

One important note that you'll see several times in this book: Make certain to switch off and unplug the computer before you do any work inside the case. This is very important to both the computer's survival and your survival.

335

consistent to installing each component. For example, the steps for changing your PC motherboard will apply whether it's a 486 or Pentium class motherboard. Likewise, whether you are installing a 6x or a 8x CD-ROM drive, the instructions we give still apply.

CASE

We talked about the types of cases you can use in your PC system (Chapter 3). In this section, we'll talk about some tips for handling cases properly.

Opening the PC case

Regardless of the type of case (e.g., desktop case, a mini-tower case or an upright case), you have three ways of opening it.

1. Case hinged on chassis.

2. Front cover attached to chassis; top moves back and/or up.

3. Front cover attached to case (independent of chassis); top and cover pulls forward.

You can easily determine which type of PC case you have. The screws are on the back of the case on upright and mini-tower cases. One screw is usually in each corner and one screw is on either side between the corner screws. Some mini-towers even have screws on the sides. Don't confuse these screws with the screws to the power supply.

Desktop cases usually also have screws on the back. Each corner will have a screw and another appears halfway between the two top corner screws. You will also find desktop cases with screws on the sides. You may have to place the case on its back to reach the screws.

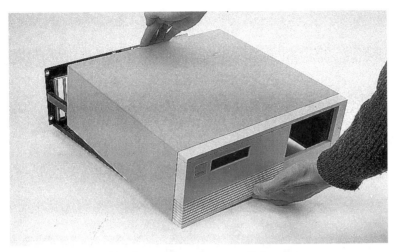

The front cover is part of the top

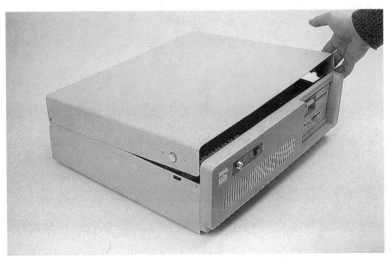

The front cover is part of the chassis

When you loosen the screws, move the top carefully in the proper direction. Move slowly and gently, as the brackets which hold the screws in place may catch on cables. Don't shake or drag the top of the case; doing so may damage the case or other components.

For now, we'll simply say that you'll probably have to add items to the case before installing any components.

New cases usually come with a package that has all the accessories you'll need to attach to the case. Sometimes you even have to attach the legs. You won't find a set of instructions. Fortunately, you do have this book.

NOTE

You should always be careful when taking the top off any case but this is especially true with desktop cases. Internal hard drives are sometimes located to the right of the power supply. This is where top of the case frequently gets stuck. If so, you must bend it past the power supply.

If you're unpacking a new case from the box to build your own PC, please read Chapter 12.

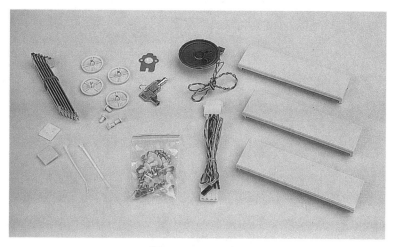

Case accessories

Install the speaker first (you might not be able to reach the area later). One installation method fits the speaker into a plastic holder in the front left of the chassis. Insert the speaker's magnet (the metal cylinder at the back of the speaker) in the plastic holder in the chassis.

A second method uses magnetized clips. You'll usually find these flaps in the front left part of the case.

Mounting rails

You may find mounting rails for hard drives and disk drives among the accessories. Save these rails because without them you will have problems installing a disk drive or hard drive.

The power switch may not be connected to the power supply. The following section ("Power Supply") describes the instructions involved in making this connection.

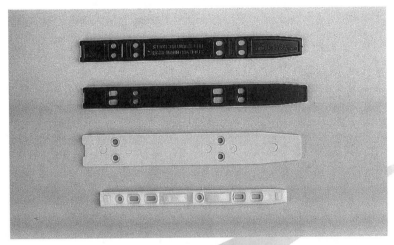

Mounting rails are all different

If you're working with a used case, you'll have to hope that any case components that aren't attached are at least somewhere in a bag. Finding the right mounting rails may be a matter of luck.

NOTE

Never drill or file anything inside or above the case. One mislaid metal filing or fragment can do a lot of damage if it bridges a connection on the power supply or motherboard. It's impossible to completely remove these fragments.

Chapter
11
Section
3

POWER SUPPLY

The power supply is one of the most important components in a computer system. It's also the most likely to fail of all the components in a computer system. Power supplies are usually self-contained (i.e., power supply and power switch built into one unit). In some cases, you may have to use a cable to connect the power supply to the power switch.

Most 486 and Pentium systems use a 200-watt power supply (compare this to the average 100 watt light bulb). The term power supply is somewhat of a misnomer. The power supply in your PC doesn't really *supply* power but *converts* the alternating current (AC) from your house or business into the 5-volt and 12-volt direct current (DC) used by your computer. The motherboard, boards and cards use the 5-volt power. The disk drive and fan motors use the 12-volt power.

Other reasons your PC needs a power supply

Power supplies do more than convert household current. They also make certain the system operates with the correct *level* of power. This is important if voltage in your area is reduced. The power supply performs an internal check and test before the system is allowed to start. The power supply sends the motherboard a special signal called the Power Good. If this signal is not present the computer does not run. Also, the Power Good signal weakens when the AC voltage drops and causes the power supply to overheat. This weakened Power Good signal forces the system to either reset or shutdown. An indication of a losing the Power Good signal is if your system fails to operate although the power switch is on and the fan and hard drives are running.

Most modern systems have an adequate power supply. A power supply usually fails from normal wear and tear and not from overloading or a power surge. Other causes of failure include thermal expansion and contraction. This results from switching the power on and off over time.

> **NOTE**
>
> Notice the large label (usually yellow - to get your attention) attached to the power supply warning you not to open the power supply. The capacitors in a power supply, even a power supply which is removed and unplugged from a socket, still have enough power to deliver a serious shock.
>
> **NEVER ATTEMPT TO REPAIR A POWER SUPPLY...SIMPLY REPLACE DEFECTIVE POWER SUPPLIES**

Most power supplies are considered universal, or worldwide. A universal power supply uses the 120-volt, 60-cycle current in the US and the 220 volt, 50-cycle current in Europe and other countries. For more information, refer to any diagrams attached to the power supply or to the documentation included with the power supply.

Maintaining the power supply

Because a power supply usually has only two moving parts (fan and power switch) little preventative maintenance is required.

An indication that your fan might have died is when your PC is suddenly very quiet but is still operating. Should that happen, save your work and shut down the PC system immediately.

Today's fast Pentium class processors generate a lot of heat; components can be damaged if a fan is unavailable to disperse this heat. Many of the Pentium class processors use a CPU-mounted fan because a simple heat sink cannot handle the job of dispersing the heat. A CPU-mounted fan is placed directly on top of the processor to disperse the heat generated by the processor. However, the disadvantage to the CPU-mounted fan is that when they fail, the processor overheats almost immediately and can quickly become damaged.

A higher capacity power supply may be the answer if you're PC is having problems that are related to overheating.

A few preventative maintenance tips for the power supply include the following:

❖ Your PC uses vents to dissipate the heat. Don't block these vents with paper, peripherals or other objects.

❖ Occasionally remove the power supply (see Chapter 14) and use compressed air to blow dust out of the fan.

❖ See Chapter 14 for additional preventative maintenance tips

Chapter
11
Section
3

341

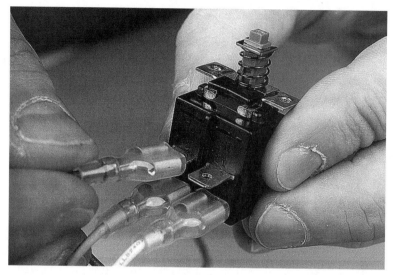

Connecting the power switch

Replacing the power supply fan

One of the few improvements you can make to the power supply is to replace the fan with a quieter model. This type of power supply fan is sometimes called a *muffin fan* because its low cylindrical design resembles an English muffin.

Several manufacturers produce very quiet fans. You can also purchase a temperature-regulated fan. This upgrade should be performed only by those with steady hands; some danger is involved because you have to open the power supply to make the replacement.

Step #1	Remove the power supply

To make your work easier, remove the power supply from the PC. Disconnect all the cables from the motherboard, the devices, and the power supply. Then remove the four screws on the back of the case. Now you can remove the power supply from the computer.

Removing the screws from the power supply

Wait at least 30 minutes before opening the power supply. This will allow time for the voltage to "die down." Use insulated tools when you perform this work. NEVER touch the inside of the power supply.

Step #2	Remove the old fan.

Open the power supply case and remove the four screws holding the old fan to the power supply case. You may also have to remove the grill from the fan. The fan usually gets power from a black and red two-wire cable. The red wire normally carries the current so it's called the *hot line* or *phase line*.

After unscrewing the old fan and removing it, see where the cable ends on the power supply. You should see a connector; if not, you may have to cut the black and red cable. If you must cut the cable, save as much of the cable leading into the power supply as possible.

Chapter
11
Section
3

343

Installing New Components

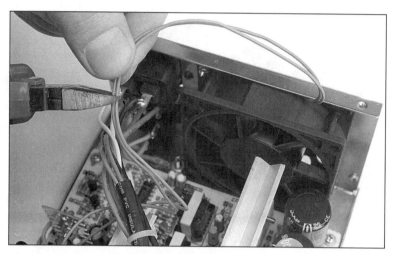

Cutting the fan cable

Step #3	Install the new fan.

Attach the ends of the cables to a two-line connector that mates with the new fan's connector. Remember to connect the wires red to red and black to black. Now reattach the screws to the new fan and reattach the fan grill. Wrap some electrician's tape around the connectors, then attach the power supply case.

The installed replacement fan

Step #4 | Test the power supply.

Reconnect the power supply to the motherboard and the other devices. Plug in a power cable and switch on the PC. Something was overlooked if the power supply only makes a soft whirring noise and doesn't operate. Otherwise, the fan will work and the PC will run normally.

Step #5 | Install the power supply.

After that you can reinstall the power supply and screw down the back of the case.

The plug with the three red cables goes toward the inside

Chapter 11

INSTALLING A DISK DRIVE

In this section we'll talk about installing a disk drive. These disk drives include a 5.25-inch drive, 3.5-inch drive and a combination disk drive. Although it's unlikely you'll ever need a 5.25-inch disk drive, there may be a time when you need some old archived file that is only available on a 5.25-inch diskette. If so, you'll need to know how to install the old 5.25-inch disk drive, too.

Considerations before installing

Installing a disk drive isn't a difficult task but you need to consider several factors before starting. Preparation is essential. Before you decide to install a second disk drive, take a good look inside your PC case. Note the starting and ending locations of cables. Considering all possibilities beforehand can help avoid costly disappointments later.

Is there a space for the drive?

The most important question is whether there is room to install another disk drive. You won't have any trouble finding room in upright cases or mini-towers. Still, it's always a good idea to take a good look inside the case to make certain the computer has enough room.

Drive mounting brackets

You usually won't have any trouble finding room in today's desktop cases, either. These cases are designed to hold two disk drives of different formats and at least one hard drive.

Older desktop cases frequently have only two mounting brackets. One bracket is for the hard drive and one bracket is for the disk drive. You may also have difficulty with cases that have three mounting brackets on top of one another if the hard drive is full height. It will block two 5.25-inch mounting brackets.

Be careful with brand name products. Manufacturers of brand name products tend to package their computers in PC cases that don't have room for a second disk drive. In those cases, you can still use an external disk drive for your second disk drive.

Are mounting rails required

After ensuring the case has enough room to install the drive, check whether you'll need mounting rails to attach the drive.

Differences between models

Check the first drive carefully. If you need mounting rails, it's a good idea to take the rails from this drive with you when you purchase rails for the second drive, since there are many types and models. It's also possible the rails are screwed into one of the free drive mounts.

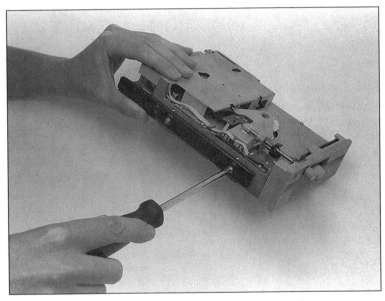

Attaching a drive with mounting rails

Is there a free power connection for the drive?

You can't always answer this question immediately with "yes." To be on the safe side, check for an unused disk drive power connection. You'll quickly run out of room quickly with power supplies that have very short cable harnesses. If you cannot find an unused power connection, you'll have to use a Y-splitter cable. You can buy these Y-cables at an electronics store.

We don't recommend homemade cables. Also, avoid making any changes to any of the existing power cables.

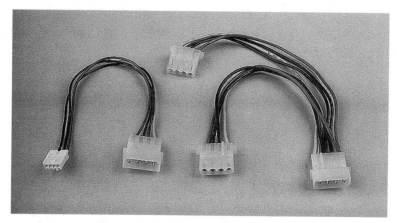

Y power splitter cable and adapter for 3.5-inch drives

3.5-inch adapter

Remember that some 3.5-inch disk drives have different power supply connections than 5.25-inch disk drives. You may have to buy an appropriate adapter (you can also get the adapter at the electronics shop). Modern PC power supplies have the correct connectors built in.

People are constantly asking us to recommend a disk drive or tell them about quiet disk drives. In our experience, we don't know of a manufacturer's products that we could either praise or criticize. After a certain amount of use, every drive gets louder.

5.25-inch disk drive installation

Preparations

We'll assume that you have a computer with an existing disk drive. The format doesn't matter. If this is not the case, skip ahead to Chapter 12. If you haven't done so, switch off the power, unplug the PC and remove the case. Make sure you have room for the second drive.

In keeping with our motto, "first test - then install", we'll start by connecting the drive and setting it up. Later we'll tighten the screws.

Step #1	Changing any settings for the drive.

You usually won't have to make any settings to the drive itself. Disk drives are preset as the second physical drive at the factory. Don't touch the jumpers on the drive. This is especially true if you don't have any documentation for the drive. The overwhelming majority of IBM compatible PCs differentiate between the first (A:) and second (B:) disk drives through the data and controller cable, instead of a drive setting.

Twist and turn

The first drive (A:) is connected to the end of the flat ribbon cable, whose data lines 10 to 16 (calculated from the marked cable side beginning at the right) are visibly twisted. These twisted lines convert the default "Drive select" jumper 2 to 1. The controller selects the drive behind the twisted lines as the first drive.

The connection for the second disk drive, from the controller's view, is in front of the twisted lines. The cable is straight and the default "Drive select" jumper 2 is preserved.

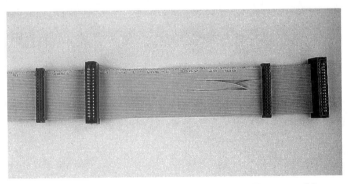

The twisted and straight ends of the floppy cable

You'll rarely find floppy cables that aren't twisted. Provided the first drive is available and has the correct setting, you won't have any problems with the second drive, since it's preset.

However, if you're replacing the first drive (e.g., because it is defective), you'll have to set the "Drive select" jumper on the drive. Several jumpers are usually available that enable settings from 0 to 3 (or 1 to 4). These jumpers are often marked "DS" for "Drive select."

Depending on where the numbers start, the "Drive select" jumper for the first drive must be set at DS0 or DS1. However, often solving the problem isn't that easy.

We recommend simply replacing the straight cable for one with a connection in front and in back of the twist.

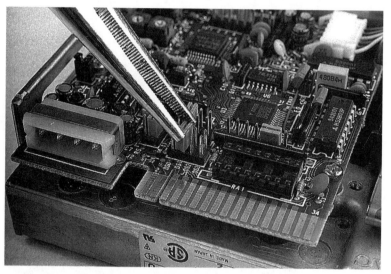

The "Drive select" jumper on the drive

Step #2	Connecting the controller and drive.

Since we're explaining how to install a second drive, the first drive is already connected with the controller card. On some computers, the cable also leads directly to the motherboard.

The first drive usually will be connected to the twisted end of the cable as we've described.

However, often the cable also has a second plug, which extends from the controller card in front of the cable twist. This is the connection for the second disk drive. If you don't have this second connection, or if it doesn't have the right plug, replace the entire cable for one that does.

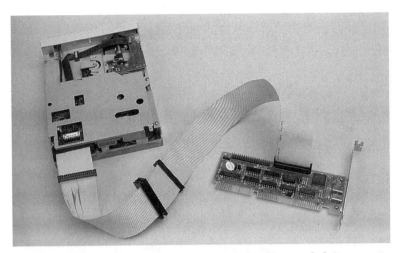

The cable connection between controller and drives

Today's PCs have two different plugs for both drives because different plugs are required depending on the drive format. The 5.25-inch drive requires a card connector that plugs into the drive card strip so the labeled side of the cable is adjacent to the side where the card strip of the drive has a notch.

It's usually impossible to twist the cable because the plug has a crosspiece that fits into this notch. If this crosspiece isn't on the labeled side of the cable, this indicates the plug wasn't attached to the cable properly.

Before setting the drive on any surface on the PC, we recommend that you place a nonconducting object on that surface (e.g., a book).

It's best to place the drive connected to the controller on its side (e.g., on the PC power supply) if the cables are long enough. For your test, simply place the drive in a position in which the head arm on the bottom of the drive can turn freely and the electronic circuitry of the drive doesn't come into contact with other metal parts.

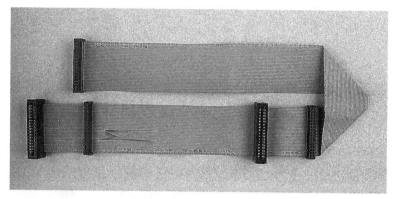

A universal floppy cable

Step #3	Supplying the drive with power.

Now take a free power cable from the power supply and connect it to the power connection on the disk drive. The outlet is made of white plastic. Four contact pins connect the plug to the power line. The shape of the socket prevents you from plugging in the plug incorrectly, as long as you don't use force. Remember that two of the four corners are round.

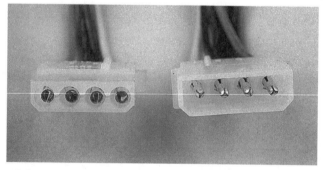

The shape of the socket prevents you from plugging in the plug incorrectly

Step #4	Setting up the drive.

Every IBM compatible PC starting with the 286 generation has a configuration memory called CMOS-RAM or AT-SETUP. You must set up the drive you just connected in AT-SETUP.

You can start SETUP either from the ROM of the computer or from a diskette. Today it's possible to call SETUP by pressing a key or combination of keys after the computer tests its RAM (main memory). If you aren't sure how to call the SETUP program on your PC, refer to Chapter 13. You can also get help by checking the motherboard technical documentation, or your PC's user manual.

Reassembly

Ensure that you have all the cables connected correctly and the connected drive isn't in contact with any live parts. Now reconnect all the other cables (keyboard, monitor, power) and boot up your computer.

Next, start the SETUP program. Many BIOS implementations recognize the existing difference between the setup configuration and the new configuration themselves and prompt you to call SETUP.

In the input window for the standard CMOS, select the proper setting for drive B:. This may be "1.2 Meg," or "High Density" (1.2 Meg drive). Otherwise, use the setting "360K", "Low Density", or "Double Density" (360K drive). Which term you must enter varies depending on the manufacturer of the BIOS.

Normally you use the cursor keys to select from default values. Refer to Chapter 13 for more information. Remember to save the new entries you make.

Step #5	Test the drive before final installation.

After connecting and setting up the drive, test it to see if it works. First, see if the PC starts up correctly. Watch the startup process carefully. After you switch on the PC, it should test RAM, briefly access the two disk drives in the proper sequence, sound a short beep (boot signal), and then load the operating system either from the hard drive or a diskette in drive A:.

Second test

If the startup process doesn't proceed as we described (both drives are accessed simultaneously, the drive LEDs light up at the same time, etc.) or you get error messages during formatting, switch off the computer and check the cable connections between the disk drives and the controller again.

You can also refer to Chapter 15 for more information.

Chapter
11
Section
3

However, if startup runs smoothly, you're almost home free. You still have to format a diskette with your new disk drive. If you're able to use the DOS FORMAT B: command successfully, and the diskette formats as it should, then you know all is well with your new disk drive.

Step #6	Install the drive and tighten the screws.

Now switch off the computer, unplug the power supply, and disconnect the cables from the drive. Install the drive in your PC case with the head arm facing the bottom or on its side (never on its back). You might have to use mounting rails. If you do use mounting rails, fasten the mounting rails with countersunk screws; otherwise you will have trouble inserting the drive.

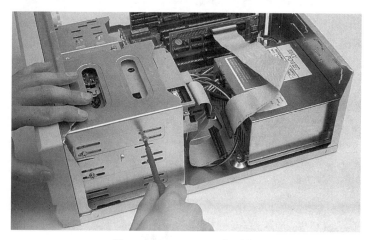

Two screws on each side

After attaching the drive, reconnect the cables on the drive. Before closing the cover, test the drive again as described in Step 5. Don't leave any screws in the computer; then tighten the screws in the case. Now you're finished installing the disk drive.

3.5-inch disk drive installation

Installing a 3.5-inch disk drive is virtually identical to installing a 5.25-inch drive. Therefore, follow the procedures described above in the "5.25-inch disk drive installation" part of this chapter for installing a 5.25-inch drive. However, we need to talk about a few special features.

Mounting kit

Not all cases have one or more 3.5-inch mounting brackets. If your case doesn't, you must buy a mounting kit for a 5.25-inch slide-in unit.

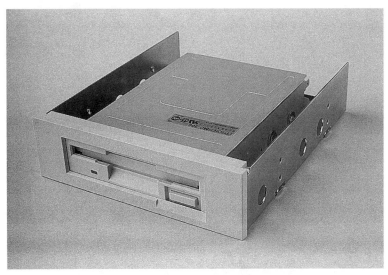

A disk drive in a mounting kit

The connector on the controller cable for connecting a 3.5-inch drive has a different appearance than the card connector used for 5.25-inch drives. To connect the drive directly, you need a post connector that will accept the 34 contact pins on the drive. Line 1 (labeled side of cable) is usually on the inside, next to the power connection. In some cases (e.g., with Chinon drives), pin 1 is outside on the edge of the drive. Normally you'll be able to see labeling on the drive board (pin 1 or 2, or pin 33 or 34).

You can also purchase small adapter boards that let you connect 3.5-inch drives to card connectors.

355

Installing New Components

Power adapter

If your 3.5-inch adapter case doesn't have the 3.5-inch mounting bracket, most likely it doesn't have the proper power connection for this kind of disk drive.

The power connection for a 3.5-inch drive has a completely different appearance than the power connection for 5.25-inch disk drives. You can buy the necessary adapter at an electronics store.

Adapter plug

The power connector isn't as clearly labeled as standard power connectors for 5.25-inch disk drives. Usually the bottom of the power connector has a small plastic object that fits in a hole in the power socket of the drive (underneath the contact pins). In any case, you should be able to plug in the power connector easily, without bending the contact pins.

If the case doesn't have the 3.5-inch mounting bracket, most likely it doesn't have the proper power connection for this kind of disk drive.

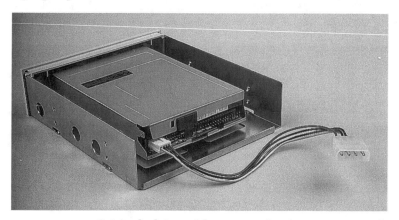

3.5-inch drive with power adapter

Combination drive installation

Combination disk drives combine a 3.5-inch disk drive with a 5.25-inch disk drive in one device. Installing a combination disk drive follows identical steps as installing a "normal" disk drive.

You cannot connect a combination drive as the second drive to a conventional combination or disk controller that's designed to manage two disk drives. If you have such a controller, you must operate the combination disk drive as the only drive.

Space advantage

Combination drives are the same size as conventional 5.25-inch disk drives. This means that you can run both drives in a single 5.25-inch mounting frame. This is an advantage for you if you own a very flat PC cases, especially if they want to install other equipment, such as a CD-ROM drive.

It's very easy to install a combination drive.

Step #1	Check the settings for the drive.

Combination drives are preset with the 5.25-inch drive as the first drive (A:) and the 3.5-inch drive as the second drive (B:). You can switch the two drives by changing the "Drive select" jumper. A jumper strip is in charge of the priority order for the two drives. To set the 3.5-inch drive as drive A:, set the jumper for this drive to DS1 and set the jumper for the 5.25-inch drive to DS2.

Step #2	Connect the controller and drive.

To connect to the combination controller, you'll need a conventional 34-pin flat ribbon cable with a post connector on the controller end and a card connector on the floppy end to accept the combination drive's edge connector.

On this end, 7 of the 34 lines must be twisted, as we explained earlier. While conventional disk drives require separate connections for A: and B:, the combination drive needs only a single flat ribbon cable connection.

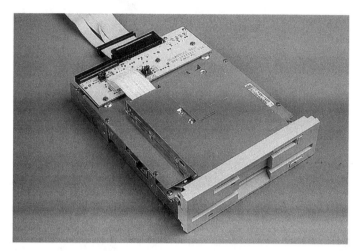

The combination drive on the twisted cable

Place the labeled side of the cable on Pin 1 on the controller and connect it to the combination drive using the notched side of the contact strip (as with typical 5.25-inch disk drives).

Step #3	Supply the drive with power.

Supply the combination drive with power in the same way you would supply a conventional 5.25-inch drive with power. The combination drive requires only one power connection. The connection jack is the same one you use with a conventional 5.25-inch disk drive.

Step #4	Using CMOS SETUP for the drives.

To set up the two drives in CMOS SETUP, follow the same procedure you would for regular disk drives. When entering the drives, use the same setting you did when selecting the "Drive Select" jumper sequence for the combination drive.

Step #5	Test the drive before final installation.

This step is identical to Step #5 from earlier in this section but we'll repeat it here so you won't need to look for the information elsewhere. After connecting and setting up the drive, test it to see if it works. See if your PC starts up correctly. Watch the startup process carefully. After you turn on your PC, it should test RAM, briefly access the two disk drives in the proper sequence, sound a short beep (boot signal) and then load the operating system either from the hard drive or a diskette in drive A:.

If the startup process doesn't proceed as we described (both drives are accessed simultaneously, the drive LEDs light up at the same time, etc.) or you get error messages during formatting, switch off the computer and check the cable connections between the disk drives and the controller again. (See Chapter 15 for additional information).

However, if startup runs smoothly, you're almost home free. You still have to format a diskette with your new disk drive. If you're able to use the DOS FORMAT B: command successfully, and the diskette formats as it should, then your new disk drive is functioning correctly.

Step #6	Install the drive and tighten the screws.

This step is identical to Step #6 from earlier in this section but we'll repeat it here so you won't need to look for the information elsewhere. Now turn off the computer, unplug the power supply and disconnect the cables from the drive. Install the drive in your PC case with the head arm facing the bottom or on its side (never on its back). You might have to use mounting rails. If you do use mounting rails, fasten the mounting rails with countersunk screws; otherwise you will have trouble inserting the drive.

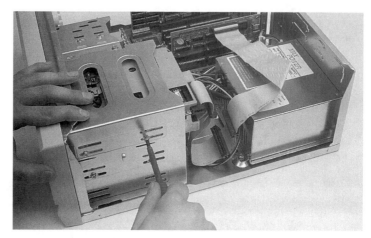

Two screws on each side

After attaching the drive, reconnect the cables on the drive. Before closing the cover, test the drive again as described in Step #5. Make certain not to leave any screws in the computer; then tighten the screws in the case. Now you're finished installing the disk drive.

Four disk drives on one PC

Now that you know how to install different types of disk drives, we'll explain how to connect more than two disk drives to a PC. This procedure usually involves replacing the current disk controller. It's important to examine the hardware requirements carefully to prepare for and execute this upgrade properly. It's absolutely necessary to examine the PC case to determine exactly what kind of controller is currently being used to control the disk drives in your PC.

So unplug the power supply cable and take a good look at inside your PC case.

Preparation: Determining the hardware requirements

The diskette controller is located on the motherboard

Suppose the flat ribbon cables from the disk drives lead directly to a connection on the motherboard. Your next move is to check the motherboard documentation or user manual to determine if the diskette controller (FDC) can be disabled "on board."

If it can be disabled, purchase a diskette controller that handles four disk drives and all formats. If you cannot disable the diskette controller, then to the best of our knowledge, there is no way to solve this problem.

The diskette controller is on a separate expansion board

Suppose the flat ribbon cable of the disk drives leads to a card in one of the expansion slots and the card isn't combined with any other devices. In this case, purchase a diskette controller (not a combination controller) that handles four disk drives in all formats and replace the installed card with the new one.

A combination controller is managing the disk drives

Suppose the flat ribbon cables for disk drives and hard drives are both connected to the same expansion board. If the card still has a 34-pin connection free, you can probably connect two more disk drives there. If not, replace the combination controller completely with a similar (MFM, RLL, AT BUS, SCSI, ESDI or IDE) combination controller that can manage four disk drives.

Another option would be to disable the diskette controller part and install another diskette controller that can manage four disk drives and has all formats. The second solution makes sense when the installed controller card contains other connections (serial and parallel ports and joystick ports).

Now that you know the hardware requirements and how to connect up to four disk drives, we'll describe the procedure for this upgrade step-by-step. Because of the many controllers for four disk drives currently on the market, some controllers may not fit our description.

Also, check the power supply of your PC case for power connections for all the drives you're installing. If there aren't enough connections, purchase Y-power splitters.

Step #1	Remove or disable the diskette controller.

To remove the diskette controller either to replace it or simply disable it, first loosen the attachment screw to the face plate on the case. Then carefully pull up the card from the expansion socket.

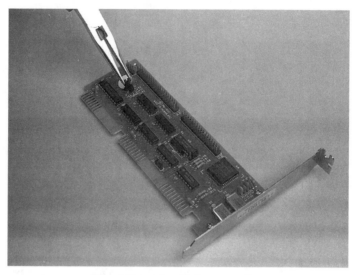

Disabling the disk controller

To disable the controller, either reset, connect or disconnect a jumper on the controller board or change a setting on a DIP switch. In either case, you must have the technical documentation for the controller board or a great deal of time and patience to make the correct setting.

Step #2	Install and connect replacement controller

BIOS or CONFIG

Depending on your hardware, now you must use another controller or an additional controller. Depending on the model, you must set switches or jumpers on the controller to let the controller BIOS know what kind of disk drives are connected. Set only those drives that have been connected up to this point.

With some quadruple disk controllers, you must also install software. You would then control the third and fourth disk drives using device drivers that must be entered in the CONFIG.SYS file. Refer to the controller documentation or installation guide for more information.

After making all the necessary settings, reconnect the cables of the existing disk drives (for combination controllers, reconnect the hard drive as well) first. Make sure that you connect the labeled side of the cable with the pin marked 1 on the controller connection.

Step #3	Plug in the computer and check the disk controller.

After all the cables are connected properly, first check whether the system functions as before. Reconnect the monitor and the keyboard, reconnect the PC to the power supply and boot up the system. If the entries in CMOS SETUP haven't been changed, the PC will have to access all the disk drives and boot without error messages. This process may take longer than before, since the controller BIOS also appears on the screen. Be patient.

If your PC doesn't start up as it should, try to eliminate the errors before connecting the rest of the drives. Read the controller documentation and Section 2 for more information.

If the PC starts up without any errors and goes to the DOS prompt, continue with Step #4.

Step #4	Connect and test the remaining disk drives.

To do this, first switch off the PC and unplug the power supply. Then set the additional disk drives on the controller in accordance with the controller documentation or installation guide. Connect the new disk drives first and try them out before installing them physically. Use the disk controller documentation as a guide.

After all the drives are properly connected and supplied with power, reconnect the system to the power supply and start up the computer. If startup runs smoothly, format a diskette in each of the disk drives (starting with drive A:). See whether you can boot from a diskette in drive A:. If all the disk drives formatted their diskettes properly, then you know everything is correct.

Chapter
11
Section
3

LASTDRIVE

However, if you're unable to address a drive, remember that DOS only defaults to five logical drive letters (A: to E:). For example, if you require six different drive letters (e.g., two hard drives and four disk drives), you must increase the maximum value for the number of logical DOS drives with the LASTDRIVE command. In our example, you must enter the line LASTDRIVE = F in the CONFIG.SYS file.

```
C:\>type config.sys
DEVICE=C:\WINDOWS\HIMEM.SYS
device=C:\WINDOWS\EMM386.EXE NOEMS
DEVICE=C:\D_D\D_D.SYS /F=C:\D_D_VOL.000
DOS=HIGH,umb
devicehigh=c:\dos\setver.exe
FILES=35
BUFFERS=30
SHELL=C:\DOS\COMMAND.COM C:\DOS\ /P
LASTDRIVE=M
STACKS=9,256
```

The LASTDRIVE command in CONFIG.SYS

If everything functions properly, disable the system, disconnect the power supply, and begin installing the disk drives physically. Follow the instructions earlier in this section.

INSTALLING A HARD DRIVE

Installing a hard drive in an IBM compatible PC isn't as easy as it might sound in a magazine article. It's actually a complicated process that requires an understanding of the technical connections to be done successfully.

Normally, the differences can be tremendous, depending on what kind of hard drive you want to install. You have to remember several items when repairing a hard drive or upgrading to a new one.

Earlier we provided a detailed description of the various hard drive systems used with IBM compatible PCs, including their advantages and disadvantages. In this section we go into detail about installing the different hard drive systems on your computer.

Similar to any upgrading procedure, once again it's a matter of identifying the requirements first.

Preparation

The most important consideration is determining the type of hard drive system with which you're dealing. If you don't have a hard drive controller or a hard drive in your PC, this process will be simple. You can choose from almost any hard drive system. If you decide to install a completely new hard drive system (consisting of hard drive, cable set, and controller card), then the most important task is already complete.

However, if your PC already has a hard drive controller, then you must buy a hard drive system that corresponds with that controller-unless you want to replace it.

This is especially true if you want to add a second hard drive to the existing hard drive/controller set. With a single exception (some RLL hard drives can also be formatted as MFM drives, at the expense of capacity), it's impossible to manage different hard drive systems from the same controller.

Identifying the existing hard drive system

If you don't know what kind of hard drive system you have, the flat ribbon cable connections can help you identify your system. The post connectors of the flat ribbon cables to the hard drives are plugged into a strip with contact pins.

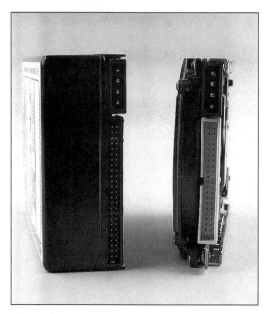

Examples of two bus controllers: SCSI (left) and AT bus (right)

The pin strips help you clearly identify the hard drive system. If this pin strip has 40 pins and only one cable goes from the controller to the hard drive, then you have an IDE or AT bus controller. A SCSI controller has 50-pin strips.

The hard drive controllers for MFM, RLL and ESDI hard drives all have a 34-pin strip for connecting the hard drive control cable and a 20-pin strip for the data cable. So there are two cables connecting the hard drive to the controller. You won't be able to identify the hard drive by the pin strips.

Instead, check the controller card for a possible model designation. If you have a hard drive connected, use the model designation in our hard drive list in the appendix to determine the type of hard drive system you have.

The two card connectors of an MFM/RLL hard drive

Buy the right material to mount the hard drive

Make certain to get the right type of material for mounting the hard drive. The hard drive must be securely fastened. You should be able to place the drive in any position except upside down or slanted to one side.

Hard drives come in a 3.5-inch format and can be installed in 3.5-inch housings in today's cases. Older desktop cases and big tower cases have only 5.25-inch mounting brackets.

The only way to install 3.5-inch hard drives into 5.25-inch mounting brackets is with the help of a mounting kit. You may also need mounting rails.

You can tell by the way the disk drives are attached. Before attempting to install a hard drive, make sure you know how you are going to mount it in the case.

The hard drive power supply

The power supplies for today's Pentium class PCs can operate many combinations of hard drives, CD-ROM drives and disk drives. These power supplies usually supply 200 watts. To be on the safe side, you should check whether your PC power supply has a free power cable to which you can connect the hard drive. If it doesn't, buy a Y-power splitter to divide the power cable into two connections.

NOTE

Make An Emergency Startup Disk

Use the emergency startup disk to start your PC if you're having problems starting Windows. Insert the startup disk in your computer and then restart your PC. Your PC starts from that disk and not from your hard drive.

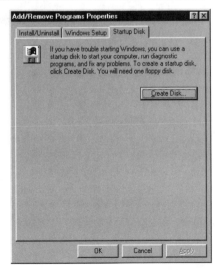

Before continuing, make certain to have a bootable emergency startup disk available. Then if your hard drive fails or cannot start Windows, use the startup disk to start your computer. To create an emergency boot disk in Windows 95, click **Start/Settings/ Control Panel**. Then double-click the Add/ Remove Programs icon and select the Startup disk tab. Follow the instructions on your screen.

367

MFM hard drive installation

We mentioned what you'll need to install a hard drive. Now let's talk about some special features that are important for installing an MFM hard drive. (See Chapter 8 for more information on what is an MFM hard drive).

We'll assume in this section that you have a functional MFM hard drive controller or an MFM combination controller as well as an MFM hard drive that's in working order. We'll discuss errors that result from defective hardware in Chapter 14 and Chapter 15.

The cable set for MFM hard drives

To install an MFM hard drive, you'll need a special cable set consisting of a wide control cable for one or two hard drives and one thin data cable for each hard drive.

The data cables have 20 lines with a post connector on one end that connects with the controller card and a card connector on the other end. This is connected to the smaller of the two contact strips on the hard drive.

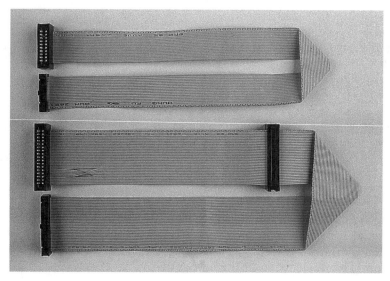

An MFM cable set

The control cable should be equipped for two hard drives (i.e., it should have three connectors). It should have a post connector for the controller and two card connectors for either one or two hard drives.

This cable is frequently twisted from line 25 to 29 (don't mix this up with the cable for disk drives, which has 7 twisted lines from 10 to 16). However, there are also cables that aren't twisted.

Special software

As we explained in Section 1 and Section 2, before an operating system can accept an MFM hard drive, the drive must undergo an initialization process. This process is also referred to as a low-level format. To do this, you'll need special software that isn't found in your operating system.

Software for making this low-level format is available. Some newer PC BIOS configurations (e.g., from AMI) frequently contain a program, called a hard drive formatter, that you can start from ROM. If you don't have such a utility, you won't be able to install an MFM hard drive. We'll explain how to use this kind of utility later.

Hard drive installation in eight steps

We broke down our instructions for installing an MFM hard drive into eight steps. We recommend reading through all the steps first so you know what awaits you. We assume that you're installing the first and only MFM hard drive in your PC. We'll discuss installing a second MFM hard drive later.

The steps involved include the following:

1. Set the "Drive Select" jumper on the hard drive

2. Connect the hard drive to the controller and the power supply

3. Set up the hard drive in CMOS SETUP

4. Low-level format

5. Partition the hard drive

6. Format the hard drive

7. Test the hard drive

8. Physically install the hard drive in the PC case

Chapter

11

Section

3

369

Installing New Components

Let's start with Step #1. We assume the case is already open and the power cable is unplugged from the PC.

Step #1	Set the "Drive Select" jumper on the hard drive.

MFM hard drives are usually preset at the factory as the first drive. The "Drive Select" jumper is set to drive "0". Generally you won't need to change the default setting on the drive. A few manufacturers set their drives as drive "1". In this case, use the twisted end of the control cable instead of the other end. The straight end is free.

If your hard drive cable is straight all the way through, then you can only use it with hard drives set as the first drive, whose "Drive Select" jumper is set to "0". So you may have to change the default setting of the hard drive or else get a different cable.

"Drive Select" jumper set to "0"

Finding the jumper

Set the "Drive Select" jumper for MFM hard drives from jumpers or DIP switches. The location of these jumpers or switches on the hard drive varies for each manufacturer. Therefore, we can't provide a general description.

370

Seagate usually places the "Drive Select" jumper for MFM hard drives between the contact strips for the cable connections. If you put a Seagate drive on the table with the board on top and look from the connection strips towards the control lamp, the "Drive Select" jumper is set to "0" when the jumper is all the way to the right.

If the jumper is on the second contact from the right, it means "Drive Select" jumper "1" is active. At any rate, the jumper has to be connected; otherwise it's impossible to address the drive.

Step #2	Connect the hard drive to the controller and the power supply.

Use the post connector to connect the 34-pin control cable to the hard drive/combination controller. It's easy finding the connection on hard drive controllers since only one 34-pin connection is present. MFM combination controllers have two 34-pin connections. If the connections aren't labeled, you can assume the connection closest to the cover plate is for the disk drives. This means that you connect the hard drive control cable to the other, inner connection.

Remember the labeled side of the cable connects with pin 1 of the connector. Generally, pin 1 or 2 or else pin 33 or 34 are labeled on the controller card. If they aren't, look at the connector from the back side of the controller board. Pin 1 usually has a square soldered joint instead of a round one.

Connecting the cables to the controller

Next, connect the 20-pin data cable to the controller. The connector is usually to the immediate left of the control cable connector. Farther left or underneath is the connector for the second data cable (important only if you use two hard drives). Connect the labeled side of this cable with pin 1 also.

Then plug the controller into any free 16-bit slot on the motherboard, as close as possible to the hard drive, and fasten the card to the back of the case with a screw. Make certain to insert the card properly.

Using the combination controller

Then connect the hard drive to a free power cable from the power supply. First, place the hard drive on the PC power supply (if possible, place a nonconducting pad on the power supply, then place the hard drive on top of the pad).

After that, connect the power and data cables to the hard drive so the labeled side of the cables adjoins the grooved sides of the contact strips. Usually the card connectors of the cables have small cross-pieces that fit into the groove so you can't plug them in the wrong way.

NOTE

Never force the plug in the socket

Pay attention to the shape of the plug and the socket. Never force the plug in the socket. Remember not to block the fan, and avoid short circuits on the bottom of the hard drive.

Installing New Components

The hard drive is connected

Check once more whether all the cable connections are correct.

Step #3	Set up the hard drive in CMOS SETUP.

Before you can continue with the next steps, you must tell your PC that you've added a hard drive. All PCs save their configuration in a special battery backed memory called CMOS RAM. The hard drive is entered in a type of configuration list there. Every time you start up the system, the PC checks whether this list matches the hardware it finds in its self-test. If something is missing or if there are too many entries, the PC will notice and prompt you to check the entries.

Start the SETUP program to make changes to this configuration list. However, before turning your PC back on, read the rest of this section. Many PC BIOS configurations allow you to start SETUP by pressing a key during the self-test. For example, after testing RAM, AMI BIOS displays the following message:

Press DEL to run SETUP

When you press Del, the PC then branches to a selection menu from which you can start CMOS SETUP or standard CMOS.

Chapter
11
Section
3

373

When you turn on your PC again, you'll notice a change in the configuration. This change causes the computer to try to access the hard drive after the self-test. This process can last several seconds. You're also likely to hear some strange noises from the hard drive.

Error messages

However, the PC can't access the hard drive since it hasn't yet been set up. So the PC displays an error message that refers either to the controller, the drive or the entry in SETUP. Here are some examples (each BIOS uses different error messages):

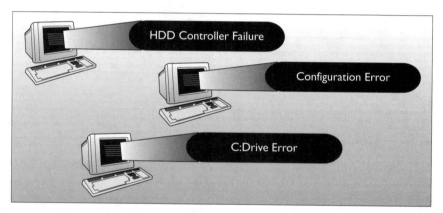

Often the error message prompts the user to run the SETUP program:

Frequently pressing the F1 key runs the SETUP program:

Now reconnect your PC to the power supply, plug the monitor and keyboard back in, and switch on the computer. Study the monitor and follow the instructions, or try to start SETUP.

When you start SETUP, the monitor displays either dialog boxes or selection menus that enable you to enter the date, time, type of disk drives, type of hard drives, kind of graphics adapter, and other items. Ordinarily, you won't be able to type anything, but you can select from a number of options. A status line often indicates how to make the selections.

Search and enter

Normally you'll use the cursor keys to move the cursor to a text box for the hard drive and select from a number of different hard drive types using the | key. Which hard drive type you select depends on the entries for cylinders and heads that go with this type. See the list of hard drives in the Appendix for the parameters of the hard drive you're installing.

Some PC BIOS configurations (especially older ones) display the current numbers of the hard drive types, but not their drive parameters. Ordinarily in such cases you can press a special key ([F1] or [?]) to display a type list.

You must select the right type and enter it. This means that you must select the type whose cylinders, heads, and sectors match those of the hard drive you're installing. For example, the Seagate ST-251 40 Meg hard drive requires an entry of 820 cylinders, 6 heads, and 17 sectors. Remember that each BIOS assigns different type numbers for these parameters.

When you cannot set the drive type that you are installing...

Although this may be annoying at first, the situation isn't hopeless. Today's PC BIOS configurations offer a "User Type" under type 47. This means that you can enter the parameters yourself under this type. The entries for cylinders, heads, and sectors (always 17 for MFM drives) are important. You can set all the other values to "0" if you don't know what they are. Don't be surprised if the memory size calculated from the entries is different from the value you expected. It doesn't mean anything.

Chapter

11

Section

3

Lower capacity

If CMOS SETUP doesn't offer a User Type either, you still have the option of setting a type with lower values than the actual values of your hard drive. If possible, choose a type that has the same number of heads as the hard drive you're installing. Although this method doesn't always work with every drive, it's better than nothing.

However, using this method will cost you a couple of megabytes in memory capacity (we explained how to calculate memory capacity from the number of cylinders and heads in Section 2).

Software solutions

Special utility programs for hard drive installation also give you the option of generating software drivers that manage the hard drive independently of the system BIOS. This is your last chance to set up a "difficult" hard drive. We'll discuss this in a special chapter on utility programs.

NOTE

Never enter more cylinders or heads than your hard drive really has. If you do, low-level formatting may destroy your hard drive. Make sure you find out the correct parameters for the hard drive you are installing.

Leave the entry for the second hard drive at "NOT INSTALLED" or "NONE".

After you finish entering the parameters for your hard drive, you must save them; otherwise they won't go into effect. Usually the monitor displays information on saving. There are always two ways to exit the dialog box for CMOS SETUP: By saving and by canceling. When you exit by saving, it reboots the system, since the entries don't go into effect until the system is reset.

When you start a PC BIOS from ROM, a confirmation prompt often appears before you save. You can answer this prompt by pressing Y for "Yes" or N for "No". Usually you also have to press Enter to confirm your choice. You are now finished setting up your hard drive.

The screen of your PC will then clear and the computer will reboot, starting with the RAM test. Be sure to have a bootable DOS diskette in the A: drive so you can load the operating system after the autoboot routine.

During the routine, however, you'll still get an error message about the hard drive or the controller, even though you made the right entries in CMOS SETUP. You may see one of the following error messages:

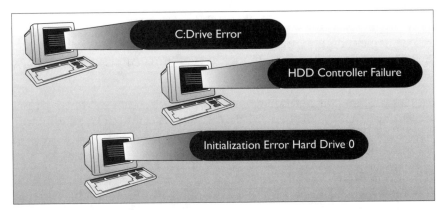

The message simply tells you the PC found a hard drive, but it cannot recognize it yet, since it hasn't been initialized (i.e., low-level formatted). That's our next step.

This error message gives you another opportunity to branch to standard CMOS or boot the PC. This time, boot the PC. Follow the instructions on the screen. The system will then try to load the operating system from the diskette in drive A:. If the operating system loads successfully, you can begin a low-level format.

Step #4	Perform a low-level format.

After cabling your hard drive and setting the correct values for formatting the hard drive cylinders and heads in the system BIOS, you're ready for low-level formatting.

Many of today's PCs, especially those equipped with AMI BIOS from American Megatrends, offer a hard drive utility as part of a diagnostic program. Like SETUP, you can also start this program from ROM. The program is actually designed to test the different hardware components. Usually you call this program like the SETUP program, by pressing [Del] after the RAM test. Watch for screen messages to this effect. You can usually select a hard drive utility from a menu item called "DIAGS".

Because there are so many different ROM BIOS routines for low-level formatting, we won't be able to provide instructions that will apply to every case.

Formatting programs included in the package

Brand name manufacturers sometimes include diskettes containing such hard drive formatting programs. Frequently, you'll also find such programs included as part of the supplied DOS licenses.

Such programs for hard drive initialization often have extensive test routines for surface analysis of the hard drives to be formatted. Depending on the size of the hard drive, such programs can easily take several hours. For more information, see the appropriate user manual.

If you don't have one of these low-level formatting programs, then you must buy your own software. Please see the related information later in this section.

Setting the interleave

Normally, these utilities read out the hard drive parameters from the CMOS RAM and provide the low-level formatting routine. Then all you have to do is confirm the routine (usually by pressing *e*). In addition, you'll also be prompted for information about the interleave factor. If you are not certain which value to specify, refer to the explanations about the interleave factor in Chapter 8. You'll find enough information there to help you make the necessary decision.

When the drive has defects

Finally, the utility gives you the option of making entries in the Bad Track Table. This table provides a list of the sectors marked as defective by the manufacturer. Usually this is a list with cylinder and head numbers that comes with the hard drive.

It's a good idea to enter these bad sectors in the Bad Track Table, since this prevents the computer from using these sectors for data reception. Hardly any MFM hard drive comes from the manufacturer completely free of defects. So don't worry if you have 10 to 20 bad sectors on your hard drive. This is typical for most hard drives.

Installing New Components

Example of a Bad Track Table that you'll find with an MFM hard drive

After you enter all the information related to the low-level format, the program displays a confirmation prompt and informs you that low-level formatting will irretrievably destroy all the data on the hard drive. Answer the prompt by pressing Ⓨ.

If all the information is correct and the hardware components are working, the utility will start counting the cylinders and heads in sequence. Depending on the hard drive model, it will make a ticking noise. When the program is finished, it displays a message on the screen, such as "Format Complete" or "Format successful."

This concludes low-level formatting. When you reboot the PC, it won't display any more error messages about the hard drive or the controller.

Step #5	Partition the hard drive.

The hardware accepts the hard drive formatting. However, the operating system won't recognize the hard drive until it finds a partition table with information about the size and division of the storage medium. To create this partition table, use the DOS command FDISK.

Partitioning with FDISK

First, start the operating system from a diskette in drive A: and then call FDISK from the diskette.

Chapter

11

Section

3

379

The DOS 6.2 FDISK main menu

DOS can manage hard drives of 1 Gigabyte in a single partition. That means that you don't have to divide the hard drive into several partitions, or logical drives. If you don't want to work with different operating systems on the hard drive you're partitioning, it's generally a bad idea to set up several logical drives. This also makes using FDISK easier.

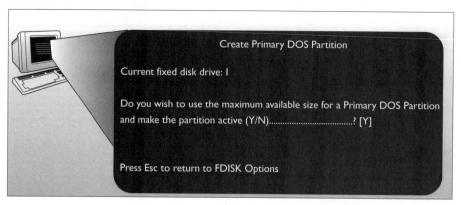

Create the primary DOS partition first

After calling FDISK, you see a selection menu on the screen. The first option in this menu is called "Create a DOS partition or logical DOS drive;." After selecting this option, another screen appears where the first option allows you to "Create Primary DOS Partition."

Select the first option from this screen also. FDISK then asks you whether you want to use the maximum available size for the primary DOS partition and make this partition active. Answer this prompt by pressing Ⓨ.

FDISK then prompts you to insert a bootable disk and press any key. After you do this, the computer reboots to create the partition table.

The PC starts up in the usual way. You shouldn't see any error messages. After you reload the operating system from diskette, DOS recognizes the hard drive.

Enter C: to access the hard drive. DOS then switches to the hard drive. You're finished partitioning the hard drive. You can now continue with Step #6 ("Formatting the hard drive").

Error messages displayed?

However, if DOS displays the error message:

Invalid Drive Letter

this means that nothing is entered in the partition table.

Any errors made during the low-level format will show up here, at the very latest. Try to run FDISK again. If your second effort fails, retrace your steps and perform another low-level format if necessary.

Installing several partitions...

You can divide the hard drive into several logical DOS drives. Generally you set up the primary DOS partition first. In this case, you would answer the question about using the maximum available size for a primary DOS partition by pressing Ⓝ.

FDISK then asks you how much space you want to reserve for the primary partition, at the same time displaying the total available space. You can specify the partition size in megabytes or as a percentage of the total capacity.

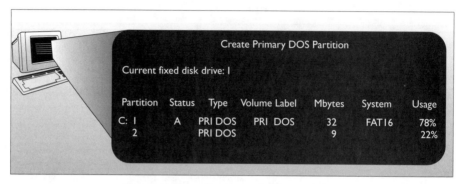

Partition	Status	Type	Volume Label	Mbytes	System	Usage
C: 1	A	PRI DOS	PRI DOS	32	FAT16	78%
2		PRI DOS		9		22%

Create Primary DOS Partition

Current fixed disk drive: 1

Determining the size of the partition

After the message "Primary DOS Partition created" appears on the screen, press
(Esc) to return to the FDISK main menu. Set up your extended DOS partition on the rest of the hard drive. FDISK supplies the corresponding values; you simply confirm them.

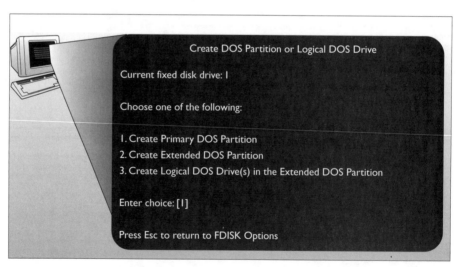

Create DOS Partition or Logical DOS Drive

Current fixed disk drive: 1

Choose one of the following:

1. Create Primary DOS Partition
2. Create Extended DOS Partition
3. Create Logical DOS Drive(s) in the Extended DOS Partition

Enter choice: [1]

Press Esc to return to FDISK Options

Select 2 to create an extended DOS partition

FDISK then begins setting up the logical DOS drives until the entire space in the extended DOS partition has been assigned logical drives. You can choose either megabytes or percentages of the extended DOS partition.

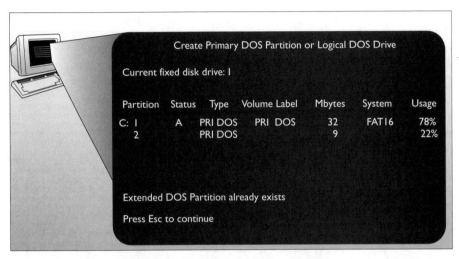

Create Primary DOS Partition or Logical DOS Drive

Current fixed disk drive: I

Partition	Status	Type	Volume Label	Mbytes	System	Usage
C: I	A	PRI DOS	PRI DOS	32	FAT16	78%
2		PRI DOS		9		22%

Extended DOS Partition already exists

Press Esc to continue

Extended DOS partition created

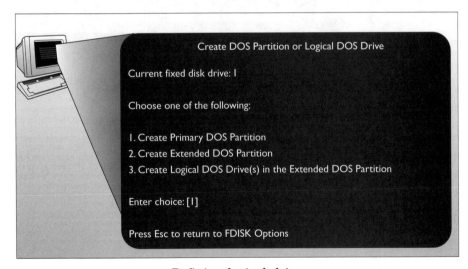

Create DOS Partition or Logical DOS Drive

Current fixed disk drive: I

Choose one of the following:

1. Create Primary DOS Partition
2. Create Extended DOS Partition
3. Create Logical DOS Drive(s) in the Extended DOS Partition

Enter choice: [1]

Press Esc to return to FDISK Options

Defining logical drives

After assigning logical DOS drives to the entire space, press [Esc] to return to the FDISK main menu. Now set the active partition. To do this, select option 2 in the FDISK main menu "Set active partition."

> **NOTE**
>
> Important! The primary partition must be active. Set the primary partition so you can start the PC from there; otherwise you won't be able to load the operating system from the hard drive.

Set the primary partition so you can start the PC from there; otherwise you won't be able to load the operating system from the hard drive.

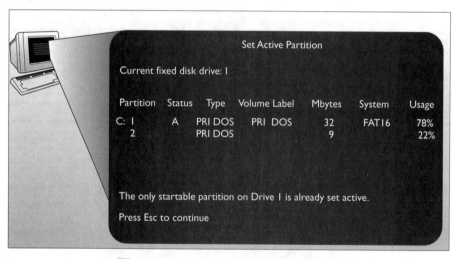

The primary partition must be active

Press [Esc] to return to the main menu. Select item 4 to display the partition table. If you like what FDISK shows you, press [Esc] to exit FDISK and warm boot the computer. This makes the partitioning active.

Working with different operating systems

To work with different operating systems, partition only the part of the hard drive that you want to use for DOS. Use the partitioning programs of the other operating systems to partition the other parts of the hard drive. However, remember that only one operating system can be the active, or boot partition.

Step #6	Format the hard drive.

A hard drive, just like a diskette, must be formatted before it can receive data. In other words, you must give the hard drive a structure that DOS can read. The DOS FORMAT program performs this task. This program should also be on the diskette in drive A:.

Transferring the system files

Switch back to drive A: and start FORMAT. When you format, remember to copy the system files so the hard drive will be able to boot the system and the command interpreter of the operating system can be loaded from the hard drive.

Use the following DOS command:

```
FORMAT C:/S
```

After formatting, DOS displays the formatted capacity of the hard drive on the monitor. This completes the process of formatting the hard drive.

Setting up several partitions

If you set up more than one partition with FDISK in Step #5, then you have logical DOS drives. You must also format these drives. You will have to run FORMAT for each logical drive:

```
FORMAT D:
FORMAT E:
etc.
```

Since the operating system is written to the boot sector of the hard drive and is always located in the primary partition, /s doesn't have to be added to the Format command. You can display the current division of your hard drive at any time. To do this, choose menu option 4 "Display Partition Information" in the main menu of FDISK.

Chapter 11

Section 3

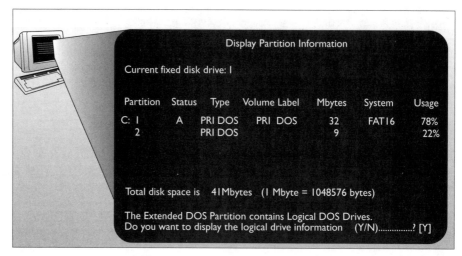

Displayed partition information

Step #7	Test the hard drive.

After formatting the hard drive and copying the system files to it, you should be able to boot the PC from the hard drive. This is the most important test for your newly installed hard drive. Remove the DOS diskette from drive A: and execute a warm boot (press Esc + Alt + Del simultaneously).

Does the PC start up all the way to the system prompt? If it does, then switch off the PC. Wait a couple seconds until the hard drive is quiet, then switch the system back on. Does the PC start up now and go all the way to the system prompt without any errors?

Now see whether you can copy to the hard drive. Create a DOS directory and copy the DOS files from the system diskettes to the directory. Then try to start DOS programs, such as CHKDSK (or SCANDISK), from the hard drive.

If everything runs smoothly, then you've successfully installed the hard drive. If it runs according to your expectations, you can install it in its mounting kit. Switch off the PC, unplug the power cable from the computer, and wait for the hard drive to stop. Then begin physically installing the hard drive.

Step #8	Physically install the hard drive in the PC case.

Before disconnecting the cables, take another look at how they connect to the hard drive. Now install the hard drive in its designated place in the PC case. Avoid any contact between the hard drive circuitry and any metal or other conductors of electricity.

Install the hard drive firmly and securely. Make certain the hard drive isn't tilted at an angle, regardless of whether you use a mounting kit.

The hard drive is installed

Now reconnect all the cables and try out the hard drive again before closing the PC case. Testing the hard drive again is worth all the trouble. If you've overlooked something, you'll have to open the PC case again. So, close the case and tighten the screws only when you're absolutely certain that everything is 100% satisfactory. This completes the installation of the MFM hard drive.

If you want to install two hard drives at the same time, or if you're adding a second hard drive to an MFM hard drive, the most critical points have to do with setting the "Drive Select" jumper and the cable connections.

The following basic rules usually apply:

387

If the hard drives are connected to the controller by a 34-pin control cable that has a straight end and a twisted end, set the "Drive Select" jumper to the same position on both drives.

If the "Drive Select" jumper is inserted in the first logical position (position 0 or 1), then connect the first drive to the straight end of the cable and the second drive to the twisted end. If the jumper is in the second logical position (1 or 2), then the first drive connects to the twisted end and the second drive connects to the straight end.

If the drives are connected to a control cable with two straight cable ends, set the "Drive Select" jumper to the first position (0 or 1) on the first drive and set it to the second position (1 or 2) on the second drive. It doesn't matter to which plug the first hard drive is connected.

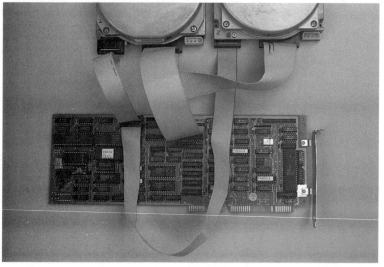

Connecting the second hard drive to the twisted cable

Mark the first and second drive according to this rule and make the connection to the 34-pin control cable. Then connect the 20-pin data cable of the first hard drive to the connector on the controller closest to the control cable connector. Then connect the 20-pin data cable of the second hard drive to the free connector.

First test

After that, enter both hard drives in the CMOS RAM. Enter the first hard drive under drive C: and enter the second hard drive under drive D:.

If one of the two drives is already completely installed, test whether you can still boot from the first hard drive after connecting and setting up the second hard drive. If you can, then both drives are probably cabled correctly.

Perform a low-level format as described in Step #4. Remember to select the second hard drive; otherwise you'll lose all the data on the first hard drive.

FDISK also recognizes the existence of a second hard drive and offers another option. Option 5 makes it possible to direct FDISK activities to the first or second drive.

Use the FORMAT D: command to format the second hard drive. Since you can only boot the PC from C:, you cannot make the second hard drive bootable. This means that you don't have to specify the parameter "/s" when you type FORMAT.

> **NOTE**
>
> When you physically install the second hard drive, be careful not to mix up the cables. This can happen more quickly than you think. It never hurts to take a second look.

RLL hard drive installation

Refer to the first part of this section for information about preparing to install. The preparations for installing an MFM hard drive are almost identical for installing RLL hard drives.

Since RLL hard drives are able to accept higher data densities, they are a little more sensitive to changes in temperature.

Therefore, when you install an RLL hard drive, make sure it is warm from running. Connect it to the PC power supply and let it run for about 30 minutes. Then read this section so you'll know what's in store for you.

Installation procedures for MFM and RLL hard drives are similar in many ways. In this section we'll concentrate on showing and explaining the differences involved in installing RLL hard drives.

Chapter 11 Section 3

389

To avoid repetition, we'll refer to our explanations listed earlier in this section whenever appropriate.

Hard drive installation in 9 steps:

We have also divided the instructions for installing RLL hard drives into steps. Here is an overview of those steps.

1. Set the "Drive Select" jumper on the hard drive

2. Connect the hard drive to the controller and the power-supply

3. The controller has its own BIOS

4. Set up the hard drive

5. Low-level format

6. Partition the hard drive

7. Format the hard drive

8. Test the hard drive

9. Physically install the hard drive in the PC case

Steps #1-2	Setting the "Drive Select" jumper and cable connections.

There are no differences in setting the "Drive Select" jumper or in making the cable connections between the hard drive and the controller.

Connect the cables exactly as you would with an MFM hard drive. The data and control cables are identical. Supply the drive with power the same way, too.

Regarding the controller, remember that you're installing an RLL controller (i.e., a controller that's capable of writing hard drives with 26 sectors per track). As you'll see in the next step, there are major differences in the controllers of the two hard drives (MFM vs. RLL).

Step #3	Answering the controller BIOS

This step isn't a part of MFM hard drive installation. For MFM installation, you simply must enter the proper drive type in the CMOS of the computer. However, for an RLL hard drive system, you must consider a few points.

RLL hard drive controllers come with their own BIOS or without a BIOS. If you're using a controller that doesn't have its own BIOS, enter the hard drive parameters in CMOS SETUP, as you would with an MFM hard drive. However, if the controller does have a BIOS, you must enter the hard drive parameters there.

First, determine which kind of RLL hard drive controller you have. If the hard drive and controller are cabled correctly, reconnect the PC to the monitor, keyboard, and power supply. Insert a bootable diskette into drive A: and switch on the PC.

Since you've just connected a hard drive that is unknown to your PC, the PC BIOS will produce an error message at first, indicating a hard drive or controller error. We presented a few possible error messages earlier in this section. Don't let this bother you. Follow the instructions on the screen, all the way to booting from the inserted DOS diskette.

Now enter the DOS DEBUG command. The PC will respond by displaying a blinking hyphen under the last command line. Use the DEBUG command with an address to be entered later to try to call the Controller BIOS. To do this, enter the following after the blinking hyphen:

```
g=c800:5
```

Then press (Enter).

If this doesn't result in immediate activity on the monitor, do a warm boot by pressing (Esc) + (Alt) + (Del). Then repeat Step 3 and enter the following instruction after the hyphen:

```
g=cc00:5
```

Press (Enter) again. If nothing happens a second time, you can assume the hard drive controller doesn't have its own BIOS. Reboot the PC and continue with Step 4.

391

If you were able to call the controller BIOS, you'll see something happening on the screen. Usually the BIOS routines will branch to a selection menu on the screen, from which you can select other options. The important menu items are the ones for starting subroutines for determining hard drive parameters or the low-level format. We'll tell you how to use them shortly.

Step #4	Use CMOS SETUP to setup the hard drive.

Setting up the hard drive varies, depending on whether you were able to call the controller BIOS.

In this case, set up the hard drive in CMOS SETUP as we described earlier in this section for MFM hard drives. You don't have to worry about the CMOS specifications for sectors and size of the hard drive type you entered. The RLL controller automatically formats 26 sectors, which provides 50% more hard drive capacity than the capacity specified for 17 sectors. However, you don't need to worry about this. Follow the instructions for Step #3 from the section on MFM drives earlier in this section.

If you were able to call the controller BIOS in Step #3, select the option for setting hard drive parameters from the menu. This option is often called "Change Parameters." Give the number of cylinders and heads. Frequently this option displays selection tables for different hard drive types which you can browse through. Select a hard drive that matches the number of heads and cylinders of the one you're installing. You must save your selection, which usually causes the PC to reboot.

Most controller BIOSes will also write an entry into the CMOS. Frequently the controller BIOS will set type "1." While this corresponds only to a 10 Meg hard drive, the purpose of the entry is to tell the system that a hard drive is connected. Other controllers would like to enter "NOT INSTALLED" for the hard drive. Sometimes RLL controllers come with documentation that includes information about this entry.

Once you save the entry about the type and reboot the computer, you're finished setting up the hard drive in the controller BIOS.

Step #5	Partition the hard drive.

The procedure for low-level formatting the hard drive also varies, depending on which result you get from Step #3:

If the controller doesn't have its own BIOS, format the hard drive the same way you would format an MFM hard drive. Refer to the information on MFM hard drives earlier in this section.

After communicating the hard drive parameters to the controller, call DEBUG again with the address in Step #3 to make the controller BIOS active. Now select an option called "Low-Level-Format" or "Preformat Harddisk" or "Initialize Harddisk".

A brief dialog with the BIOS routine follows. At the end of the dialog, low-level formatting occurs. The formatting routine works through the specified cylinders and heads. If low-level formatting is successful, you'll see one of the following messages:

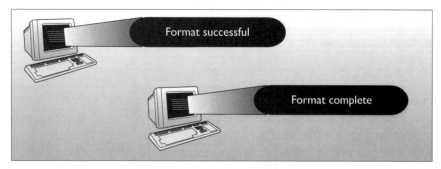

Format successful

Format complete

This concludes the initialization of the hard drive.

Steps #6 - 9	Partition, format, test and mount the hard drive.

These steps are the same ones used for an MFM hard drive. Follow the instructions relating to the MFM hard drives earlier in this section.

If any errors occur, retrace the steps; maybe you overlooked something.

Installing a second RLL hard drive is like installing a second MFM hard drive. Refer to the information on the MFM hard drives earlier in this section for more information.

SCSI hard drive installation

Some of the hard drive information we've talked about in this chapter applies to SCSI drives. However, there are several important differences to installing a SCSI hard drive.

One important difference is the flat ribbon cable between the hard drive and the controller. Since the SCSI interface is fundamentally different from the ST-506 interface (which supports the MFM, RLL, and ESDI hard drives we've been discussing), the SCSI also requires a different cable to the controller.

A typical SCSI cable consists of 50 lines and integrates control lines and data lines in a single cable. The cable is straight (i.e., it doesn't have any twisted ends typical of the other hard drive cables).

Hard drive installation in 9 steps

We've divided the instructions for installing a SCSI hard drive into steps. The following summarizes those steps.

1. Set the "Drive Select" jumper on the hard drive

2. Connect the hard drive to the controller and power supply

3. Set up the hard drive

4. Partition the hard drive

5. Format the hard drive

6. Test the hard drive

7. Physically install the hard drive in the PC case.

Low-level format isn't required

If you already have experience installing another hard drive type (MFM or RLL), remember this overview of the steps for installing a SCSI hard drive doesn't include low-level formatting.

NOTE

SCSI hard drives come from the manufacturer already prepared. The SCSI controller recognizes the physical parameters of the hard drive by means of identification marks already placed on the hard drive. Check with your manufacturer for details, and whether you need to low-level format your SCSI drive.

One belief is that SCSI hard drives shouldn't, under any circumstances, be low-level formatted by normal means. According to this belief, performing a low-level format would destroy the drive ID entries that are so vital to the SCSI controller. If this occurs, the hard drive would be useless.

Step #1	Set the "Drive Select" jumper on the hard drive.

You distinguish the various devices that a SCSI controller can manage by a SCSI-ID that you set on the device. This SCSI-ID is basically an address where the device (in our case, the hard drive) can be found, and controlled.

These addresses range from 0 to 7 because the SCSI controller can manage up to eight different devices. Set the address on the hard drive either through jumpers or a set of DIP switches. If you're installing the hard drive as the first, and only SCSI device in the computer, set the SCSI-ID to "0".

Step #2	Connect the hard drive to the controller and power supply.

Like other hard drive systems, this one is also connected to the controller by a flat ribbon cable. As we mentioned, the SCSI interface uses only a wide 50-line cable that combines the control and data wires.

The cable has 50-pin post connectors on both ends. Connect the cable to the controller so the labeled side of the cable with PIN 1 connects to the 50-pin connector strip on the controller. Connect the cable to the hard drive in the same way.

The same rule applies to connecting with the hard drive. Usually Pin 1 of the hard drive connector is on the inside, next to the power connector. Ordinarily Pins 1 and 2 or 49 and 50 on the hard drive electronic circuitry are also labeled.

Chapter
11
Section
3

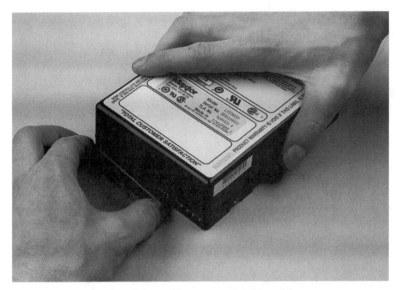

Attaching the 50-pin SCSI cable

After making all the cable connections between the hard drive and controller, insert the controller in a free 16-bit slot on the motherboard.

Supply the hard drive with power the same way you would for all other hard drive systems. Plug in the drive to a free power connection from the power supply. The plug and socket are "keyed" (designed to fit snugly), so it's impossible to plug them in the wrong way unless you use force.

Step #3	Set up the hard drive.

After making all the cable connections, place the hard drive on the PC power supply with the electronic circuitry facing up. Place it on a pad if possible.

Now reconnect the keyboard, monitor, and power supply to the PC. Then insert a bootable DOS diskette in drive A: and switch on the PC. After the autostart routine, the SCSI BIOS of the hard drive controller starts up. It can take a while for the SCSI controller to find the hard drive and display it on the monitor. In a sense, the hard drive sets itself up on the controller.

Do not set up SCSI hard drives in CMOS SETUP. The correct entry for a SCSI hard drive is "NOT INSTALLED" or "NONE". If a hard drive type happens to be set, the PC displays an error message.

If this happens, be sure to correct the setup entries. We explained how to start SETUP earlier in this section.

If a hard drive isn't entered in CMOS, the PC will load the operating system from the diskette after a message from the hard drive controller.

Steps #4 - 7	Partition, format, test and tighten the screws.

Follow the instructions for installing an MFM hard drive for steps 4 through 7. The steps are identical to the steps for MFM hard drives. If you perform all the steps and no errors occur, you are finished installing the SCSI hard drive.

Installing two SCSI hard drives...

In this case, remember the flat ribbon cable that connects the controller with the drive has two connectors for hard drives, and the SCSI-ID on the second hard drive should be set to "1". The sequence in which you connect the hard drives to the cable doesn't matter to the controller.

You must also run the DOS FDISK and FORMAT programs for the second hard drive. After starting FDISK, be sure to change to the second drive before choosing any other option. Use drive D: for the second drive when you format it; omit the "/s" switch, since you only have to have the system files on the first hard drive (e.g., FORMAT D:).

AT bus hard drive installation

All today's powerful Pentium class PCs use hard drives as their primary storage device. AT bus hard drives are the easiest hard drives to install. This is true as long as the PC motherboard has a BIOS that's familiar with the parameters of the AT bus hard drive you're installing or has a "user defined" hard drive type. We'll discuss this in more detail later in this section.

The installation procedure is basically the same procedure described in the section on installing an MFM hard drive. However, there is no low-level formatting. Because of this, you also don't need any special initialization programs; all the necessary utilities are part of the operating system.

The following list summarizes the installation steps involved. This first part talks about installing one hard drive. We'll cover installing a second AT bus hard drive in a separate section.

397

1. Set the Master/Slave jumper on the hard drive

2. Connect the hard drive to the controller and power supply

3. Set up the hard drive in CMOS SETUP

4. Partition the hard drive

5. Format the hard drive

6. Test the hard drive

7. Physically install the hard drive in the PC case

Again, we assume that you've already opened the PC case and that you have unplugged the power cable from the computer.

Step #1	Set the Master/Slave jumper on the hard drive.

Except for SCSI hard drives, all the other hard drive types we've discussed require setting the "Drive Select" jumper on the hard drive. AT bus hard drives work according to a different principle. We've discussed the Master/Slave principle in Section 2.

Generally, AT bus hard drives are preset as "masters without slaves" at the factory. This means the drive is informed, by the jumper configuration, that it is the "master drive" and the only drive.

Unfortunately, the jumpers are not uniformly labeled. Each manufacturer uses its own labels, so it's impossible for us to provide a general description of the jumper positions (see photo on the following page).

NOTE

AT bus hard drives made by Seagate also have a jumper that regulates the function of the control LED on the hard drive. This jumper keeps the LED switched off. You have to set the jumper if you want the LED on the drive or case to go on when the drive is busy. Usually the jumper is labeled "ACT".

You can usually accept the default settings for the first and only hard drive.

398

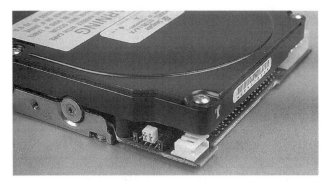

Seagate drives have the jumpers on the side

Step #2	Connect the hard drive to the controller and power supply.

There are three peculiarities about AT bus hard drive cables that clearly differentiate them from regular hard drive cables. First, AT bus cables are wider and have 40 lines, while other hard drives use 34-line cables. Secondly, AT bus hard drive cables combine control and data lines in a single cable. Thirdly, AT bus hard drive cables are straight. You won't find any twisted cables on an AT bus hard drive cable.

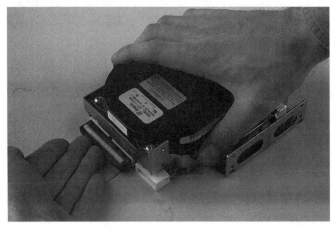

Connecting the cable

Chapter
11
Section
3

399

The cable connects to both controller and hard drive with the labeled side of the cable adjacent to Pin 1 of the contact strips. It isn't possible to plug in the cable incorrectly. Remember to find a free power cable to connect the hard drive to the power supply. The wrap connections are like the ones on other hard drives.

After cabling the hard drive, place it on its back, resting on a nonconducting surface atop the PC power supply. Try it out before physically installing it.

Step #3	Use CMOS SETUP to set up the hard drive.

After making all the cable connections, you can reconnect the PC to the power supply and switch it on.

After the RAM test, your PC will display an error message related to the hard drive. Although the PC is able to find the drive, it discovers the drive hasn't yet been set up. For example, you might see one of the following messages:

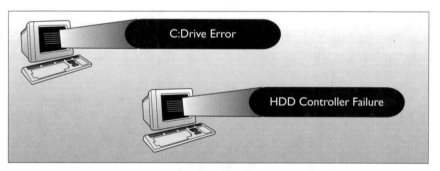

Also, the PC prompts you to start the SETUP program. Follow the instructions on the screen and enter the connected hard drive in CMOS SETUP.

You don't use physical parameters to enter the drive in CMOS SETUP, as you would if you were setting up an MFM or RLL hard drive. Instead you use logical values (i.e., values that are valid for "Translation mode"). Ask about this information when you buy the hard drive. The Appendix also contains a list of hard drive parameters. You will also find AT bus hard drives with the valid values for translation mode.

However, you'll find entries that are suitable only for smaller AT bus hard drives (40 Meg) in the hard drive types known to BIOS. The only way to set up bigger AT bus hard drives is to make your own entry under "User type". Ignore the entries for "Write Compensation" and "Landing Zone" and set them to "0".

After entering the parameters, save the configuration. See the section on installing an MFM hard drive for more information. Instructions on saving are usually displayed.

Try the default types

Often the logical parameters of the hard drive don't correspond to any standard type and there isn't a user defined hard drive type in BIOS either. This is frequently the case with older 286es that have an AWARD BIOS or a PHOENIX BIOS. If this happens to you, try out all the default types that correspond to the values of the hard drive you're installing in memory capacity:

```
capacity in bytes = cylinders * heads * sectors * 512
```

To try out these values, enter the type, save it, and reboot the computer. If the PC boots up without displaying any error messages, you can run the hard drive with the parameters you entered. If the BIOS gives you a drive error or controller failure, you must change the entry.

If this method is also unsuccessful, you can still try to enter parameters for the hard drive that are lower than the correct values. For example, the PC may accept the hard drive if the number of cylinders is smaller, but you use the right number of heads. You'll be able to tell whether you made the right entry when you boot the PC. If the boot process runs smoothly and the operating system can be loaded from the diskette, the proper entry was used. Save this entry and continue with the next step.

However, this last method always results in a hard drive with reduced capacity.

Steps #4 - 6	Partition, format and test the hard drive.

If the PC boots up and goes to the DOS prompt after you set up the hard drive, start FDISK to make the hard drive a logical DOS drive. We discussed using FDISK and FORMAT in the section on using an MFM hard drive as an example. Use the same procedure on the AT bus hard drive. Then use the same method to test the hard drive.

Step #7	Physically install the hard drive in the PC case.

If the hard drive worked smoothly during the test, you can begin physically installing the hard drive. Unplug the power cable and disconnect all the cables to the hard drive.

Do you need a mounting kit?

There's nothing special about installing an AT bus hard drive. It will easily fit into a 3.5-inch mounting bracket on your PC case. However, you'll need a mounting kit to install it in a 5.25-inch box, as well as mounting rails for older cases. You can also buy mounting brackets that screw into the long sides of the hard drives to make them wider.

AT bus hard drive with mounting bracket

Don't use the wrong screws!

Remember to use the right screws (i.e., ensure they're not too long). If you use screws that are even slightly longer, you can bore into the hard drive circuitry with the screw. To be on the safe side, check the length needed for the screw before tightening the screws to the hard drive.

If you own a Seagate hard drive, remember that once the hard drive is physically installed, it no longer has access to the jumper for the "Activity LED" light.

After reconnecting all the cables for the hard drive, controller, and power supply, double-check the cabling. If the operating system loads from the hard drive, you're ready to close the case.

As we mentioned at the beginning of this section, AT bus hard drives are connected to a straight, 40-line cable. It doesn't matter which drive is connected to the cable first. The first hard drive can be connected to the end of the cable and the second one can be connected to the middle of the cable.

Step #1	Determine Master/Slave configuration.

The "Master/Slave configuration" is the deciding factor in distinguishing the first and second hard drive. Set and/or clear small jumpers on the hard drive to make this configuration.

The position of these jumpers varies depending on the manufacturer. For example, Seagate places the jumpers for its 40 to 120 Meg hard drives on the side of the drives. Other manufacturers place the jumpers on the control circuitry, or on the front side, next to the power connection. The labeling on the jumpers also varies.

Therefore, we cannot provide a general description of the correct jumper position. Instead, we can only tell you how to locate this position.

Always configure the first drive (i.e., the hard drive entered as C: in CMOS SETUP) as the "Master Drive". This is the drive from which you boot up the PC. The MASTER jumper might be labeled "MS" or "CD". If there is a second drive under the master, a second jumper informs the drive there is a "Slave" drive. This jumper is often labeled "SP" (Slave Present).

Tell the first hard drive (the master) that it has a second (slave) hard drive. Tell the second drive that it is not a master. In other words, clear the "Master" jumper on the second drive. Then both the first hard drive and the second one will understand the second hard drive is the slave.

Once you understand this principle, you probably won't have any trouble adapting the drives to each other.

Chapter 11

Section 3

403

| Step #2 | Use CMOS SETUP to set up both hard drives |

Enter the second hard drive with its translation mode values in the CMOS table as drive D:. As long as it's possible to make both entries, you won't have any trouble. We'll discuss potential problems later.

After saving these entries, the PC will boot up and try to load the operating system from the disk drive if the first hard drive hasn't already been formatted as the boot drive. If the first hard drive is formatted as the boot drive, the PC will start from drive C:.

| Step #3 | Partition and format the second hard drive. |

After successfully partitioning the hard drive and rebooting, you still must format the second hard drive. Type the following to format your second hard drive:

FORMAT D: [Enter]

Problems with the second AT bus hard drive

NOTE

Be careful with FDISK. We assume the first hard drive is already formatted and that it contains data. If so, be very careful when using FDISK. If the computer has a second hard drive that is already setup, FDISK will display an extra option. "Select next hard drive" as well as to which drive the displayed options refer. Before partitioning, switch to the second hard drive and install a primary DOS partition there.

If you have problems installing a second hard drive, first ensure the second drive works and is free of technical defects.

To do this, connect the (second) hard drive in place of the first (and up to now, only) hard drive and set the jumpers to "Master without Slave". Make the necessary entry in the CMOS and then run both FDISK and FORMAT. If you are able to format the drive without any trouble, you can assume that it is in good working order.

You should not have any problems if both hard drives are from the same manufacturer. This is especially true if both hard drives are the same model.

However, if you're using two different hard drives, you may have problems with the Master/Slave configuration. Usually you won't have any problems combining drives from different manufacturers. Unfortunately, we cannot give you a list of which hard drive types are incompatible and which ones are compatible with each other.

If two drives aren't working together properly, although everything is properly cabled and the Master/Slave setting is correct, the cause isn't necessarily the hard drive models. There can be other causes.

Often two hard drives that won't work together on a specific motherboard, work fine when connected to another motherboard. However, the first motherboard may be able to work with two other hard drives.

We are not aware of the technical reasons for two hard drives not being able to work together. Sometimes the only way to solve the problem is to replace one of the hard drives with another compatible model.

Occasionally a pair of hard drives won't work together unless a particular drive is "Master". As soon as you try to make this drive the "Slave", the combination no longer works. So, if you find a particular combination of hard drives that works, stick with it.

The System BIOS can also cause problems. As we mentioned, normally you can set up only larger AT bus hard drives with the user defined setup entry. You use type 47 to set up the drive (USER TYPE). If the second drive also must be entered as type 47, it can place a burden on the BIOS.

New PHOENIX or AWARD BIOS configurations offer two user-defined hard drive types to compensate for this (types 47 and 48). The latest AMI BIOS offers another solution. It's able to distinguish between type 47 for drive C: and type 47 for type D:. Older AMI BIOS configurations cannot make this distinction.

It's easy to determine the capabilities of your BIOS. Start the SETUP program and enter different values under type 47 for drives C: and D:. If BIOS is able to distinguish the two different type 47s, then SETUP will display different parameters for C: and D: under type 47 after you save and reboot. Otherwise, you'll see the same entry for both drives. This means you can set up only one drive as user defined. In this case, you won't be able to avoid entering one of the two drives at a lower capacity, as we described.

Installing a removable disk system

Lately removable disk systems have been making a comeback. First let's talk about the difference between a true removable disk drive and a normal hard drive in a removable frame.

Installing New Components

We'll start with a hard drive in a removable frame. In this case, we're dealing with an ordinary hard drive (e.g., AT bus) that's screwed into a frame. The hard drive is plugged into the back of the frame. The plug looks like the Centronics plug of a printer cable. The hard drive gets both current and data from this plug.

Hard drives in removable frames

The companion to this frame is screwed into a 5.25-inch case. The same connectors that are usually located on a hard drive are on the back of this inner frame. On the inside, these connectors lead to a socket that is the counterpart to the "Centronics plug" on the hard drive. You enter this hard drive in CMOS SETUP, as you would a normal hard drive, and the installation procedure is also the same. AT bus hard drives are usually in removable frames because they are so flat.

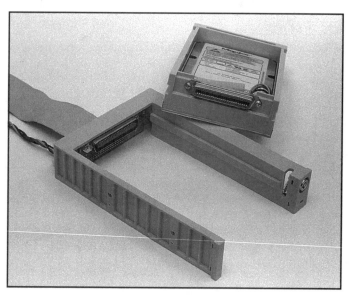

AT bus hard drive in a removable frame

You can also pull out the removable frame and replace it with another hard drive in a different removable frame. You should always use the same kind of hard drive; otherwise you must continually change the CMOS entry.

It's also possible to install a true removable disk system. While you remove the entire drive from the computer with the hard drives that come in removable frames, removable disk systems change only the data disks. This is similar to using diskettes that have a 40 Meg capacity.

Removable hard drives are SCSI devices

The actual drive is a SCSI device controlled by a SCSI controller. All you need is a simple SCSI controller, since the removable hard drives are quite slow. Since SCSI devices don't have to be set up in CMOS, this system can coexist with, for example, two AT bus hard drives connected to a combination controller. The System BIOS and the SCSI BIOS won't conflict with one another. Installation is identical to that of a SCSI hard drive.

Using utility programs

You should use one of the following programs only when you can't perform a low-level format on a hard drive using DEBUG, an integrated BIOS routine, or one of the low-level format programs, and you know that no defects exist in the hardware.

The two most popular utility programs for installing hard drives are Speedstor from Storage Dimensions and Disk Manager from Ontrack. You can use either program to install almost all hard drives.

Both programs contain the data for several hard drives and you can enter the hard drive parameters. We think that Speedstor is the more flexible of the two programs since it is user-friendly and has a larger variety of hard drives. We'll discuss both in this section.

Manual or automatic?

Both programs can automatically perform all the necessary steps to complete a DOS format in a single pass. This includes low-level formatting, setting up partitions, and creating a device driver. However, you can also perform each of these steps manually. It's usually better to do this because you can use the device drivers the software generates only when it's impossible to set up the hard drive correctly in the usual way.

Chapter
11
Section
3

407

Chapter 11

Instead of discussing SpeedStor in detail, we'll briefly explain how to use this program. We'll assume that you've connected the hard drive and entered it correctly in the CMOS. Boot the PC from a diskette and insert the Speedstor program diskette in the disk drive.

Main menu

After you start SSTOR.EXE (or HARDPREP.EXE if you have an older version of Speedstor), the Speedstor main menu appears. Select the "TYPE" option from the main menu to display a selection list of hard drives sorted by the manufacturer. Try to find your hard drive model and select it. Speedstor then returns to the main menu. The parameters of the hard drive type you selected appear in the data line.

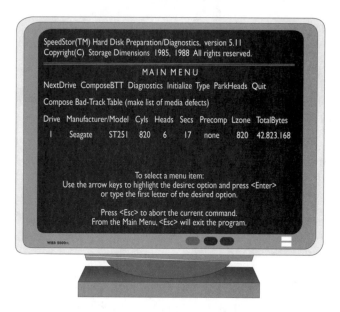

The Speedstor main menu

Speedstor then prompts you for the disk drive number. After you select "DRIVE ONE", a list of several hard drive manufacturers appears on the screen.

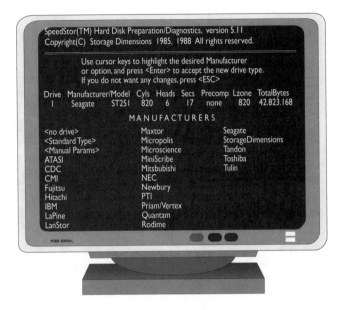

Move the pointer to the appropriate manufacturer (our example selected "NEC") and select it by pressing Enter. Speedstor then displays another selection menu listing the various models of hard drives from this manufacturer. This list could be several screen pages in length-use Pg Up and Pg Dn to scroll through the list. Select the proper hard drive model (we selected model D5146).

Now select "Initialize". Speedstor goes to the initialization menu and waits for your input. To low-level format the complete hard drive, highlight the "StandardInit" option. After that, SpeedStor prompts you for more information and gives you the option of entering bad sectors on the hard drive in the BTT (Bad Track Table). If your hard drive came with such a list of bad tracks, enter them here. Another security prompt appears at the end of the dialog and then the program begins running.

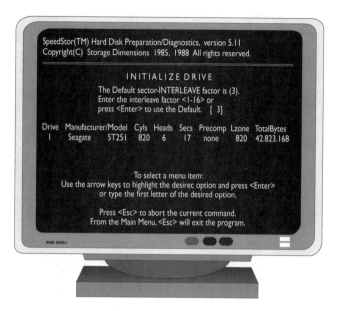

SpeedStor(TM) Hard Disk Preparation/Diagnostics, version 5.11
Copyright(C) Storage Dimensions 1985, 1988 All rights reserved.

INITIALIZE DRIVE
The Default sector-INTERLEAVE factor is (3).
Enter the interleave factor <1-16> or
press <Enter> to use the Default.   [3]

Drive	Manufacturer/Model		Cyls	Heads	Secs	Precomp	Lzone	TotalBytes
1	Seagate	ST251	820	6	17	none	820	42.823.168

To select a menu item:
Use the arrow keys to highlight the desirec option and press <Enter>
or type the first letter of the desired option.

Press <Esc> to abort the current command.
From the Main Menu, <Esc> will exit the program.

Cancel the program in case of error

Under normal circumstances (i.e., if the hardware is all right), the program will process all the cylinders. The program begins at the top, works its way down, and then goes back up. This process shouldn't take more than 5 minutes per 20 Meg of hard drive capacity. If the program takes a long time, this means something is wrong. Press (Esc) to cancel the program.

After successful initialization, Speedstor displays the message "Initialization successful". Select "Quit" to return to the DOS prompt so you can continue working with FDISK and FORMAT.

Speedstor also accepts manual entries

If the hard drive model you're installing doesn't appear in Speedstor's list, you can also enter your hard drive parameters manually. Speedstor has an option called "ManualParams" for this purpose. However, don't make any entries here unless you are certain they match those of your hard drive. Low-level formatting a hard drive with the wrong values can damage the hard drive, especially if the values are too.

410

Creating a device drive

If none of the previous procedures work, because BIOS doesn't support the drive type, you must have Speedstor generate a device driver that will make the hard drive usable in DOS, provided the device driver is loaded at system startup.

Use the "INSTALL" command to start this program routine from the Speedstor diskette. The program will then determine your partition sizes for the hard drive in a dialog with you. Then it initializes, partitions, and formats the hard drive. The program creates a "HARDRIVE.SYS" device driver and enters it in the CONFIG.SYS file. This device driver manages the hard drive independently of the system BIOS.

However, setting up a hard drive that isn't supported by BIOS is very complicated. You must experiment with different solutions. Doing this requires a lot of experience so you can interpret the error messages correctly or the aberrant behavior of the PC system in this situation. Quite often you will fail and the entire undertaking becomes a frustrating experience. The best way to avoid these difficulties is to be properly prepared.

DiskManager also provides a number of hard drive models for your selection. However, these are only models manufactured by Seagate. You can also use DiskManager to process hard drives from other manufacturers as long as the parameters match those of the Seagate drive you specify.

To run only the routine for low-level formatting, start the program from the diskette by entering:

dm [Enter]

The opening provides a list of Seagate hard drive models. Choose the model most like the one you're installing as the default. Later DiskManager gives you an opportunity to change these default settings manually.

DiskManager

Now save these hard drive parameters and change from the "Main Menu" to the "Initialization Menu" to low-level format the hard drive.

Generating a driver for the hard drive

You can also manually enter parameters. Run DiskManager by entering:

dm/m [Enter]

This enters the "Initialization Menu" after you select the hard drive model. From here, you can change the default drive parameters, which allows you to process a hard drive, not made by Seagate, with different data. Select the "Configuration Menu." Select the Seagate model that most closely matches your own hard drive. DiskManager then gives you the option of changing each hard drive parameter.

INSTALLING TAPE DRIVES

Because hard drive capacities are constantly increasing, backing up data to diskettes can be a problem. It's almost impossible to back up 100 to 200 Meg of data onto diskettes, mainly because of the time this process would take. So tape drives are becoming more popular for data backups.

In Chapter 8 we talked about the different kinds of tape drives. We won't repeat those differences here. However, along with these technical considerations, there are also practical considerations that can influence your decision for or against a particular tape drive.

Additional adapter required

If you decide to install a floppy tape backup drive, it's important to know whether one or two drives are connected to the diskette controller. If two drives are already connected, you will need an additional controller since you can no longer connect the tape drive directly to the diskette controller.

However, purchasing a SCSI tape backup drive makes sense only if you already have a SCSI controller, or you intend to hook up other SCSI devices in the future.

What you will need

To install the drive, you'll need a free 5.25-inch mounting unit, and an unused power connector from the PC power supply (or a Y power splitter cable). Before buying a tape drive, determine what comes with it.

A data cable for connecting to the controller is almost always part of the package. Sometimes, it may be too short, which can be especially troublesome for owners of tower cases. The package doesn't always include backup software, even though it's impossible to perform backups from a tape drive.

Finally, determine whether you will need mounting rails to install the drive in an unused 5.25-inch drive bay in your case.

413

Installing a floppy tape drive

The procedure for installing a floppy tape drive differs, depending on the number of connected disk drives. You won't have to change any settings or jumpers on the drive. You can install it directly into the case.

How many drives are connected?

If only one disk drive is connected, you can use the other unused connection for the second disk drive to hook up the tape drive to the diskette controller. Connect the floppy cable to the tape drive so the notched side of the contact strap covers the labeled side of the floppy cable. Connect the tape drive to an unused power cable from the power supply as well.

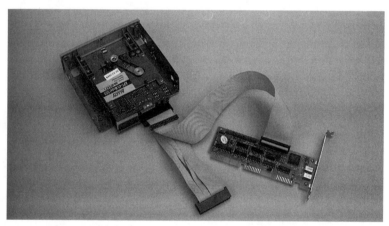

The floppy model tape drive on the straight cable

It's not necessary to set up the tape drive since the system doesn't assign a logical drive letter to the device. This fact alone explains why it is impossible to copy to a tape drive in the normal way (e.g., with the DOS COPY command). To DOS, the tape drive doesn't even exist. The software supplied with the tape drive, and only this software, is able to find the drive at a port address specified in the software configuration.

When two disk drives are already connected

In this case, you won't be able to hook up the tape drive right away, because the diskette controller is completely occupied by two disk drives. There are two ways to solve this problem.

First, you could replace the controller for a model that can manage more than two disk drives. The advantage of this solution lies in the fact that you aren't filling up any additional expansion slots.

Card without settings

Second, you could use an interface card. Plug it into an unused slot and use a straight flat ribbon cable to connect it to the diskette controller. The labeled side of the cable goes on Pin 1 of the connector pin strip. The interface card has a 34-pin connector strip for the cable to the disk drives and for the flat ribbon cable to the tape drive. You cannot change or make any settings on this card.

Frequently these interface cards have a socket for a branch connection from the power supply. It is used to supply power to an external device. If you have already connected the tape drive to the power supply, don't make another connection here. This could destroy the card or the drive.

Installing the backup software

After connecting the tape drive to the controller and the power supply, you're ready to install the backup software. Installation will vary depending on the product you are installing. Usually the installation diskette has a file called INSTALL or SETUP that you call to start an automatic installation routine. Some tape drive models use data compression. This means the software is able to store either 120 Meg of uncompressed data, or 240 Meg of compressed data on one tape. The software will use data compression only if you specify this during installation.

After you finish installing the software on the hard drive and insert a tape cartridge, you can usually determine whether the tape drive will be addressed by simply calling the tape backup software formatting a tape. Frequently a message appears before the main menu, such as "Waiting for tape...", while the tape drive rewinds the tape to its beginning. You can hear the drive working.

Chapter
11
Section
3

415

Determining a successful installation

Format a tape to determine whether installation was successful. Usually there is an option for this purpose in the "Utilities" menu item. For example, formatting a tape could take about 60 minutes for a 120 Meg cartridge. If the drive formats the tape completely, you can almost assume that everything is all right-at least between the backup software and the tape drive.

However, the purpose of the device is to back up data from the hard drive. So first try to back up the DOS directory to the tape. Options for backing up to the tape are called "Backup" options while the ones for restoring are called "Restore" options. Learn a little about the software and do the following test:

1. Create a TEST directory on the hard drive.

2. Copy data from another directory to this directory.

3. Back up the TEST directory to an empty tape.

4. Delete the contents of TEST from the hard drive.

5. Now restore the backup.

6. Check the restored contents of the TEST directory.

If this test was successful, you're finished installing the tape drive.

Installing a SCSI tape drive

Another, more expensive model of tape drive works with a SCSI interface. You can run such a SCSI tape drive on any controller that conforms to the SCSI standard. This means that you can operate a SCSI drive along with hard drives, scanners, and other SCSI devices from a single controller. The number of SCSI devices you can connect to a SCSI controller justifies its high price.

Here is an overview of the installation steps:

1. Confirm settings on the tape drive

2. Connect cables

3. Install backup software

4. Install device driver in the CONFIG.SYS file

5. Format and test a tape

6. Mount the tape drive in the PC case

Step #1	Confirm settings on the tape streamer.

As you'll remember from our discussion about SCSI hard drives, a SCSI device requires only a valid SCSI-ID to be recognized by the controller. When setting the ID, it's important to know how many SCSI devices are already connected, or which identification numbers between 0 and 7 are still free.

Suppose that you already have one SCSI device running on your computer, such as a hard drive. During installation, this device is assigned a SCSI ID of "0". Then you would assign an ID of "1" to the drive when you install it. You can make this setting on the tape drive with jumpers or DIP switches.

Step #2	Connect the cables.

After that, connect the drive to the same cable that connects the first SCSI device to the controller. Connect it so the labeled side of the 50-line SCSI cable is covered by Pin 1 of the SCSI connector on the tape drive. The drive also gets a power connection directly from the power supply.

Step #3	Install the backup software.

You cannot access the tape drive without special backup software. Backup software is either bundled with the tape drive or you can buy it separately.

Now follow the instructions in the user manual for installing the software on your hard drive. Backup programs that include the drive may also install the device driver necessary for addressing the tape drive and make changes to the CONFIG.SYS file. In such cases, skip Step #4.

Chapter

11

Section

3

Step #4	Install device driver in the CONFIG.SYS file.

To be able to address the tape drive from the SCSI interface, you must enter a device driver in the CONFIG.SYS file that will be loaded into resident memory at every system start. This driver file comes on diskette either with the tape drive or the SCSI controller.

You have to copy the driver somewhere on the hard drive also. It's best to copy it to the same directory as the backup software and enter the complete search path. Depending on the product, the driver could have a different name. Make the necessary entry in the CONFIG.SYS file, in the root directory of your hard drive, by adding the following line:

```
DEVICE=C:\[Path specification]\[Device driver name]
```

Only by installing this driver and resetting the system can you access the tape drive using the backup software.

Step #5	Format and test a tape.

After formatting a tape, it presents itself during the system start. At the same time, the computer accesses the tape drive and you will see the control LED light up.

Now insert a new tape cartridge and start up the backup software. First try to format the tape. Usually you will find the right option under "Utilities". After you select this option, the tape drive should start moving the tape. It may need to rewind to find the beginning of the tape.

This could take a few minutes, depending on the size of the tape. If the tape drive formats the tape without any problems or error messages, everything should be fine. Perform the test described earlier in this section.

However, if you have formatting problems not attributable to using the wrong tape, then you didn't install the drive correctly. Usually the problem lies with the configuration of the backup software. Check the configuration again using your manuals. Generally, you'll also find a list of error messages and their meanings in the manual.

Step #6	Mount the tape drive in the PC case.

After testing, you are finally ready to fasten the drive to the PC case. It fits into a 5.25-inch mounting unit, just like disk drives. Check whether the tape drive works a second time before closing the PC case.

External tape drives

Although becoming less popular, we should nevertheless talk about installing external tape drives. The basic difference between an external and an internal backup drive is that external devices either have their own power supply, independent of the PC power supply, or they have to be supplied with power from the data cable.

Older external tape drives usually come with their own power supply. Newer models come with a separate controller card. The controller card has a female, 25-pin socket for the tape drive connector cable.

The controller card plugs into an unused slot on the motherboard, and must also be hooked up to an available power supply line from the power supply. You usually won't need to make any settings on the card; the devices are set by default.

An example of an external tape drive

Hardware installation before software installation

You may have address problems or other trouble with other cards in the PC. In these instances, you can use jumpers to change the hardware configuration of the card. Please refer to your manual for more information. Remember that making changes to the hardware means changing the software as well.

After cabling the PC and the streamer, install the backup software on the hard drive. Do the same test we described earlier in this section.

INSTALLING A CD-ROM DRIVE

It's easy to install a CD-ROM drive. A CD-ROM drive is connected to its own controller card or to a sound card that already has the adapter (e.g., Sound Blaster 32 from Creative Labs). This adapter is usually part of the CD-ROM drive package. After connecting the drive to the adapter, you must also link a device driver to the CONFIG.SYS file so you can address the CD-ROM drive like a DOS drive.

Here are the necessary steps:

Step #1	Install controller card.

The controller card usually doesn't require any settings. It's often impossible to make any settings to the controller card. Insert the controller card, as is, into a free slot on the motherboard.

Step #2	Connect the cables.

Now connect the controller card to the CD-ROM drive with the flat ribbon cable. Use the connection side labeled "1" on the adapter card and the CD-ROM drive to connect with the labeled side of the flat ribbon cable. You must also connect the CD-ROM drive to the PC power supply using a free power line. Often you have to use a Y-power splitter cable because there are no more free cables on the power supply.

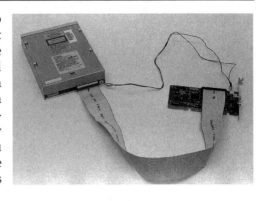

Step #3	Add device driver to CONFIG.SYS

Now copy the supplied software to a directory on the hard drive. Next enter the complete search path of the device driver for the drive in the CONFIG.SYS file. Please refer to the installation manual for information about entering the search path, including information about the entry and any extra parameters.

Step #4	Configure DOS (if necessary).

When you enter the device driver in the CONFIG.SYS file, you also determine which logical drive label DOS uses to address the CD-ROM drive. If this logical drive letter is "greater" than "E:", you must also add the line LASTDRIVE=z before the device driver in CONFIG.SYS. Otherwise, DOS will recognize only drive letters A: to E:.

Step #5	Test CD-ROM drive.

If all the settings are correct and the driver has been installed correctly, nothing else can go wrong. Reset the PC and check the monitor for error messages. Insert a CD and display the directory using the DOS DIR command and the drive letter you assigned to the CD-ROM drive. For example, if E: is your CD-ROM drive, type the following:

```
DIR E:  [Enter]
```

Chapter

11

Section

3

421

If that doesn't work, check the cable connections. Also, look at the device driver in the CONFIG.SYS file.

Step #6	Physically install drive in the PC case.

If the drive functions properly, you're almost finished. All you have to do is physically install the drive. When you install the CD-ROM drive, follow the same procedure we described for installing disk drives.

MOTHERBOARD

In this section we'll discuss the motherboard and the components installed on it. Be very careful when working on or with the motherboard; most importantly, take your time. Remember, without the motherboard, nothing will run on your PC. Besides, replacing a damaged motherboard is expensive.

You may not need to remove expansion cards or drives from the motherboard when you're working on it. However, you'll have to loosen cables (e.g., to reach the memory sockets). Note

NOTE

Be careful with the pins because they break easily. Avoid all types of shock. Store the processor in a safe place where it won't fall to the floor. When you insert the replacement CPU, make certain to watch the beveled corner of the chip surface with the corresponding marking on the processor socket.

422

the appearance of cable connections and to what it connects before loosening it. Take your time and be careful when you work with the motherboard. The material you're working with is fragile and some of it is quite expensive.

You can usually replace motherboards of generic PCs with each other quite easily. The mounting holes and spacing of the expansion slots have been standardized. Remember you're also replacing the BIOS along with the board. This can, however, lead to some problems.

You won't have any trouble replacing the old motherboard with a new one if the BIOS of the new board isn't older than the BIOS on the old board. This is especially true if both BIOS configurations were made by the same manufacturer.

If each BIOS was made by a different manufacturer, determine whether you'll be able to enter the hard drives on the new board as they were entered on the old board. BIOSes from Phoenix or Award don't have a USER TYPE in every version that allows you to enter the hard drive parameters yourself. If you want to continue running two hard drives, determine beforehand whether the "new" BIOS also allows this distinction between two different user defined entries. If it doesn't allow this distinction, you'll encounter problems with your hard drive configuration.

The new motherboard may also be too fast for some cards. This happens frequently when adapter cards have their own BIOS, such as VGA video cards. For example, some older VGA cards won't run on all 486 motherboards. Not all manufacturers offer a replacement for the video card BIOS. Certain AT bus hard drive controllers can also cause trouble on faster boards. Fortunately, you can easily replace such controllers.

Frequent problems occur when 386 or 486 boards are combined with an old MFM or RLL controller. Remember that problems will probably occur if you use some Western Digital controllers on fast motherboards. Frequently, the hard drives are able to boot up, but may have write errors for no reason at all. This also applies to older MFM or RLL controllers from other companies.

So if you intend to install a new motherboard, determine which problems you'll encounter. We've found that motherboards with NEAT chip sets are especially dangerous. Models with chip sets from Chips & Technologies are very common, especially 386 systems. If you want to save yourself a lot of trouble, don't use these models, especially if you're buying a used board. Buy your motherboard from a dealer. The dealer can always give you qualified advice about any problems you have with the motherboard.

Chapter

11

Section

3

423

Installing or replacing the motherboard

Remember, we're talking about replacing the motherboard with a new one. This is an entirely different task than installing a motherboard in a new case. Keep a notepad handy because you will probably need it. Before talking about the details, we'll summarize the steps involved.

1. Keep a notepad ready

2. Remove the necessary cables

3. Remove expansion cards

4. Remove the old motherboard

5. Add memory chips to the new motherboard and test it (outside the case)

6. Install the new motherboard

7. Test the new motherboard (inside of case)

8. Reconnect cables to case

9. Reinstall expansion cards

10. Reconnect the rest of the cables

11. Make entries in CMOS

12. Test the motherboard again

As you can see, replacing the motherboard involves many steps. Therefore, errors can occur in several places. The following information should help you perform the job properly. We're assuming you're replacing only the motherboard of your PC. We're also assuming that your current peripherals and cards (the same disk drives, hard drives, video cards, and all other expansion boards) will be installed on the new motherboard.

Step #1	Keep a notepad available.

Before you start to take your PC apart, make notes about a couple of things that you will need later.

424

Installing New Components

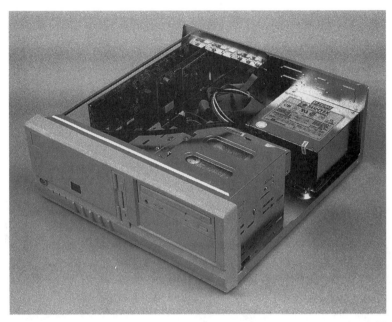

Before taking your PC apart, write down important notes that you'll need later

First, write down the hard drive parameters you entered in the CMOS of the "old" motherboard. It's not enough to know the number of the type that's currently set. Types vary depending on the manufacturer of the BIOS. So write down the parameters that follow the type. This means you'll have to run CMOS SETUP on your computer one more time to copy these parameters. Some BIOS don't display the parameters on the screen immediately; all you'll see is the set type number. In these instances, press [Esc] or [F1] to view a list of the available parameters.

After recording the hard drive parameters, note all the entries for the PC components that you won't be able to activate from memory. After that, exit CMOS SETUP and turn off your computer.

Another bit of advice is to back up your data. Nothing is more frustrating than losing data you've worked hard to compile. Take the time now and back up.

Installing New Components

Step #2	Remove the necessary components.

First, unplug the power cable from the computer, then free the PC of all connected peripherals including the keyboard and the monitor. Draw a diagram with all the cable connections so you can plug everything back in when you're finished installing the motherboard.

You'll also have to remove the thin colored cables from the control LED on the case to the connections on the motherboard. This includes the loudspeaker as well as the Turbo and Reset switches. Remove these cables and move them out of the way.

Then disconnect the cables on the diskette and hard drive controller. Remember where they were plugged in. You should draw a small diagram on your notepad. Combination controllers often have connections for serial and parallel ports as well.

Remove any cables from these two connections also. Remember exactly where and how the cables were plugged in. Flat ribbon cables have a colored side that will help. Try to move these cables out of the way so they don't disturb you while you're working.

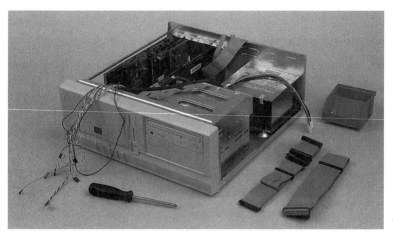

After removing all the cables

Disconnect all the cables that could hinder you while you are working on the expansion cards. Carefully note the position and direction of the connectors if you are not certain how to connect the cables.

Step #3	Remove expansion cards.

Now remove the expansion cards. To do this, loosen the screw from the back of the case. Carefully pull the card from the socket. Put the cards in a safe place away from the case. You don't need to remember the sequence in which the cards were installed; this isn't important on a motherboard with an ISA bus.

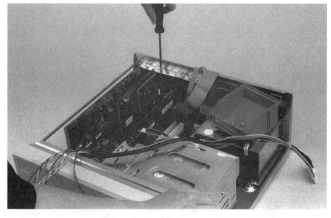

Loosen the screws before removing the expansion card

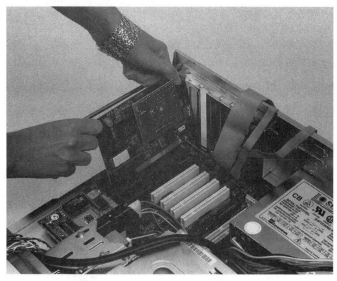

Carefully pull the card from the socket

427

Installing New Components

If you have several multi I/O cards installed, with serial ports connected through narrow 10-line cables, be sure to write down which interface jumper is connected to which card. Also note the devices that are connected to these ports.

Step #4	Remove the old motherboard.

Next, remove the old motherboard. To do this, disconnect the power cables that come from the power supply from the board. Note how they're connected to the motherboard. The three red cables adjacent to each other point to the inside of the board.

Remove the screws holding the board to the bottom of the case

Remove the screws holding the board to the bottom of the case. Two screws are usually located at the upper edge of the board between the keyboard connection and the upper-left corner (but they may be located elsewhere). Unscrew the Phillips head screws carefully and remove them from the holes. Make sure the screw driver doesn't slip and touch something other than the screws.

Make sure that you really have removed all the screws holding down the board. If your PC is in a desktop case, you should be able to move the board about one centimeter to the left, or away from the power supply. Hold the board gently with both hands on the left and right edges underneath the board and try to move it to the left. Don't force the board. Often the plastic spacers get stuck. If you can manage to move the motherboard to the left, you should be able to lift it up out of the sliding rails. Be very careful and gentle when you do this.

428

Older cases, especially hinged cases, don't have sliding rails for the spacers. The spacers are fastened to the bottom of the case. It's almost impossible to get the board out of the case cleanly. There are two ways to do this. First, try to pinch the tips of the spacers together and then pull up the board (difficult, since you can't do it simultaneously with all the spacers) or close the case, turn the computer upside down, and use a sharp knife to cut off the thin plastic disks holding the spacers to the case. Although you'll need to buy new spacers, the board is out of the case. Then simply remove the rest of the spacers from the motherboard slots.

It's much easier to remove the motherboard from mini-towers or upright cases, since you also have access to the back of the motherboard. Many of the mini-towers or uprights allow you to completely remove the bottom of the case. This makes it much easier to remove and install motherboards.

If you managed to remove the motherboard from the case without damaging the spacers, use pliers to remove the spacers from the holes in the motherboard and use them with the new motherboard.

429

Installing New Components

If you try to use the installed memory elements on the new motherboard, remove them from the old motherboard now, before we go on to the next step.

Lift SIP modules (the small miniboards) up and out of their sockets carefully. Using a small thin screwdriver, carefully pry out SIMM modules from the socket. If the modules are fastened on both sides, loosen the clamps and lift out the modules.

Removing SIMMs

DRAM chips must be pulled up out of their sockets carefully without bending or breaking off the legs.

Step #5	Add memory chips to the new motherboard and test it (outside the case).

Before installing your new motherboard in the case, add the necessary memory chips and test it while it's outside of the case. Now install the appropriate memory modules on the new motherboard and check whether all the jumpers or DIP switches are set correctly for the memory size you have chosen.

Check whether all the jumpers or DIP switches are set correctly

Use the technical documentation to make this determination. Be sure you have the correct setting for the display switch, which is a jumper or switch that differentiates between monochrome graphics and color graphics. Always set the switch to color for a VGA card.

Insert and tilt the SIMMs; 2 SIMMs fill up 1 bank in most Pentium-class PCs

Another important switch toggles between external and internal batteries. If the board has an internal battery, you can tell by the blue accumulator that it's soldered directly onto the board next to the keyboard input (other locations are possible).

Chapter 11

Section 3

If so, set the jumper to internal battery. Otherwise, the CMOS won't be able to retain the system configuration after you switch off the computer.

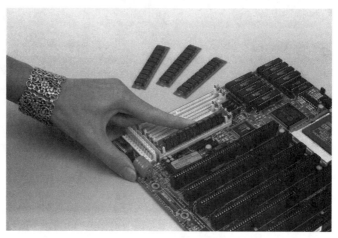

On this "temporary" motherboard you can keep using four 30-pin SIMMs

After checking all the relevant motherboard jumpers, or switch settings, put a cardboard box or similar sturdy support base on the case and then place the motherboard on top of it so you can test the motherboard. To test the motherboard, plug in the power supply cable to the motherboard so the three red cables are in the middle of the board while the only orange or white cable is outside on the upper edge. You can't plug in the cable incorrectly because of its shape.

Black cables are in the center: Connecting the motherboard power supply

After you're certain the motherboard works with the power supply, carefully plug in the video card, reconnect the keyboard and monitor, and plug the power cable back into the power supply of the computer.

When you switch on the power, the new motherboard should display a picture on the screen, if you inserted the memory modules into the motherboard correctly, all the jumpers are set correctly, and the video card also works with the new motherboard.

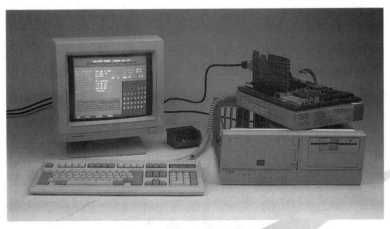

Testing the motherboard

If the motherboard displays a picture, you can assume that it's compatible to the memory modules and the video card. Obviously, you may encounter problems during everyday use. However, you can assume at this point everything is correct. Switch off the power supply and dismantle your test platform.

Now unplug the power cable from the computer power supply also.

NOTE

Electrostatic energy (or static electricity) is capable of damaging computer circuits in some of the components. To prevent damaging them, you'll need to discharge yourself of electrostatic energy before handling the components.

A simple way to do this is to ground yourself. When your power supply is plugged into a three-prong wall outlet, the computer case is grounded as well. To discharge yourself of the electrostatic energy, touch the metal computer case.

433

Step #6	Install the new motherboard.

Before physically installing your new motherboard in the case, check whether the small screw sockets and the screws for the motherboard will also fit in the holes on your new board. You won't need more than two mounting screws. Remove any screws that you don't need from the case, since they could cause ground contact between the case and back of the board.

Find two places where you can connect the new motherboard and remove the rest of the screw sockets.

Now carefully place the board on the sliding rails and try to get the spacers in the proper position. Then move the motherboard about one centimeter to the right toward the power supply. Sometimes the spacers can get caught. Use as little force as possible to free them. If you own a mini-tower or upright this will be easier because you can also reach the board from underneath.

The new motherboard is installed

The motherboard is properly seated when you can move it back and forth without using much force. Find the position in which the screw sockets cover the mounting holes and carefully screw in the mounting screws until you're sure they will hold the motherboard without sliding. Then connect the motherboard to the power supply as described in Step #5. This concludes the physical installation of the motherboard.

Step #7	Test the motherboard.

The purpose of this test is to determine whether the motherboard is in contact with the case in a place where it shouldn't be. If this happens, the board won't even run. Reinstall the video card and reconnect the keyboard and the monitor. Reconnect the power supply and switch on the PC again.

If there is a picture on the monitor, then the test is almost complete. If a picture doesn't appear, and you haven't made any changes to the board since Step #5, you can assume the motherboard is in ground contact somewhere. Carefully disassemble the motherboard and check things over.

The correct memory size should be displayed on the screen. The memory size should be displayed accurately to within 384K. So a PC that counts up to 4096K (4 Meg), but stops at 3712K, is completely normal. However, if the same PC counts only to 1024K, most likely the jumper configuration on the motherboard is incorrect. If the amount of variance between the physically installed memory size and the memory size recognized by the computer isn't greater than 384K, everything is fine.

Don't be surprised if you see your first error messages after the memory test. You're getting the messages because you haven't yet made any entries in the CMOS, and you haven't connected a drive from which you can load the operating system. We'll discuss this shortly.

We're finished with the most important part; the board is in the case and running properly.

Step #8	Reconnect cables to case.

Next, reconnect the connection cable between the motherboard and the control LED on the front of the case. Now is the ideal time, since you won't be able to reach it so easily after everything is installed. Usually the connections are in the lower-left corner of the board, at the bottom.

To avoid mixing up the cables, try to follow their path from the light and button so you find the proper plug.

Use a two line blue (or blue and white) cable with a two-pin jumper to connect the Reset button to the motherboard. The cable is almost always marked "RESET" or "HWRS" (for hardware reset). If you have trouble finding the cable, either

NOTE

This step requires you frequently reach inside the case to do a lot of testing. Take the time to turn off the PC every time you unplug a cable.

Never work inside the case while the PC is still turned on. Ground yourself at regular intervals.

check the documentation of the motherboard, or wait and see what's left over after you finish everything else. The best way to determine whether you used the proper cable is to press the key after switching on the computer (picture must be on the screen). After you press the Reset button the screen clears and the system reboots.

The speaker

This is the easiest connection to find. It's unique because it has four pins. However, only two of the pins are used. For this reason, the speaker cable almost always has a four-pin plug, but only two cables. The connection is usually labeled "SPK" (for speaker).

Power LED and keyboard lock

These two functions are often on a combined connection. Although the connection is five-pin, only four of the pins are used. The plug is also usually combined and five-pin. One position is missing. One of the cables is almost always green. Connect this green cable to the "1" connector pin. After you turn on the computer, this green power LED should light up immediately. If the light doesn't go on, the plug is plugged into the connector strip incorrectly.

What to do with the lock

Sometimes the connection cables aren't five-pin combination plugs. In this case, remember the cable for the power LED is usually green and white. The two cables lead to the two outer pins, with green going to Pin 1. The two-pin cable from the keyboard lock plugs in between, with both pins plugged next to each other. One pin is free. Use the keyboard lock to determine which pin is free.

This cable is easy to find. It's usually three-pin (black-white-orange) but fits into a two-pin connector. The Turbo switch on the board is marked "Turbo SW" or "TB". Depending on whether this switch must be open or closed to set the board to high frequency, it may have come from the factory with a jumper on the connector pins. This sets the PC to a particular frequency.

To switch the system clock, remove the jumper and plug in the three-pin cable from the turbo switch. One line is left over. The only way you can tell whether the switch is working at this point is to watch the monitor during the memory test. In one setting of the switch, the test should run more slowly; otherwise the plug isn't seated properly.

The case connections

Turbo LED

This connection can get complicated if the PC case has a digital display. In this case, the Turbo LED is linked to this display because the displayed megahertz number corresponding with the Turbo switch should be a variable.

Setting the speed display can be dangerous, since it should be set while the computer is running. So there is a great danger of a short circuit when you fumble around with jumpers in a confined area behind the case cover, right above the power switch (its contacts aren't always fully insulated). This could damage individual PC components. A short circuit could even cause critical injuries.

If there is no display, connect the yellow and black cable from the Turbo LED to the Turbo LED connection. The connection is usually labeled "LED" or "TBLED". Since this is a diode, it plugs in only one way. You must experiment to determine the correct one. You must also do the same until the Turbo LED lights up when the PC is running in Turbo, which is its normal frequency.

Chapter

11

Section

3

437

The hard drive LED is usually connected to the hard drive controller instead of the motherboard. Usually the connector cable is red and white or red and black. This cable also plugs in only one way. Almost always, the red cable goes to Pin 1 of the connection on the controller. That should be all the case cables. Let's proceed to the next step.

Step #9	Reinstall expansion cards.

After reconnecting all the cables, you're ready to install the expansion cards. Place the expansion cards in the slots using your best judgment. Remember that with many boards, you can't use all cards in the slot closest to the keyboard connection (usually an 8-bit socket) since the accumulator that powers the CMOS is also there. Normally you can't even insert interface cards there. Avoid touching the accumulator with any expansion cards or connectors.

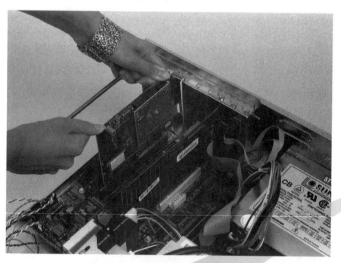

Now the cards are installed

Physically install the expansion cards on the back of the case.

> **NOTE**
>
> Keep a slot free between the cards if possible. This will help maximize heat dispersion. A few motherboards have the memory sockets arranged so poorly that long plug-in cards will touch them. Avoid this at all costs as it can lead to heat damage.

Step #10	Reconnect the rest of the cables.

You still haven't connected the drives to the diskette and hard drive controller. However, this should be simple if you took detailed notes. Let's start with the cable for the disk drives. Either the controller has only one obvious connection for this 34-line cable or it goes in the connection closest to the mounting screw. Connect the labeled side of the cable with Pin 1 of the connector.

If more than one cable from the hard drive leads to the controller, start again by connecting the one closest to the mounting screw. Once again, the labeled side of the cable connects with Pin 1 of the connector.

If there is only one cable leading from the hard drive to the controller, you'll recognize the connector on the controller by its width alone (40-pin or 50-pin). Again, connect Pin 1 with the labeled side of the cable. Finally, connect the hard drive control LED on the case with the appropriate connector on the controller (see Step #8).

The hard drive control LED connected to the controller

Step #11	Make necessary entries in CMOS.

For everything to run smoothly, you must make the necessary entries in CMOS. Reconnect the monitor and keyboard and plug the PC back into the power supply. After ensuring that all the cards are seated properly in their slots and the cable connections are correct, switch the PC back on.

If something goes wrong

If something goes wrong after you switch on the PC (e.g., a picture doesn't appear or the speaker emits a steady "beep"), switch off the computer immediately and try to find the error. Remember that in Step #7 everything was still working.

Remove the cards again and test after each card until you find the error. For more information on finding errors, see Chapter 15.

If the PC displays a screen, shows the startup message, and executes the POST (power-on self-test), it will probably display a series of error messages with a prompt to start CMOS SETUP. Modern BIOS configurations indicate which key to press to start up CMOS SETUP.

Giving the computer the right information

Now start CMOS SETUP. This program is probably a little different than the one from your old computer. First, familiarize yourself with the operation of the program and then enter the correct values for the disk drives, hard drives, graphic cards, etc., in the standard CMOS. Unfortunately, we cannot provide instructions for making the settings because these vary depending on your PC's BIOS configuration.

In Chapter 13 we discuss CMOS settings using an AMI BIOS as an example. If you have questions or problems with CMOS settings, please refer to Chapter 13.

Save again

Modern PC BIOS hardware automatically recognizes the memory size of computers. Normally you cannot make an entry here. If the BIOS displays an error message regarding the memory size ("RAM size error"), but the correct information was already entered after you called CMOS, simply save again. BIOS won't accept the entries until you save this second time.

After you make all the relevant entries and save, your PC should start up from the hard drive and go all the way to the DOS prompt without any error messages.

| Step #12 | Test the motherboard again. |

In the tests, we assume that your PC was in proper working order before you installed the new motherboard and that you were able to load the operating system from the hard drive. Press the Reset button and watch what happens.

Everything is working properly if your PC does the following:

1. Screen turns black after reset
2. VGA/EGA-BIOS message appears (if VGA/EGA card exists)
3. System BIOS message appears
4. Memory test
5. Briefly accesses disk drive A:
6. Briefly accesses disk drive B:
7. Briefly accesses hard drive C:
8. Boot signal from loudspeaker
9. Accesses drive A: (tries to boot)
10. Accesses hard drive C: (tries to boot)
11. Operating system loads from the hard drive

If your PC performs these steps, there shouldn't be any problems. Before closing the case, check the disk drives to see whether they still work. To do this, format a diskette in each drive. Also test the hard drive. Try starting and quitting your programs. Call a directory. Try writing to the hard drive. Call CHKDSK (OR SCANDISK) a few times. In other words, give the PC several different tasks.

If errors occur, or if you see error messages on the screen, turn to Chapter 15 and try to find the problem.

Chapter
11
Section
3

The installation process is complete

Remember, don't tighten the screws on the case until you're convinced that everything is in working order.

Expanding RAM

Expanding the memory available for programs and data is becoming one of the most important and popular ways to upgrade a computer. This has occurred because of falling prices and the increasing demands of new software. Recent developments in semiconductor technology are producing more powerful memory modules that are smaller. So it's possible to install up to 32 Meg of RAM on a normal motherboard. Actually, there are even motherboards with 64 Meg.

Class differences

In Section 2 we discussed memory management of the various processor classes and the related address boundaries in detail. We don't want to repeat this information here. However, this information is important in order to understand the steps relating to memory expansion.

At the beginning of this section we tried to provide some general rules about physical memory installation. The following statements apply to all processor classes. The only differences are in the memory module used and memory expansion through a RAM card.

442

Expanding RAM "on board"

Even old 286 systems could be expanded to a maximum of 4 Meg of memory "on board" (5 Meg in exceptional cases) by adding memory modules. In very rare cases, primarily with motherboards that have NEAT chip sets, you can install as much as 8 Meg on the motherboard. 386SX boards are usually expandable to a maximum of 8 Meg. This is generally done using SIMM or SIP modules.

Motherboards with 386DX or 486 processors can almost always have at least 32 Meg and sometimes as much as 64 Meg "on board". Users upgrade almost exclusively with SIMM memory modules.

The following rules apply to physical memory division on motherboards of IBM compatible computers beginning with 286 processors:

1. Memory on board is distributed over two banks (Bank 0 and 1).

2. Each bank contains half of the maximum possible memory. Other divisions are possible if there is mixed distribution on SIP/SIMM sockets and dynamic RAM chips.

3. A bank must always be fully equipped.

4. You cannot mix memory modules of differing capacity within a bank.

5. It's not always possible to combine two memory banks with different capacities.

As far as memory organization is concerned, boards with NEAT chip sets are exceptions: Almost every NEAT board is different.

Empty banks stay empty

Older 286 and 386SX boards may use 4-bank technology. The banks are marked from bank 0 to bank 3. Actually, however, only two of these banks can be used, depending on whether you want dynamic RAM chips (up to 1 Meg) or SIMM/ SIP modules (up to 4 Meg). Combining all the banks is only possible in exceptional cases (5 Meg). You must use jumpers or switches to determine whether you address bank 0/1 or 2/3.

By remembering these rules, you can decide how to upgrade a 286 motherboard on board, if you can determine which modules you can use on your board.

443

Installing New Components

Example 1:

A motherboard that has 36 combination sockets for dynamic RAM chips can take either 256K chips or megabit chips. All the sockets are filled with 256K RAM modules, totaling 1 Meg. To add another Meg to memory, giving you a total of 2 Meg, you would have to first remove the installed modules, since each socket is already occupied.

You would have to use megabit modules as replacements (actually 18 modules for 2 Meg). Bank 0 would be full, while bank 1 remained free. By adding another 18 modules in bank 1, you attain the maximum capacity of 4 Meg.

Example 2:

Some 286 motherboards were built with the "apparent" 4 bank technology we mentioned earlier. Banks 0 and 1 consist of four sockets each for quadruple 256 chips (256K*4) and two sockets each for simple 256 RAM chips. These sockets are full. The installed memory size is at 1 Meg. Banks 2 and 3 have two SIP sockets each, and will accept both 256K modules and 1 Meg modules.

You want to upgrade the main memory (RAM) to 2 Meg. If it's possible to run all four banks (manually), there are two options. First, remove all the RAM chips and fill up one of the two SIP banks with megabit modules (2 modules of 1 Meg each = 2 Meg). You can also leave the RAM chips and fill all the SIP sockets with 256 modules (4 modules * 256K = 1 Meg plus 1 Meg in DRAMs = 2 Meg).

Different options

The first option is certainly the better of the two, since it allows for an additional upgrading to 4 Meg by simply adding extra modules. The second option, however, fills up the entire board. You would have to remove some installed modules to upgrade, thus forfeiting the use of those modules. As you can see, it's very important to plan the most economical way to upgrade memory.

You can use the same principles for larger memory capacities. Suppose that you have a 386 motherboard with eight SIMM sockets equipped with 4 Meg. How many modules do you have in how many sockets?

4 Meg modules

The only possibility is that bank 0 consists of 4 SIMM sockets and is filled with 1 Meg modules. There are only two options for an upgrade based on the installed memory.

First, you could expand to 8 Meg by filling bank 1 with 1 Meg modules. Secondly, you could upgrade to 20 Meg by filling bank 1 with a total of four 4 Meg modules. However, this will work only if the board is able to process these modules (check your documentation).

Now let's discuss how to use these options to upgrade memory.

Step #1	Remove "old" memory modules (if necessary).

If you're removing memory modules, you must remove some or all the currently installed modules, then you must begin with Step #1. Make enough room inside so you can easily access the RAM banks. Remove cards that are in your way.

> **NOTE**
>
> Be careful when removing dynamic RAM chips from their sockets. Don't bend any of the chip pins. You can buy special chip pliers from your computer dealer or use the bent side of one of the cover plates from one of the free expansion slots. Hold the front side of the chips. Carefully lift the chips until you can pull them out easily. Don't lift up on the sockets.

Grab SIP modules with both hands on the two upper corners and pull them slowly from their sockets. If the modules are seated too tightly, try carefully prying them up with a plastic tool. Remember the pins on the SIP modules are very delicate.

SIMMs come with snap connectors and wrap connectors. SIMMs with snap connectors are easy to remove. Undo the clips, unsnap the modules, and remove them from the sockets.

Removing a RAM chip

Chapter
11
Section
3

445

If the SIMMs are seated in wrap connectors, then you will also find a plastic clip that snaps into the round lock holes on the sides of the modules. Bend the clip back while pulling it up. It's a good idea to take a small plastic pen and pull the modules to the top.

Pulling SIPs from wrap connectors

Step #2	Insert the new memory modules.

Next, insert the new modules. This isn't very difficult with SIMM or SIP modules. You can't insert SIMM modules the wrong way because they have a notch on one side.

Usually, line 1 on both the line and the socket is labeled. SIP modules don't have this notch, but they are also usually labeled. If you bend any pins, simply place the module on a smooth flat surface and straighten out the pins with a sturdy, square object (e.g., a 3.5-inch diskette as shown in the illustration on the right).

Inserting dynamic RAM chips requires a certain amount of dexterity. Ensure that you insert the chips correctly.

446

Every RAM socket has a notch or some other mark on its front side. RAM chips are also notched or marked accordingly. Both marks or notches must go together. First, turn the case so the sockets are crosswise, with the marks on either the right or the left. Insert one side of the chips into the socket so the pins of this side are sticking out in the holes. Gently insert the other side and push in the chips.

This takes some practice. So, check each chip carefully to ensure that it's seated correctly. If one chip is out of place or bent, problems can occur.

Let's discuss how the memory banks on the boards are marked. Usually a row of memory sockets is marked as either bank 0 or bank 1. However, some boards have the SIMM sockets marked from 0 to 7. In these instances, the first four sockets in the bank are bank 0.

You'll also find the following distribution: SIMMs 0,2,4,6 make up bank 0, while SIMMs 1,3,5 and 7 are bank 1. Generally you can get the necessary information from the documentation to the motherboard. If you're not sure, you must experiment. A picture won't be displayed until bank 0 is filled up.

Step #3	Setting up the new memory.

After inserting all the modules correctly, read the documentation to your motherboard to determine whether any jumpers or DIP switches should be set. Most likely, you will have to set one of these. Often this is how you indicate the module size with which you're working.

Memory recognized!

If all the switches are correctly set, the computer will immediately recognize your new memory size during the power on self test. The computer will recognize the new memory size, even if another value is entered in the CMOS.

However, this isn't the case with NEAT chip sets. Here you must make the correct entry in the Extended CMOS before the system recognizes the memory. To determine how much memory the system recognizes, reconnect the PC to the power supply, the monitor, and the keyboard. Then switch on the PC.

The memory size should match

After the BIOS message, the system counts the memory. The value can deviate as much as 384K from the intended memory size, since some BIOS systems deduct the disk space required for the shadow option. If the value doesn't match the memory size you installed, double-check whether all modules are correctly seated and whether all the switches on the motherboard are correctly set.

If the system recognizes the correct amount of memory, the system BIOS will immediately output an error message after the power on self test is completed. For example, you might see the following error message:

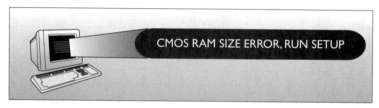

CMOS RAM SIZE ERROR, RUN SETUP

If you start CMOS SETUP then, you may be surprised. In many cases (e.g., with AMI BIOS), the new RAM size is already entered correctly; simply save it again. In other cases, you must enter the new amount manually. Remember that you would enter 4096K of memory, for example, as 640K "Base Memory" and 3072K "Extended Memory". The 384K between 640K and 1 Meg are used for the Shadow option.

In Chapter 13 we discuss CMOS settings using an AMI BIOS as an example. Refer to this chapter for more information.

Now save these settings. The PC will then reboot and should continue all the way to the DOS prompt without any error messages. You are finished expanding RAM.

Using memory expansion cards

Memory expansion cards are becoming less popular because the RAM capacities that can be achieved on board have been increased significantly through the new semiconductor technology.

However, memory expansion cards are still used and, in many cases, they are quite useful. Generally, you don't use a memory expansion card until you've filled up the motherboard.

RAM cards are also organized into banks. The same rules we mentioned for memory organization on motherboards also apply to RAM cards. Some RAM cards can be equipped with DRAMs, but you can also use SIMMs on memory expansion cards.

A 16-bit RAM card

Setting the start address

A memory expansion card usually has a row of switches for setting the start address of the card, as well as the type and size of the upgrade. The start address refers to the memory size at which memory physically begins on the card, and is no longer on the motherboard. So if the motherboard is at full capacity with 8 Meg, in this case you would set the start address of a memory expansion card at 8192K. To make the proper settings, you must have technical documentation.

You must also set up the card memory (i.e., enter the total RAM size in CMOS SETUP). This is the total amount of memory both on board and on the card.

Installing expanded memory (EMS)

In Section 2 we provided a detailed description of installing expanded memory. The most important factor for configuring EMS memory is the processor.

You can easily configure EMS memory for 486 motherboards. The hardware doesn't have to be changed. All you need is MS-DOS 6.2. To install 1024K of expanded memory, add the following three lines in the same sequence to your CONFIG.SYS file.

```
DEVICE = C:\DOS\HIMEM.SYS
DOS=HIGH
DEVICE = C:\DOS\EMM386.EXE 1024
```

If you don't specify a special size, the system uses the default setting of 256K reserved for EMS. To enable the setting, reboot the computer. The size and division of the EMS memory you've installed appears on the screen. For a closer look at the EMS memory, press (Pause) to halt screen output.

You must use jumpers or DIP switches to set 286 motherboards to EMS. However, this isn't possible with all 286 motherboards. If this is possible with your motherboard, you still need the right EMS driver for your motherboard. If you don't have the right driver, an EMS driver designed for other motherboards probably won't work on your motherboard.

If your board is able to configure Expanded Memory, you must enable specific switch settings on the board. When you enable these settings, the motherboard switches off a portion of the memory, which no longer appears during the power on self test. This portion of memory is also removed from the CMOS (i.e., the entry refers only to the remainder of the memory).

Then copy the supplied EMS driver, from the diskette that came with the board, to the appropriate directory, specifying the complete directory path, if necessary. Then, enter the following line in the CONFIG.SYS file:

```
DEVICE = EMS.SYS (size in kilobytes)
```

Also, the specified memory size must match the actual memory size.

After rebooting, depending on the memory size you specified, you set up some memory pages of expanded memory. The driver could have a different name. However, usually the letters "EMS" or "EMM" will appear somewhere in the name.

Replacing the system BIOS

Occasionally, you must also replace the BIOS, for example, to enter other hard drive types.

When you replace the BIOS you can never be sure that your motherboard will run with the new BIOS. Often, everything seems to be all right at first.

Only later do you notice mistakes. Replacing the system BIOS with a BIOS from another manufacturer can always cause problems.

Because of these problems, you must ensure that you use the right BIOS with the right board (e.g., use a 486 BIOS with a 486 board).

The system BIOS usually consists of two EPROMS. The EPROMS have labels that list the manufacturer, a copyright notice, and a serial number. The two sockets are usually marked "High" and "Low." The newer boards often have only one EPROM.

Basically, you must experiment. Remember that as long as the power is disconnected and you frequently ground yourself, you can't destroy anything. Pull out the two BIOS EPROMS from their sockets and then install the replacement EPROMS.

Ensure that you connect the new EPROMS correctly. Sometimes a keyboard BIOS is included; this is usually longer and plugs into a socket near the keyboard input.

If you don't see a picture on your screen within seconds after switching on the computer, switch the two chips around; "High" and "Low" may be mixed up. If that doesn't work either, you won't be able to use the new BIOS.

If your board runs with the new BIOS, first make all the necessary entries in the CMOS and save them. Then try working with the system (format diskettes, write to the hard drive, tap the memory).

Reset the system a couple of times in a row. In short, test your PC to determine whether it runs as it should. If it does, then you've successfully replaced the BIOS.

Installing New Components

Expanding cache memory

Today most normal motherboards with 486 or Pentium processors have external memory caches. These external memory caches consist of static RAM chips. The standard size of a cache on a 386 motherboard is 64K. The external cache is up to 256K for a 486 and Pentium processor.

When the first motherboards equipped with caches were introduced, some of them had only 32K capacities. You can upgrade some of these boards to double the cache capacity.

The architecture of the board is more important than the size of the cache upgrade. The user's manual included with the motherboard contains this information.

In Section 2 we mentioned that upgrading the memory cache of a DOS computer usually isn't useful. However, we'll provide some practical tips for doing this.

Since there is no uniform cache organization on the various motherboards, we can't provide instructions that apply to all motherboards. However, this procedure is similar to upgrading RAM.

The cache also has two banks, one of which must always be full. Also, you may have to remove the old modules before you can upgrade. The memory chips look like long dynamic RAM chips.

Since the terms used to describe cache models can be very confusing, you should take your documentation to a dealer and ask him/her to find the proper cache elements.

Ensure that you plug in the new cache modules correctly. You may also have to change the settings of a jumper on the motherboard to the new cache size.

Not all system BIOS display the cache size on the monitor during the power-on self-test. It's not necessary to set up the external cache in CMOS SETUP.

However, you often have the option of completely disabling the cache memory in CMOS Setup. You should definitely take a closer look at this setting.

Replacing the processor

The CPU should be replaced for only two reasons. One reason is that you suspect the installed CPU is defective and you want to replace it to see if you're right. The other reason is that you have a multiprocessor board on which you can use different 486 CPUs (486SX/20, 486DX/25, 486DX/33). In this case, the clock of the CPU will probably have to be replaced also.

It's very difficult to replace processors of the 386SX generation. The CPUs are usually soldered directly to the motherboard. The 386 and its successor the 486 are in a pin grid case seated on a normal socket in open access.

> **NOTE**
> Be careful with the pins because they break easily. Avoid all types of shock, and store the processor in a safe place where it won't fall to the ground. When you insert the replacement CPU, be sure to match the beveled corner of the chip surface with the corresponding marking on the processor socket.

Installing New Components

Using a "chip puller" to remove a 486 processor

An alternative is to use a thin screwdriver to gently lift the processor out of the socket by its sides. Be very careful if you use this method.

Using a thin screw driver to remove a 486 processor (1 of 2 pictures)

Using a thin screw driver to remove a 486 processor (2 of 2 pictures)

We mentioned that when you upgrade a multiprocessor board, you must replace the quartz (clock) along with it. Read the board documentation for more information. You'll also have to change a switch that provides information about the processor type.

Installing/Replacing the coprocessor

Installing a math coprocessor should take about five minutes. First, find the socket that holds the coprocessor.

On 386 boards, this is a square socket covered with a two or three tiered plate with holes punched in it. Three tiered sockets will hold either a 387 coprocessor or a Weitek coprocessor.

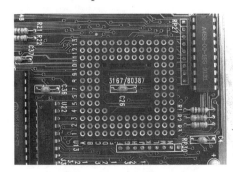

Insert the 387 coprocessor so the outer tier of holes is free. Ensure that you plug it in correctly. The beveled corner of the coprocessor chip must match the appropriate marking on the socket.

The math coprocessor's cycle with 386es is synchronized to the main processor. This is why the coprocessor must be designed for the highest CPU cycle. However, some 386 boards give you the option of using a slower coprocessor. In such cases, the coprocessor gets its own clock. However, you must set this change to another clock through jumpers on the board. Often, you have to use jumpers or a CMOS entry to set up the coprocessor. After installation, call the CMOS SETUP program and check whether the coprocessor must be set up. The entry for this is usually located in "Advanced or Extended CMOS".

The 80287 coprocessor is a long, rectangular chip that looks like a keyboard processor. Plug it in its socket and enable it from a jumper on the motherboard. Usually you must also set it up in SETUP.

The only reliable way to test the coprocessor is to use the test programs that came with the coprocessor. Most system information programs, such as the Norton System Info program, display only the existence of the chip. So you still don't know whether the coprocessor is working properly.

INSTALLING AN INTEL OVERDRIVE PROCESSOR

Intel's OverDrive processors are for upgrading the Intel family of 486 processors (including the 486SX, 486DX, 486SX2 and 486DX2). Installing these processors is very simple with most PC systems. By installing an OverDrive processor, most software will run faster on your existing 486 system.

Before buying an OverDrive Upgrade kit

Check the following before buying an OverDrive Upgrade kit:

❖ Determine the type of 486 chip is installed

❖ Determine how it is installed on the motherboard

The OverDrive processor is a good choice if you're upgrading a 486 and want an excellent cost-to-performance increase in your PC's performance. Notice in the following photo that the Intel OverDrive box includes a chart for your convenience. You should use the chart to determine which Overdrive chip you can use.

Installing an OverDrive chip

Installing an OverDrive chip involves three steps.

1. Locate and identify the Intel 486 chip installed in your PC. This is the processor which we want to remove.

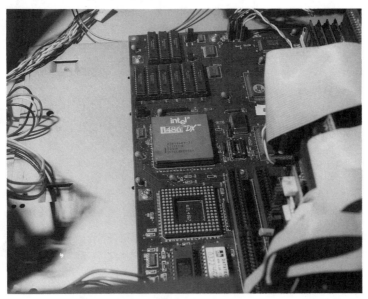

The location of the Intel 486DX processor which we want to remove

2. Use the chip removal tool included by Intel to remove the chip from the motherboard.

3. Insert the Overdrive chip and test it.

457

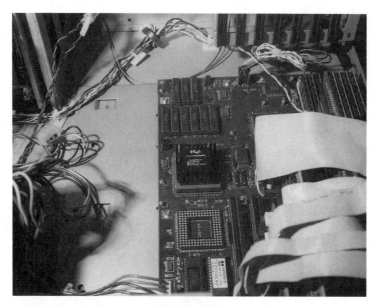

The Intel DX40DPR100 processor installed successfully

Intel includes a processor demo and diagnostics software with the OverDrive. The software includes an excellent hands-on graphic demonstration of how to install the Intel OverDrive chip.

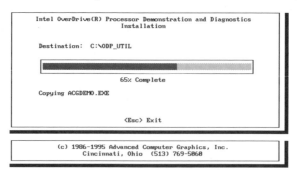

Installing the demonstration

What's included with the package

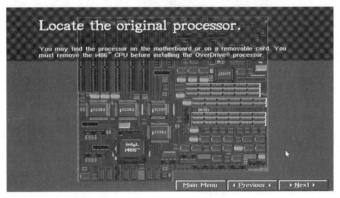

A typical PC motherboard with Intel 486

INSTALLING DIFFERENT EXPANSION CARDS

Many PC users install expansion cards on their PC. However, even though this procedure usually doesn't require much technical understanding or manual dexterity, many users have problems with expansion cards. Before explaining how to install an expansion card, we'll ask some basic questions.

Installing New Components

Is the proper slot still available?

Although this may not seem important, this requirement frequently causes problems. This is especially true if you have a name brand machine with a nonstandard motherboard or if you own a PC in a slimline case. In these instances, you may not have an extra slot.

So, what is the correct slot? As you probably know, most motherboards have two types of slots and each has different lengths. One type is a short 8-bit slot. The other type is the longer 16-bit slot and represents the actual AT bus.

8-bit or 16-bit

Regardless of the type of slot in which they're inserted, 8-bit cards will perform the tasks for which they were designed.

However, this doesn't apply to 16-bit cards. These cards must be plugged into a 16-bit slot. If you try to insert a 16-bit card into an 8-bit slot you can damage the hardware. At the very least, the 16-bit card won't work. At the very worst, if the contacts of the 16-bit card touch components on the motherboard, you could short circuit the board.

Does the plug fit?

Some manufacturers make the hole in the back of the case for the expansion card so close or so square there isn't enough room to plug in anything near some of the slots (e.g., a printer cable).

The local requirements of an expansion card can also be important. For example, you may not be able to add a long card because other PC components are blocking the card's path. The mounting kit of a floppy disk drive or a hard drive usually causes this problem. However, sometimes the memory banks of the motherboard can be an obstacle for the expansion card, especially if the memory banks are filled with SIMMs or SIPs.

Determining space

Before buying your expansion card, determine how much space is available in your PC. A quick glance at the back of the case isn't sufficient. Open the case and determine whether you have a free slot. Expansion cards that don't have an outer connector might otherwise look like a simple cover plate. If you open the case and discover there's not enough space, don't give up hope. Sometimes you can make room by transferring an existing card to a different slot and then plugging your new expansion card into the slot you just freed up.

Switching places

You may be able to use this procedure when you want to install a 16-bit card, but only find an 8-bit slot that's free. Perhaps your system has an 8-bit card plugged into a 16-bit slot somewhere. If you plug this card into the 8-bit slot, you can free up a 16-bit slot.

Cable connections are also important. A cable that is too short will add extra work and potential problems because, in this case, you may have to make several switches.

You can use almost any slot providing it meets the criteria we mentioned. If you're fortunate to be able to choose from several slots, consider the following suggestions.

If you plan on making future upgrades, you should try to keep as much room free as possible. Avoid long cable paths that might have to lead through other expansions. Also, if you install a long card, remember that you may no longer be able to reach some components of the main board, such as the coprocessor socket or the SIMM or SIP banks.

The video card can be occasionally affected if the PC power supply is divided. This results in a noticeable decrease in the quality of the picture (swimming). This problem frequently occurs when the monitor cable is poorly shielded. Because of this, we recommend installing the video card far from the power supply. Usually, the best slot is the one on the far left.

Chapter
11
Section
3

461

Most cards, especially add-ons, must be set from jumpers or DIP switches. For example, you must specify which interrupt or DMA channel the card can use. Standard expansion cards are usually preset. However, always check this setting before installing the card. Once the card is screwed into the slot, you won't be able to recognize much. If you use a pair of pliers or a screwdriver to change settings on the jumpers once the card is installed, you could damage the card.

When the card isn't compatible

You should determine whether a card is compatible before purchasing the card. Not all expansions are compatible with the installed components in the system. For example, usually you won't be able to install a modem card in addition to four existing serial ports. Usually it's also impossible to install a second game port. If you have a card (e.g., a Sound Blaster card), which has an additional game port, make certain you cannot switch it off by changing the setting of a jumper.

This also applies to installing a second printer port or a scanner card. If you aren't sure whether the expansion you're planning could cause problems, read the appropriate chapter in Section 2 before beginning the installation. The chapters in the first part of the book discuss the special problems linked with IRQs, DMAs and port addresses.

General installation procedures

The procedure for installing a card is basically the same for all the various cards. We'll give you a general description of this procedure in 10 steps. Then we'll discuss the special features involved in installing the most common expansion cards.

Step #1	Prepare the central unit.

Place your computer on a sturdy surface and remove all exterior cable connections. Most importantly, remove the power supply cable. Don't force the cables. If you cannot pull out a plug easily, it's probably also attached with screws. Use a small screwdriver to remove the screws from the sides of the plug and then pull out the plug.

Step #2	Open the case.

Next, open the case as we described in the "Case" section earlier in this chapter.

Step #3	Prepare the slot.

Now find an appropriate free slot or rearrange your existing expansion cards to free up a slot. Then remove the cover plate from the slot on the back of the case. Use a Phillips head screwdriver to unscrew the screw on the top of the blank filler and then carefully pull out the blank filler from the slot.

Removing a slot cover plate

If the screw falls while you're unscrewing it, stop what you're doing and find the screw. Otherwise, the next time you switch on the system, the screw could cause a short circuit and destroy the entire motherboard.

Step #4	Make some room!

Give yourself enough room to work (i.e., remove anything that might get in your way when you install the card). Usually, the cables from the other cards will get in your way. Make notes about where the cables go and how to plug them in and then pull them out. Doing this is much easier than trying to repair a damaged cable.

Step #5	Configure the card.

Check the jumper positions or DIP switch settings. Correct them if necessary. If your card requires cables inside the computer, determine if there will still be enough room for the cable when the card is installed. Then attach the cables. Make sure you plug the cable in correctly; otherwise you'll have to remove the card to turn the plug around.

Step #6	Insert the card.

Now insert your new card in its slot. To do this, grab the card with both hands and plug it into the slot.

Inserting an expansion card

Don't handle the contact strip on the bottom of the card, and avoid putting any pressure on the components. Otherwise you may damage something. Then push the card down into the slot with your thumbs. Don't use force because the card may jam in the slot.

Now pull the card out again and notice how it was seated when you installed it. Your expansion card may not fit properly in a slot on an inexpensive case. If this happens, try a different slot. This usually solves the problem.

You could also use cutting pliers to snip off the pointed extension at the bottom of the card. However, before doing this, make certain this is the reason the card is jamming. Remember, cutting the card usually voids the manufacturer's warranty automatically.

Step #7	Physically install the card.

Now screw the mounting bracket of the card to the back of the case. Ensure the card remains seated. With inexpensive cases, cards sometimes become unseated. This usually occurs because of loose mounting brackets. Loosen the screws (usually there are two), shift the bracket to the desired position, and then tighten the screws again.

Tightening the screws on an expansion card

Step #8	Attach the cable.

Now connect the cable to the card (if you haven't done this already) and return any cables or other parts, which you have moved, to their original positions.

Step #9	TEST

Perform a test on the card to see whether it works while the case is still open. That way, if you have to make any changes, you'll have an easier time getting to the parts.

465

Step #10	Close the case.

Close the case in the reverse order in which you opened it.

Installing or replacing the video card

If you remember the following points, installing a video card usually isn't a problem.

Make certain the DIP switch on the motherboard is positioned correctly

You must set a jumper for a monochrome or color adapter with most motherboards. Set the mono/color jumper to the proper position. The entry for this jumper in CMOS SETUP must also correspond to the actual circumstances.

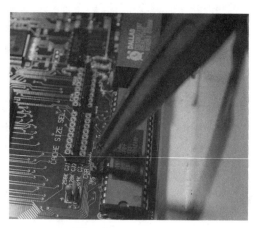

The display switch

VGA cards and monitor types

If you're using a VGA card, you must set a DIP switch for the type of monitor you're using. You can also specify with VGA cards whether the 15-pin analog outlet or the 9-pin TTL connector is active. If your card has a switch that you can access from the back, you can even change this setting while the card is installed. However, the change won't be activated until you reboot your PC.

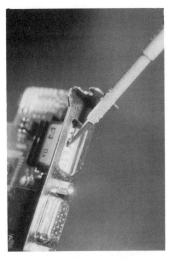

Setting the monitor type on the card

Check for an "interlace" jumper?

Use this jumper to set the scanning frequency for higher resolutions. You can use Super VGA cards only if your monitor is also able to reproduce the high frequency of non-interlaced mode. If you don't have a Super VGA card, set this jumper to "interlaced"; otherwise you could destroy your screen.

Watch out for the power supply

Use a slot far from the power supply. This reduces the loss of picture quality that's caused by "noise" and magnetic interference from the power supply. Sometimes high frequency emissions from a neighboring network card can interfere with the picture signal. This problem can also be solved by selecting a different slot.

Using a SCSI controller or a network card on your system

SCSI address conflicts can also occur when you install a VGA card. Only a few video cards allow you to make changes to their BIOS address. So normally you must make this setting on the SCSI controller or network card. If you've installed software (e.g., driver software for a floppy model tape streamer) that accesses these addresses, then you must also reconfigure the software. Unfortunately, this also applies to all network software.

467

Use shadow RAM

If you upgrade from a Hercules compatible video card to an EGA or VGA adapter with its own BIOS, don't miss the speed advantage that's available by installing shadow RAM. Make the necessary entry in SETUP or load the appropriate driver in CONFIG.SYS if your CMOS SETUP doesn't allow such an entry.

Installing an interface card

If you want to install a multi I/O card in your computer as the only interface card, you won't need to make any changes. By simply plugging in the card, you get one parallel port, two serial ports and a game port. The IRQs and port addresses should already match the card.

Pin 1

The most frequent reason a serial port doesn't work is because the cable leading from the card to the back of the case isn't plugged in correctly. So, be sure that you plug in this cable properly. The marked lead of the flat ribbon cable, usually red, must match Pin 1 of the post connector.

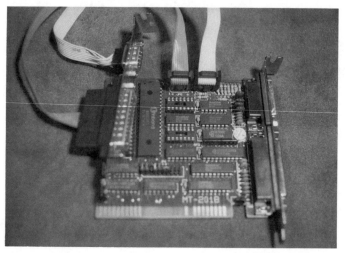

Connecting the serial interfaces correctly

Sometimes Pin 1 isn't marked on an interface card. If not, first check the user's manual for the interface. If you don't find any information there, maybe one of the soldered joints of the post connector on the back of the card is square, unlike all the other joints, which are round. This soldered joint identifies it as Pin 1.

Your last resort is to experiment (there are only two possibilities) or contact the store where you purchased the card.

Locations for the cables

Most multi I/O cards have the connections for the printer and the game port on the mounting bracket of the card. The two serial ports have external cable connections. The plugs from these cables can either fit through holes on the back of the case or can be used together with a mounting bracket in place of a slot cover plate. This means that you won't be able to use that slot for anything else.

If you determine that you won't need the slot later, you should use the slot for this purpose. Otherwise, you'll have to remove the plug and push it through the holes in the case. To do this, use a flat or combination pliers to open the hexagon bolts.

You could also use a socket wrench if you have the right size (usually about .25 inches or 6 mm).

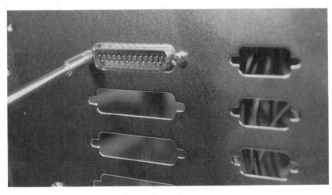

Tightening the screws

Maximum upgrade

In Section 2 we discussed the options for combining specific ports. Now we'll summarize those options.

469

Chapter 11

You can easily install four serial (COM1-COM4) ports and three (LPT1-LPT3) parallel ports, as well as a GAME port (for two joysticks) in your system. If you have more than two serial ports, at least two of them must share an interrupt. Only the first printer port gets an interrupt.

> **NOTE**
> Be careful when you tighten the screws. Since the threading is made of plastic, it's easy to strip the threading. Therefore, don't make the bolts too tight.

One game port is enough for two

Installing a second game port isn't necessary because you can use a Y-power splitter cable to connect two joysticks. Also, installing a second game port will affect the first adapter or even damage or destroy it.

To install extra ports, remember how the existing cards are set and configure the new cards so there isn't any overlapping.

Installing a sound card

The problems that occur when you install a sound card are almost related to the settings on the card itself.

Game ports

If the card has a game port but your system already has one, you must disable one of the game ports. It's best to disable the game port on the sound card, since it's readily available. Consult the card's documentation to determine which jumper disables the game port. Sometimes the jumper itself will be marked "GAME en/dis".

470

Disabling the game port

If the sound card uses the same interrupt as the printer port, this may lead to conflicts that could interfere with printer output or the way the sound card functions, especially if you're printing in the background from a printer spooler.

Usually the two interrupts are IRQ 5 and 7. Try to configure your printer port to use a different interrupt than your sound card. If you can't do this (e.g., because you don't have any documentation for your interface card or you don't have a test program for displaying the interrupt distribution in the system), you can also change the default value for the IRQ of the sound card.

As a result, you may have to reinstall some programs that use this interrupt. Otherwise, the programs won't run at all, especially the demo programs that are included with most cards.

Port address used by the card

Normally the card uses address 220 Hex. If this default address is already being used by a different adapter in the system, enter a different value here. First, try 240 Hex, and then try all the other possible addresses in sequence. Fortunately, conflicts with the port address rarely occur.

Don't be surprised if you hear strange noises from the speaker instead of music or if error messages appear about the sound card when you start certain programs. This is especially true with a 486 machine. It's usually a program error and not a hardware problem. Try starting the programs with the Turbo button switched off or disable the internal cache memory of your 486 in BIOS SETUP.

Determining where to install the card

Find a slot that provides easy access to the volume control. However, ensure that you won't damage any cable connections behind the computer.

The volume control of a sound card

Installing a modem card

The modem card, or internal modem, is simply an extra serial port. Once you realize this, most of the questions you have about installing it are answered.

Determining which COM port to install the card

If possible, set the modem to COM4. Otherwise, set it to COM2. If you don't use a mouse, you could also set it to COM1. The reason for this sequence is related to do the assignment of interrupts to the COM ports. We discussed this problem in Section 2.

Don't set the card to a port that already exists in your computer. In other words, if you already have four serial ports, you must do without one of them by disabling it on the card when you change the setting on the jumper or by removing the card from your computer.

Pulse or tone dial?

Many modems give you the option of switching between pulse dialing or tone. Select whatever dialing system your telephone uses.

472

Setting the volume control

Some modems have an internal loudspeaker. Usually, there is a volume control on the back of the card. If you try to use the volume control, be sure to choose a slot for the modem that enables you to access the volume control easily, without having to feel your way through a jungle of cables.

CMOS BATTERY

All computers include a battery that is used to keep a small amount of memory active (or alive). This battery contains the CMOS (complementary metal oxide semiconductor) information for your PC. This CMOS information is important. Otherwise, you would need to enter your CMOS configuration each time you turn on your PC. The CMOS memory is "read" by your PC to learn the hardware configuration of your system. This includes the amount of memory, number of disk drives, hard drives, CD-ROM drives and the video configuration of your PC.

One of the first steps you should do is print your CMOS SETUP or write down the information and attach it to the underside of your computer case lid. Keep a second copy in a safe place where you'll be able to find it. Then you're certain to have it available if you need it.

You can see the CMOS configuration by running the SETUP program or the CONFIG program. When the CMOS SETUP information is displayed, press the [Print Screen] key to print it. SETUP may have a specific option to print the information. It's important to have a copy of your CMOS setup in case it is wiped out by a dead battery.

You can also check the effectiveness of the CMOS battery by typing the following:

```
TIME
```

and press [Enter].

Check your watch for an elapsed time. Repeat the step and compare the elapsed time to your watch. If your PC is losing time, you may want to change your battery. Although PC batteries usually last for five years or more, if you're upgrading your PC consider buying a new one now.

Chapter 11 Section 3

473

The most obvious clue that you need a battery is when you turn your PC on and it displays the following message:

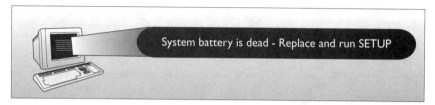

System battery is dead - Replace and run SETUP

Or, when you turn on your PC and see the following message:

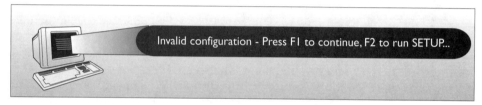

Invalid configuration - Press F1 to continue, F2 to run SETUP...

You press F1 and see the following message:

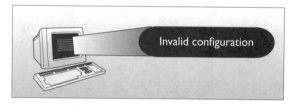

Invalid configuration

If you get either of these messages you'll need to setup your CMOS every time you switch on your machine.

Replacing a CMOS battery

Before replacing a CMOS battery, make certain to discharge yourself of static electricity (now more frequently called "electrostatic energy"). You must unplug your computer and remove the case. Look inside and locate the battery. It's usually located near the power supply attached to the chassis by Velcro.

It should be attached by two wires (red and black) twisted together that go to a connector on the motherboard. Although it is located inside your computer, we call it an external CMOS battery.

474

Battery types

The PC will have one of three types of batteries:

1. Soldered

If you find that your CMOS battery is soldered in, we recommend taking it to a computer repair shop unless you're proficient in desoldering and soldering circuit boards. CMOS memory and battery may be together in one module on some Pentium class computers. If so, look for "Benchmarq" or "Dallas".

2. NiCad

A NiCad battery is located on the motherboard and looks similar to a large watch battery. If you have a NiCad battery, carefully remove it with a screwdriver. Note which side of the battery is showing. It will be either a '+' or '-' sign. When you replace it with a new one, place it carefully back the same way.

3. External pack

If you have an externally connected battery, carefully disconnect the wired connector located on the motherboard. Note the locations of the red and black wires. Caution: always look carefully at the present installation and if necessary, mark the wires and/or write down what you see. When you replace the battery, you will need to plug it back into the motherboard the same way.

You can purchase a battery from your local computer retail store, computer superstore or other national electronics store. Take your old CMOS battery too when you buy a new CMOS battery. Then you're certain to match its voltage and buy the correct battery. The cost of a battery usually ranges from about $3.00 to $12.00.

After you've replaced your battery and turned on your PC, compare the configuration of your CMOS with the previous configuration. If the new configuration matches the previous configuration, you're set with the new battery. Otherwise, you'll need to enter the previous settings and save those settings for the new CMOS configuration.

Chapter

11

Section

3

475

Building A Multimedia PC

Although multimedia became a new buzzword in the 1990s, the idea of multimedia goes back many years before then. Multimedia simply means the ability to disseminate information in more than one form (using text, audio, graphics, animated graphics and full-motion video). The term first appeared in education during the 1960s and 1970s, when it described new media supporting the learning process in classroom instruction. Now, it involves integrating different applications of entertainment electronics such as video, sound and graphics.

Most areas of computing is narrowly defined. However, multimedia does not suffer because few people understand it but rather everyone understands it differently. You may have noticed some manufacturers have claimed their products are "multimedia". The manufacturers should take responsibility for this because few standards exist between products. By simply adding full color graphics or special sound effects to a traditional word processor, manufacturers immediately labeled the software as multimedia.

After a slow start, PCs (both DOS and Windows based systems) are now "multimedia capable." Previously, only a few complex applications were multimedia capable. The components deliver information in many ways, but achieve their greatest effectiveness through their interaction. Information, images and sounds are technically and aesthetically integrated, then focused on a single product.

477

Building A Multimedia PC

The MPC standard

MPC (Multimedia PC) standard is a CD-ROM and hardware standard developed by Microsoft and other leading hardware and software manufacturers. The Multimedia PC Marketing Council was established to administer the program and license the MPC logo and trademark.

The standard was intended to make work easier for software manufacturers to identify minimum requirements for their products. It was to apply to future developments in PC multimedia. The Windows graphical interface forms the foundation of this standard, enhanced by multimedia software components and programming tools.

Initially the Microsoft Windows multimedia Extension provided the software interface to Windows 3.0 for multimedia products from a variety of manufacturers. The corresponding multimedia drivers and interfaces have since been incorporated into Windows 3.1.

Using CD-ROM drives for memory-intensive graphics and sound file processing places rigorous demands on PC hardware. Both sound cards and CD-ROMs are specified as components of the multimedia PC (MPC) standard.

A PC configuration must include all components and meet all specifications defined in the standard to qualify for the MPC seal.

Hardware manufacturers wishing to submit their products for MPC approval must apply to the multimedia PC Marketing Council in New York. Approval certifies the product fulfills the requirements of the MPC standard.

A personal computer system that has qualified for the MPC title has specific characteristics that make it suitable for multimedia use.

The MPC standard attempts to set the first standards for personal computers capable of sound and video through hardware and software ports. The first standard, called MPC Level 1, was modest enough so owners of Intel 80286 based computers could enjoy the benefits of multimedia. Its specifications were introduced in 1990. It defined the a system that was considered to be a minimal base for running multimedia applications and presentations.

The MPC Level 2 was introduced in 1993. It reflected how computer technology evolved since Level 1 was introduced. The following table shows the differences between these two specifications:

MPC Level 3 Standard (Minimum requirements for a multimedia PC)		
	MPC Level 1	MPC Level 2
RAM	2 Meg	4 Meg
Microprocessor	386 SX	486SX/25
Hard Drive	30 Meg capacity	160 Meg capacity
CD-ROM Drive	150 KB/second transfer rate 1 second or less seek time Mode 1 capable	300 KB/second transfer rate 400ms or less seek time CD-ROM XA ready Multisession capable
Audio	8-bit digital sound 22 KHz sampling rate (DAC) 11 KHz sampling rate (ADC)	16-bit digital sound 44.1 KHz sampling rate (DAC) 44.1 KHz sampling rate (ADC)
Video	VGA	VGA with 64K colors at 640 x 480
System Software	Windows with Multimedia	Windows 3.1 Extensions

Although the specifications of MPC Level 1 were later upgraded, they formed the first definition of the MPC standard.

Explaining everything about multimedia would fill volumes. For this chapter, we'll focus on computers that meet the MPC (MMPC) standard.

Most applications will run faster on the MPC Level 3 standard introduced in May, 1995. These changes reflect the changes in technology since the MPC Level 1 and 2 were published. Software based video will perform better on Level 3 multimedia PCs. Also, photo CD applications which are not supported on Level 1 MPCs will run on these machines with double speed CD-ROM drives.

NOTE

The MPC logo does not guarantee the quality of the products, only the products have met the specifications of the MPC Council. Therefore, you should look for the MPC specifications and not necessarily the MPC logo when shopping for a multimedia system.

Chapter 12

MPC Level 3 Standard (Minimum requirements for a multimedia PC)	
RAM	8 Meg
Microprocessor	75 MHz Pentium or equivalent
Hard Drive	540 Meg capacity
CD-ROM Drive	600 KB/second sustained transfer rate 250ms average access time CD-ROM XA ready, multisession capable
Audio	16-Bit digital sound, wavetable, MIDI playback
Speakers	Measured and tested at 3 watts/channel.
Video PlayBack	MPEG1 (hardware or software) with OM-1 compliance Frame buffer resolution of 352 x 240 at 30 fps or 352 x 288 at 25 fps
System Software	Windows 3.11 and DOS 6.0

Besides the peripherals and components listed in the table above, we'll add the following:

Floppy Drive	1.44 Meg 3.5 inch disk drive
Serial interface	(9 or 25 pin) 9600 minimum
Parrallel Interface	Bi-directional
Video Card	SVGA with 800 x 600 pixel resolution with 256 colors
Mouse	2 or 3 button
Joystick	Analog (IBM-compatible)

The technology for connecting video recorders, cameras, and televisions to PCs is constantly changing and no true standards yet exist. So we'll describe how to assemble a custom PC outfitted with a CD-ROM drive and a digital audio system. According to Multimedia PC specifications, this is a "Multimedia PC."

First, we'll list the steps involved in building your own multimedia PC. Take enough time to do all the steps in sequence. It should take from two to four hours to perform all the steps (depending on your experience and ability).

We assume that you have all the necessary equipment, including the documentation and software for these components. You also must have the original diskettes for the software and operating system you're going to install.

Building a multimedia PC in 29 steps

The multimedia PC we'll build in this chapter involves only 29 steps (listed below). These steps are explained in more detail over the next several pages.

1. Be certain you have all the components, software and documentation

2. Open and prepare the case

3. Equip the motherboard with memory module chips

4. Test the motherboard, memory, and video card outside of the case

5. Install the motherboard in case

6. Install the video card

7. Test the motherboard, memory, and video card inside case

8. Install the combination controller with ports

9. Plug in disk drive A: and test

10. Plug in disk drive B: and test

11. Install disk drives and tighten screws

12. Plug in hard drive and set it up

13. Partition, format and test hard drive

14. Install hard drive and tighten screws

15. Install MS-DOS 5.0 on the hard drive

16. Make manual changes to start and configuration files

17. Install Windows 3.1 on the hard drive

18. Install video card driver software

19. Prepare sound card

20. Install sound card

Chapter 12 Section 3

> **NOTE**
>
> Be sure to read or reread Chapter 10. It lists several rules and suggestions explaining the dangers of working on PCs.

Building A Multimedia PC

21. Connect external speakers

22. Install software for sound card

23. Try out sound card

> **NOTE**
>
> You can stop after Step #17 or Step #18 if you don't want the multimedia options. This gives you a complete, custom built PC system, configured as above except without the sound card and CD-ROM drive.

24. Link sound card to Windows 3.1 (or Windows 95) and test

25. Connect CD-ROM drive

26. Set up CD-ROM drive under DOS

27. Try out CD-ROM drive

28. Install CD-ROM drive and tighten screws

29. Close case

When you have all the components and a place to work, you're ready to start.

Step #1	Be certain you have all the components, software and documentation

The first step is to make certain you have all the necessary parts available. Remember the components must be complete.

The multimedia PC consists of many parts

Big tower case

The tower case comes with case faceplates, a key for the keyboard lock, a bag with spacers and mounting screws, a PC loudspeaker, documentation of the settings for the digital speed display, and a power cable (the accessories are usually in a small cardboard box inside the case).

Motherboard (Pentium processor)

The motherboard comes with at least 64K SRAM modules for external cache, sockets for at least 8 SIMM modules, current BIOS and technical documentation.

4 SIMM modules

Each with 1 Meg capacity, 70 ns access time.

5.25-inch disk drive

3.5-inch disk drive

A 5.25-inch mounting kit with mounting screws

AT bus combination controller with ports

This includes an AT bus 16-bit controller card with one parallel and joystick port on the cover plate, 1 additional case cover plate with two mounted serial sockets (9-pin and 25-pin) with two 10-line connector cables, one flat ribbon cable for disk drives (34-line) with two plugs per drive position, one end twisted, 1 flat ribbon cable for hard drive connection (40-line), and technical documentation.

Hard drive with IDE port

3.5-inch format, 540 Meg capacity, Conner Model CP30104

VGA video card with ET4000 chip

This includes 1 Meg RAM, various driver diskettes, and technical documentation.

Sound card

Sound Blaster 32 from Creative Labs comes with 1 cable for stereo, various diskettes and technical documentation.

1 pair stereo speakers

Make certain the speakers are shielded.

Chapter
12
Section
3

483

CD-ROM drive

Internal drive from Matsushita. This includes a flat ribbon cable for connection to the CD-ROM controller on the sound card, various diskettes, 1 compact disk in the caddy, 1 cable for the audio input of the sound card, and technical documentation.

102 key keyboard, MF/2 format

Serial Microsoft compatible mouse

This includes a driver diskette that can't be used under Windows 3.1. Frequently also comes with additional software, a mouse pad or an adapter for a 25-pin connection.

14-inch analog color monitor (17-inch monitor is a good alternative)

Dot pitch 0.28mm, frequency band 31.5-35.5 KHz, maximum resolution 1024 x 768 pixels, glare free CRT, cable for connection to the PC, and power cable.

MS-DOS 6.2

This includes various diskettes and program documentation. For this project, make sure you create a "bootable emergency startup" diskette (see Chapter 8 for more information).

This diskette should contain FORMAT, FDISK, COMMAND.COM and other important files that you'll need in case you cannot boot from the hard drive. We'll call this the STARTUP diskette in this chapter.

Windows 3.x or WfWG 3.11 (Windows 95 is a good alternative)

This includes the installation CD-ROM or diskettes and program documentation.

A data CD of your choice for testing purposes

If you have everything on our list, combine all the technical documentation in one pile. Later, you won't have to look for the information you need. Also, keep the software and the components together so they don't get lost.

Step #2	Open and prepare the case

After taking the tower case out of the package, place it on your worktable, with the back facing you. You won't always be able to access the case screws right away. Frequently, you must first use a screwdriver to pry off a plastic cover from the back of the case.

Then use a Phillips head screwdriver to unscrew the six case screws, which are in each of the four corners and between the top and bottom corners on the left and right.

So you don't misplace them, place all the screws in a small cup.

485

Building A Multimedia PC

Removing the plastic cover from the back of the case

After unscrewing the case, you'll be able to pull up the cover of the case. The accessories are contained in a small carton inside the case. These accessories include the following:

❖ A small bag containing screws and spacers

❖ Several plastic guide rails

❖ Additional items

We'll discuss all the accessories later. After unscrewing the top (see photo next page), set the carton aside for now.

Building A Multimedia PC

Unscrewing the case

Removing the cover from the case

Building A Multimedia PC

For the tower case in our example, you must connect the power switch with the cable harness from the power supply first. Check your case and power supply documentation for more information.

One type of power switch connection

Now that you've connected the power switch with the power supply unit, move the case to a comfortable working position. Place the tower on the table with the front facing you and the mounting brackets for the drives on the right hand side.

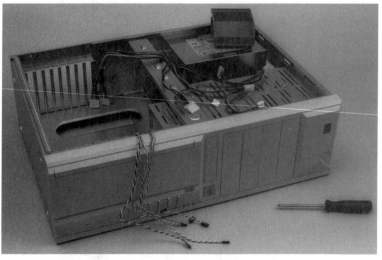

Place the tower on the table with the front facing you for easier access

Building A Multimedia PC

Next, find the carton with the case accessories. Inside the carton you should find a small bag containing screws and spacers.

Place the contents of this bag into the cup you're using to hold the screws. Set the case faceplates aside for now; you'll install them last. The bag should also contain several plastic guide rails. These rails are designed for longer boards. Mount these rails across from the grooves for the expansion slots by clamping them into the predrilled holes with the plastic slots.

You won't need the rest of the contents of the carton until later. Move the carton out of the way for now.

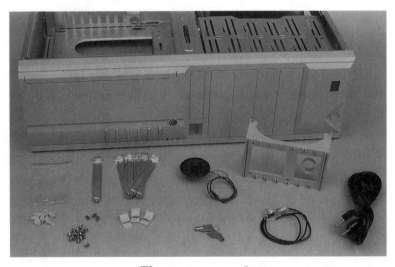

The case accessories

Step #3	Equip motherboard with memory module chips

Now that you've got the case ready to receive different components, plug the memory modules into the motherboard.

Now take the motherboard from the package and place it flat on a nonconducting material (i.e., a piece of foam). Refer to the documentation or the label on

> **NOTE**
>
> Touch the tower case before touching the motherboard and the memory modules to discharge any electrostatic energy charges that may have built up in your body.

the board to determine which of the eight SIMM sockets is bank 0. Now plug in one of the four 1 Meg SIMM modules in each of the four sockets of bank 0.

Unless you use force, there's no chance of plugging the modules in incorrectly. Make certain that each module is in full contact with the sockets and rock them back and forth until the clips lock in place.

Step #3 is completed when you finish installing the four modules in the plan.

Installing the SIMM modules

Step #4	Test the motherboard, memory and video card outside the case

To avoid problems later, test the memory installation and the motherboard now to see whether they work. Place the motherboard with the installed memory on the nonconducting material. Then place the nonconducting material on the open PC case so that you can easily plug in the motherboard connection cable from the power supply to the connection on the motherboard.

The motherboard gets its power from the two plugs marked "P8" and "P9" from the PC power supply unit. These two plugs are easy to recognize because, unlike other cables from the PC power supply unit, they have six leads each.

The plugs are connected to the motherboard so the three red cables next to one another point to the middle of the board, while the only orange or white cable is at the keyboard input. It's impossible to plug the boards in wrong.

The board plugs of the power supply unit

If you mix up the plugs, the motherboard won't work. However, mixing up the plugs shouldn't result in a short circuit.

You'll also need the video card for your test. Take it out of the package and insert it in one of the expansion slots on the motherboard.

Now connect the monitor with the video card and plug the keyboard into the motherboard. Finally, connect the PC with a power cable and then plug it into an outlet. Make certain the power switch is set to "off".

NOTE

Be careful when you insert the video card, since the motherboard isn't screwed in yet. Don't use force either. Make sure the case faceplate of the video card doesn't lift up the motherboard.

Chapter
12
Section
3

Main board ready for testing

Check all the connections you just made. Is the video card inserted properly in the slot? Is the motherboard connected with the power supply unit? It's very important the motherboard doesn't touch any metal.

Now turn on both the PC and the monitor. After a moment, the BIOS of the video card and then the system BIOS appear on the screen. Then the computer performs the autostart routine, counting 4096K of memory. Everything is all right if the computer displays an amount between 3712K and 4096K.

You can ignore the error messages following the memory test. We only needed to test whether the motherboard and video card worked and the computer recognized the correct amount of memory.

Now turn off the power and unplug the power cable. Unplug everything again, pull the video card from the slot and disconnect the motherboard from the power supply. This step is finished.

Step #5	Install motherboard in case

Since you're certain the motherboard and the installed memory work properly, you can begin installing these components. First, screw in two hexagonal threaded bolts (from the bag of screws accompanying the case) into the mounting plate for the motherboard. The mounting screws for the motherboard fit into these bolts. The case mounting plate has threaded holes for this purpose.

Building A Multimedia PC

Place the motherboard on the mounting plate to check whether the threaded holes of both parts match. Then use a small socket wrench to screw the threaded bolts in the right holes.

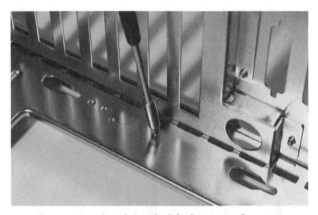

Screwing the threaded bolts into the case

Then put the plastic spacers on the motherboard (also in the bag of screws) that will later screw into the guide holes on the mounting plate of the case. Insert the spacers into the threaded holes that cover the guide holes from the bottom of the board with the pointed end up. After you finish inserting all the necessary spacers, you're ready to insert the motherboard.

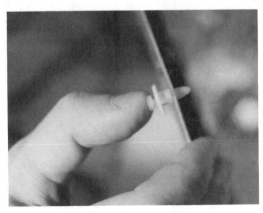

Inserting the spacers

Building A Multimedia PC

Insert the board with the spacers in the guide holes and then move the board slightly to the right, until the holes are covered by the threaded bolts. Use two screws to fasten the motherboard to the case. Turn the screws carefully; it's enough if the motherboard no longer slips. Finally, plug the power cables from the power unit into the board, as you did in the last step.

Inserting the board

The central component, the motherboard, is now in the case. Consult the documentation to ensure the jumpers and switches are set correctly. Now is the time to check because you still have free access. Later, when the case is full, it will be more difficult to find the jumpers and change the settings.

Tightening the screws on the motherboard

Step #6	Install video card

Next, we'll reinsert the video card. Compare the settings of the jumpers or switches on the card with the documentation accompanying the video card. Often you must set the correct monitor type. You can install the card once it has the proper settings. Find a 16-bit slot as far to the left as possible.

Since you won't need to cable the video card to other components of the PC, install it a little farther to the left. Plug the video card into a 16-bit slot and screw it to the back of the case. Now you can set the display switch on the motherboard.

The display switch is either a jumper that you have to set or a switch on a DIP switch block. The documentation of the motherboard contains this information. Set the display switch to color.

495

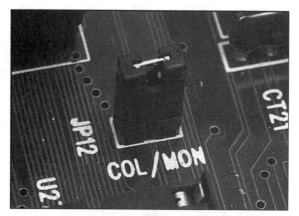

The display switch is a jumper you must set or a switch on a DIP switch block

Configuring and inserting the video card

Building A Multimedia PC

Step #7	Test motherboard, memory, and video card inside case

After you screw in the motherboard and the video card, connect the PC speaker. Its beeping will help you when you're troubleshooting. The two-lead cable (usually red and black or yellow and black) from the PC loudspeaker ends in a four-pin plug; only the outer pins are used.

The motherboard has its counterpart, a four-pin strip that is often marked "SPK" (for speaker). Your motherboard documentation should provide detailed information about where this connection is located. Find it and plug in the loudspeaker cable.

The first step in connecting the speaker

497

Building A Multimedia PC

The second step in connecting the speaker

Next we'll perform an intermediate test to detect possible errors as early as possible. When you install the motherboard, there's a chance the case could be touching it somewhere, resulting in a short circuit. Your motherboard won't work after a short circuit. So let's reconnect all the cables between the PC, monitor, and keyboard and get ready to turn on the PC. Remember to plug the PC back into the power supply.

Check the motherboard for screws you may have forgotten. As soon as everything seems to be in order, turn on the PC.

The PC system displays the video card BIOS and system BIOS messages on the screen. Now, since you hooked up the speaker, you should be able to hear the PC counting the memory. If you don't do anything else, the computer will then check the configuration and you won't see anything else on the screen.

When the computer finishes checking, you'll probably hear a beep and see an error message on the screen, listing errors or prompting you to press a key. For now we won't worry about error messages. Instead, we'll connect the cables of the case. First, switch off your PC.

First, connect the Reset button to the motherboard. Find the cable leading from the Reset button on the front of the case. This is a two-lead cable that's usually blue and white. You should be able to find its counterpart on the motherboard, a pin strip with two pins. Often the Reset connection is labeled "RST" for Reset or "HWR" for hardware reset.

Next, find the cable for both the power LED and the keyboard lock. Both functions are usually on a combined connection on the motherboard. The connector has five pins, unlike any of the other connectors. However, only four of the five pins are occupied. Usually the plug is also combined and has five pins. One position is missing. One of the cables is usually green; it's the cable you connect to the connector pin marked "1" on the motherboard connection.

Connecting the Reset button, Turbo button, keyboard lock and LED

In rare cases, the connection cables aren't combined into a 5-pin plug. If you don't have a combination plug, remember the power LED cable is usually green and white. The two cables fit into the outer pins, with green going on Pin 1. The two-pin cable from the keyboard lock goes in between, and one pin is free. We'll find out which one later when we test the keyboard lock.

499

We still must find the cable for the Turbo switch. Usually the cable is three-pin (black-white-orange), but you almost always connect it to a two-pin connector on the motherboard.

The connector on the motherboard is marked "Turbo-SW" or "TB". Depending on whether this switch sets the board to maximum frequency when closed or open, the factory may already have put a jumper on the connector pins. This automatically sets the PC to a frequency.

Replace the jumper with a three-pin cable from the Turbo switch to make it possible to change the frequency of the system clock from the case switch.

Connecting the turbo control LED can be very complicated if you include the digital speed display. We discussed this in the "Motherboard" section of Chapter 7.

The speed display's cable is a two-lead, black and yellow cable. The connector on the motherboard is almost always next to the contact for the Turbo switch, and is usually marked "LED".

> **NOTE**
>
> In this example, since we're interested only in the Turbo switch, we'll connect only the Turbo LED. We won't discuss the speed display.

After making all the relevant case connections for the motherboard, you must check them. Switch the PC back on and wait for the memory test to start. Then press the Reset button to clear the screen. The start routine automatically begins in approximately 10 seconds. If this doesn't work, the motherboard and the video card may be incompatible. Until you replace the video card, continue pressing Reset.

During the memory test you can test the Turbo switch. This changes the "counting rhythm," which you should be able to hear. In the fast setting, the yellow Turbo LED should light up; otherwise it's plugged in wrong. The green power LED should light up at the start and stay lit; the keyboard lock prevents keyboard input when you lock it. A locked keyboard results in an error message, such as "Keyboard locked", after the memory test.

If all the control lights and switches function correctly, you can switch off your PC. This step is finished.

Step #8	Install combination controller with ports

It's not difficult to install the combination controller. For this purpose, choose a 16-bit slot as close as possible to the drive mounting brackets so the cables will reach. The ports on the card are usually preset at the factory with all ports set to default addresses and all installed ports active. The IRQ layout of the serial ports also corresponds to the default settings (COM1=IRQ4, COM2=IRQ3).

Inserting the combination controller

Nevertheless, check these settings against the model you're using to ensure they match. Correct the jumper settings if necessary. Often the diskette controller and the hard drive controller can be switched off separately. Check these settings as well. Both controller functions should be enabled.

Tighten the screws on the combination controller

Now insert the card in the slot and screw its faceplate to the case. Then plug in the two connector cables of the serial port faceplate to the appropriate contacts on the controller card. The connector labeled "ASYNC 1" is reserved for the first serial port. Use this port for the mouse cable.

Cable connections of the port faceplate

Then connect the other port to ASYNC2, the second serial port (COM2:).

Connect the cables to the connector pins so the labeled side of the cable is connected to the connector pin marked "1". The last time you'll notice any errors is when you install Windows and the mouse won't work.

Now all you have to do is select which slot you're going to block by fastening the serial port faceplate. Unfortunately, there is no way to avoid doing this. Many cards are so big that you can't use the neighboring slot anyway.

NOTE

Another possibility would be to use an 8-bit socket, which is only useful for port or scanner cards anyway.

Now fasten the port faceplate to the back of the case with a screw.

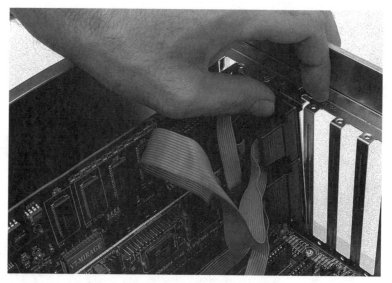

Installing the port faceplate

Step #9	Plug in disk drive A: and test

Now let's install the first disk drive. For now, connect the disk drive. We'll install it later. Plug the long end of the 34-lead floppy cable into the post connector on the contact strip of the combination controller. The width of the cable indicates the location of the controller connection. The labeled side of the cable connects to connector pin "1" on the controller.

Connecting the floppy cable to the combination controller

Place the disk drive (we assume it's a 5.25-inch disk drive with 1.2 Meg capacity) on its side on the power supply or the mounting unit with the control LED in view. Connect a power cable from the power supply unit to the appropriate connector on the disk drive.

Then plug the card connector on the twisted end of the floppy cable into the contact strap on the drive so the labeled side of the cable connects with the grooved side of the contact strap.

The disk drive is cabled

Our next task is to enter the disk drive in CMOS SETUP. Switch on the PC and note the message that appears after the memory test. This message should read "Press [DEL] to run Setup" or something similar. Now press [Del]. Select the item "STANDARD CMOS" from the selection menu.

In the input window that appears, select "1.2 Meg" or "5.25-inch" for drive A:. Normally, you'll use the [Page Up] and [Page Down] keys to scroll through the entries and make your selection. For now, leave the B: drive and the hard drive set to "NOT INSTALLED"; we'll discuss those settings later.

"Primary Display" or "Video" should already be set to "VGA/EGA". If there is a setting for "Keyboard", set it to "Installed". The memory size should already be entered correctly.

Press [Esc] to exit the input window and then choose "Write to CMOS and Exit". Answer the confirmation prompt that appears by pressing [Y].

When the computer reboots, it briefly accesses the disk drive following the memory test. It may display an error message as well. In any case, the computer then prompts you to insert a diskette with the operating system and press a key.

Insert the STARTUP diskette mentioned at the beginning of this chapter. Once the DOS system prompt appears, type the following:

```
FORMAT A:
```

and press Enter.

The computer prompts you to remove the STARTUP diskette from the drive and insert a blank high-density diskette. Then press Enter to confirm the formatting procedure. If the diskette formats without any errors, you can concentrate on the second disk drive. Switch off the PC for now.

Step #10	Plug in disk drive B: and test

We'll also connect, set up, and test the second disk drive before physically installing both disk drives. Take the second disk drive and try to determine where "Pin 1" is located on the connector strip of the disk drive. Usually there is a matching label on the control board. Connect the drive's connector to the cable leading to the controller. Again, the side of the cable with writing on it matches "Pin 1".

Then attach the power connection of the disk drive to a power cable from the power supply unit.

When you turn on the PC again, first set up the disk drive in the STANDARD CMOS, as you did in Step 9. However, this time the entry is different; use either 3.5-inch or 1.44 Meg. After saving the entry and rebooting, the PC

NOTE

Don't use force because it's possible to plug in these plugs incorrectly. Examine each one very carefully. Place this disk drive on its side on the power supply unit as well. Make certain you can see the control LED.

accesses both disk drives briefly and then tries to start from A:.

Insert the STARTUP diskette in drive A: and reboot. Repeat the formatting process in Step 9 for drive B:. If this disk drive also formats diskettes correctly, you're almost finished. Try switching to drive B:, read the directories of the diskette, switch back to drive A: and display that diskette's directories as well.

If everything is correct, switch off the computer and unplug the power cable. You're finished with this step and are ready to physically install the disk drives.

Step #11	Install disk drives and tighten screws

Since both disk drives work well, you can install them. First, determine which side of the 3.5-inch drive had the marked side of the cable. It's important to do this now because later it will be more difficult to distinguish the markings. Then disconnect all cables from the drives.

Install the A: drive in the second mounting bracket from the top and install the B: drive directly below it. To do this, you must temporarily place the tower in an upright position.

> **NOTE**
>
> Larger tower cases often have problems with the length of the cables. That's why it's better to leave the upper part of the tower free.

The 3.5-inch disk drive needs an installation kit

When you install the drives, always start with the 3.5-inch disk drive. Insert the drive into a 5.25-inch mounting kit and tighten the screws so the head arm points down. In our example the 3.5-inch drive is in position B: (the third mounting bracket from the top).

Building A Multimedia PC

Now insert the drive with its frame in the case and tighten the four screws (two on each side). Be sure that you're using the right screws; they should screw in easily. If you're using a plastic mounting kit, you'll often use self-tapping (sheet metal) screws.

Slide them in and tighten the screws

Before you physically install drive A:, reconnect all the cables for drive B: while they're still easy to reach. Note the side of the cable that contains writing. When all the cables are correctly installed, drive A: (5.25-inch) slides into the second unit from above, with the head arm pointing down. This drive also has two screws on either side.

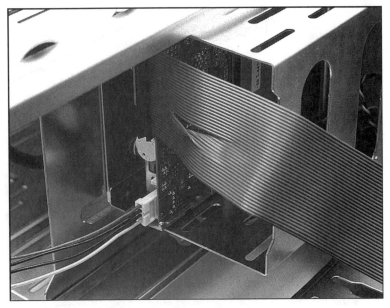

Cable drive B: first

Now reconnect all the cables for this disk drive.

If all the cable connections are correct and the disk drives are installed, you can place the tower case on its side again. Switch on the PC for a minute to check your work. Try accessing both disk drives and loading the operating system from the STARTUP diskette. Then switch off the PC and unplug the power supply. You're finished installing the disk drives.

Step #12	Plug in hard drive and set it up

AT bus hard drives are usually preset as "Master drive" in the setting "First and only hard drive".

For the Conner CP 30104, this means the middle jumper, "C/D", is enabled.

While other conditions apply for all other hard drives, as we have said, you usually won't have to check.

NOTE

Don't risk your hard drive. When the power to the PC is switched on, don't move, lift, or turn the hard drive. Even after switching off the power, wait one more minute before moving the hard drive.

The hard drive cannot slip, fall or move while it's running. Although we suggest to "test first before installing", don't jeopardize your hard drive during testing. If necessary, install the hard drive first before testing.

Checking the Master/Slave setting

Now connect one end of the 40-wire AT bus hard drive cable to the correct connector on the controller card. Make certain that "Pin 1" goes on the labeled side of the cable. Connect the other end to the connector block to the hard drive. Wire "1" on our Conner hard drive is on the inside, next to the power connection.

The connectors of most hard drives are organized in the same way. The hard drive also requires another power connection from the power supply unit. Now let's set up the hard drive on the system.

The hard drive is connected

Reconnect the PC to the power supply and switch it on. After the memory test, the PC soon displays an error message about discovering an unknown hard drive. The end of the message reads either of these two messages:

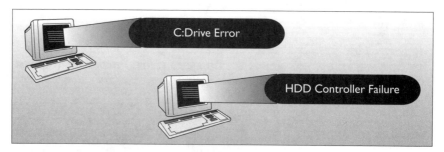

At the same time, the computer either prompts you to start CMOS SETUP or starts the program itself. Now enable the input window for STANDARD CMOS, then select type 47 (User Type) under "C:" or "Disk 1".

You can define this hard drive type yourself. Enter the parameters of the installed hard drive here. The only important values are the ones for cylinders, heads, and sectors. Use the following entries for our Conner CP 30104:

Item	Value
Cylinders	997
Heads	14
Write Precompensation	0
Landing Zone	0
Sectors	7

The second hard drive contains the entry "NOT INSTALLED". Save the entries and exit the input window again ("Write to CMOS and Exit"). The computer reboots but this time doesn't display an error message about recognizing the hard drive. However, you're still not finished with the hard drive. You have to prepare it for the operating system. We'll do this in the next step.

The current 486 BIOS manufactured by AMI contains a setting option for the "System Boot Up Sequence" entry in ADVANCED CMOS SETUP. This is the sequence of drives used by the computer to search for the operating system.

The success of the next step depends on setting the "System Boot Up Sequence" to "A:;C:", meaning the PC searches A: and then C: for the operating system. The "Floppy Drive Seek At Boot" entry should be "enabled".

To find these settings, go to ADVANCED CMOS SETUP after calling the CMOS SETUP program. Check these settings and make any necessary corrections. Press ⬜ to exit the menu and save the settings by selecting "Write CMOS and Exit".

For more information about ADVANCED CMOS SETUP, refer to Chapter 13.

Step #13	Partition, format, and test hard drive

After setting up your hard drive in CMOS SETUP, you must prepare it for working with MS-DOS. Insert your STARTUP diskette in drive A: and press the Reset button. The system boots from the diskette.

A simple DOS prompt, showing the current drive as drive A:, appears:

```
A>
```

Next, call the partitioning program to set up the hard drive partition by typing:

```
FDISK  Enter
```

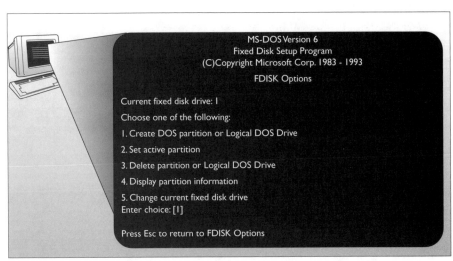

The FDISK main menu

In the main menu, select the first menu item, "Create DOS partition or Logical DOS Drive". Since the value "1" is already preset in the line "Enter choice:", confirm by pressing (Enter).

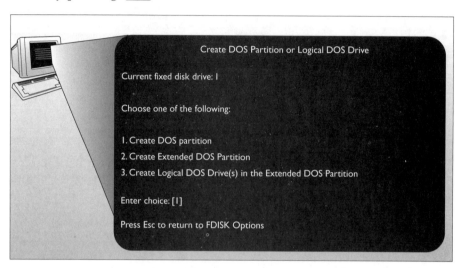

The second step

In the "Create DOS partition or Logical DOS Drive" submenu that follows, select the "Create Primary DOS Partition" (default) option again.

Then press (Enter). The following question appears:

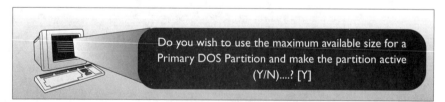

Press (Y) to select the default "Y" value and press (Enter).

Now watch the computer access the hard drive as it creates your partition. Then the computer displays the following message on the screen:

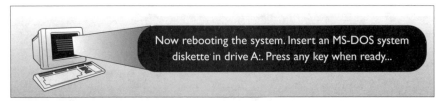

Now rebooting the system. Insert an MS-DOS system diskette in drive A:. Press any key when ready...

Since you already have your STARTUP diskette in the drive, press `Enter`. The system performs a warm boot and is loaded again from the diskette. Now you're ready to format your hard drive. To do this, type the following:

```
FORMAT C:/S
```

and press `Enter`.

Answer the following security prompt:

WARNING! ALL DATA ON NON-REMOVABLE DISK DRIVE C:WILL BE LOST!
Proceed with Format (Y/N)?y

by pressing `Y` and then `Enter`.

The computer formats the hard drive. Notice the hard drive LED blinking and a ticking noise. The format routine keeps you updated on the progress of the formatting:

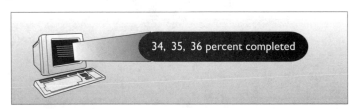

34, 35, 36 percent completed

Then you see the following two messages:

Chapter
12
Section
3

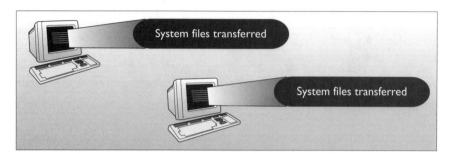

Answer the following prompt by pressing Enter:

Then you'll see a summary of available space on your new hard drive.

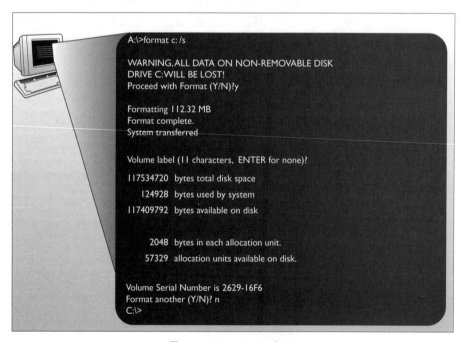

Formatting complete

Since the hard drive is completely formatted, you can now copy the operating system, programs, or other data to the drive. Remove the diskette from drive A: and press Reset to see whether the hard drive also boots.

After the new operating system prompts you for the date and time (press `Enter` to bypass the prompts), it displays the following lines:

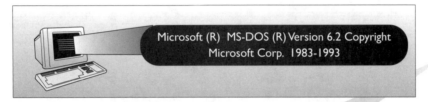

> Microsoft (R) MS-DOS (R) Version 6.2 Copyright Microsoft Corp. 1983-1993

Switch off the computer and physically install the hard drive.

Step #14	Install hard drive and tighten screws

First, disconnect all cable connections to the hard drive. All modern tower cases have a kind of metal box for installing a 3.5-inch hard drive. Usually this box is under the disk drive mounting brackets. This box is specially designed for installing 3.5-inch hard drives.

NOTE

Be careful when fastening the screws. If they're too long, they could bore through the control board of the hard drive (especially Conner hard drives). To be safe, test the screws first. Make certain the electronic circuitry of the hard drive doesn't touch other components. Then reconnect all the cables.

You should also connect the cable between the hard drive control LED on the front of the case and the hard drive controller. This is usually a red and black or red and white two-wire cable.

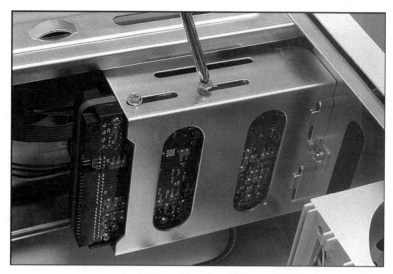

Installing the hard drive

The combination controller has either a two-pin or four-pin connector. The red wire of the cable goes on Pin "1" of the connector. Test the connection by checking the control LED. The control LED indicates hard drive activity.

The hard drive control LED is connected to the controller

After you finish physically installing the hard drive, you can begin installing the operating system.

Step #15	Install MS-DOS 6.22 on the hard drive

Insert diskette 1 into drive A: and run A:SETUP. It boots from the diskette and displays the MS-DOS SETUP screen. Press Enter to go to the next menu.

NOTE

You need **all** the original MS-DOS 6.22 diskettes to install MS-DOS 6.22.

To change settings, select the menu item and press Enter.

In the menu that now appears on the screen, select the "MS-DOS Shell:" option and press Enter. From this submenu, select "Do not run MS-DOS Shell on startup." and press Enter. We're selecting this option because later we'll install MS-Windows.

If all settings are correct, select "Continue Setup: The information above is correct." and press Enter. Follow the instructions on your screen.

During installation, MS-DOS prompts you to insert different diskettes into the appropriate drive. After you've inserted all the diskettes, the computer displays a message that installation is complete. Remove the diskette from the drive and reboot your computer.

After rebooting, type the following command

```
DIR
```

to make certain the DOS Setup program created a directory called

```
C:\DOS
```

on your hard drive.

This completes installing DOS. Now you can begin configuring the operating system.

Step #16	Make manual changes to start and configuration files

We'll begin the system configuration adapting configuration files with the CONFIG.SYS file. We'll use the editor included with DOS. To call the Editor, type the following line:

Chapter
12
Section
3

519

```
EDIT CONFIG.SYS
```

The editor screen should appear. Look for a line that reads:

```
DEVICE=C:\DOS\SETVER.EXE
```

Move the cursor to this line, and press Ctrl and Y simultaneously.

The following line should be the first line of CONFIG.SYS:

```
DEVICE=C:\DOS\HIMEM.SYS
```

Use the arrow keys to move the cursor down one line so it's at the beginning of the second line and press Enter. A blank line appears above the cursor. Move the cursor to this blank line and type the following text:

```
DEVICE=C:\DOS\EMM386.EXE  NOEMS
```

Then go down one line and add ", UMB" to the line

```
DOS=HIGH
```

so the third line of your configuration file now reads:

```
DOS=HIGH, UMB
```

Now add another blank line as described and type:

```
DEVICEHIGH=C:\DOS\SMARTDRV.SYS
```

Change the number 10 in the FILES line to 30, so it reads:

```
FILES=30
```

Your new CONFIG.SYS file is ready. Press Alt and F to activate the **File** menu and select **Exit**. Press Enter and answer the question about saving the loaded file by pressing Enter. Your new CONFIG.SYS file is now in the root directory of your hard drive.

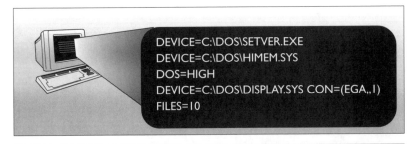

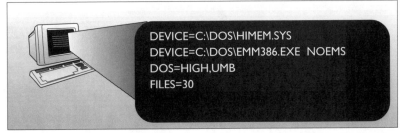

The "old" CONFIG.SYS (top) and the "new" CONFIG.SYS (bottom)

You can similarly update the AUTOEXEC.BAT file. Load it in the DOS Editor by typing:

`EDIT AUTOEXEC.BAT`

When the file appears on the screen, first delete all lines beginning with

`MODE CON CODEPAGE`

by moving the cursor to each line and pressing Ctrl Y. Add the following as the last line of AUTOEXEC.BAT:

`VER`

Exit the program as described for the CONFIG.SYS file.

Chapter
12
Section
3

521

Building A Multimedia PC

The "old" AUTOEXEC.BAT (top) and the "new" AUTOEXEC.BAT (bottom)

Make certain your changes are correct by typing the two following lines:

```
TYPE CONFIG.SYS
```

```
TYPE AUTOEXEC.BAT
```

Then reboot your computer. After booting up, type

```
MEM
```

to find out that your DOS applications have 627728 bytes available, although you installed a hard drive cache.

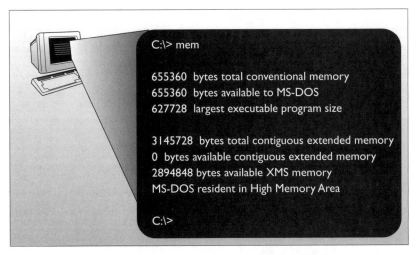

Example of free memory under DOS 6.2

However, when you install Microsoft Windows 3.1, this configuration changes again.

Step #17	Install Windows 3.1 or Windows for Workgroups

Start the installation by inserting the diskette labeled "Diskette 1 - Setup" into drive B: (for 3.5-inch diskettes).
Switch to drive B: by typing:

B: `Enter`

Call the installation program by typing:

SETUP

NOTE

If you're installing Windows 95, please read the installation instructions that accompanied the Windows 95 CD-ROM.

You'll need the Windows 95 installation CD-ROM or the original Windows 3.1 diskettes in this step.

After a short wait, you'll see the welcome screen of the Windows or Windows for Workgroups 3.11 Setup program. Press `Enter` to exit this screen and go to the next menu where you can choose either a user defined installation or a standardized installation of Windows.

Press E to select Express Setup for a faster and easier setup.

Next, Windows Setup checks the configuration of your hardware and begins transferring Windows files. Occasionally, the program prompts you to insert another diskette into drive B:. After you insert the diskettes, remember to press `Enter` again. The screen eventually changes to Windows.

Make certain the mouse works

If you installed the mouse port properly, you can now use your mouse for the first time. Move the mouse back and forth to see whether the mouse pointer (the little white arrow on the screen) also moves.

Now you must type in your name. You need your keyboard to do this. Type your name in the appropriate box; you can also include your company's name or anything else that seems important.

Move the mouse pointer to the appropriate box and click the left mouse button. When you're finished typing in the name, click the `Continue` button to exit this menu. Windows then asks you whether the name is correct. Confirm by clicking `Continue` again.

Installing the printer

When the dialog box for printer setup appears, don't select any printer for now.

After one or two more diskettes, Windows begins building its program structure. You can follow this process on the screen. Then Windows searches your hard drive for applications that are already installed. It will find two programs, DOS-EDIT and QBasic. Since we don't want to run these programs under Windows, click the `Cancel` button.

Since we also think it would be better to skip running the tutorial after Windows is completely installed, click the `Do not run tutorial` button. Then, you go to the last step of Windows Setup. Select the button that completely reboots the system.

After the computer finishes booting, type the following:

MEM `Enter`

You'll probably be surprised to discover the amount of your computer's free memory has increased again, even after installing Windows. Now you have 632352 bytes.

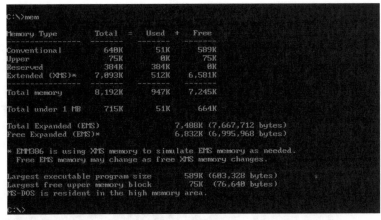

```
C:\>mem

Memory Type        Total   =   Used  +   Free
--------------    -------     ------    ------
Conventional        640K        51K      589K
Upper                75K         0K       75K
Reserved            384K        384K       0K
Extended (XMS)*    7,093K       512K    6,581K
                  -------     ------    ------
Total memory       8,192K       947K    7,245K

Total under 1 MB    715K        51K      664K

Total Expanded (EMS)             7,488K (7,667,712 bytes)
Free Expanded (EMS)*             6,832K (6,995,968 bytes)

* EMM386 is using XMS memory to simulate EMS memory as needed.
  Free EMS memory may change as free XMS memory changes.

Largest executable program size    589K (603,328 bytes)
Largest free upper memory block     75K  (76,640 bytes)
MS-DOS is resident in the high memory area.

C:\>
```

Example of modified memory map after installing Windows

You now have more memory because of the improved HIMEM and SMARTDRV drivers used by Windows. Setup made the necessary changes in CONFIG.SYS and AUTOEXEC.BAT automatically. Check WINDOW's work by typing:

TYPE CONFIG.SYS [Enter]

and

TYPE AUTOEXEC.BAT [Enter]

Then type

DEL *.OLD [Enter]

to delete the backup copies of the old configuration files.

Chapter
12
Section
3

525

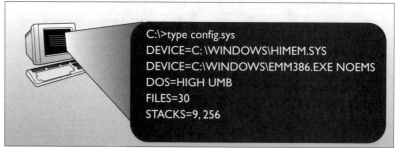

The modified startup files

Now you can start your new program, Windows, for the first time. Type the following at the DOS prompt:

`WIN` Enter

The Windows logo is followed by an open window called the Main group. Notice the name "Main" in the title bar at the top of the window. This group combines the main functions of Windows. Before doing anything else in Windows, let's set up a permanent swap file. Double-click the "Control Panel" icon. This takes you to a new window with an icon called "386 Enhanced". Double-click this icon and click on the Virtual Memory... button in

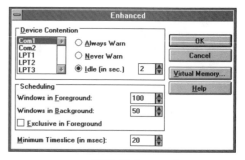

386 Enhanced

the 386 Enhanced submenu. You go to another submenu where you'll find information about the Windows swapfile.

Now click on the (Change) button (on the right) and watch the window increase in size. This new area at the bottom contains some options related to the size and type of the Windows swap file. Windows also has a default setting for each option.

Accept Windows' setting by clicking the (OK) button. Don't worry about the size of the file (you can change it any time you wish) or the confirmation message that follows ("Are you sure you want to ...?"). Then click on the (Restart) button to affect the changes.

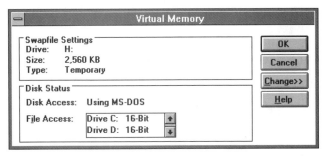

Accept Windows' settings

Step #18	Install video card driver software

To do this, double-click the "Windows Setup" icon in the "Main" group. A window opens on the screen with information about your current configuration. Select the **Options** menu, and then click on **Change System Settings....**

The next window displays your video card type (probably VGA or SVGA) in the Display: line. Notice the small arrow to the right of this entry that points down. Click on this arrow to activate the drop-down list box for Display:.

Now move the cursor down to the last position, called "Other display (Requires disk from OEM)...".

Chapter

12

Section

3

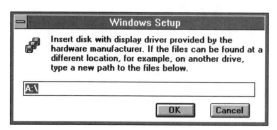

You'll need a driver diskette

As soon as this option is selected (highlighted), press [Enter] and insert the Windows driver diskette into drive A:. After Windows finishes reading the diskette, you'll see a small menu with various graphics resolutions. Select **640*480 in 256 Colors** and click on [OK].

After loading the driver, you must still insert a Windows original diskette. Change to the appropriate drive, click on [OK] and follow the instructions on the screen.

Then restart Windows to make the video driver active.

Step #19	Prepare the sound card

Installing Microsoft Windows 3.1 meets the basic requirements for hardware and software installation of a sound card and a CD-ROM drive. Remember, by following these steps, you can install either a SB16, AWE32 or other Sound Blaster compatible board correctly.

Before physically installing the Sound Blaster 16 card, check the default settings and make any necessary modifications. The default setting "IRQ 7" usually won't cause problems, as long as you don't make both the sound card and the printer active simultaneously.

NOTE

Windows 95 has made several improvements in how sound cards are installed and used. If you're upgrading to Windows 95, look for the sound cards that are plug'n'play compatible with Windows 95.

The plug'n'play compatible sound cards are very easy to install. You simply "guide" Windows 95 to the new device. Windows 95 will then install the sound card correctly.

528

The jumper on the card labeled "JP19" is on when IRQ 7 is used. If another IRQ is changed, the various application and demo programs must be informed of this during installation. In other words, leave this setting unchanged. This also applies to the port address set to 220 Hex through JP13.

Since two different joystick ports aren't necessarily compatible on one PC and the combination controller card already has one active game port, you must disable the joystick port on the sound card. Use the jumper called "J4" on the Sound Blaster 16 card to disable the port. Simply remove the jumper on J4 to set the integrated game port to "disabled."

The configuration jumper on the sound card

Step #20	Install the sound card

It's easy to install the Sound Blaster 16 card or any other card by inserting it into any 16-bit slot.

It's also important to remember the Sound Blaster 32 card contains the controller for the CD-ROM you plan to install. So don't install the sound card too far from the CD drive (use the cable length as a guide). There is also an audio cable between the CD-ROM and the sound card to

NOTE

Remember the card shouldn't be too close to any other expansion cards. The card contains several components that are sensitive to heat. To prevent heat buildup, leave one slot free between the sound card and the other cards.

consider. Choose the right slot and fasten the card to the back of the case with a screw.

Inserting the sound card

Step #21	Connect the external speakers

Connect a boom box, stereo system, or amplified speakers, to fully use the Sound Blaster 32 card's capabilities. To do this, connect the supplied cable for connection to the stereo and the sound card output. Set the volume control of the sound card to a medium level.

Connecting the speakers to the sound card

Step #22	Install the software for the sound card

Use the sound card's original installation diskette. Insert the diskette into drive A: and begin installation by typing:

```
A: Enter
INST_HD C: Enter
```

The automatic installation routine starts and prompts you to specify the settings made on the card.

Continue using the default values (IRQ7, DMA1 and port address 220). Next, the installation routine creates a directory called SB32 and copies the various supplied programs into separate subdirectories of this directory.

The SB32 directory also contains some batch files that you can run to call the programs for you. Then the installation program adds the following to your AUTOEXEC.BAT file to configure the Sound Blaster 32 card through the BLASTER and SOUND environment variables:

```
SET BLASTER=A220 I7 D1 T2
SET SOUND=C:\SB32
```

The expanded AUTOEXEC.BAT

This concludes the installation of the Sound Blaster 32 software. Now let's find out if the card works.

Step #23	Test the sound card

To test the sound card, reboot the system by pressing Ctrl + Alt + Del to make the changes in the system settings active.

Then type the following

```
CD SB32
```

to change to the SB32 directory and type DIR to view the number of programs. Experiment with some of the programs and learn about the options and limitations of your Multimedia PC. Then, we'll move on to the next step.

Step #24	Link the sound card to Windows 3.1 (or Windows for Workgroups 3.11)

To begin actual Multimedia installation, first load Windows, by typing:

```
WIN
```

Then call the Windows "Control Panel" in the "Main" group. Once you're in the Control Panel, click on the "Drivers" option. Then click on the Add button and select "Unlisted or Updated Driver".

Selecting a MIDI driver

Then, a dialog box appears, prompting you to insert a diskette with the OEMSETUP.INF file or specify the path for this file. Enter following in this box:

```
C:\SB32\WIN31
```

Now you'll see a list of the available drivers. Install each of these drivers and specify the default values for IRQ, DMA and the port address.

After each driver, Windows prompts you to restart the computer to make the driver active. Select "No Restart" until you have installed the last driver. Then select "Restart Windows". Then you return to the Program Manager.

Now select **File/New/Program Group** to add a new group file to the Program Manager. Name the group file BLASTER and then copy the MMCBOX.EXE, MMJBOX.EXE, and SBMIXER.EXE programs to this file. These program files are in subdirectories of C:\SB32.

Run the "Drivers" icon again to install sound drivers, and "MIDI Mapper" to select a MIDI driver to match your sound card (this may require setting MIDI ports to match the sound card, rather than the default MIDI Out).

Then select "Media Player" from the "Accessories" group. Choose a piece of music by selecting **File/Open...**. You can play back any file with the .MID extension (e.g., CANYON.MID). To play the file, click on the PLAY icon of the Media Player. It resembles a play button on a video cassette recorder.

Step #25	Connect the CD-ROM drive

Your multimedia PC still needs a CD-ROM drive. Connect this drive and do a test run before you attach it into the case.

Inserting a CD-ROM controller

First connect one end of the flat ribbon cable for data transfer to the connector block of the controller, which is on the Sound Blaster 16 card in our example. The other end of the cable is a 40 wire AT bus cable on our Matsushita drive. Connect it to the post strip on the drive.

When you connect this cable, the marked side of the cable goes with Pin "1" of the connector. If you find a free outlet on the power supply, use it for the CD-ROM drive. Otherwise, you must use a Y power splitter. For now, position the CD-ROM drive on the tower case.

Connecting the audio cable to the sound card

Don't forget the audio cable

Finally, connect the audio cable to the CD-ROM drive and the sound card so you can play audio CDs from the Sound Blaster 32 in addition to data CDs.

The Sound Blaster 32 has a special software program for this purpose. The sound card and CD-ROM drive that we chose won't cause any problems with incompatible plugs or plug layout.

Step #26	Set up the CD-ROM drive under DOS

Installing the software for your CD-ROM is similar to installing the Sound Blaster software. First, insert your original installation diskette into drive A: and type

```
A: Enter
INST_CD C: Enter
```

to begin installation. Confirm the default settings for IRQ, DMA, and the port address, and follow the other instructions.

The installation routine now installs the software for the CD-ROM in the C:\SB32\DRV directory and adds the following line to the CONFIG.SYS:

```
DEVICE=C:\SB32\DRV\SB32CD.SYS  /D:\MSCD001  /P:220
```

535

However, you have to add the following line to your CONFIG.SYS file:

```
DEVICE=C:\DOS\SETVER.EXE
```

Run the DOS Editor as follows:

```
EDIT CONFIG.SYS
```

Add the above device line, following the EMM386 driver.

To assign a drive letter to your CD-ROM, call the following batch file from the C:\SB32\DRV directory:

```
CDDRIVE
```

This executes the MSCDEX program with a few parameters. To be able to address the CD-ROM drive at all times, type:

```
EDIT AUTOEXEC.BAT
```

Add the following to your AUTOEXEC.BAT file:

```
CALL C:\SB32\DRV\CDDRIVE.BAT
```

Then insert your CD and reboot the system. When the computer finishes booting, type

```
D:
```

to change to your CD-ROM drive, as if it were a normal hard drive.

Step #27	Test the CD-ROM drive

Type

```
DIR
```

to take a look at your new drive. Copy some files to your hard drive or run a program on the CD-ROM drive. Don't be afraid to experiment. By experimenting, you test the drive and become more familiar with the technology.

Try deleting a file on the CD-ROM. Although the CD-ROM drive behaves like a completely normal hard drive for the Windows File Manager too, you cannot write to the drive.

After you load Windows, you'll have a drive D: available. Use the multimedia software to test the CD-ROM drive. Also, run any programs or demos your CD might have on it. As soon as you think everything is working properly, finish putting your computer together.

Removing the 5.25-inch drive faceplate...

Step #28	Install the CD-ROM drive and tighten the screws

Now that you've adapted your CD-ROM drive for use under DOS and Windows, you're ready to physically install it.

Disconnect all the cables from the drive. Disconnect all the cables from the PC and the power supply too, since you're finally ready to move the case to an upright position. The CD-ROM drive is the last device to be installed.

It's time to close the case. Place the CD-ROM drive underneath the two disk drives in the closest free bracket and fasten it to the case as you did with the two disk drives, with two screws on either side. Then reconnect all the cables (data cable, audio cable, power cable). This concludes the installation of the CD-ROM drive.

Chapter

12

Section

3

537

Building A Multimedia PC

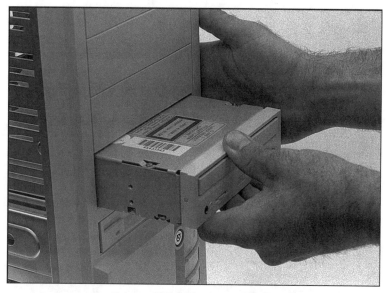

...and installing the CD-ROM drive

Step #29	Close the case only if everything functions correctly

Does everything function correctly? If so, there's no reason to leave the case open. If some screws haven't been used, try to find the ones for the tower case (there are probably six of them).

Disconnect all the cables so you can put the top of the case back on. Some tops have small guide rails at the bottom that fit into grooves on the bottom of the case. Then tighten all six screws to the case.

Congratulations, you did it. Your multimedia PC is now ready for use. Have fun with it.

The finished multimedia PC

FINAL SUGGESTIONS AND HELPFUL TIPS

Sound cards and speakers

A sound card, like a stereo system, is only as good as its speaker system. They can be either active or passive. Active speakers include built-in amplifiers and volume controls. These speakers boost the sound received from the sound card output.

Power supply for speakers

Active speakers require batteries or a separate power supply. We recommend using a power supply since batteries can wear out quickly. Passive speakers play whatever comes from the sound card without further modification. Volume is controlled at the card itself. With a sound card capable of 4 watts at 4 ohms per stereo channel, ordinary passive speakers, like those used on most stereo systems, are acceptable.

539

Building A Multimedia PC

Make certain to use shielded speakers. Speakers contain magnets which are strong enough to distort the picture on the monitor. Since you're likely to place at least one speaker near the monitor, the distortion could be quite noticeable. Shielded speakers on the other hand have no affect on your monitor because they shield the magnetic field.

See Chapter 9 for more information on speakers

Car speakers also work well since they're compact and produce high-quality sound. You could also use speakers designed for a Walkman-type personal stereo/cassette player. They're enclosed in finished cases and are affordable. However, they seldom produce the desired quality from a 32-bit sound card or even a 16-bit sound card that you'll need in your multimedia presentations. We recommend using these speakers only in preliminary work or if they're your only choice.

You could also use your stereo by connecting the auxiliary input jack on your stereo. Since stereo speakers are designed for quality output, the quality of control of the sound is quite good. However, this requires that your computer system and stereo equipment be close together. You also lose the portability of external speakers.

Microphone connector

A sound card meeting MPC specifications must have a microphone connector. A microphone allows you to record voice or sound effects. Then you can create, edit and play your sound files by using a sound editor such as those from Voyetra Technologies, Turtle Beach Systems, Inc. and others. The table on the right lists the features which a good microphone should include.

Feature	Ideal setting
Impedance	600 ohms
Sensitivity	74 decibels (dB) or higher

The purpose of a microphone is to receive external sound and then turn those signals into electrical impulses that are sent to your sound card.

The three types of microphones that can be used with sound cards are dynamic microphones and two types of condenser microphones.

Condenser microphones

Condenser microphones are also called electret microphones. This is the type of microphone that is typically included with sound cards. You can also buy them separately for less than $10. As their low cost suggests, the construction of a condenser microphone is usually less than solid. Furthermore, condenser microphones aren't known for a great frequency range. Therefore, a condenser microphone would have to be positioned fairly close to the input source to produce good recordings. They also sometimes requires a preamp so you can adjust its volume. Unfortunately, this can add noise and distort quality.

Some condenser microphones need batteries to operate. These batteries need to be replaced eventually. The condenser microphone must usually have its battery installed in order for it to work properly with sound cards.

If you are considering using your microphone only for voice recognition, the inexpensive condenser microphone will likely be acceptable.

Dynamic microphones

However, for more professional results, use a dynamic microphone. This is especially true for recording music vocals or a sound files for a business presentation. The dynamic microphone doesn't require an external power supply. It's a very durable and sturdy microphone. Dynamic microphones are either desktop or handheld microphones.

A dynamic microphone has more power, usually larger in size and have a better range compared to a condenser microphone. The results of recordings using this type of microphone will usually be of higher quality than the condenser microphones.

Although dynamic microphones suffered from poor response in high frequencies, newer models have been improved. However, even today's models of dynamic microphones are not noted for good response at either end of the audio spectrum. They distort less than the condenser microphones and can handle a heavier load of high volume sounds.

If you're considering buying or using a separate microphone, ask the sound card manufacturer to see which type of microphone works best with their sound cards. Also make certain whether your sound card will work with a stereo microphone

Chapter
12
Section
3

541

Joystick connector

You may need to calibrate an analog joystick before you can use them in a game. Refer to the documentation for our applications for more information on joystick calibration.

See Chapter 9 for more information on joysticks

Sound cards generate, record or play back sounds of any kind. These sounds include speech, music and sound effects. Besides recording over a microphone or stereo system connected to your sound card, you can create and record your own musical compositions on special synthesizers or keyboards attached through a MIDI interface.

Sound card connection options

Besides the general performance capabilities of a sound card, its connections to external audio sources is also important. You should be able to connect your sound card to a microphone and to a stereo system.

See Chapter 9 for more information on sound cards

These capabilities allow you to make music, radio and voice recordings. You can even mix microphone input with other audio signals.

As an alternative to direct microphone input, you can connect your sound card to another device (e.g., a tape player) throughout the Line-in connector. This allows you to record sounds at remote locations and then transfer them to your computer.

Speaker connection

Another important connection is for speakers. As we mentioned, you can use active or passive speakers depending on your needs and your sound card's output capacity.

Software volume control

Volume is usually controlled by appropriate software. Most sound cards include a mixer program.

Additional features you should look for in sound cards include the following:

❖ Mixer programs to regulate output volume.

❖ Mixer program which enables separate volume control for each input and output signal.

❖ Balance control (independent settings for the left and right stereo channels).

❖ Volume control on the back of the card.

Volume control for the Sound Blaster 16

MIDI interface

Another important connection, which is also part of the MPC standard, is a MIDI interface. MIDI (Musical Instrument Digital Interface) is a standardized (manufacturer-independent) file format for recording and exchanging musical instrument sound data.

Besides the actual musical notes, a MIDI file contains information such as dynamics, articulations, and instrument types. When played, the music is created by a sound card's synthesizer chips or by a synthesizer connected through a MIDI interface.

The MIDI interface is a special connector over which MIDI data is sent to a MIDI devices, such as synthesizers for reproducing songs and keyboards for entering songs. Sequencer programs can also create MIDI files.

These programs usually display an organ-like keyboard on the screen. You can use your mouse or computer keys to "play" the organ-like keyboard. You can record your own compositions and store them in MIDI format.

For example, Midisoft Studio for Windows is a powerful sequencer program that can help you record keystrokes from an external keyboard (real time sequencer) and edit complete MIDI files, note-for-note, on the screen (single-step sequencer).

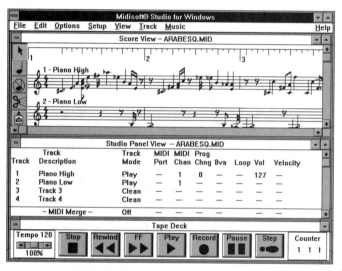

The different views in Midisoft

MIDI files can subsequently be edited by any program that processes the MIDI format.

Built-in amplifier

Another factor to consider when evaluating sound reproduction capability is power.

Power is measured in watts, as it is for stereo systems. Typical sound cards deliver from 1 to 6 watts per stereo channel at 4 ohms. Although this doesn't sound like much, it's actually quite sufficient. Most stereos, even the less expensive ones, are capable of at least 35 watts per channel. However, only 1 to 2 watts are needed for normal room listening volume.

> **NOTE**
>
> Some sound cards allow you to use a CD-ROM drive, usually by means of an integrated AT bus on the card. In other cases, a CD-ROM drive is connected through a SCSI interface, which requires an additional controller.
>
> It's also possible to connect a CD-ROM drive to a sound card so audio data is played over the sound card directly.

Another measure of sound reproduction capability is the number of synthesizer voices that can be produced per stereo channel. The process of frequency modulation can generate some very pleasant synthesized sounds.

In frequency modulation, the electrical oscillations that represent a sound can be adjusted, thus generating a different type of sound. Although this process may seem complicated, it's easily accomplished with the proper software and hardware. Most sound cards offer 11 voices per stereo channel.

The special FM chips found in sound cards (e.g., Yamaha) create the familiar background for many games and other synthesizers.

MPC specification

The following lists the major sound card requirements of the MPC standard:

External connections

- ❖ Microphone
- ❖ Speakers / headphones
- ❖ Stereo system
- ❖ MIDI devices
- ❖ CD-ROM drive

Input and output

- ❖ Built-in amplifier
- ❖ Synthesizer
- ❖ Stereo channels
- ❖ 16-bit (or 32-bit) DAC / ADC
- ❖ 22.05 KHz sampling rate (44.1 Khz recommended)

Chapter
12
Section
3

545

CMOS Setup With AMI BIOS

One major advantage of an XT or AT computer is its ability to be upgraded and changed. You can select from hundreds of hard drives and use many different types of graphics cards. You can start your computer from a 5.25-inch 360K disk drive, a 3.5-inch drive at 1.44 Meg or a network card with boot ROM.

You can add a large amount of memory to RAM or change the number of ports. Since your computer doesn't automatically recognize these changes, you must give it the opportunity to read this information. This is the purpose of CMOS memory and SETUP. All relevant information for operating the computer is stored in CMOS memory. A battery stores this information when you turn off the computer.

You use the SETUP program to change this information. In other words, you must use this program to tell your computer about any changes you make to the hardware.

SPECIAL AMI SETUP FEATURES

Older computers didn't have an integrated ROM SETUP program. Instead, you had to load the SETUP program from a bootable diskette. Now most computers have motherboards with an integrated ROM SETUP program.

Chapter 13

The AMI BIOS has one of the best SETUP programs on the market today. Along with the standard settings, the AMI BIOS has many enhanced setting options that are easy to use because of AMI BIOS' menu-driven system.

Also, the AMI BIOS has become very popular because of its reliability and low price. Most motherboards now include a BIOS from American Megatrends, Inc.

Safety precautions

The AMI BIOS has a security measure that reduces the chance of your making a drastic error while running the program. AMI BIOS even prevents you from making the mistake. You must confirm every important change you make in this program through a security prompt before the program executes the change.

If you are ever uncertain about how to answer the questions, press [Esc] to return to a more familiar part of the program. To exit the program without saving, simply switch off the computer.

However, the most important safety precaution in AMI SETUP is the option for ignoring the settings of advanced SETUP when you switch on the computer. To do this, hold down the [Ins] key when you switch on the computer until the memory test starts. Try this option first if your system doesn't react.

RUNNING AMI SETUP

The AMI SETUP program is executed before the computer loads the operating system. Therefore, device drivers aren't installed yet. Your mouse won't work either, so you'll have to run SETUP from the keyboard.

Keyboard layout

This presents our first problem. Since whatever keyboard driver you use isn't loaded yet either, your keyboard will act like an American keyboard. This also happens when you boot up the PC without running the AUTOEXEC.BAT file. Remember this if you use a keyboard layout that's different from the U.S. layout.

A confirmation dialog box appears every time you make a change or want to exit SETUP. Press Ⓨ to confirm this prompt. Depending on your type of BIOS, the program either ignores any other letter or interprets it as NO.

The following illustration lists and describes the keys you can use in AMI SETUP. Although the keys have the same function throughout the program, certain options may not always be available.

Available keys in AMI SETUP

Key	Function
Esc	Exits
← → ↑ ↓	Selects a menu item
Pg Up Pg Dn	Modifies the settings of an active menu item
F1	Displays a help screen for the selected menu item
F1 F3	Change the screen colors
F5	Retrieves the settings that were in effect when you started SETUP
F6	Loads the default values in BIOS for advanced CMOS SETUP and advanced SETUP
F7	Loads the startup defaults for advanced CMOS SETUP and advanced SETUP
F10	Saves the changes and exits the program

THE MAIN MENU

To access the main menu, press Del after BIOS completes the POST (Power On Self Test).

The main menu is divided into three areas: The copyright notice, the selection menu and the help line. At the bottom of the screen, an overview of the possible key functions is displayed. Use the cursor keys to move the selection bar to the individual menu items. When a menu item is selected, the help line displays a description of the selected option. We'll give you a detailed description of each option later in this section.

Chapter 13

Press the ⌈Ins⌋ key to execute the selected option. SETUP prompts you to press any key. Then you move to either another menu or SETUP prompts you to confirm your selection again.

Standard CMOS SETUP

Menu entry	STANDARD CMOS Setup

This is probably the most important option in SETUP. In the STANDARD CMOS SETUP screen you make all the basic settings for your computer. This menu contains the drive sizes, the hard drive parameters, RAM size, and many other settings.

Press any key to clear the warning from the screen.

You're now in the STANDARD CMOS SETUP screen. This screen is divided into six areas. The upper border displays the

> **NOTE**
>
> After selecting this menu item, first you'll see the warning we discussed. You can change settings in this menu that will crash your system. If this happens, hold down the ⌈Del⌋ key and turn on the computer.

copyright notice. Underneath this is the actual work window. Here you can select options by pressing the cursor keys.

In the upper-right corner of this window is a small area displaying the current memory size as determined by POST. You cannot switch to this window; AMI BIOS sets the memory size automatically. A small calendar in the lower right displays the current day saved in CMOS.

To the left of the date on some systems, you'll find the Help window. A list of the possible settings for each selected menu item appears here. You don't have to press ⌈F1⌋ because the help window is always active. Below the help window, in the lower-left corner, you'll find a reference to the keys and their functions.

Modifying standard CMOS settings

To modify the standard CMOS settings, select the corresponding menu item with the cursor keys. Then use ⌈Pg Up⌋ and ⌈Pg Dn⌋ to change the settings.

Choose from the following options:

Date:

Use (Pg Up) and (Pg Dn) to change the day and the year. The day of the week is automatically displayed.

Time:

Use (Pg Up) and (Pg Dn) to set the hours, minutes, and seconds. You can also enter the numbers directly from the keyboard.

Daylight Saving:

You can enable or disable this setting.

Hard drive types C: and D: (Hard drive C:/D: type)

This is where you define the standard type of your hard drive(s). AMI BIOS displays the parameters next to the hard drive type for you. So, if you don't know what type of hard drive you have, use the (Pg Up) and (Pg Dn) keys to browse through the default values and find the correct hard drive type.

If you don't find the correct type among the 46 default settings, you can also enter the parameters manually. To do this, select user defined hard drive type 47 (the user defined hard drive). Then use the cursor keys to select hard drive parameter entries.

Use the numeric keys to enter the appropriate values for your hard drive:

1. Number of cylinders (Cyln)

2. Number of heads (Head)

3. Precompensation (WPcom)

4. Land zone (LZone)

5. Number of sectors (Sect)

NOTE

If you don't know what to enter under points 3 and 4, we recommend entering the last track of your hard drive for land zone (i.e., the highest possible value) and either a 0 (always precompensation) or 65535 (no precompensation) for precompensation.

551

Chapter 13

It's sometimes necessary to set up two different hard drives, C: and D:, as user defined. Ami Setup also gives you this option. Hard drive type 47 for drive C: is not the same as hard drive type 47 for drive D:.

Floppy drives A: and B:

Enter the installed drive type here. Use the ⎡Pg Up⎤ and ⎡Pg Dn⎤ keys to make your entry. The information you enter here must be correct; otherwise you may no longer be able to boot from a diskette.

Primary display:

Enter the graphics card installed on your system here. If you have a Hercules (compatible) card, select "Monochrome". If you have a monochrome VGA screen, use the VGA/PGA/EGA option.

The Color 40x25 or 80x25 settings are for a CGA card. However, these settings will also usually work with an EGA/VGA card without producing an error message. You won't have any trouble with graphic output until later. Select this option only if you actually have a CGA card installed. The numbers refer to the number of characters that can be displayed in text mode.

Keyboard:

You can choose between switching off the keyboard test here. If you enter "Not installed", the POST won't perform the keyboard test. This will make the system start go faster.

ADVANCED CMOS SETUP

Menu entry	ADVANCED CMOS Setup

ADVANCED CMOS SETUP is one of the special features of the AMI BIOS. Use ADVANCED CMOS SETUP to make settings independent from the chip set of the motherboard. Unfortunately, the layout of this menu item varies from computer to computer. It's possible you won't find every menu item of your BIOS in the list discussed below. In these instances, press ⎡F1⎤ for the AMI BIOS Help system.

Special functions

After reading the usual warning, you'll move to the ADVANCED CMOS SETUP screen. Most options can be enabled or disabled. Some items have more than two settings.

Setting typematic frequency (Typematic Rate Programming)

If you hold down a key on your keyboard, the character is repeated after a certain delay on the screen. If you set this option to Enabled, then you can set the delay from the "Typematic Rate Delay (msec)" menu item and you can set the speed of the character repetition from the "Typematic Rate (Chars/Sec)" menu item.

Above 1 MB memory test

If your system takes too long to start up and you don't want to press Esc to skip the memory test (pressing Esc takes you to SETUP on some computers), then you can skip the test for memory above 1 Meg by setting this option to "Disabled".

Memory test tick sound

Set this option to "Disabled" if the ticking bothers you.

Memory parity error check

Enter "Disabled" here if you don't want the computer to check the parity bits.

NOTE
Since entering "Enabled" isn't practical, you should keep it set at "Enabled".

Press <Del> message display

Choose "Disabled" for this setting if you don't want the message to appear on the screen when you boot the computer.

Hard drive type 47 RAM area

AMI BIOS requires 1K of RAM for the user-defined hard drives (type 47). Use this option to determine whether this area should be in base system memory at 0:300 Hex, or in free DOS memory. Choose free DOS memory only if the base system memory is already occupied.

Chapter
13
Section
3

Chapter 13

Wait for <F1> if any errors

This setting determines whether the boot process should be interrupted until you press F1 if POST finds an error. Set this option to "Disabled" only if you are unable to eliminate an error but the system is still running.

System bootup <NumLock>

The external numeric keypad is usually set to numeric display when you boot the system. Set this option to "Disabled" if you don't want the keypad to be set to numeric display.

Numeric processor

Not all Setup programs have this option. If your computer cannot perform this setting automatically, then set "Present" if you have a WEITEK coprocessor.

Weitek processor

The POST cannot recognize the existence of an EK processor. If you installed an EK processor in your system, set this option to "Present".

Floppy Drive Seek At Boot

Set this option to "Disabled" to remove the typical boot-up noise. It also saves you time in the system test.

System Boot Up Sequence

Normally, the computer first tries to boot from the diskette. If a system diskette isn't in the drive, the computer tries to boot from the hard drive. Today, most computers start from the hard drive. So if you set this option to "C:,A:", you'll speed up the process while also protecting your computer from unauthorized access.

External/internal cache memory

Choose "Disabled" to slow down your computer, or if you have problems with expansion cards.

Password checking option

You can choose to have the computer prompt for the password every time you start up the system ("Always"), or only when you enter Setup ("Setup"). Select "Disabled" to remove the password prompt.

Turbo video mode

You'll occasionally find this option on some newer motherboards. Because Turbo Video Mode is set to "Disabled" by default, picture construction under MS-DOS is extremely slow. If your SETUP program has this function, be sure to set it to "Enabled".

Video ROM shadow C000, 16K

Use this option to copy the ROM-BIOS in the system to the root directory extension. This significantly speeds up your PC system. You should definitely set the Video and System ROM shadow to "Enabled". The Adapter ROM Shadow only makes sense if you have an adapter with BIOS. In these instances, enable only the address area that matches the address of your adapter ROM. For example, for a hard drive controller this area is usually at C800.

ADVANCED CHIPSET SETUP

Menu entry	ADVANCED CHIPSET Setup

The options of this menu depend on the chipset used on the motherboard. The options may appear differently on your computer, or may not appear at all. Since it would be impossible for us to cover all the versions of chipsets, press F1 for Help.

NOTE

The options of advanced chipset setup usually do more damage than good. If you aren't certain about the purpose of an option, press F7 to accept the default setting.

Hidden refresh

Set this option to "Enabled" to have the computer perform a RAM refresh without pausing the CPU. Sometimes the computer succeeds, but usually this option causes problems. We recommend leaving the option set to "Disabled" because the advantage in speed is only minimal.

ATBUS slow refresh

Choose "Enabled" for this setting to perform the RAM refresh only every fourth time.

AT cycle wait state

Enter "Enabled" here to add another wait state to the AT Bus. Sometimes this is a way to solve problems with older expansion cards.

DRAM read/write wait state

This setting allows you to choose from 0 to 3 wait states for read and write accesses. This setting depends on the access time of your RAMs and the recommendations in the manual for your motherboard.

> **NOTE**
>
> If you encounter memory problems (PARITY ERROR) while running your computer, try to solve the problem by setting all the wait states to their highest values.

Cache write W/S

Normally you can run static RAM of cache memory without wait states. The only time you must assign a wait state ("1W/S") is with the 40ns SRAM chips, which are rarely used.

Auto Configuration with BIOS DEFAULTS

Menu entry	AUTOCONFIGURATION WITH BIOS DEFAULTS/POWER-ON DEFAULTS

These options are part of the security functions provided by the AMI BIOS.

Use the first option, BIOS DEFAULTS, to set all the parameters of advanced SETUP back to their old values (i.e., the values stored in CMOS before you loaded the Setup program). For example, this option is useful when you make changes to settings and then decide you want to return to the old settings but you can't remember them.

The second option, POWER ON DEFAULTS, loads specific settings from a list in the BIOS ROM. Use this option to set all the parameters of advanced SETUP functions to harmless values (e.g., if the computer is no longer able to load its operating system, or if other disturbances occur during operation that could be related to the SETUP configuration).

Because both options are protected by a security prompt, you must press Ⓨ to confirm them again before they can be activated.

Then, select WRITE TO CMOS AND EXIT to quit SETUP.

> **NOTE**
>
> We recommend running this option before changing any settings of advanced Setup when you configure your motherboard for the first time. Frequently, even new motherboards have several possible changes available in advanced Setup that can result in computer crashes.

Protecting your data with a password

| Menu entry | CHANGE PASSWORD |

After you activate the menu item for changing the password, the program prompts you to enter the current password: ENTER CURRENT PASSWORD. If you haven't used a password before, the default password is "AMI".

Notice that your keystrokes won't appear as letters on the screen. Remember, no one else is supposed to know your password. After you enter the correct password, the program prompts you for the password: ENTER NEW PASSWORD.

Now enter the new password, which can contain up to six letters, and press the (Enter) key. The program then prompts you to enter the new password again with the following message:

RE-ENTER NEW PASSWORD

This is for your own security. If you make a mistake typing in the new password, an error message is displayed:

Then you'll return to the main menu. You can try again from here at any time.

HARD DRIVE HELP PROGRAM

Menu entry	HARDDISK UTILITY

This program lets you perform a low-level format on your hard drive, run a surface test, and set the interleave ratio. Each of these processes irretrievably destroys the data on your hard drive.

If you don't have other software to perform this task, use this formatting routine only if you have an MFM or RLL hard drive. We recommend using this program very carefully.

> **NOTE**
> Avoid this option if you have data on your hard drive that aren't backed up or you aren't certain whether you have an AT-bus hard drive installed in your computer (AT bus hard drives cannot be low-level formatted).

Since all versions of AMI BIOS aren't identical, a separate chapter is needed to thoroughly describe all the different options. We already talked about low-level formatting in the chapter on installing hard drives.

First, compare the hard drive parameters in the top half of the screen with the parameters of the hard drive installed on your computer. You can change these settings through standard CMOS Setup. Next, select the Hard Disk Format option and answer all the questions. Enter any bad tracks in the appropriate window and confirm the security prompt by pressing Ⓨ.

Quitting Setup

Menu entry	(DO NOT) WRITE TO CMOS AND EXIT

You can exit the SETUP program with or without saving the changes you made.

To exit SETUP:

1. To save your changes, either select WRITE TO CMOS AND EXIT or press F10. SETUP asks you whether you really want to save the changes and exit the program:

The default response is "N". Change it to "Y" and press Enter. The Setup program now writes your entries to the CMOS and, if everything is correct, the computer will run properly.

2. To exit SETUP without saving the changes, either select "DO NOT WRITE TO CMOS AND EXIT" or press Esc. Once again, you have to answer a security prompt:

The default value is "N". Select "Y" and then Enter to exit SETUP.

Chapter

13

Section

3

Maintaining Your PC

Naturally you want your PC and its peripherals to work flawlessly for a long time. However, for this to happen, you must take care of your PC system. You're only asking for trouble if you don't follow certain preventive procedures. These procedures include avoiding harmful actions and performing simple maintenance measures regularly. These measures help minimize wear and tear on your PC. They'll also help prevent major defects caused by dirt buildup on various components. Furthermore, when it comes time to sell your PC, its resale value will increase if you follow a strict preventive maintenance schedule now.

In this chapter we'll discuss the problems that can occur because of different conditions. Besides dust and smoke, other sources of problems include temperature changes, magnetic fields, and moisture.

However, remember these different factors do not affect all PC components to the same extent. For example, a keyboard and a mouse are subject to higher physical demands and external influences than a hard drive.

PLAN BEFORE YOU BUY

If you're planning to buy a new PC, consider service and support to be as important as any component in the system. For example, consider any warranty options the dealer or manufacturer offers. Most will offer extended warranties besides the normal warranty. Extended warranties are typically two-year or three-year warranties.

Warranties and extended warranties

The warranty has become an important selling point for many manufacturers. Regardless of where you buy your PC system, read the warranty carefully. Make certain you understand the exact terms of service and support provided in the manufacturer's warranty. For example you should be able to answer these questions:

1. Buying from a mail order company has certain advantages. However, if you need to return the complete system or exchange a part, make certain you know beforehand who pays the shipping costs. This includes shipping both there and back.

2. How often is phone support available? Many vendors offer support only on weekdays or during daytime hours. Other vendors offer unlimited phone and online support available 24 hours a day every day.

3. Is software support free or is an extra charge involved?

4. It's possible the vendor will come to your house or business to make a repair. If so, make certain you know how soon the technician(s) will appear.

5. See if the service center provides a "loaner" PC while yours is being repaired. This is especially important if the repair takes a few days.

Don't be afraid to ask other users about their experiences with different manufacturers. Check the Internet newsgroups or America Online's PC Hardware Forum (Keyword, PC Hardware) or CompuServe's Consumer Forum (Go SAVE).

Extended warranty

Most extended warranties cover parts and labor. However, make certain you know exactly what you'll be getting for your money. Some companies give you the option of buying a warranty that covers parts only. Therefore, you may not need to pay labor you'll never use if you're comfortable installing parts yourself. All you need is some basic troubleshooting skills, tools and access to parts. Then you can eliminate part or maybe all of an extended warranty.

Some extended warranties take effect at time of purchase but others take effect when the original factory warranty expires.

> **NOTE**
>
> One point to consider about extended warranties: Most hardware failures occur within a few months of purchase. However, if you feel more comfortable with a comprehensive support and service plan, buy an extended warranty.
>
> Also, buying an on-site warranty doesn't necessarily mean a technician will rush to your house and fix your problem. It often means that the technician will ask you to troubleshoot every possible source of the problem. They'll appear at your location only when necessary.

Third party warranties

Many third-party tech-support services claim to offer better and faster service and support than the manufacturer. Many third party warranties are typically 5% to 10% of the purchase price of the system. So, for a $2000 system, a third party warranty costs about $200. A few third-party extended warranties may include on-site repair, parts and labor. In addition, some warranties may include the cost of sending the technician to your site or for overnight shipping.

You probably don't need all this coverage. An extended warranty is usually a way for the dealer or manufacturer to make extra money. The cost of extended warranties is usually so high that it can only be justified for critical systems (file servers, print servers, etc.). However, if you buy an extended warranty, make sure you're buying superlative service. Also, the warranty should include free shipping (both ways) for hardware that cannot be serviced on site. This hardware would include printers, laptops and monitors.

Chapter
14
Section
3

A few manufacturers let you renew your warranty (called *recertification*). However, the manufacturer is likely to charge fee to send out a technician to your location to check the condition of your PC. After the warranty expires it's usually to your advantage to have your PC serviced only when it's needed. This is especially true if you have an older (three years plus) system. Remember, too, that as the price of PCs continue to fall, you're still paying a lot of money to maintain older technology.

Finding a good service center

A good idea to save time and frustration is to know where the reputable service centers are located in your area before you need them. Follow these steps to find a good repair shop:

1. Call your system's manufacturer. They'll refer you to a certified dealer in your area.

2. Ask other users for recommendations. The best advertising is often word-of-mouth.

3. Check to see who repairs the systems at your workplace. Usually, a repair firm that services large companies on an ongoing basis is very reputable.

4. Post an E-mail message in an online service or a local bulletin board that deals with computer repair and support questions.

5. Contact your local computer users group or SIG (Special Interest Group). These groups are a great source of information.

If you need to take your PC to the service center, follow these suggestions:

1. Get the repair person to talk about your problem.

2. Make certain you understand the problem(s) entirely. Know what needs to be fixed.

3. How long will the repair take.

4. How much will the repair cost.

5. Get everything above in writing.

HARD DRIVE MAINTENANCE TIPS

You can easily customize the following tips and techniques to your normal work schedule with your PC.

The following rules may seem obvious to many users but you may be surprised how few user follow them.

Back up your data

Use a floppy disk, tape or removable storage device (see Chapter 8) to back up important files. Windows 3.1, DOS 6.x and Windows 95 all feature built-in backup programs. Otherwise, several commercial programs are available that can do the job very easily for you.

Back up your hard drive at least once a month if you use your computer mainly for entertainment. Otherwise, back up at least once a week if you keep your finance records, work files or other important documents/files on your PC.

Before backing up any data, make certain to exit programs and shut down your PC properly. Then restart the PC. Otherwise, you risk losing data.

Keep your hard drive organized

Keep your files and folders organized. Your PC will run faster if it has to look through fewer files and folders. You should make program and file maintenance a routine task. Check the contents of your hard drive occasionally. Determine the files that you still need and delete unwanted files. Archive files you want to keep but no longer use. Assign a specific directory or folder for all applications when storing data files. Deleting files not only creates more room on your drive, it also makes organizing your files easier.

Maintaining Your PC

Many programs, such as Microsoft Word, automatically save backup copies of their data files (usually having a .BAK extension). Although this is a fairly practical function, it can require a great deal of hard drive space. Other programs create temporary files (files with a .TMP extension). Delete these files regularly.

Run a defragmenting utility. It will reorganize the files on the hard drive so the pieces that make up the file are grouped together. Defragging your drive will also usually speed up its performance level. Your hard drive's read/write head won't jump around as much on a defragmented drive. See Chapter 8 for information on running a defragger.

Treat your hard drive with respect

Don't jostle your system while it's running. Hard drives operate like record players: A delicate read/write head retrieves data from spinning magnetic platters. Slight bumps can make the read/write heads crash into the platters and possibly corrupt data and even damage the disk. Also, keep your PC on a sturdy, level spot to avoid sudden shifts.

Checking your hard drive

Use CHKDSK (Windows 3.x) or ScanDisk (Windows 95). These utilities will look for file fragments and other problems and repair them. See Chapter 8 for more information.

PREVENTIVE MAINTENANCE TIPS

Emergency boot disk

When a serious problem emerges with a DOS/Windows PC, your system will often issue an error message (Configuration Error, Invalid Setup, or Boot Disk Failure, for example) and then lock up. You can't diagnose and repair the problem until you get your system up and running. The only way to override these messages is to restart your computer from drive A, rather than from the hard drive. To do this, you'll need an emergency boot floppy disk, which you can create from any blank floppy disk.

Windows 3.x

If you're running Windows 3.x, you'll first need to quit Windows. Then insert the new floppy diskette into drive A. At the C:\> prompt, type the following:

```
FORMAT /S A:
```

and press the Enter key. This will format the floppy disk and copy crucial system files to it. Now you'll want to add some other key startup files. Type each of the lines below, pressing the Enter key at the end of each one and waiting for the C:\> prompt to return before typing the next line:

```
COPY C:\AUTOEXEC.BAT A:
COPY C:\CONFIG.SYS A:
COPY C:\WINDOWS\SYSTEM.INI A:
COPY C:\WINDOWS\WIN.INI A:
```

Your boot disk is now complete. Keep it in a cool, dry place.

Windows 95

Windows 95 lets you create an emergency startup disk during installation or at a later time. Insert a blank floppy diskette in drive A. Open the Add/Remove Programs application in Control Panel. Click on the "Startup Disk" tab and click on the Create Disk... button. Windows will walk you through the steps.

Consult your PC's manual to learn how to visit your computer's CMOS setup screen (look up Setup in the index). This screen lists how much base memory and extended memory is installed in your PC; write this information on the boot floppy's label. Your boot disk is now complete. Keep it in a cool, dry place.

Chapter **14** Section **3**

567

Maintaining Your PC

Avoiding nicotine, dust and heat buildup

A layer of dust will cover your computer's housing if it isn't cleaned regularly. The unused interior of the PC will remain relatively free of dust. Very little dust can enter the PC through its vents.

However, dust can quickly and completely cover the interior of a PC that is used several hours a day. The fan unit in the power supply pulls warm air out of the PC interior. As a result, fresh air enters the PC housing through its openings. This fresh air carries dust and other particles, particularly nicotine.

Since floppy drives aren't sealed units, air and dirt can also enter through their openings very quickly. Dust particles and nicotine are deposited on the drive's read/write heads. These substances will eventually affect the drive's operation.

Humidity can cause the coating of dust on the inside of your PC to form a type of insulating layer. This leads to heat buildup in the PC's components. Excessive heat can shorten the life span of or even destroy processors and other components inside your PC.

Dust also can contain chemicals that are good conductors of electricity. These chemicals could cause minor short circuits or create electrical signal paths where none should exist. The chemicals in the dust could also cause rapid corrosion of cable connectors, socket installed components, and where areas where boards plug into slots.

Although Pentium class computers do not use a math coprocessor, some 486 processors still need math coprocessors. These coprocessors were especially sensitive to dust and temperature changes. Even a slight temperature increase in a PC tower case located over an under floor heating system may lead to hardware damage. In this case, a coprocessor might first return incorrect values and eventually will not function.

NOTE

Excessive temperature changes are never good for your PC. The ideal temperature range for operating personal computers is between 65 and 75 degrees Fahrenheit. Too much heat can easily destroy electronic components or the processor and coprocessor. These components are designed for a constant operating temperature range.

Hard drive systems using high data densities, for example RLL or ARLL systems, may produce read errors at exceedingly high or low temperatures. In these instances, the temperature extremes simply cause the data carrier to expand or contract too much.

Moisture and liquids

You've probably heard warnings about placing food or drinks near your PC. However, too many PC users still place coffee mugs and other drinks dangerously close to their PCs. So, unfortunately, accidents can happen, and something can be spilled onto your PC motherboard.

If an accident does occur, never use a hair dry to dry the wet components. Although this method will eventually dry your hardware, it may also destroy components through overheating. Disassemble your PC into its individual components. Then use a lint-free cloth to dab the components gently. Allow the components to air-dry for several days before reassembling your PC.

Preventing moisture buildup inside your PC

Whenever you're transporting your PC system over long distances, we recommend placing a small bag of moisture absorbent material (such as silica gel) in the interior of your PC. Use tape or a rubber band, if necessary, to fasten this bag to the interior of the case. This will keep the bag from jostling components and expansion cards.

You should also follow this tip when you store your PC in the trunk of your car overnight or if you won't be using your PC for a very long time. This helps absorb any moisture that condenses inside the PC.

Such bags of moisture absorbent material are usually available at camera supply stores or electronics and computer stores.

NOTE

Never immediately turn on a computer which was exposed to cold temperatures and then returned to a heated room. Wait at least thirty minutes (preferably longer) to allow any condensed moisture of your PC to evaporate. Also, allow the components to reach room temperature before turning on the PC.

Excessive moisture or humidity levels will corrode metal surfaces over longer periods of time. Corroded cable contacts are extremely rare in PC systems; they usually occur only under very poor conditions.

However, corrosion results in error symptoms that are usually very difficult to diagnose. Usually these symptoms will be intermittent (one time it works, another time it doesn't). You should occasionally check your system's cable connections for corrosion.

Magnetic and radio frequency interference

Your PC and its peripherals are susceptible to interference by strong magnetic fields. These magnetic fields are produced by other electronic devices or even the computer's peripherals. For example, power supplies that are insufficiently shielded produce such magnetic fields. These fields can cause your monitor's picture to become blurred. Other common sources of interference include the following:

❖ Locating a laser printer too close to the monitor.

❖ Poorly shielded printer cables that are in close contact with electrical power cords may also result in faulty printer output.

❖ Using speakers that are not shielded.

Magnetic fields can also destroy information stored on data carriers. Therefore, do not place diskettes, removable storage cartridges, etc., near any source of magnetic fields. This is true even for a short time.

Even screwdrivers with magnetic tips can destroy your DOS diskettes. So always keep tools at a very safe distance.

Speakers and even sound cards also present an interference potential. Make certain to use shielded speakers. So, use care in placing these speakers, avoiding diskettes and other data carriers.

All speakers contain magnets. So, the magnets in speakers can damage data on diskettes or even on hard drives. Make certain to use speakers designed with magnetic shielding built into their cases. This shielding will prevent damaging data or interfering with the monitor.

Static electricity

Static electricity is the little spark you feel when your finger comes close to a door knob after you've walked across a carpet on a dry day (called an "ESD event"). You probably won't notice or feel an ESD event below 3,000 volts. In order to feel this electrostatic discharge (ESD), the charge must be around 3,500 volts. However, a sensitive computer part can be destroyed or become damaged with charges as low as 250 volts

Fortunately the damage caused by an ESD event often is minor. It usually requires simply rebooting, reprinting or restarting. However, the damage is cumulative. In other words, too many shocks will damage the computer to the point of where it's inoperable. Also, ESD can not only erase floppies and hard drives but fry the electronics inside and between computer chips.

Furthermore, some research has recently suggested that the electrostatic field between the user and the computer system causes a number of health related risks to users who spend as little as two hours daily in front of a computer. These problems range from sore eyes to nausea all the way to a rash on face, neck and arms. Whether these health concerns are justified is open to debate. However, what isn't debatable is the potential damage ESD event can do to your PC system.

Preventing ESD events and ESD damage

Preventing ESD damage is quite simple. The first step is to understand there is a potential danger in ESD. Then, follow these simple rules and techniques:

❖ Safely ground yourself before working on your PC.

❖ Use an antistatic mat beneath the computer. Touch the mat before touching any part of the computer (see Chapter 10).

❖ When shipping or storing computer parts, use a static dissipative, static shielding, or complete environmental barrier material.

❖ Make certain the building or house is grounded properly by using an outlet tester.

❖ Other devices include range from the simple (antistatic grounding wrist straps) to the exotic (target area ionizers)

Chapter

14

Section

3

571

Chapter 14

Never underestimate the dangers of static electricity if you're working inside your PC or when handling chips or cards. A static discharge that is not routed to the ground can destroy or damage a computer component. Always ground yourself first by touching the computer case of by touching the bracket of a card or adapter.

PREVENTIVE MAINTENANCE AND CARE

Personal computers are almost completely maintenance-free devices. However, you can easily perform a few simple maintenance and care measures yourself. Simply make a habit of thoroughly cleaning your PC system twice a year.

Diskette care

Although a 3.5-inch diskette is durable in its plastic shell, it's not indestructible. So by following a few simple tips, you can prolong the life of your program and data diskettes:

❖ Avoid extremes of temperature. If a disk becomes hot or cold, let it reach room temperature before placing it in the drive.

❖ Keep disks away from magnets. Don't place diskettes near the monitor or speakers - they have their own magnetic fields.

❖ Keep diskettes dry and in a dust-free protective case.

❖ Listen for sounds of trouble. Grinding and grating noises or squeaks and squeals are indications that a floppy diskette is quickly becoming useless.

Cleaning the interior and exterior of your PC

A good preventative maintenance plan always includes regular cleaning of the PC. Both the interior and exterior should be cleaned thoroughly. The best way of cleaning the interior of your PC is by using a fine brush. These types of brushes are used to clean paintings. Make certain that the power is switched off (better yet - remove the plug from the electric socket). Touch a metal side of the case to discharge static before reaching into it. Clean the motherboard thoroughly with this brush.

Use a can of compressed air with a long nozzle tube to get at hard-to-reach places or for large dust bunnies. Most electronic stores sell cans of compressed air. Make certain to buy and use compressed air that is designed for cleaning or dusting off computer equipment. The compressed air is used like a blower to remove dust and gunk. This makes it easy to remove dust anywhere in your system. Never wipe PC components with moistened cloths. Use only dry methods of removing dust from your PC.

Clean the exterior of your system's power supply unit. The holes in the unit's casing collect a large amount of dust and nicotine. If these holes become clogged, the PC's ventilation system won't work properly. This can lead to heat buildup and, ultimately, hardware damage. Use either a brush, compressed air or cotton swabs to clear the fan blades and screen.

Check the fan for buildup of gunk. Air should flow smoothly through the fan to cool off your PC.

Cleaning the drive(s)

Like all PC components that rely on moving mechanical parts, disk drives are susceptible to wear and tear. Regular maintenance can increase their life span considerably. Remove the drives from your system. Use compressed air to blow all dust deposits completely from their interior. Before re-installing the drives, use a cotton swab dampened with rubbing alcohol to clean the read/write heads gently.

Be careful not to bend any components, and do not open the drive housing under any circumstances. You should always keep your diskettes in their dust sleeves. Also, try to keep the area around your drives clean so the heads don't become dirty too quickly.

573

Hard drives are designed to be maintenance-free PC components. They're sealed to prevent contaminants like dust or nicotine from entering the hard drive. You can minimize the chance of hard drive surface damage by preventing sudden movements or shocks to your PC.

Cables and connections

While cleaning your PC you should also check all the cable connections inside and outside your PC. Make sure the cables are seated securely. Clean any contacts that show signs of corrosion. Cover unused connectors of free cables with electrical tape to prevent contamination and dirt buildup.

Cleaning the keyboard

Keyboards are probably second to a mouse in collecting gunk. However, never shake your keyboard to remove gunk. Doing so usually just traps the gunk under the key caps. Instead, tip the keyboard upside down and use a can of compressed air to blow out the spaces between individual keys.

The best way of cleaning your keyboard is the following. First, make certain to switch off the computer. Then open the keyboard housing. Use a fine brush to clean the keyboard interior thoroughly. Clean the keyboard housing and the keys using a cloth dampened with water and very mild detergent. Some users also find household window cleaner with ammonia a good cleaner for keyboards.

You should be able to remove the keycaps from your keyboard. This makes cleaning the keyboard much easier. If any liquids enter the keyboard, be sure that it dries out completely before using it again.

Cleaning the mouse

Your mouse is probably the number collector of gunk in your PC system. They use a rubber ball that rolls against wheels inside the unit. Since this ball also contacts the table or desk surface as the mouse is moved, it picks up dirt and dust. This debris soon finds its way into the interior of the mouse. This buildup of dirt and dust eventually affects the mouse's operation.

Fortunately, they're easy to clean. Rotate the small disk on the bottom of your mouse to release the roller ball from the housing of the mouse. Clean the ball regularly using a damp cloth. The small rollers that contact the roller ball can be cleaned with cotton swabs and rubbing alcohol.

To minimize this problem, make certain the mouse pad or surface on which you use the mouse is clean. Clean the mouse pad occasionally as well.

Cleaning the monitor

Don't forget to include the monitor in your regular PC cleaning jobs. Make certain to switch off your monitor before you start to clean it. Simply use household glass cleaner to clean both the screen and the monitor housing. Never spray the liquid on the monitor. Instead, spray the cleaner onto the cloth first and then wipe off the monitor. You don't want any liquid entering any openings or cracks in the monitor.

COMPUTER VIRUSES

A problem that has remained serious for several years is that of computer viruses. This problem continues because of the increasing number of PC users sharing data, using worldwide networks and using electronic mail systems.

As you probably already know, many viruses don't become active immediately after infecting a program. Instead, they remain dormant for a certain time. Their usual task is to become resident in the PC's memory when their host program is started. Then they infect programs that are executed later.

NOTE

Since viruses are simply clever programs, they take up space on the diskette on which they are residing. Therefore, when a virus attaches itself to a program file, that file's size increases. The unexplained increase in a program file's size always indicates a likely virus. If you're not checking file sizes regularly, the viruses go undetected. However, not only program files can be infected, but any type of file type.

The virus starts only when several predetermined factors are combined. These factors can include the date (Michelangelo virus) or a specific number of times the host program is started. The result of a virus infection ranges from humorous to completely destructive. This range includes crumbling screen pictures with raining letters as well as the irrevocable destruction of all hard drive contents.

Printing directories

Print a hardcopy of the directories on your hard drive at regular intervals. Compare this printout with earlier printouts. This is a very simple way of detecting viruses that may have infected your hard drive. Use this method with diskettes, too.

To obtain a hardcopy of any directory, simply reroute your screen output to the printer using the following DOS command:

```
DIR > PRN
```

You may also use "LPT1:" or "LPT2:" instead of "PRN", depending on which parallel port your printer is connected.

Anti-virus programs

Thousands of computer viruses have been written and new ones appear daily. Be sure to compare how frequently different manufacturers update their virus protection programs when looking for this type of software. The effectiveness of an anti-virus program depends on its ability to detect current or new viruses. So, you should buy virus protection software only from manufacturers who update their products regularly. One of the best known is from McAfee Associates. For more information see *McAfee Anti-Virus for Beginners* from Abacus.

Effective virus protection

No fail-safe methods of virus protection exist. However, you can minimize your computer's chance of becoming infected by virus. The following guidelines will help you:

1. Only use original software

   The best way to prevent virus infection is to use only data carriers that are write-protected by the manufacturer. This write protection is irreversible on 5.25-inch diskettes. The slot on the side of the diskette, which must be exposed to write to the diskette, is simply missing.

   If such a diskette is copied while a virus is resident in the PC's memory, the copy will be infected with the virus. Most likely this infection will be completely unnoticed.

   If your system becomes infected with a virus, you must reinstall your software without contracting the same virus again. This is when the software's original diskettes are invaluable.

   Often you can buy used software. You can usually save quite a bit of money by buying programs this way. As long as the software is on original diskettes, with the irreversible write-protection we mentioned above, it should be safe.

2. Never let others use your PC, for example, to make copies of diskettes. Your PC system will also be infected if a virus has infected the files being copied. Always think twice about placing an unknown diskette in your floppy drive. This is exactly the way that viruses, just like other programs, get onto your hard drive.

3. Avoid downloading software through your modem, from other PCs or from mailboxes. This is how most computer viruses are transmitted.

   You must make informed decisions about how to use your system. Remember, don't allow third parties to use your computer and use only original programs. These are the easiest ways of preventing a computer virus.

Chapter 14

OTHER TIPS & TECHNIQUES

Write-protect data

You're probably aware of the importance of write-protecting important floppy disks. By moving the small tab until the square hole appears prevents you from accidentally writing to it. You can also change the attribute of a file on your hard drive to "read-only" so it isn't accidentally deleted.

Password-protection isn't foolproof but it can keep some users away from areas where they shouldn't be. Some commercial programs are available that allow you to password-protect programs and files on your hard disk..

Registering software

Registering the software you buy has several advantages:

❖ Faster access to technical support phone lines

❖ You'll be notified of bug fixes

❖ Discounts on new versions (sometimes big discounts)

❖ Discounts on the company's other products

❖ No hassle replacement of damaged disks

Calling technical support

If or when you need to call technical support, have the following information available. This will help the technician determine your problem and solution faster:

❖ The amount of memory installed in your system

❖ The amount of free disk space you have

❖ The version of the operating system you are running

❖ For DOS/Windows PCs, printouts of your AUTOEXEC.BAT and CONFIG.SYS files from your root directory

❖ For Windows PCs, printouts of your WIN.INI and SYSTEM.INI files from the Windows directory.

❖ The version number of the program (when calling about a specific program)

Preventing electrical interference

Any electrical devices will produce some interference. Put your speakers too close together and they may shriek and squeal. Also, some devices can affect the images your monitor; more importantly, some electrical interference can damage data on floppy diskettes, tapes and even hard drives.

Make certain to buy and use shielded speakers and shielded power supplies. Otherwise, they can produce enough interference to affect the monitor's colors and image quality. The easiest solution is to keep magnetic devices as far away from one another as possible. Also, fluorescent lamps, radios, stereos, televisions and printers discharge electrical interference. Keep them as far away as possible from your PC, too.

Power and spike protection

Protect your PC from spikes and surges. Make certain to plug your PC's and its components' into three-pronged, grounded outlets. Switch off your PC and all peripherals before connecting or disconnecting any cables or adding new hardware. Plugging a keyboard, monitor, printer, or CD-ROM drive into your system while electricity is flowing can turn your system and the peripheral into expensive paperweights.

A surge suppressor is a good idea. Surge suppressors intercept power surges and high-voltage spikes that occasionally affect power lines. Make certain it meets the UL 1449 standard and is rated to at least 330 volts.

For even more protection, consider an uninterruptible power supply (UPS). It acts as a backup battery for your PC. When the electrical power stops or dips too low to run your PC, a UPS automatically powers on and saves important data.

Chapter

14

Section

3

579

Troubleshooting Problems

15

Although your computer is usually very reliable, you've probably also experienced occasions when it hasn't worked properly. For example, maybe you've been unable to print documents or use your new modem to access the Internet. A problem somewhere in the PC system can frustrate even the most humble person.

Therefore, having a system for locating errors can be very helpful. By using this system, you can not only find the source of an error, you can probably correct the problem. In many cases this is possible even if you don't know much about the technical aspects of your computer.

Unfortunately, this process is much more difficult than it sounds. Computers are complicated and sensitive machines. So, solving problems can be frustrating and time-consuming. One reason it's difficult to locate errors on computers is that a symptom doesn't always lead to the cause of a problem. For example, a defective printer port could be the cause of formatting problems on the printed page. Also, a keyboard problem could cause the computer to "hang up" during booting. Perhaps you may think there is a hard drive error because the hard drive control LED is flashing.

Most errors, even obvious ones, can have completely different causes than their symptoms indicate. It's important to remember this when you're trying to locate errors, even when you're using a specific system.

POSSIBLE SOURCES OF PROBLEMS

This section talks about sources of some general or typical problems you're likely to have.

Genuine defects

Errors caused by genuine defects involve defective electronic components. For example, the problems may be the result of a defect in an expansion card, the CPU, RAM or another component of the motherboard, etc.

A genuine defect is rare. However, of all the possible errors, these errors are the one most likely to fool users (i.e., they usually cause problems in areas for which they aren't even responsible). Therefore, these defects make it very difficult to find the source of the error.

Cable problems

The flat ribbon cables used to connect disk drives and hard drives are very sensitive. Additional connections can often cause loose contacts when the PC heats up. This results in drive problems.

If your printer or mouse stops working, a defective printer cable or mouse cable is much more likely to be the cause of the problem than the printer port or mouse port. Fortunately, this type of error usually occurs immediately after you install the expansion card. So, it's fairly easy to diagnose.

Usually specific jumpers for setting port addresses, IRQs, or DMA channels are incompatible with other components in the system that have the same settings.

Expansion cards installed wrong

Another cause of errors is an incorrectly installed expansion card. For example, the card could shift when you screw it into the slot.

Also, you could try an "impossible" configuration, such as installing a second combination controller that isn't designed to be a second controller (i.e., the controller is intended for use as a first controller).

582

CMOS SETUP problems

One of the most common causes of problems involves CMOS SETUP. The problem is usually caused by an old accumulator or an empty battery. This results in the loss of all the setup data. Since the PC can no longer recognize the hard drive, the system cannot be started.

Entering the wrong drive type or video adapter can also cause problems.

It's especially difficult if the system BIOS has an advanced SETUP (usually AMI BIOS) that changes the bus clock or the RAM Refresh. AMI's ADVANCED CMOS SETUP allows settings that will completely lock up your computer.

The only solution is to delete all the CMOS data, either by holding down i when you switch on the computer, or by discharging the accumulator (there is a jumper on the motherboard for doing this).

It's difficult to differentiate between these types of problems and genuine defects.

Software problems

Software that has been installed incorrectly, used incorrectly, or is simply defective can cause almost any kind of error. These errors can range from write errors on a disk drive or hard drive to a memory parity error, which causes a system crash.

It's beyond the scope of this book to analyze software problems. This is due primarily to the sheer number of different programs that are available. Another reason is that programs behave differently, depending on the computer configuration.

Therefore, we'll only talk about hardware errors and problems in this chapter.

Chapter 15

FINDING THE SOURCE OF ERRORS

As you saw in the previous section, many errors can be divided into categories based on their source. However, what do you do when a problem has several symptoms but you can't determine their sources?

We'll use an example to demonstrate how difficult it can be to find the source of a problem. Suppose that your mouse suddenly stops working. You believe the only possible reason for this to happen is that your mouse is defective. So, you buy a new mouse. However, when you try this mouse, it doesn't work either. So, still believing the problem is with the mouse (even with a new mouse), you return it to your dealer to exchange it for a different mouse.

However, even this second mouse doesn't work. Now you're suspicious that the mouse isn't the source of your problem. So, you take both the new mouse and your original mouse to a friend's house and try both on her PC. She checks both of these mice on her computer and discover they both work.

So, nothing is wrong with the mice, and you haven't made any changes to your software or hardware configuration, except for installing a battery. This means that something must be wrong with the serial port.

When you open the computer to replace the interface card, you notice that battery box, which is taped to the power supply with electrical tape, is very close to the interface card.

When you installed the battery you didn't make any changes to the expansion card. However, you remember that you disconnected one of the flat ribbon cables to find the contacts for connecting the external CMOS battery to the motherboard. Then you plugged the cable back in, just as the cable from the second serial port was plugged in.

However, the interface card didn't contain any information about how the flat ribbon cable should be plugged in. So, you realize that you may have plugged the cable in incorrectly. When you turn the cable around and plug it back in, the port works again.

The cable of the second serial port was also plugged in upside down. Most likely it was like this when you purchased the computer. However, you didn't notice this because you didn't use the second port.

This example illustrates two basic problems in identifying and eliminating errors on PCs. First, it shows that it's helpful to try out components, which you think are defective, on another computer before replacing them. However, not many users have access to more than one computer.

The example also shows how important it is to consider the source of the error from all different points of view. The source of the error can be in an entirely different area than you might have first guessed.

Narrowing down potential sources

To save yourself from time-consuming repairs like the one in the example, especially ones that are expensive, ask yourself the following questions before you take any action:

When did you first notice the error?

For example, did you notice the error after installing software, moving the PC, etc.? The answer to this question may help you find the solution to a problem, especially if the change doesn't seem related to the problem.

When exactly does the error occur?

Knowing when the error occurs (e.g., before, during or after the booting process), can also help you find the source of the problem.

Can you reproduce the error?

Try to accurately describe the conditions under which the error occurred. A time error that takes place before the computer warms up will definitely have a different source than an error that always occurs after you call a program (e.g., a specific DOS command).

What does the error look like?

Being aware of the computer's other actions when an error occurs can also help you find the source of the error. For example, the number and duration of beeps that sound when you switch on your computer provides useful information.

Any other changes to the computer can also be important. Does the fan or the hard drive run, do the LEDs light up, etc.?

Troubleshooting Problems

After narrowing down the sources of the error by answering these questions, you can begin to solve the problem.

Before making any major changes, such as removing a CD-ROM drive, always check all the cable connections and how these connections fit together. This usually saves you a lot of work.

If you can borrow PC components, start by replacing the parts you think are defective. If replacement parts aren't available, you might solve the problem by removing all the components that aren't needed to run the computer or the

> **NOTE**
>
> As with all actions on the computer hardware, the advice we gave at the beginning of Chapter 9 applies here. Above all, never change anything while the power supply is switched on, and always ground yourself. After all, we want to eliminate errors, not cause new ones.

components that obviously have nothing to do with the error. Sometimes removing such a part also removes the error.

COMMON ERRORS

This section describes the most common errors according to their symptoms. We'll use these symptoms to determine the source of the error accurately.

Unfortunately, because of the difficulties described, we won't always be able to do this. It's also possible that your symptom won't appear in the following list because there are so many possible sources. In these instances, a description of a similar problem may help.

After certain changes, such as installing expansion cards, refer to the section or chapter that discusses the change. You may have made a mistake or overlooked something.

Errors after startup

Errors / Problems	You switched on the computer, the screen stays dark, the fan and hard drive won't run, LEDs don't light up

If the power supply cord and the outlet are working properly, most likely there's problem with the power supply.

Open the computer (not the power supply) to determine whether the power supply itself is defective or some other computer part is causing a short circuit.

Then separate each component, one by one, from the power supply. Each time you do this, switch the computer on and off to check whether the fan for the power supply works.

Start with the floppy drives and then continue with the hard drive(s). If the fan begins running again, reconnect the last component and switch on the PC again. The fan may have a short circuit if it still continues not to work. Unfortunately, it's usually not cost effective to replace or repair a fan.

If you still haven't found anything, separate the motherboard from the power supply next. Before switching on the computer, make sure you reconnect something to the power supply. It's best if you connect a hard drive. You cannot run most power supply units unloaded.

If the fan still won't run, your power supply unit is probably defective. Remove it from the computer and take it to your computer dealer for a second opinion.

However, if the vent starts running and the hard drive you connected also works, the error is on the motherboard. Reconnect the motherboard (make certain to switch off the power supply first). Remove all the expansion cards. Switch on the PC each time you remove a card to check for improvement.

If you still haven't eliminated the short circuit after removing the last card, the source of the error is then the motherboard itself. Ensure that the power supply runs without the motherboard connected and then remove the motherboard.

It's usually cheaper to exchange the motherboard than have it repaired. (This is especially true if you can still use the memory components and the CPU.)

Troubleshooting Problems

Chapter 15

Errors / Problems	Computer beeps, fan runs, screen stays dark

The beeping is an error message from the Power-On Self-Test (POST). The POST beeps because the system error is so serious that even simple screen output is no longer possible. You can identify the different errors by the duration and number of beeps. You'll find a summary of these acoustical error messages at the end of this chapter.

Errors / Problems	One or more three digit or four digit numbers appear on the screen, computer stalls

This is also a POST message. The numbers are codes for different hardware errors. You'll also find a list of these codes at the end of this chapter.

Errors / Problems	Computer stalls while counting memory, no error message

This error generally occurs only on compatible devices whose POSTs don't produce error messages.

If the cause of the error is a defective memory component, the computer will always stall in the same place. If the motherboard has a defect, the computer could also stall at different times.

If your computer has a memory expansion card, remove it. If this eliminates the error, either the expansion card is defective or the memory starting address is configured incorrectly. If the address is configured incorrectly, it may conflict with the memory on the motherboard.

Refer to the expansion card's installation information for the correct DIP switch or jumper setting.

Errors / Problems	Computer counts too little memory (e.g., 896K instad of 1024K) but otherwise works satisfactorily

This is probably not even an error but simply a result of using shadow RAM.

When you use shadow RAM, a part of the expanded memory is reserved for data from the BIOS ROM and the video BIOS. The speed advantage gained by using shadow RAM during the boot process and in picture construction usually makes up for the slight memory loss. Otherwise, some versions of SETUP have a special option that lets you disable shadow RAM.

Errors / Problems	Screen remains dark, cursor in upper-left corner, no error message, computer eventually boots (performs drive test and accesses hard drive)

It's possible the mono/color jumper for configuring the graphics card is set incorrectly.

You may have changed graphics cards or added a second graphics card, but not informed the motherboard of this change.

Set the Color/Monochrome jumper to the other position or configure your graphics card as the first or second adapter. If you're not certain which adapter to use, follow the manufacturer's specifications.

For more information about installing a different or second graphics card, see the "Installing Different Expansion Cards" section in Chapter 11.

Chapter
15
Section
1

Errors / Problems	"CMOS Configuration Error" or similar message appears, computer beeps and locks up

This error message usually occurs after you make changes to the hardware. Another possibility is if the CMOS battery is dead or too old and weak.

The message indicates that the data stored in CMOS don't match the hardware configuration determined during the POST.

Enter the correct data in SETUP. Make certain that any jumpers on the motherboard for configuring RAM or the graphics card are in the correct position.

If this error occurs frequently or if you lose the CMOS entries you made, install an external battery as described in Chapter 11.

Errors / Problems	Computer cannot boot from hard drive

Because there are so many possible sources of this problem, it's one of the most common errors. It is also one of the worst errors you'll see.

Fortunately, this error rarely indicates a defective hard drive. Instead, most of the problems result from a defective configuration or deleted system files.

Now we'll briefly describe a normal case (i.e., we'll list what is required for a hard drive to run perfectly).

Correct CMOS entry

Let's begin with CMOS SETUP. You must set up the hard drive correctly. The number of heads, tracks, and cylinders must match those of the hard drive type you enter in SETUP.

Also, if your SETUP has an entry about the bus clock, make certain the bus clock doesn't exceed that of a normal IBM AT. Otherwise, the controller may break down, especially with some old MFM systems.

Low-level format

Next, you must low-level format the hard drive. The only exception to this is an AT bus hard drive, which is already low-level formatted by the manufacturer. Users shouldn't initialize an AT bus hard drive because it could destroy the hard drive.

Partitioning with FDISK

Before DOS formatting, use FDISK to set up at least one DOS partition on the hard drive. This partition should be active (i.e., it must be selected for BIOS as the boot partition).

DOS formatting with system files

The regular DOS format is next. Use the /S switch to transfer the files of the operating system kernel to the boot sector.

Then copy the COMMAND.COM file to the root directory of the boot drive. Some versions of DOS also let you copy this file to a subdirectory and point to it using a COMSPEC entry in the CONFIG.SYS file. In these instances, losing the CONFIG.SYS file is equivalent to deleting the command interpreter itself.

So, to boot from a hard drive, it must be low-level formatted, partitioned and activated. Also, you must DOS format the hard drive (/S), and provide a command interpreter.

Therefore, before considering a hard drive error, check all these requirements first. Boot your computer from a diskette and then try to access the hard drive.

If you manage to access the hard drive, check the root directory for the COMMAND.COM file or determine whether the COMSPEC entry in the CONFIG.SYS file points to this file.

CHKDSK displays the system kernel

Use the CHKDSK program to confirm that the hidden system kernel files (i.e., MSDOS.SYS and IO.SYS) are on the hard drive. CHKDSK displays the hidden files in a list.

Then use FDISK to determine whether there is an active DOS partition.

If none of these solutions work, you have the option of setting up the hard drive again. This involves performing all the steps listed from the entries in SETUP to creating an active partition and DOS formatting.

Then reinstall your software. Remember that by doing this you're losing all data on the hard drive.

AT bus drives

Another common error occurs with AT bus drives that have different translation parameters. AT bus drives use different SETUP entries that have different capacities.

Some AT bus hard drives already have a partition when you buy them. However, if you need to use FDISK to set up an active partition and then change the entry in SETUP, you may be able to DOS format the drive and transfer system files. However, the boot process will always be canceled.

Therefore, before changing the SETUP parameters of AT bus drives, delete all the partitions on the hard drive and recreate them again later.

The only way to localize a hardware error on the hard drive system (which may not the problem) is to replace the controller and the hard drive. Also remember the possibility of a defective cable.

Everything said about other serious errors also applies to this situation. Remove all parts from your computer that aren't related to the problem. For example, the improvement in their hard drives after removing the game card has surprised many users.

Troubleshooting Problems

Errors when you're using your PC

Errors / Problems	Computer locks up or crashes

When the computer "locks up", it refuses to react to anything you try. Usually the contents of the screen are "frozen;" sometimes the screen even turns black. Pressing the Num Lock key won't even toggle the LED. All you can do is reset the system.

There are many causes for this type of computer crash. Pay close attention to the conditions under which the error occurred. For example, a hard drive or floppy LED that's lit can indicate an error in the drive or controller.

If you have a hardware BIOS with ADVANCED CMOS SETUP, your system may be crashing because you made the wrong setting in ADVANCED CMOS SETUP. In this case, increase the redraw waitstate if possible, and disable any hidden refresh or slow refresh functions.

Usually SETUP has an option in its main menu called "Restore BIOS defaults". This option specifies default settings for all the delicate, tricky options. Don't worry about hurting vital settings like hard drive type or drive size because this option doesn't change those settings.

If the error keeps occurring in specific parts of a program, it could be a software error. For example, if a program tries to use a coprocessor that your computer doesn't have or a graphics mode not supported by your installed graphics card, a system crash may occur.

However, if the problem happens arbitrarily, depending on certain situations, or if the problem seems to be linked to warming up the computer, you probably have a defective CPU, coprocessor, or motherboard.

To narrow down the problem, remove everything from the computer that's not absolutely necessary to run it and determine if anything changes.

Perhaps you can borrow a friend's motherboard or test your computer with a different CPU at a computer store. Remember that the test CPU should also be suitable for the clock speed of your motherboard (i.e., it must be at least as fast as your own motherboard; it can also be faster).

So, you can put a 33 MHz CPU on a 20 MHz board without any trouble. However, putting a 20 MHz CPU on a 33 MHz board will destroy the processor.

Owners of 386SX computers usually cannot exchange their CPUs because they are soldered on the motherboard. In this case, you must exchange the entire motherboard.

Errors / Problems	Parity error (at Hex ....)

This error message usually indicates a memory reading error or a checksum error.

When such a checksum error occurs, it triggers a special interrupt that stops the CPU and causes an error message to appear on the screen, usually with the hexadecimal address of the memory component that caused the error.

Since it's no longer possible to continue working on the computer, this condition is locking up the system. Unfortunately, this error message doesn't always indicate a memory error. Almost every component, which has direct or indirect access to the bus, can trigger such an interrupt. This makes it much more difficult to find the error.

Therefore, follow the same steps to localize the error that we described in the previous section about hanging the computer. First, check your settings in CMOS SETUP, especially the settings for waitstate and refresh. Then start removing components.

The RAM installed on your graphics card can also cause memory errors. If you can borrow another graphics card, test it on your PC to determine whether this is the cause.

If you get a parity error after putting together a new computer or after putting new memory chips on the motherboard, this usually means that the DRAM access time is insufficient.

Occasionally problems will also occur with SIMM or SIP chips, on which memory modules with different access times are being used. You should be able to exchange these for another brand. Ask your computer dealer for more information.

Troubleshooting Problems

Errors / Problems	Both drive lights are on, but the drives don't work

This error occurs after you've worked on the drive cable. It occurs because a cable for the 3.5-inch drive isn't plugged in correctly.

Check the floppy cable. It must be connected to the floppy or combination controller with a post connector; the red or blue wire of the 34-pin flat ribbon cable should go to Pin "1". The floppy cable connects to the floppy drives from a card connector (5.25-inch drive) and a post connector (3.5-inch drive).

The end of the cable, with part of the wires twisted, goes to drive A:; the drive selects should both be at DS1. Once again, the labeled wire goes to Pin "1".

Errors / Problems	The printer won't print

This is a frequent error. It can be a problem with the printer, the cable, the PC, or the software. It's usually caused by a defective printer cable or poorly installed software.

Try printing from DOS. Either press ⓟ or use the PRINT command. For example, you could enter PRINT AUTOEXEC.BAT. The printer must be switched on and online. Then run a printer self-test to determine whether the printer is defective. With most printers, you do this by holding down the Formfeed button, or some other button, when you switch on the printer. Check the printer manual to determine which button you must press to enable the self-test.

If the self-test is successful, check the printer cable. Either borrow a cable that works or try printing with your cable on another system. If you still haven't found the error, your printer port is probably defective or configured incorrectly. If you have an AMI BIOS, check the system configuration table that appears on the screen after the self test to determine whether the system even recognizes the port.

If you still can't find the error, either the card is defective or it's in conflict with another expansion. For example, a second parallel port on the monochrome video card could be accessing the same port addresses or IRQs. Remove everything from the computer that you don't need and then try printing again.

ERROR MESSAGES

BIOS runs several tests every time you start the system. For example, BIOS checks the memory, checks for disk drives, and checks the specified parameters to see whether they are correct. The tables in this section list the most common error messages.

POST is an acronym for Power-On Self-Test. It's a series of diagnostic tests that your PC perform automatically when you switch it on or restart it.

If POST detects an error that is serious, it will prevent your PC from booting completely. Instead, it will display an error message that will help you determine the source of the problem(s). These error messages are called (appropriately) fatal errors.

The following lists the three types of output messages with which POST usually works:

❖ POST audio error messages

❖ POST visual error codes

❖ POST hexadecimal numeric error codes

We'll talk about each of these error codes in this section.

Audio error messages

POST audio error messages are, as the name suggests, a series of beeps. The number of beeps determines the source of the error. For example, if you hear several short beeps, POST detected a problem with the motherboard. However, if you hear one short beep when you start your PC, then POST detected no errors.

The following table lists the POST audio error messages and their likely problem(s).

POST Audio Error Messages		
Signal	Sound pattern	Meaning
No tone		Power out
Continuous tone	_____	Power supply defective
Several short beeps	- - - - - - - - -	Defective motherboard
1 long	_	RAM Refresh
1 long, 1 short	_-	Defective motherboard or ROM-BASIC
1 long, 2 short	_--	Video card error or dip switch (XT)
1 long, 3 short	_---	Error on EGA card
2 long, 1 short	_ _ -	Synchronization of monitor adapter
2 short	--	Parity error (incorrect memory checksum)
3 short	---	Errors in the first 64K of RAM
4 short	----	Timer or counter defective
5 short	-----	Processor failure or video RAM
6 short	------	Error in keyboard processor
7 short	-------	Virtual processor mode set (AT)
8 short	--------	Incorrect writing to Video RAM
9 short	---------	Wrong ROM BIOS checksum

POST error messages

These error messages use a three or four number code to indicate the source of the problem. The first number indicates the device number. The following numbers indicate the error. For example the POST error message of 102 indicates a motherboard error (1) and a problem in the timer error (02). A display of 100 means no errors were detected in the motherboard. In other words, "00" always means no errors.

Error Messages During POST	
Error	**Meaning**
01x	Non-defined error
02x	Error in power supply
1xx	**Motherboard error**
100	No errors detected
101	Interrupt error
102	Timer error
103	Timer interrupt error
104	Defective Protected Mode (AT)
105	Last 8042 command not accepted
106	Converting Logic (Expansion bus) defective
107	"Sticking" NMI
108	Defective bus timer
109	DMA error
110	Parity error (PS/2)
111	Defective expanded memory (PS/2)
121	Unexpected hardware interrupt
161	CMOS checksum wrong (AT)
162	Defective configuration (AT-CMOS)
163	Wrong date or time (AT-CMOS)
164	Defective memory size (AT-CMOS)
199	Specified configuration defective
2xx	**Memory errors**
2xx	No errors detected
201	Memory error, address specified
202	Address error, A0 -A15
203	Address error, A16-A23
215	Memory error (PS/2)
216	Memory error (PS/2)

Chapter

15

Section

1

Error	Meaning
Error Messages During POST (continued)	
3xx	**Keyboard errors**
300	No errors detected
301	Keyboard reset defective or key stuck
302	Keyboard locked
303	Keyboard defective
304	Defective keyboard control
4xx	**MDA errors**
400	No error detected
401	Defective adapter self test, memory error
408	Defective character attributes
416	Defective character set
424	Cannot set text mode 80x25
432	Defective parallel port (PS/2)
5xx	**CGA errors**
500	No error detected
501	Defective adapter self test, memory error
508	Defective character attributes
516	Defective character set
524	Cannot set text mode 80x25
532	Cannot set text mode 40x25
540	Cannot set graphics mode 320x200
548	Cannot set graphics mode 640x200
6xx	**Disk drive errors**
600	No error detected
601	Defective disk drive self test
602	Invalid boot sector
606	Diskette change not displayed
607	Write-protect
608	Defective diskette status
610	Formatting not possible
611	Disk drive doesn't react, timeout

Error	Meaning
\multicolumn{2}{l}{Error Messages During POST (continued)}	
6xx	**Disk drive errors (continued)**
612	Defective controller chip
613	DMA error
616	Defective number of rotations
621	Defective positioning
622	CRC error
623	Sector not found
624	Defective address
625	Defective positioning, controller error
626	Defective data compare
7xx	**Math coprocessor errors**
700	No error detected
9xx	**Error in first parallel port (LPT1)**
900	No error detected
901	Defective port self test
10xx	**Error in second parallel port (LPT2)**
1000	No error detected
1001	Defective port self test
11xx	**Error in first serial port (COM1)**
1100	No error detected
1101	Defective port self test
12xx	**Error in second serial port (COM2)**
1200	No error detected
1201	Defective port self test
13xx	**Error in game port**
1300	No error detected
1301	Defective port self test
1302	Defective joystick
14xx	**Printer error**
1400	No error detected
1401	Defective printer self test
1404	Defective dot matrix printer

Chapter

15

Section

1

599

Error Messages During POST (continued)	
Error	**Meaning**
15xx	SDLC adapter error
1500	No error detected
16xx	Terminal emulation error
1600	No error detected
17xx	Hard drive error
1700	No error detected
1701	Defective hard drive self test
1702	Defective controller
1703	Defective hard drive
1704	Non localizable error
1780	Defective hard drive 0
1781	Defective hard drive 1
1782	Defective controller
1790	Defective hard drive 0
1791	Defective hard drive 1
18xx	Expansion card errors
1800	No error detected
1801	Defective card self test
1810	Defective enable/disable
1811	Defective extender card test
1812	Defective addressing
1813	Error in wait state
1814	Defective enable/disable
1815	Error in wait state
1818	Defective disable
1819	Defective wait request
1821	Defective addressing
19xx	3270 PC attachment card errors
1900	No error detected
20xx	Errors in first BSC adapter
20xx	No error detected

Error Messages During POST (continued)	
Error	Meaning
21xx	Errors in second BSC adapter
2100	No error detected
22xx	Cluster adapter errors (LANs)
2200	No error detected
24xx	EGA error (on PS/2 VGA error)
2400	No error detected
2401	Defective adapter self test, memory error
2408	Defective character attributes
26xx	Errors of XT/370
2600	No error detected
27xx	Errors of AT/370
2700	No error detected
28xx	Errors of 3278/79 emulation adapter
2800	No error detected
29xx	Color printer errors
2900	No error detected
30xx	Errors of first PC network adapter
3000	No error detected
31xx	Errors of second PC network adapter
3100	No error detected
33xx	Compact printer errors
3300	No error detected
36xx	Errors on General Purpose Interface Bus
3600	No error detected
38xx	Data Acquisition Adapter errors
3800	No error detected
39xx	PGA error
3900	No error detected
3901	Defective adapter self test, memory error
71xx	Voice Communication Adapter errors
7100	No error detected

Error	Meaning
Error Messages During POST (continued)	
73xx	External 3.5-inch disk drive errors
7300	No error detected
7301	Defective disk drive self test
7306	Diskette change not displayed
7307	Write-protect
7308	Defective diskette status
7310	Formatting not possible
7311	Disk drive doesn't react, timeout
7312	Defective controller chip
7313	DMA error
7316	Defective number of revolutions
7321	Defective positioning
7322	CRC error
7323	Sector not found
7324	Defective address
7325	Defective positioning, controller error
7326	Defective data compare
85xx	Expanded memory errors
8500	No error detected
86xx	Digitizer errors on PS/2
8600	No error detected
89xx	Digitizer errors on PS/2
8900	No error detected
104xx	ESDI controller errors on PS/2
10400	No error detected
10401	Defective self test
10402	Defective controller
10403	Defective hard drive
10404	Non localizable errors

Error Messages During POST (continued)	
Error	Meaning
10480	Defective hard drive 0
10481	Defective hard drive 1
10482	Defective controller
10490	Defective hard drive 0
10491	Defective hard drive 1

Chapter
15
Section
1

What's On The Companion CD-ROM

We hope **Upgrading & Maintaining Your PC** will be an indispensable reference guide to upgrading and maintaining your PC. The companion CD-ROM contains dozens of practical and helpful utilities for testing and maintaining your PC. This chapter details the programs on the companion CD-ROM.

FILES YOU'LL FIND ON THE ROOT DIRECTORY

The following table lists the files you'll find on the Companion CD-ROM root directory.

File name	Explanation
ACROREAD EXE	Adobe's Award Winning Portable Document Reader
BOOKFILE PDF	Requires AcroRead - Load this file to view book.
CD_DIR TXT	Complete text file listing all the programs with descriptions.
MAINFILE PDF	The main file for viewing the contents of book.
README TXT	This file.
THREED VBX	Required file.
VBRUN300 DLL	Required file.
WRKSHEET PDF	PRINT THESE WORKSHEETS using Acrobat Reader.

605

What's On The Companion CD-ROM

You can experiment with using the various utilities and diagnostic programs. You can install them from the companion CD-ROM or copy them to a new directory on your hard drive and then run them. The programs are shareware or evaluation programs (or both) written and copyrighted by the authors and companies. Please register the programs you use with the respective author.

USING THE COMPANION CD-ROM

You must first load the MENU.EXE program located in the root directory to use the companion CD-ROM. When the program is loaded, you'll have various buttons to select your utilities. Insert the CD-ROM into your CD-ROM drive. We're assuming in this chapter that the letter assigned to your CD-ROM drive is "D:". If not, simply substitute your CD-ROM drive letter instead of "D:"

Loading the MENU in Windows 3.x

Select the **File/Run...** command in the Windows Program Manager:

This opens the Run dialog box. Then type the following in the Run dialog box:

606

```
d:\menu.exe
```

The Run dialog box should now look like the following:

Then press the Enter key or click the OK button. The main MENU program will start. This MENU program is used to install or test various shareware utilities.

Loading the MENU in Windows 95

Select the Start menu and then the **Run...** command:

Chapter
16
Section
3

What's On The Companion CD-ROM

Chapter 16

This opens the Run dialog box. Then type the following in the Run dialog box:

`d:\menu.exe`

The Run dialog box should now look like the following:

What's On The Companion CD-ROM

Then press the Enter key or click the OK button. The main MENU program will start. This MENU program is used to install or test various shareware utilities.

Installing Adobe's Acrobat Reader

Adobe's Acrobat Reader is a utility allowing you to view PDF files. Three PDF files are available on the companion CD-ROM:

Filename	Information
WRKSHEET.PDF	Printable work sheet form in the book
CATALOG.PDF	Current Abacus Book and Software catalog
MAINBOOK.PDF	Complete Upgrading... book in electronic form

If you already have Acrobat Reader, skip the next steps and go on to the CYRIX notes.

Follow these steps to install Acrobat Reader on your hard drive:

What's On The Companion CD-ROM

Chapter 16

1. Make certain there's enough room on your hard drive. Adobe Acrobat requires approximately 2 Meg.

2. Insert the companion CD-ROM in your CD-ROM drive.

3. Load Windows 3.x or Windows 95.

4. From the Windows Program Manager, select the **File/Run** command.

5. Type the following command:

```
D:\ACROREAD.EXE
```

and press the Enter key.

A screen similar to the following should appear:

Simply follow the instructions and prompts which appear on your screen. Double click the Acrobat Reader icon to load it. After Acrobat Reader is loaded, go to **File/Open...** and select "MAINFILE.PDF" to view or read *Upgrading & Maintaining Your PC* on the companion CD-ROM.

Special Cyrix instructions

We've included the instructions for performing the Cyrix's upgrade test. This test will determine whether or not you can upgrade your older 386 PC to a 486 with a Cyrix chip. Please read it carefully.

The files required for this test are in the directory CYRIXTST. Please read the README.TXT in this directory for instructions.

A SPECIAL NOTE ON SHAREWARE, FREEWARE AND PUBLIC DOMAIN SOFTWARE

Many of the programs included on the CD-ROM are fully functioning "shareware evaluation versions" of the best programs available today. Because shareware is copyrighted, the authors ask for payment if you use their program(s). You may try out the program for a limited time, typically 10 to 30 days, and then decide whether you want to keep it. If you continue to use it, you're requested to send the author a nominal fee. Shareware benefits both the user and the author as it allows prices to remain low by avoiding distribution, packaging, and advertising costs.

The shareware concept allows small software companies and program authors to introduce the application programs they have developed to a wider audience. The programs can be freely distributed and tested for a specific time period before you have to register them. Registration involves paying registration fees, which make you a licensed user of the program. Check the documentation or the program itself for the amount of registration fee and the address where you send the registration form.

After registration you will frequently get the current full version of the program without restrictions and shareware notes as well as the option of purchasing upgraded versions later for a reduced price. As a rule, larger applications include a users manual. Shareware programs usually feature the complete performance range of the full versions. Some programs use special messages to indicate they're shareware versions. The message usually appears immediately after program startup or can be called from the Help menu.

Chapter
16
Section
3

Chapter 16

The **Upgrading & Maintaining Your PC** companion CD-ROM will show the variety of shareware. To ensure that the program authors continue writing programs and offering them as shareware, we urge you to support the shareware concept by registering the programs that you plan to use on a permanent basis.

You will find program instructions as well as notes on registration for the shareware programs in special text files located in the program directory of each program. These programs are usually called READ.ME, README.TXT or README.DOC. As a rule, the TXT, WRI or DOC extensions are used for text files, which you can view and print with Windows 95 editors.

Some of the programs on this CD-ROM are distributed as freeware or public domain. You can use these programs without paying a registration fee. Keep in mind that freely distributed programs cannot be used for commercial purposes and are sometimes subject to separate restrictions.

The Menu program is a part of the companion CD-ROM. It's neither shareware, freeware nor public domain. Please do not redistribute the Menu program from Abacus.

DIRECTORIES AND THEIR CONTENTS

The directories and their contents are included in one convenient file on the companion CD-ROM called CD_DIR.TXT. You may print this text file or view it separately from the MENU program.

Listed below are the programs that we have included on the companion CD-ROM of *Upgrading & Maintaining Your PC*. Each is listed with the directory name and then a comment about the program. Again, these programs are either shareware or freeware.

586TEST

Checks PC system for the infamous "math" bug that plagued certain versions of the Intel Pentium processor.

What's On The Companion CD-ROM

The 586TEST program

95BOOTR2

Copyright (c) Fred Salerno. All rights reserved. (requires Windows 95)
Previously called "95 Dual Booter v1.0", this program is a dual boot utility for
Windows 95. It allows you to select the way to boot up Windows 95.

The 95BOOTR2 program

Chapter 16

AAASSS

Copyright (c) Scandere Software All rights reserved.
AAASSS AZ Utilities - Graphs directories and/or sub-directories to a color Windows Pie Chart. Graphs directory and/or sub-directories on a color window pie chart. Simultaneously charts percentages and sizes of directories many levels deep. Easy and fun to use. Shows at a glance which directories and their subs are using up the most disk space. Uses memory only, no need to write large disk maps.

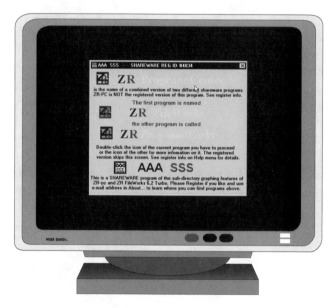

The AAASSS program

ABACUS

A directory FULL of Abacus product announcements and catalog.

BMPVIEW

Copyright (c) Daniel Brum. All rights reserved.
This is a Windows 95 graphics viewer.

What's On The Companion CD-ROM

The BMPVIEW program

CDTA

Copyright (c) Eric Balkan. All rights reserved.
CD-ROM Timing Analyzer determines the data transfer rate of your CD-ROM drive.

CHIEF200

Copyright (c) Dr. Abimbola Olowofoyeku.   All rights reserved.
A handy installer and uninstaller for Windows programs. This program is an "off the shelf" installation package for Windows programs. It can be used to install Windows packages of almost any size (up to 64 installation disks). The files may be compressed (with MS COMPRESS.EXE) or uncompressed. Both types of file are handled transparently. The installer will optionally create Program Manager groups and icons.

615

What's On The Companion CD-ROM

Chapter 16

The CHIEF200 program

CYRXTST

This directory contains the test for Cyrix Upgrade Microprocessors.

DLL

A directory of additional dynamic link libraries you may need.

ISPY250

Copyright (c) Dean Software Design. All rights reserved.
InfoSpy is a general purpose system viewer that has many extras. It's a general purpose Windows environment viewer that lets you view heap, tasks, windows, classes, modules, file handles, DOS and memory information. You can trace messages, stack and set up automatic timers to provide real-time tracing on virtually every aspect of Windows.

What's On The Companion CD-ROM

The InfoSpy program

MSSINFO

Copyright (c) 1994 Mathews Software Services, Inc. All rights reserved.
MemStatus shows the current memory status of either Windows 95 or NT. This
includes physical memory in use, paging file in use and overall memory load.
As a percentage of use increases, its bar becomes redder, its background darker
blue. Anything above 80% will cause the percent digits to become red.

The MemStatus program

MSTAT32

Copyright (c) by Mark Gamber. All rights reserved.
This utility displays the current memory status of Windows 95 including the
total and available physical RAM, total and available paging memory, total and
available virtual memory and free system resources.

The Memory Status (MEMSTAT) program

NOMO4

A demonstration copy of Abacus NoMouse for Windows software.

What's On The Companion CD-ROM

P90TEST

Copyright (c) by Inside Technologies. All rights reserved.
This utility from Inside Technologies (3535 Dewey Street, Boise, ID. 83703) will
do the "math" to check if you need to replace your Pentium chip. This excellent
and fast utility is a very useful program for Pentium owners.

To run P90TEST type:

```
P90TEST
```

and press (Enter).

The P90TEST program

PC_CARE

Copyright (c) by American Megatrends. All rights reserved.
PC_CARE is a Windows based PC diagnostic utility from American Megatrends,
Inc. who also make AMI BIOS.

Chapter
16
Section
3

What's On The Companion CD-ROM

Chapter 16

PC_CARE

REGSRCH

Copyright (c) 1995 by Steven J. Hoek Software Development. All rights reserved.

Registry Search & Replace (REGSRCH.EXE) is a Win32 utility which can be used to simplify maintenance of the Windows NT 3.5 and Windows 95 registration databases (the "registry"). For more complete information on what this utility offers, how to use it or about its author, see the accompanying help file.

Registry Search & Replace (REGSRCH.EXE)

SAF_TNET

Copyright (c) Ron Parker (CT Software). All rights reserved.
Safety Net is a utility for backing up key files. It has once default setting (backup key Windows and system files) and three user configurable options. For example, use Safety Net to backup all your DOC, database files or both. An added function is that the files can be ZIPped to disk. It can also print your directory tree. Safety Net requires VBRUN300.DLL.

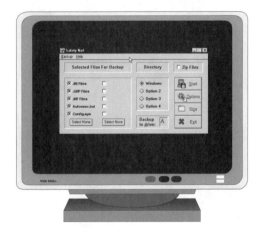

Backup Utility Safety Net (SAF_TNET)

SCAN4D

Software Innovations (Freeware).
Use this program to discover what DLLs are used by a particular program (useful when you want to remove a Windows program from your system).

Chapter 16

The SCAN4D program

SPEEDY11

Copyright (c) J. Lin. All rights reserved.

Speedy is a Windows graphics performance benchmark. The program can be used in many ways to compare the relative performance of different graphics hardware and display driver combinations.

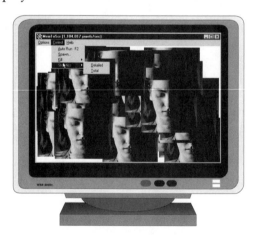

The SPEEDY11 program

622

What's On The Companion CD-ROM

SYSCACHE

Copyright (c) Advanced Personal Systems. All rights reserved.
SYSCACHE is a system information program from Advanced Personal Systems of Milpitas CA.

The SYSCACHE program

SYSCEN

Copyright (c) 1994 Mathews Software Services, Inc. All rights reserved.
System Census for Windows v1.1 is a system configuration reporting tool that you can use to keep track of your system. It reports on elements of your Windows, DOS, network (if applicable) and hardware subsystems, providing you with the information necessary to keep your system running in top shape. As a Windows application, System Census for Windows has access to all the information relevant to your system.

What's On The Companion CD-ROM

Chapter 16

The System Census for Windows v1.1 program

TESTCARD

Copyright (c) Graham Lemon. All rights reserved.

Video Testcard runs video tests to set up your EGA/VGA/SVGA/XGA/Multisync screens. It provides a reasonably complete method for all TV engineer types to set up your EGA/VGA/SVGA/XGA/Multisync screens. It provides many screens ranging from color bars to a barrel distortion circle.

The Videotest card program (TESTCARD)

What's On The Companion CD-ROM

VAULT

Copyright (c) Pocket-Sized Software. All rights reserved.
Vault stores your information as an outline and organizes your information into categories and subcategories that you specify.

The Vault program

WINSPEED

Copyright (c) Chris Hewitt. All rights reserved. (Freeware)
WinSpeed measures the CPU, disk and video performance of your system from the point of view of Windows. It uses API calls where appropriate. The Help file which is included with this utility explains the meanings of the figures. It offers some suggestions on tuning Windows. Since this program is freeware, please copy and pass a copy to your friends.

What's On The Companion CD-ROM

Chapter 16

The WinSpeed program

WINTACH

Creates a system performance index to compare the performance of your PC to other PCs.

The WinTach program

What's On The Companion CD-ROM

WINTUNE

Copyright (c) Windows Magazine. All rights reserved.
Excellent "tune up" kit for your PC by John Ruley.

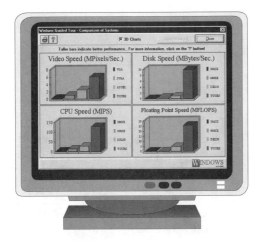

The WinTune program

WINDSOCK

Copyright (c) Technical Pixies. All rights reserved. (Freeware)
WindSock 3.30 is a windows performance analysis utility by Chris Hewitt.

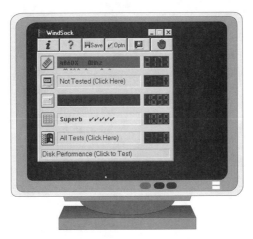

The WindSock program

627

What's On The Companion CD-ROM

Chapter 16

WITS

Copyright (c) 1993 Jon Peddie Associates. All rights reserved.
Windows Integrated Test Suite tests your PC for performance. WITS is intended to measure graphics board performance in actual Windows applications, including: Microsoft Word for Windows (version 1.x & 2.x); Microsoft Excel (version 2.1, 3.0 & 4.0); Corel Draw! (version 3.0); Aldus PhotoStyler (version 1.0); QuarkXpress (version 3.1).

The Windows Integrated Test Suite program

WUBENCH

Copyright (c) 1993 Reed Business Publishing. All rights reserved.
Windows Users Benchmarks is a collection of benchmarks for PC components.

What's On The Companion CD-ROM

The Windows User Benchmarks program

SPECIAL INSTRUCTIONS

NoMouse 4 Demo

Some brief notes regarding NoMouse Version 4 Demo... This is a 10 minute demonstration version of NoMouse Version 4. This demo has all the features of NoMouse Version 4.

Installation

To Install NoMouse from the Program Manager, select the **File** menu and then the **Run...** command. Click the [Browse...] button. Select the following directory :

  c:\abacus\nomo4

Select the program SETUP and press [Enter]. Click on the [OK] button. Click again on the [OK] button. Follow the directions and NoMouse will be installed.

Chapter 16

Super shot of the NoMouse setup screen

This version of NoMouse includes an on/off toggle so users can easily use the cursor keys to move the mouse pointer or the I-beam in Windows applications. NoMouse can be configured so that a single key will toggle the cursor keys between moving the mouse pointer or the I-beam cursor in applications.

This is done by setting the NoMouse ON/OFF hotkey to a single key, the default is the [End] key. Pressing the NoMouse ON/OFF hotkey [End] key twice rapidly (double-clicking) will turn the mouse functions on. Pressing the NoMouse ON/OFF hotkey key once will turn OFF the mouse key functions and allow normal cursor movement in a Windows application. Holding down the NoMouse ON/OFF hotkey key and then pressing a cursor key will move the mouse pointer.

Important

To configure NoMouse, call up the NoMouse Configuration dialog box by pressing [Ctrl]+[Alt]+[Q].

Pressing the NoMouse ON/OFF hotkey, the default is the [End] key, twice rapidly (double-clicking) will turn the mouse functions on, pressing the NoMouse ON/OFF hotkey, the [End] key, once will turn OFF the mouse key functions and allow normal cursor movement in a Windows application, such as WORD or EXCEL. Holding down the NoMouse ON/OFF hotkey, the [End] key, and then pressing a cursor key will move the mouse pointer. Experiment with this, it will take some practice.

630

Cyrix System Upgradability Test

Introduction

Some of the early 386SX-16MHz computers are not upgradable with Cyrix's Cx486SRx2 Upgrade Microprocessor due to the lack of a float pin on the 386SX Microprocessors.

This System Upgradability Disk will determine if your 386SX-16MHz system can be upgraded with Cyrix's Upgrade Microprocessor. If you are upgrading a 386SX-20 or 25 MHz system, verification is not necessary as all 386SX-20 and 25MHz systems are compatible with the 486SRx2-20/40 and 486SRx2-25/50 respectively.

If you have a 386SX-16Mhz system you can verify your system's compatibility by following the procedures described here. If you have any questions, please call Cyrix's Technical Support at 1-800-848-2979.

System Verification Procedure

First, review this section, then follow the steps listed below to verify your 386SX 16MHz system's compatibility.

1. Insert the disk with the Cyrix System Upgradability test into Drive A. Enter the following command at the DOS prompt (then press Enter):

    ```
    A:SXTEST
    ```

2. After a few moments, the program will ask you to reboot the computer. Please leave the Cyrix System Upgradability Disk in drive A while rebooting the computer.

After rebooting, the test program will inspect your system and return one of the following messages. If no message is returned, please call Cyrix's Technical Support at 1-800-848-2979 for assistance.

Chapter 16 Section 3

What's On The Companion CD-ROM

Messages

Message #1

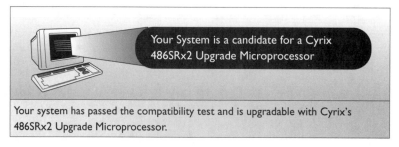

Message #2

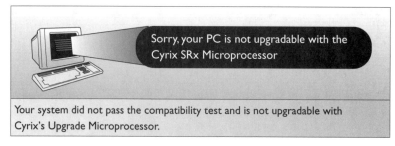

Message #3

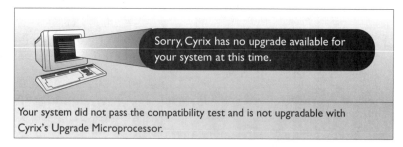

Your system did not pass the compatibility test and is not upgradable with Cyrix's Upgrade Microprocessor.

What's On The Companion CD-ROM

Message #4

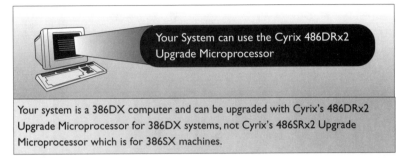

Your system is a 386DX computer and can be upgraded with Cyrix's 486DRx2 Upgrade Microprocessor for 386DX systems, not Cyrix's 486SRx2 Upgrade Microprocessor which is for 386SX machines.

Message #5

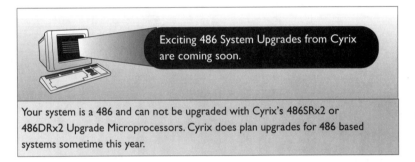

Your system is a 486 and can not be upgraded with Cyrix's 486SRx2 or 486DRx2 Upgrade Microprocessors. Cyrix does plan upgrades for 486 based systems sometime this year.

Section 4:
Appendices

Contents

Appendix A

BIOS Hard Drive Parameters

Appendix A lists the BIOS hard drive parameter tables for several ROM BIOS versions which is useful when you're installing one of these drives. The columns in Appendix A have the following meanings:

Cyl	Cylinder		WPC	Write precompensation
Kb	Kilobytes		LZ	Landing Zone
Meg	Capacity (Megabytes)			

IBM-AT-BIOS Hard Drive Parameters							
Type	Cyl	Heads	WPC	Kb	LZ	Sectors	Meg
1	306	4	128	0	305	17	10.16
2	615	4	300	0	615	17	20.42
3	615	6	300	0	615	17	30.63
4	940	8	512	0	940	17	62.42
5	940	6	512	0	940	17	46.82
6	615	4	-	0	615	17	20.42
7	462	8	256	0	511	17	30.68
8	733	5	-	0	733	17	30.42
9	900	15	-	8	901	17	112.06
10	820	3	-	0	820	17	20.42

BIOS Hard Drive Parameters

Appendix A

IBM-AT-BIOS Hard Drive Parameters (continued)							
Type	Cyl	Heads	WPC	Kb	LZ	Sectors	Meg
11	855	5	-	0	855	17	35.49
12	855	7	-	0	855	17	49.68
13	306	8	128	0	319	17	20.32
14	733	7	-	0	733	17	42.59
15	Locked						
16	612	4	0	0	663	17	20.32

OLIVETTI-/TRIUMPH-ADLER-BIOS Hard Drive Parameters							
Type	Cyl	Heads	WPC	Kb	LZ	Sectors	Meg
1	615	4	0	0	614	17	20.42
2	973	5	-	0	972	17	40.38
3	823	4	0	0	822	38	61.08
4	529	8	0	0	528	39	80.59
5	776	8	0	0	775	33	100.03
6	762	8	0	0	761	39	116.09
7	683	16	0	0	682	38	202.77
8	Locked						
9	Locked						
10	Locked						
11	Locked						
12	Locked						
13	Locked						
14	Locked						
15	Locked						
16	Locked						

BIOS Hard Drive Parameters

AMI-BIOS Hard Drive Parameters							
Type	Cyl	Heads	WPC	Kb	LZ	Sectors	Meg
1	306	4	128	0	305	17	10.16
2	615	4	300	0	615	17	20.42
3	615	6	300	0	615	17	30.63
4	940	8	512	0	940	17	62.42
5	940	6	512	0	940	17	46.82
6	615	4	-	0	615	17	20.42
7	462	8	256	0	511	17	30.68
8	733	5	-	0	733	17	30.42
9	900	15	-	8	901	17	112.06
10	820	3	-	0	820	17	20.42
11	855	5	-	0	855	17	35.49
12	855	7	-	0	855	17	49.68
13	306	8	128	0	319	17	20.32
14	733	7	-	0	733	17	42.59
15		Locked					
16	612	4	0	0	663	17	20.32
17	977	5	300	0	977	17	40.55
18	977	7	-	0	977	17	56.77
19	1024	7	512	0	1023	17	59.50
20	733	5	300	0	732	17	30.42
21	733	7	300	0	732	17	42.59
22	733	5	300	0	733	17	30.42
23	306	4	0	0	336	17	10.16
24	925	7	0	0	925	17	53.75
25	925	9	-	8	925	17	69.10
26	754	7	754	0	754	17	43.81
27	754	11	-	8	754	17	68.85
28	699	7	256	0	699	17	40.62
29	823	10	-	8	823	17	68.32
30	918	7	918	0	918	17	53.34

Appendix

A

Section

4

639

BIOS Hard Drive Parameters

AMI-BIOS Hard Drive Parameters (continued)							
Type	Cyl	Heads	WPC	Kb	LZ	Sectors	Meg
31	1024	11	-	8	1024	17	93.50
32	1024	15	-	8	1024	17	127.50
33	1024	5	1024	0	1024	17	42.50
34	612	2	128	0	612	17	10.16
35	1024	9	-	8	1024	17	76.50
36	1024	8	512	0	1024	17	68.00
37	615	8	128	0	615	17	40.84
38	987	3	987	0	987	17	24.58
39	987	7	987	0	987	17	57.35
40	820	6	820	0	820	17	40.84
41	977	5	977	0	977	17	40.55
42	981	5	981	0	981	17	40.72
43	830	7	512	0	830	17	48.23
44	830	10	-	8	830	17	68.90
45	917	15	-	8	918	17	114.18
46	1224	15	-	8	1223	17	152.40
47		User-defi	1	306	4	128	0

AWARD-BIOS Hard Drive Parameters							
Type	Cyl	Heads	WPC	Kb	LZ	Sectors	Meg
1	306	4	128	0	305	17	10.16
2	615	4	300	0	615	17	20.42
3	615	6	300	0	615	17	30.63
4	940	8	512	0	940	17	62.42
5	940	6	512	0	940	17	46.82
6	615	4	-	0	615	17	20.42
7	462	8	256	0	511	17	30.68
8	733	5	-	0	733	17	30.42
9	900	15	-	8	901	17	112.06
10	820	3	-	0	820	17	20.42

BIOS Hard Drive Parameters

Type	Cyl	Heads	WPC	Kb	LZ	Sectors	Meg
		AWARD-BIOS Hard Drive Parameters (continued)					
11	855	5	-	0	855	17	35.49
12	855	7	-	0	855	17	49.68
13	306	8	128	0	319	17	20.32
14	733	7	-	0	733	17	42.59
15		Locked					
16	612	4	0	0	663	17	20.32
17	977	5	300	0	977	17	40.55
18	977	7	-	0	977	17	56.77
19	1024	7	512	0	1023	17	59.50
20	733	5	300	0	732	17	30.42
21	733	7	300	0	732	17	42.59
22	733	5	300	0	733	17	30.42
23	306	4	0	0	336	17	10.16
24	977	5	-	0	976	17	40.55
25	1024	9	-	8	1279	17	76.50
26	1224	7	-	0	1223	17	71.12
27	1224	11	-	8	1223	17	111.76
28	1224	15	-	8	1223	17	152.40
29	1024	8	-	0	1023	17	68.00
30	1024	11	-	8	1023	17	93.50
31	918	11	-	8	1023	17	83.82
32	925	9	-	8	926	17	69.10
33	1024	10	-	8	1023	17	85.00
34	1024	12	-	8	1023	17	102.00
35	1024	13	-	8	1023	17	110.50
36	1024	14	-	8	1023	17	119.00
37	1024	2	-	0	1023	17	17.00
38	1024	16	-	8	1023	17	136.00
39	918	15	-	8	1023	17	114.30
40	820	6	none	0	820	17	40.84

Appendix

A

Section

4

641

BIOS Hard Drive Parameters

PHOENIX-BIOS Hard Drive Parameters							
Type	Cyl	Heads	WPC	Kb	LZ	Sectors	Meg
1	306	4	128	0	305	17	10.16
2	615	4	300	0	615	17	20.42
3	615	6	300	0	615	17	30.63
4	940	8	512	0	940	17	62.42
5	940	6	512	0	940	17	46.82
6	615	4	-	0	615	17	20.42
7	462	8	256	0	511	17	30.68
8	733	5	-	0	733	17	30.42
9	900	15	-	8	901	17	112.06
10	820	3	-	0	820	17	20.42
11	855	5	-	0	855	17	35.49
12	855	7	-	0	855	17	49.68
13	306	8	128	0	319	17	20.32
14	733	7	-	0	733	17	42.00
15		Locked					
16	733	3	0	0	733	17	19.00
17	965	5	300	0	965	17	41.00
18	965	10	-	0	965	17	82.00
19	977	5	512	0	977	17	42.00
20	615	8	300	0	615	17	42.00
21	820	4	300	0	820	17	28.00
22	820	6	300	0	820	17	42.00
23	612	4	0	0	612	17	21.00
24	872	7	-	0	872	17	52.00
25	872	8	-	8	872	17	60.00
26		Locked	754	0	754	17	43.81
27		Locked	-	8	754	17	68.85
28		Locked	256	0	699	17	40.62
29		Locked	-	8	823	17	68.32
30		Locked	918	0	918	17	53.34

BIOS Hard Drive Parameters

Type	Cyl	Heads	WPC	Kb	LZ	Sectors	Meg
PHOENIX-BIOS Hard Drive Parameters (continued)							
31		Locked	-	8	1024	17	93.50
32		Locked	-	8	1024	17	127.50
33	615	4	-	8	615	26	32.00
34	615	6	-	8	615	26	48.00
35	745	4	-	8	745	26	40.00
36	733	3	-	8	733	26	30.00
37	733	2	-	0	733	26	48.00
38	733	7	-	8	733	26	67.00
39	820	4	-	8	820	26	43.00
40	820	6	-	0	820	26	64.00
41	799	5	-	8	799	26	64.00
42	782	2	-	8	782	26	20.00
43	782	4	-	8	782	26	41.50
44	782	6	-	8	782	26	61.00
45	745	4	-	0	745	28	42.00
46	776	8	-	8	776	33	102.00
47	1148	4	none	8	1148	36	83.00

Type	Cyl	Heads	WPC	Kb	LZ	Sectors	Meg
COMPAQ-BIOS Hard Drive Parameters							
1	306	4	128	0	305	17	10.16
2	615	4	128	0	638	17	20.42
3	615	6	128	0	615	17	30.63
4	1024	8	512	0	1023	17	68.00
5	805	6	-	0	805	17	40.09
6	697	5	128	0	696	17	28.93
7	462	8	256	0	511	17	30.68
8	925	5	128	0	924	17	38.39
9	900	15	-	8	899	17	112.06
10	980	5	-	0	980	17	40.67

BIOS Hard Drive Parameters

COMPAQ-BIOS Hard Drive Parameters (continued)							
Type	Cyl	Heads	WPC	Kb	LZ	Sectors	Meg
6	697	5	128	0	696	17	28.93
7	462	8	256	0	511	17	30.68
8	925	5	128	0	924	17	38.39
9	900	15	-	8	899	17	112.06
10	980	5	-	0	980	17	40.67
11	925	7	128	0	924	17	53.75
12	925	9	128	8	924	17	69.10
13	612	8	256	0	611	17	40.64
14	980	4	128	0	980	17	32.54
15	Locked						
16	612	4	0	0	612	17	20.32
17	980	5	128	0	980	17	40.67
18	966	5	128	0	966	17	40.09
19	754	11	-	8	753	17	68.85
20	733	5	256	0	732	17	30.42
21	733	7	256	0	732	17	42.59
22	524	4	-	0	524	40	40.94
23	924	8	-	0	924	17	61.36
24	966	14	-	8	966	17	112.26
25	966	16	-	8	966	17	128.30
26	1023	14	-	8	1023	17	118.88
27	832	6	-	0	832	33	80.44
28	872	14	-	8	872	52	308.03
29	1240	7	-	0	1240	34	143.90
30	615	4	128	0	615	25	30.03

644

BIOS Hard Drive Parameters

COMPAQ-BIOS Hard Drive Parameters (continued)							
Type	Cyl	Heads	WPC	Kb	LZ	Sectors	Meg
41	1631	15	-	8	1631	52	618.18
42	1023	16	-	8	1023	63	501.49
43	805	4	-	0	805	26	40.88
44	805	2	-	0	805	26	20.44
45	748	8	-	0	748	33	96.42
46	748	6	-	0	748	33	72.32
47	966	5	128	0	966	25	58.96

Appendix B

Hard Drive Parameters

The tables in Appendix B list the hard drive parameter tables for several manufacturers. The column in Appendix B have the following meanings:

Cyl	Cylinder	Sect	Sectors
Cap	Capacity	AT	Access time
WPC	Write precompensation	Proc	Procedure

Atasi Hard Drive Parameters								
Model	Heads	Cyl	Sect	WPC	Cap	AT	Proc	Port
3046	7	645	35	323	80		RLL	
3051	7	704	35	352	88		RLL	
3085	8	1024	17	-	70		MFM	ST 506
3051+	7	733	35	368	91		RLL	

Hard Drive Parameters

Appendix B

BASF Hard Drive Parameters								
Model	Heads	Cyl	Sect	WPC	Cap	AT	Proc	Port
6185	6	440	17	220	22		MFM	ST 506
6186	4	440	17	220	15		MFM	ST 506
6187	2	440	17	220	7		MFM	ST 506
6188-R1	2	612	17		10		MFM	ST 506
6188-R3	4	612	17		20		MFM	ST 506

CDC Hard Drive Parameters								
Model	Head	Cyl	Sect	WP	Cap	AT	Proc	Port
94155-120	8	960	17	-	64	28	MFM	ST 506
94155-129	8	925	26	-	97		RLL	ST 506
94155-129	8	922	26		155		RLL	ST 506
94155-135	9	960	26	-	110	28	RLL	ST 506
94155-135	9	960	17	-	72	28	MFM	ST 506
94155-19	3	697	17	128	17		MFM	ST 506
94155-21	3	697	17	128	17	28	MFM	ST 506
94155-25	4	615	17	128	20		MFM	ST 506
94155-28	4	697	17	128	23		MFM	ST 506
94155-36	5	697	17	128	29	28	MFM	ST 506
94155-38	5	733	17	128	30	28	MFM	ST 506
94155-48	5	925	17	128	38	28	MFM	ST 506
94155-51	5	989	17		43		MFM	ST 506
94155-57	6	925	17	128	46	28	MFM	ST 506
94155-67	7	925	17	128	54	28	MFM	ST 506
94155-77	8	925	17	128	61		MFM	ST 506
94155-85	8	1024	17		68	28	MFM	ST 506
94155-85P	8	1024	17		68	28	MFM	ST 506
94155-86	9	925	17	128	69	28	MFM	ST 506
94155-96	9	1024	17		77	28	MFM	ST 506

Model	Head	Cyl	Sect	WP	Cap	AT	Proc	Port
94155-96P	9	1024	17		77	28	MFM	ST 506
94166-101	5	969	34	-	84		RLL	ESDI
94166-141	7	969	34	-	117		RLL	ESDI
94166-182	9	969	35	-	155		RLL	ESDI
94186-265	9	1412	34	-	220			ESDI
94186-324	11	1412	34	-	269		RLL	ESDI
94186-383	13	1412	34	-	318		RLL	ESDI
94186-383	15	1224	34	-	318		RLL	ESDI
94186-442	15	1412	34	-	367		RLL	ESDI
94204-65	8	941	17		62	28	MFM	ST 506
94204-71	8	1024	17		68	28	MFM	ST 506
94205-51	5	989	17	128	41	32	MFM	ST 506
94205-77	5	989	26	-	63	28	RLL	ST 506
94295-51	5	989	17	990	41	28	MFM	ST 506
94335-100	9	1072	17	-	80	15	MFM	ST 506
94335-150	9	1072	26	-	123	25	RLL	ST 506
94335-55	5	1072	17	-	45	25	MFM	St 506
94351-128	7	1068	36		131		RLL	SCSI
94351-160	9	1068	36		169		RLL	SCSI
94351-200	9	1068	36		169		RLL	SCSI
94351-200	9	1068	36		169		RLL	ST 506
94356-200	9	1272	34	-	190	18	RLL	ESDI
BJ7D4A	4	671	17		22		MFM	ST 506
BJ7D5A	5	671	17		28		MFM	ST 506

Hard Drive Parameters

Appendix B

CMI Hard Drive Parameters								
Model	Head	Cyl	Sect	WP	Cap	AT	Proc	Port
CM 3206	4	306	17		10		MFM	ST 506
CM 3426	4	612	17	256	20		MFM	ST 506
CM 5205	2	256	17	128	4		MFM	ST 506
CM 5206	2	306	17	128	5		MFM	ST 506
CM 5410	4	256	17	128	8		MFM	ST 506
CM 5412	4	306	17	128	10		MFM	ST 506
CM 5616	6	256	17	128	13		MFM	ST 506
CM 5619	6	306	17	128	15		MFM	ST 506
CM 5826	8	306	17	128	20		MFM	ST 506
CM 6213	2	640	17	256	10		MFM	ST 506
CM 6426	4	615	17	256	20		MFM	ST 506
CM 6626	4	640	17	256	21		MFM	ST 506
CM 6640	6	640	17	256	32		MFM	ST 506
CM 7660	6	960	17	512	48		MFM	ST 506
CM 7880	8	960	17	512	64		MFM	ST 506

Conner Hard Drive Parameters								
Model	Head	Cyl	Sect	WP	Cap	AT	Proc	Port
CP-2024	2	653	32	21			IDE	
CP-3000	5	980	17	42	28		IDE	
CP-30100				120	19		SCSI	
CP-30104	14	997	17	120	19		IDE	
CP-30204				212	16		IDE	
CP-3022	2	636	27	20	26	RLL	IDE	
CP-3024	2	636	33	21			IDE	
CP-3040	2	1047		41	25	RLL	SCSI	
CP-3044	2	1047	40	41	25	RLL		
CP-3100	8	776	33	104	29	RLL	SCSI	

650

Hard Drive Parameters

\multicolumn{10}{c	}{Conner Hard Drive Parameters (continued)}
Model	Head	Cyl	Sect	WP	Cap	AT	Proc	Port
CP-3102A	8	776	33	104	26	RLL	IDE	
CP-3102B	8	776	33	104	26	RLL	IDE	
CP-3104	8	776	33	105	25		IDE	
CP-3184	6	832	33	82			IDE	
CP-3200	8	1348	39	210	19	RLL	SCSI	
CP-3200F				212	16		SCSI	
CP-3204	16	683	38	210			IDE	
CP-3204F	16	683	38	210	16		IDE	
CP-321	4	612	17	21	19	MFM	IDE	
CP-340	4	788	26	40	29	RLL	SCSI	
CP-342	4	805	26	42	26	RLL	IDE	
CP-344	4	805	26	42	26	RLL	IDE	
CP-4024	2	627	34	21			IDE	
CP-4044	2	1105	34	42			IDE	
RCP-3200				212	16	RLL	SCSI	

\multicolumn{9}{c	}{Core Hard Drive Parameters}
Model	Head	Cyl	Sect	WP	Cap	AT	Proc	Port
AT 30	5	733	17		30	26	MFM	ST 506
AT 32	5	733	17		30	21	MFM	ST 506
AT 40	5	924	17		38	26	MFM	ST 506
AT 63	5	988	26		63	26	MFM	ST 506
AT 72	9	924	17		70	26	MFM	ST 506
HC 100	6	969	35		100	9	MFM	ESDI
HC 150	9	968	35		154	16	RLL	ESDI
HC 310	12	1582	32		310	16	MFM	ESDI
HC 380	15	1412	35		377	16	MFM	ESDI
HC 40	4	564	35		39	10	RLL	ESDI

Appendix
B
Section
4

651

Hard Drive Parameters

Appendix B

Core Hard Drive Parameters (continued)								
Model	Head	Cyl	Sect	WP	Cap	AT	Proc	Port
HC 650	16	1938	35		647	16	MFM	ESDI
HC 90	5	969	35		83	16	RLL	ESDI
OP 70	9	918	17		70	26	MFM	ST 506
OPTIMA 30	5	733	17		30	21	MFM	ST 506
OPTIMA 40	5	963	17		40	26	MFM	ST 506
OPTIMA 70	9	918	17		70	26	MFM	ST 506

Data General Hard Drive Parameters								
Model	Head	Cyl	Sect	WP	Cap	AT	Proc	Port
MOD 6526	8	1024	17		70	28	MFM	ST 506
MOD 6535	15	1224	35		320	18		ESDI
MOD 6537	15	1224	17		157	30	MFM	ST 506

Fuji Hard Drive Parameters								
Model	Head	Cyl	Sect	WP	Cap	AT	Proc	Port
FK301	4	306	17	128	10		MFM	ST 506
FK302-13	2	612	17	307	10		MFM	ST 506
FK302-26	4	612	17	307	20		MFM	ST 506
FK302-39	6	612	17	307	30		MFM	ST 506
FK303-52	8	615	17	616	41	50	MFM	ST 506
FK305-26	4	615	17	616	20	80	MFM	ST 506
FK305-39	6	615	17	616	31	80	MFM	ST 506
FK305-39R	4	615	26		31	50	RLL	ST 506
FK305-58R	6	615	26		47	50	RLL	ST 506
FK308S-39	4	615	17		20	50	MFM	SCSI
FK308S-58	6	615	17		30	50	MFM	SCSI
FK309-26	4	615	17	300	20	80	MFM	ST 506
FK309-39	4	615	26		31	80	RLL	ST 506
FK309-39R	4	615	26		31	80	RLL	ST 506
FK309-58	6	615	26		47		RLL	ST 506

Hard Drive Parameters

Fujitsu Hard Drive Parameters								
Model	Head	Cyl	Sect	WP	Cap	AT	Proc	Port
2230 AS	2	320	17		5		MFM	ST 506
2233 AS	4	320	17		10		MFM	ST 506
2234 AS	6	320	17		16		MFM	ST 506
2235 AS	8	320	17		21		MFM	ST 506
2241 AS	4	754	17		25		MFM	ST 506
2244E	5	823	35		70	25	RLL	ESDI
2244SA	5	823	35		70	25	RLL	SCSI
2245E	7	823	35		98	25	RLL	ESDI
M 2225D	4	615	26		31	35	RLL	ST 506
M 2225DR	4	615	26		31	35	RLL	ST 506
M 2226D2	6	615	17		31	35	MFM	ST 506
M 2226DR	6	615	26		47	35	RLL	ST 506
M 2227D2	8	615	17		41	35	MFM	ST 506
M 2227DR	8	615	26		63	35	RLL	ST 506
M 2230AS	2	306	17		5		MFM	ST 506
M 2230AT	2	306	17		5		MFM	ST 506
M 2231	2	306	17		5		MFM	ST 506
M 2233AS	4	306	17		10		MFM	ST 506
M 2233AT	4	306	17		10		MFM	ST 506
M 2234AS	6	306	17		15		MFM	ST 506
M 2235AS	8	306	17		20		MFM	ST 506
M 2241AS	4	754	17	375	25		MFM	ST 506
M 2242	7	754	17	375	44		MFM	ST 506
M 2243AS	11	754	17	375	69		MFM	ST 506
M 2243R	7	1186	26		105	25	RLL	ST 506
M 2243T	7	1186	17		69	25	RLL	ST 506
M 2245SA	7	823	35		98	25	RLL	SCSI
M 2246E	10	823	35		141	25	RLL	ESDI
M 2246SA	10	823	35		141	25	RLL	SCSI
M 2247E	7	1243	35		149	25	RLL	ESDI

Appendix

B

Section

4

653

Hard Drive Parameters

Appendix B

Fujitsu Hard Drive Parameters (continued)								
Model	Head	Cyl	Sect	WP	Cap	AT	Proc	Port
M 2249E	15	1243			302	18	RLL	ESDI
M 2249SA	15	1243			300	18	RLL	SCSI
M 2261E	8	1658	53		357	16		ESDI
M 2261SA	8	1658	53		357	16		SCSI
M 2263E	15	1658	53		670	16	RLL	ESDI
M 2263SA	15	1658	53		670	16	RLL	ESDI
M 2266SA	15	1658	85		1080	30		SCSI
M 2611S	2	1334			43	25	RLL	SCSI
M 2611SA	2	1334	34		45	25		SCSI
M 2611T	4	667	33		45	25		IDE
M 2612S	4	1334			89	20	RLL	SCSI
M 2613ESA	6	1334	34		135	20		SCSI
M 2613ET	12	667	33		135	20		IDE
M 2613S	6	1334			134	20	RLL	SCSI
M 2614ESA	8	1334	34		182	20		SCSI
M 2614ET	16	667	33		180	20		IDE
M 2614S	8	1334			177	20	RLL	SCSI
M 2616ESA	4	1542	34		104	20		SCSI
M 2616ET	8	771	33		104	20		IDE
M 2622SA					330	12		SCSI
M 2622T					326	12		IDE
M 2623SA					420	12		IDE
M 2623T					420	12		IDE
M 2624SA					520	12		IDE
M 2624T					513	12		IDE
M 2652SA					1700	11		SCSI

Hard Drive Parameters

Hitachi Hard Drive Parameters								
Model	Heads	Cyl	Sect	WPC	Cap	AT	Proc	Port
DK 301-1	4	306	17		10	85	MFM	ST 506
DK 301-2	6	306	17		15	85	MFM	ST 506
DK 511-3	5	699	17	300	29	30	MFM	ST 506
DK 511-5	7	699	17	300	41	30	MFM	ST 506
DK 511-8	10	823	17	400	68	23	MFM	ST 506
DK 512-12	7	823	17		48	23	MFM	ESDI
DK 512-17	10	823	17		68	23	MFM	ESDI
DK 512-8	5	823	17		34	23	MFM	ESDI
DK 512C-12	7	823	35		99	23	RLL	SCSI
DK 512C-17	10	819	35		140	23	RLL	SCSI
DK 512C-8	5	823	35		70	23	RLL	SCSI
DK 521-5	6	823	17	400	41	25	MFM	ST 506
DK 522-10	6	823	36		87	25	RLL	ESDI
DK 522C-10	6	819	35		84	25	RLL	SCSI

Hewlett-Packard Hard Drive Parameters								
Model	Head	Cyl	Sect	WPC	Cap	AT	Proc	Port
HP 97544E	8	1457			340	17	ESDI	
HP 97544T	8	1447	56		331	17	SCSI	
HP 97548E	16	1457	57		680	17	ESDI	
HP 97548T	16	1447	56		663	17	SCSI	
HP 97549T/P	16	1918	64		1000	18	SCSI	
HP 97556E	11	1680	72		681	15	ESDI	
HP 97556T	11	1670	72		673	15	SCSI	
HP 97558E	15	1961	72		1080	15	ESDI	
HP 97558T/P	15	1952	72		1000	15	SCSI	
HP 97560E	19	1961	72		1370	15	ESDI	

Hard Drive Parameters

Appendix B

Hewlett-Packard Hard Drive Parameters (continued)								
Model	Head	Cyl	Sect	WPC	Cap	AT	Proc	Port
HP 97560T/P	19	1952	72		1300	14	SCSI	
HP C2233A	5	1260	72		234	13	IDE	
HP C2233S	5				234	13	SCSI	
HP C2234A	7	1260	72		328	13	IDE	
HP C2234S	7				328	13	SCSI	
HP C2235A	9	1260	72		422	13	IDE	
HP C2235S	9				422	13	SCSI	

Iprimis Hard Drive Parameters								
Model	Heads	Cyl	Sect	WPC	Cap	AT	Proc	Port
94166	7	969	34		113		RLL	
9415-536	5	697	17		29		MFM	ST 506
9415-538	5	733	17		30		MFM	ST 506
94155-120	8	960	26		97		RLL	ST 506
94155-135	9	960	26		110		RLL	
94155-135P	9	960	26		110		RLL	
94155-48	5	925	17		39		MFM	
94155-56	9	925	17		69		MFM	
94155-57	6	925	17		46		MFM	
94155-67	7	925	17		54		MFM	
94155-77	8	925	17		61		MFM	
94155-85	8	1024	17		68		MFM	
94155-85P	8	1024	17		68		MFM	
94155-86	9	925	17		69		MFM	
94155-96	9	1024	17		77		MFM	
94155-96P	9	1024	17		77		MFM	
94156-48	5	925	17		38		MFM	
94156-67	7	925	17		54		MFM	
94156-86	9	925	17		69		MFM	
94166-101	5	969	34		80		RLL	

Iprimis Hard Drive Parameters (continued)								
Model	Heads	Cyl	Sect	WPC	Cap	AT	Proc	Port
94166-182	9	969	34		145		RLL	
94204-65	8	941	17		62		MFM	
94204-71	8	1024	17		68		MFM	
94205-51	5	989	17		41		MFM	
94205-77	5	989	26		63		RLL	
94216-106	5	1024	34		85		RLL	
94354-135	9	1072	26		122		RLL	
94354-160	9	1072	29		137		RLL	
94354-172	9	1072	36		170		RLL	
94354-200	9	1072	36		170		RLL	
94355-100	9	1072	17		80		MFM	
94355-150	9	1072	26		122		RLL	
94356-11	5	1072	36		94		RLL	
94356-155	7	1072	36		132		RLL	
94356-200	9	1072	36		170		RLL	
Wren II 85 P FH	9	1024	17		69	28	MFM	ST 506
Wren II FH	9	924	17		72	28	MFM	ST 506
Wren II HH	5	989	17		40	28	MFM	ST 506
Wren II HH AT	5	1032			71	28	RLL	
Wren III FH	9	969			153	17	RLL	ESDI
Wren III FH	9	969			151	17	RLL	SCSI
Wren III HH	5	1024			90		RLL	SCSI
Wren III HH	5	1024			90		RLL	ESDI
Wren IV FH	9	1549			340	17		SCSI
Wren V 383 H	15	1224			338	15	RLL	ESDI
Wren V FH	15	1546			635	17		SCSI
Wren V HH	5	1544			188	18		SCSI
Wren VI FH	15	1632			700	17	RLL	ESDI
Wren VI HH	7	1747			335	16	RLL	ESDI
Wren VI HH	7	1747			333	16	RLL	SCSI
Wren VII FH	15	1937			1010	17		SCSI

Appendix

B

Section

4

657

Hard Drive Parameters

Appendix B

Kontron Hard Drive Parameters								
Model	Heads	Cyl	Sect	WPC	Cap	AT	Proc	Port
SQ 555	2	1278			42	25	RLL	SCSI

Kyocera Hard Drive Parameters								
Model	Heads	Cyl	Sect	WPC	Cap	AT	Proc	Port
KC20A	4	615	17	300	21		MFM	ST 506
KC20B	4	615	17	300	21		MFM	ST 506
KC30A	4	615	26	-	31		RLL	ST 506
KC30B	4	615	26	-	31		RLL	ST 506
KC80C	8	788	27		86		RLL	SCSI

Lanstor Hard Drive Parameters								
Model	Heads	Cyl	Sect	WPC	Cap	AT	Proc	Port
LAN-64	8	1024	17	-	70		MFM	ST 506
LAN-115	15	918	17	-	117		MFM	ST 506
LAN-140	8	1024	34		140			ST 506
LAN-180	8	1024	26	-	107		RLL	ST 506

Lapine Hard Drive Parameters								
Model	Heads	Cyl	Sect	WPC	Cap	AT	Proc	Port
3062	4	306	17	0	10		MFM	ST 506
3512	4	306	17	0	10		MFM	ST 506
3522	4	306	17	0	10		MFM	ST 506
LT 200	4	615	17	0	20	60	MFM	ST 506
LT 2000	4	615	17	0	20	61	MFM	ST 506
T-10	2	615	17		10		MFM	ST 506
T-20	4	615	17	0	20	61	MFM	ST 506
T-30	4	615	27		32	65	RLL	ST 506
T-300	4	615	27		32	65	RLL	ST 506

Maxtor Hard Drive Parameters								
Model	Heads	Cyl	Sect	WPC	Cap	AT	Proc	Port
4230E	9	1224	36		203	16		ESDI
7040A	5	980	17		40	19		IDE
7060AT	7	1024	17		62	15		IDE
7080A	10	980	17		80	19		IDE
7120AT	14	1024	17		125	15		IDE
7120S	4	1498	39		125	15		SCSI
8051A	5	977	17		40	28		IDE
8760E	15	1632	54		676	16	RLL	ESDI
8760S	15	1632	54		676	16	RLL	SCSI
AT-120	16	918	17		120	26	MFM	ST 506
AT-160	16	1224	17		160	28	MFM	ST 506
AT-70	9	1024	17		70	27	MFM	ST 506
LXT-213A	16	683	38		213	15		IDE
LXT-213S	15	918	30		213	15		SCSI
LXT-340AT	16	654	63		340	13		IDE
LXT-340S	15	1560	24		340	13		SCSI
LXT-535S	11	1560	61		535	13	RLL	SCSI
MPO-1,2S	19	1216	85		1000	13		SCSI
MPO-1,7S					1500	13		SCSI
XT-1065	7	918	17	-	55	28	MFM	ST 506
XT-1085	8	1024	17	-	70	28	MFM	ST 506
XT-1105	11	918	17	-	87	27	MFM	ST 506
XT-1120	8	1024	26	-	104	27	RLL	ST 506
XT-1120R	8	1024	26	-	104	27	RLL	ST 506
XT-1140	15	918	17	-	117	27	MFM	ST 506
XT-1240	15	1024	26	-	195	27	RLL	ST 506
XT-1240R	15	1024	26	-	195	27	RLL	ST 506
XT-2085	7	1224	17	-	73	30	MFM	ST 506
XT-2140	11	1224	17	-	112	30	MFM	ST 506
XT-2190	15	1224	17	-	157	29	MFM	ST 506

659

Hard Drive Parameters

Appendix B

Maxtor Hard Drive Parameters (continued)								
Model	Heads	Cyl	Sect	WPC	Cap	AT	Proc	Port
XT-4170E	7	1224	36	-	157	14	RLL	ESDI
XT-4170S	7	1224	36	-	157	14	RLL	SCSI
XT-4280S	11	1224	34	-	233		RLL	SCSI
XT-4380	15	1224	17	-	142	16	MFM	ST 506
XT-4380E	15	1224	35	-	338	16	RLL	ESDI
XT-4830S	15	1224	36	-	338	16	RLL	SCSI
XT-8380E	8	1632	54	-	344	14	RLL	ESDI
XT-8380S	8	1632	48	-	320	16	RLL	SCSI
XT-8760	15	1632	54	-	646	16	RLL	IDE
XT-8760S	15	1632	48	-	601	16	RLL	SCSI

Memorex Hard Drive Parameters								
Model	Heads	Cyl	Sect	WPC	Cap	AT	Proc	Port
321	2	320	17	128	5		MFM	ST 506
322	4	320	17	128	10		MFM	ST 506
323	6	320	17	128	16		MFM	ST 506
324	8	320	17	128	21		MFM	ST 506
450	2	612	17	350	10		MFM	ST 506
512	3	961	17	480	24		MFM	ST 506
513	5	961	17	480	40		MFM	ST 506
514	6	961	17	480	48		MFM	ST 506

Micropolis Hard Drive Parameters								
Model	Heads	Cyl	Sect	WPC	Cap	AT	Proc	Port
1302	3	830	17	400	21		MFM	ST 506
1303	5	830	17	400	34		MFM	ST 506
1304	6	830	17	400	41		MFM	ST 506
1323	4	1024	17	-	34	28	MFM	ST 506
1324	6	1024	17	-	51	28	MFM	ST 506
1325	8	1024	17	-	70	28	MFM	ST 506
1333	4	1024	17	-	34	28	MFM	ST 506
1334	6	1024	17	-	51	30	MFM	ST 506
1335	8	1024	17	-	68	30	MFM	ST 506
1352	2	1024	36		36	23	RLL	ESDI
1353	4	1024	36		72	23	RLL	ESDI
1354	6	1024	36		108	23	RLL	ESDI
1355	8	1024	36		144	23	RLL	ESDI
1373	4	1024	36		72	23	RLL	SCSI
1374	6	1024	36		108	23	RLL	SCSI
1375	8	1024	36		144	23	RLL	SCSI
1551	7	1024	17	-	60	30	MFM	ST 506
1554	11	1224	17	-	122	30	MFM	ST 506
1555	12	1224	17	-	122	30	MFM	ST 506
1556	13	1224	17	-	132	30	MFM	ST 506
1557	14	1224	17	-	142	30	MFM	ST 506
1558	15	1224	17	-	152	30	MFM	ST 506
1624					667	15		SCSI
1324A	7	1024	17		61		MFM	ST 506
1333A	5	1024	17		42	30	MFM	ST 506
1352A	3	1024	36		54	23	RLL	ESDI
1353A	5	1024	36		90	23	RLL	ESDI
1354A	7	1024	36		126	23	RLL	ESDI
1373A	5	1024	36		90	23	RLL	SCSI
1374A	7	1024	36		126	23	RLL	SCSI

Hard Drive Parameters

Appendix B

Micropolis Hard Drive Parameters (continued)								
Model	Heads	Cyl	Sect	WPC	Cap	AT	Proc	Port
1518-15					1340	15		ESDI
1538-15					1050	15		ESDI
1548-15					1750	14		SCSI
1556-11	11	1224	35		238			
1557-12	12	1224	35		258			
1557-13	13	1224	35		280			
1558-15	15	1224	36		337	18	RLL	ESDI
1568-15					676	14		ESDI
1578-15	15	1220	35		325	18	RLL	SCSI
1580-15					668	16		SCSI
1598-15					1030	14		SCSI
1653-4	4	1249	36		88	16	RLL	ESDI
1653-5	5	1249	36		110	16	RLL	ESDI
1654-6	6	1249	36		132	16	RLL	ESDI
1654-7	7	1249	36		154	16	RLL	ESDI
1664-7					345	14	RLL	SCSI
1674-7					158	16		SCSI
1683-4	4	1776	54		187	14	RLL	SCSI
1684-7					340	14		SCSI
1773-5	5	1140	48		134	15	RLL	SCSI
1774-6	6	1140	48		160	15	RLL	SCSI
1774-7	7	1140	48		187	15	RLL	SCSI

Microscience Hard Drive Parameters								
Model	Heads	Cyl	Sect	WPC	Cap	AT	Proc	Port
4050	6	1024	17		51	18	MFM	ST 506
4060	6	1024	26		67	18	RLL	ST 506
4090	8	1024			93	18	RLL	ST 506
5100	7	855	36		105	18	RLL	ESDI
6100	7	855	36		105	18	RLL	SCSI
7040	3	855	36		45	18	RLL	ESDI
7100	7	855	36		105	18	RLL	ESDI
HH-1050	5	1024	17	-	42	28	MFM	ST 506
HH-1060	5	1024	26		65	28	RLL	ST 506
HH-1075	7	1024	17		60	28	MFM	ST 506
HH-1090	7	1314	17		76	28	MFM	ST 506
HH-1095	7	1024	26		91	28	RLL	ST 506
HH-1120	7	1314	26		117	28	RLL	ST 506
HH-2120	7	1024	33		115	28	RLL	ST 506
HH-2160 F	8	1276			160	18	RLL	ESDI
HH-312	4	306	17	-	10		MFM	ST 506
HH-315	2	612	17	-	10		MFM	ST 506
HH-3160 F	8	1314			190	18	RLL	SCSI
HH-325	4	615	17	-	20	80	MFM	ST 506
HH-330	4	612	26		31		RLL	ST 506
HH-4050	5	1024	17		42	18	MFM	ST 506
HH-4060	5	1024	17		42	18	MFM	ST 506
HH-4070	7	1024	17		60	18	MFM	ST 506
HH-4090	7	1024	17		60	18	MFM	ST 506
HH-612	4	306	17	-	10		MFM	ST 506

Hard Drive Parameters

Appendix B

Microscience Hard Drive Parameters								
Model	Heads	Cyl	Sect	WPC	Cap	AT	Proc	Port
HH-625	4	612	17		20		MFM	ST 506
HH-7100	7	960	35		110	18	RLL	IDE
HH-712	2	612	17	-	10	105	MFM	ST 506
HH-725	4	612	17	-	20	105	MFM	ST 506
HH-738	4	612	26		31	105	RLL	ST 506
HH-8040	2	1024	40		40	19		IDE
HH-825	4	615	17		20	65	MFM	ST 506
HH-830	4	615	26		31	65	RLL	ST 506

Miniscribe Hard Drive Parameters								
Model	Heads	Cyl	Sect	WPC	Cap	AT	Proc	Port
3012	2	615	17	300	10		MFM	ST 506
3053	5	1024	17		42		MFM	ST 506
3085	7	1170	17	512	62		MFM	ESDI
3138	4	615	25		31		RLL	ST 506
3145	4	615	17	300	20		MFM	ST 506
3425	4	615	17	300	20		MFM	ST 506
3438	4	613	26	128	31	85	RLL	ST 506
3650	6	809	17	-	40	61	MFM	ST 506
3675	6	809	17	-	40	61	MFM	ST 506
6032	3	1024	17	512	25	28	MFM	ST 506
6053	5	1024	17	512	42	28	MFM	ST 506
6074	7	1024	17	512	60	28	MFM	ST 506
6085	8	1024	17	512	68	28	MFM	ST 506
6128	8	1024	26	512	104	28	RLL	ST 506
8138	4	615	26		32		RLL	ST 506
8425	4	615	17	128	20	68	MFM	ST 506
8438	4	615	26	128	31	61	RLL	ST 506
8450	4	805	26		42	68	RLL	ST 506
3130E	5	1250	35	-	110			ESDI
3180E	7	1254	35	-	150	17	RLL	ESDI

Miniscribe Hard Drive Parameters (continued)									
Model	Heads	Cyl	Sect	WPC	Cap	AT	Proc	Port
3180S	7	1250			155	17	RLL	ESDI
8051A	4	745	26	300	28	42	RLL	ST 506
8051S	4	615	17	300	20		MFM	ST 506
8125S	4	612	17		20		MFM	SCSI
8138F	4	615	26		32		RLL	ST 506
8425F	4	615	17	-	20	68	MFM	ST 506
8425S	4	612	17		21		MFM	SCSI
8438F	4	615	26	128	31	61	RLL	ST 506
9230E	9	1224	35	-	188	17	RLL	ESDI
9380E	15	1224	35	-	330	16	RLL	ESDI
9380S	7	1255			345	16	RLL	SCSI
9780E	15	1224			650	17	RLL	SCSI
9780S	15	1661			666	17	RLL	ESDI

Mitsubishi Hard Drive Parameters								
Model	Head	Cyl	Sect	WPC	Cap	AT	Proc	Port
MR 335-OOM	7	743	17		41	20	MFM	ST 506
MR 522	4	612	17	300	20		MFM	ST 506
MR 533	3	977	17	X	25		MFM	ST 506
MR 535	5	971	17	X	41	28	MFM	ST 506
MR 535-OOM	5	977	26		63	28	RLL	ST 506'

NEC Hard Drive Parameters								
Model	Heads	Cyl	Sect	WPC	Cap	AT	Proc	Port
D 3142	8	642	17	128	43	28	MFM	ST 506
D 3146H	8	615	17		42	35	MFM	ST 506
D 3155	4	1251			105	25	RLL	IDE
D 3661	7	915	26		117	23	RLL	ESDI
D 3735	2	1074			45	25	RLL	IDE

Appendix
B
Section
4

665

Hard Drive Parameters

Appendix B

NEC Hard Drive Parameters (continued)								
Model	Heads	Cyl	Sect	WPC	Cap	AT	Proc	Port
D 3755	8	625	41		102			IDE
D 3756	8	625	41		102			IDE
D 3756	4	1251			105	19	RLL	IDE
D 3835	2	1074			45	25	RLL	SCSI
D 3841	8	642	17		42	28	MFM	ST 506
D 3855	4	1251			105	25	RLL	SCSI
D 3856	4	1251			105	19	RLL	SCSI
D 3861	7	914	36		117	23	RLL	SCSI
D 5124	4	306	17	-	10	85	MFM	ST 506
D 5126	4	612	17	128	21	85	MFM	ST 506
D 5126H	4	612	17	300	21	85	MFM	ST 506
D 5127H	4	615	26	-	32		RLL	ST 506
D 5128	4	612	17	300	21	80	MFM	ST 506
D 5146	8	615	17	128	42	85	MFM	ST 506
D 5146H	8	615	17	128	42	85	MFM	ST 506
D 5147H	8	615	26	-	63		RLL	ST 506
D 5452	10	823	17		71		MFM	ST 506
D 5652	10	823	36		134	21	RLL	ESDI
D 5655	8	1224	36		140	18	RLL	ESDI
D 5662	16	1224	36		300	18	RLL	ESDI
D 5852					147	21		SCSI
D 5862	15	1221	36		325	18	RLL	SCSI
HD135 AT					114	20	RLL	IDE
HD180					179	18	RLL	ESDI
HD385 S					384	18	RLL	SCSI
HD760					758	18	RLL	ESDI

666

Hard Drive Parameters

Newburry Hard Drive Parameters								
Model	Heads	Cyl	Sect	WPC	Cap	AT	Proc	Port
NDR320	4	615	17		20		MFM	ST 506
NDR340	8	615	17		40		MFM	ST 506
NDR1085	8	1024	17	-	73		MFM	ST 506
NDR1105	11	918	17	-	90		MFM	ST 506
NDR1140	15	918	17	-	121		MFM	ST 506
NDR2190	15	1024	17	-	140		MFM	ST 506

Priam Hard Drive Parameters								
Model	Heads	Cyl	Sect	WPC	Cap	AT	Proc	Port
514	11	1224	17	-	115		MFM	ST 506
519	15	1224	17	-	157		MFM	ST 506
ID 160-SC	7	1218			160	18	RLL	SCSI
ID 250-SC	11	1218			250	18	RLL	SCSI
ID 330-EC	15	1218			330	18	RLL	ESDI
V 130	3	987	26	-	38		RLL	ST 506
V 150	5	987	17	-	41		MFM	ST 506
V 170	7	987	17	-	57		MFM	ST 506
V 185	7	1166	17	-	68		MFM	ST 506

Procom Hard Drive Parameters								
Model	Heads	Cyl	Sect	WPC	Cap	AT	Proc	Port
PIRA 40	4	745			43	28	RLL	
PIRA 100	8	776			100	25	RLL	

Appendix

B

Section

4

667

Hard Drive Parameters

Appendix B

PTI Hard Drive Parameters								
Model	Heads	Cyl	Sect	WPC	Cap	AT	Proc	Port
PT225	4	615	17	300	21		MFM	ST 506
PT234	4	820	17	544	28		MFM	ST 506
PT238R	4	615	26	300	32		RLL	ST 506
PT251R	4	820	26	544	42		RLL	ST 506
PT338	6	615	17	300	32		MFM	ST 506
PT351	6	820	17	544	42		MFM	ST 506
PT357R	6	615	26	300	49		RLL	ST 506
PT376R	6	820	26	544	65		RLL	ST 506
PT4102	8	820	26	544	85		RLL	ST 506
PT468	8	820	17	544	57		MFM	ST 506

Quantum Hard Drive Parameters								
Model	Heads	Cyl	Sect	WPC	Cap	AT	Proc	Port
120AT	9	814	32		120	15		IDE
170AT	10	968	34		168	15		IDE
210AT	13	873	36		210	15		IDE
330AT	12	1520	51		331	14		IDE
40AT	5	965	17		42	19		IDE
425AT	16	1520	51		426	14		IDE
80AT	10	965	17		84	19		IDE
LPS 105AT	16	755	17	755	100	17		IDE
LPS 52AT	8	751	17	751	50	17		IDE
ProDrive 80	6	834	34		80	19	RLL	IDE
Q 520	4	512	17	256	17	17	MFM	ST 506
Q 530	6	512	17	256	25	17	MFM	ST 506
Q 540	8	512	17	256	34	17	MFM	ST 506

668

Hard Drive Parameters

Appendix B

Rodime Hard Drive Parameters								
Model	Heads	Cyl	Sect	WPC	Cap	AT	Proc	Port
RO 202E	4	640	17	-	21	55	MFM	ST 506
RO 203	6	321	17	0	16	85	MFM	ST 506
RO 203E	6	640	17	0	32	55	MFM	ST 506
RO 204	8	321	17	0	21	85	MFM	ST 506
RO 204E	8	640	17	0	42	55	MFM	ST 506
RO 3/287	7	868			105	18	RLL	SCSI
RO 3055	6	872	17	650	44	28	MFM	ST 506
RO 3057S	5	680	26		44		RLL	SCSI
RO 3065	7	872	17		51	28	MFM	ST 506
RO 3075R	6	750	26	650	57		RLL	ST 506
RO 30858	7	750	26		68	28	RLL	SCSI
RO 3085R	7	750	26	650	67		RLL	ST 506
RO 3085S	7	750	26		68		RLL	SCSI
RO 3128 A	7	868			105	18	RLL	IDE
RO 3130T	7	1053			103		RLL	SCSI
RO 5090	7	1224	17	-	71	28	MFM	ST 506
RO 5125E	5	1224	36	-	112		RLL	ESDI
RO 5125S	5	1219			100		RLL	SCSI
RO 5130R	7	1224	26	-	113		RLL	ST 506
RO 5175E	5	1224	36		112		RLL	ESDI
RO 5180E	7	1224	36	-	155		RLL	ESDI
RO 5180S	7	1219			142		RLL	SCSI
RO 5180T	7	1219			142		RLL	SCSI
RO 703E	6	640	17		33		MFM	ST 506

Hard Drive Parameters

Appendix B

Seagate Hard Drive Parameters								
Model	Heads	Cyl	Sect	WPC	Cap	AT	Proc	Port
ST 1057A	6	1024	17	-	52	18	ZBR	IDE
ST 1090A	16	335	29	-	79	17	RLL	IDE
ST 1096N	9	1024	17		80	28	MFM	SCSI
ST 1102A	10	1024	17		89	19	ZBR	IDE
ST 1111A	10	402	48	-	98	15	RLL	IDE
ST 1111E					95	15	RLL	SCSI
ST 1126A	16	469	29	-	110	17	RLL	IDE
ST 1133A	8	477	60	-	117	15	RLL	IDE
ST 1144A	14	1024	17		124	19	ZBR	IDE
ST 1156A	9	536	56	-	138	15	RLL	IDE
ST 1162A	9	1024	31		143	15		IDE
ST 1162A	16	603	29	-	143	15	RLL	IDE
ST 1186A	9	636	56	-	163	15	RLL	IDE
ST 1186N					160	15	RLL	SCSI
ST 1201A	9	1013	38		177	15	RLL	IDE
ST 1201E					178	15	RLL	ESDI
ST 1201N					170	15	RLL	SCSI
ST 1239A	14	818	36		211	15	RLL	IDE
ST 1239N	9	1302	35		210	15	RLL	SCSI
ST 125	4	615	17	300	20	40	MFM	ST 506
ST 125A	4	614	17	300	20	28	RLL	IDE
ST 138	6	615	17	-	31	40	MFM	ST 506
ST 138A	6	615	17	-	31	28	RLL	IDE
ST 138R	4	615	26	-	31	40	RLL	ST 506
ST 1400A					330	14	ZBR	IDE
ST 1400N					330	14	ZBR	SCSI
ST 1401A					340	12	ZBR	IDE
ST 1401N					340	12	ZBR	SCSI
ST 1480A	15	985	62	-	420	14	ZBR	IDE
ST 1480N					426	14	ZBR	SCSI

Seagate Hard Drive Parameters (continued)								
Model	Heads	Cyl	Sect	WPC	Cap	AT	Proc	Port
ST 1481N					426	14	ZBR	SCSI
ST 151	5	977	17	-	42	28	MFM	ST 506
ST 157A	7	733	17		44	28	RLL	IDE
ST 157N	6	615	26	-	47		RLL	SCSI
ST 157R	6	615	26	-	47	40	RLL	ST 506
ST 177N	5	921			60	24	RLL	SCSI
ST 213	2	615	17	300	10	65	MFM	ST 506
ST 2182E					160	16	RLL	ESDI
ST 225	4	615	17	300	20	65	MFM	ST 506
ST 2274A	10	873	54	-	240	16	RLL	IDE
ST 227R	6	820	26	-	65	28	RLL	ST 506
ST 2383A	14	874	54		338	16	RLL	IDE
ST 2383E	7	1747	54		338	16	RLL	ESDI
ST 238R	4	615	26	300	30	65	RLL	ST 506
ST 2502N					442	16	ZBR	SCSI
ST 250R	4	667	31	-	40	70	RLL	
ST 251	6	820	17	-	41	40	MFM	ST 506
ST 251R	6	820	26	-	62	40	RLL	ST 506
ST 274A	8	941	17	-	64	28	RLL	IDE
ST 277N	6	818	26	-	62	28	RLL	SCSI
ST 277R	6	820	26	-	62	40	MFM	ST 506
ST 280A	8	1024	17	-	70	28	RLL	IDE
ST 296N	6	820			85	28	MFM	SCSI
ST 3096A	10	1024	17	-	88	15	ZBR	IDE
ST 3120A	12	1024	17	-	105	16	ZBR	IDE
ST 3144A	15	1001	17	-	124	16	ZBR	IDE
ST 325A	4	615	17	300	21	28	RLL	IDE
ST 3283A					245	12	RLL	IDE
ST 3283N					245	12	RLL	SCSI
ST 3500N					426	10	ZBR	SCSI

Appendix

B

Section

4

Hard Drive Parameters

Appendix B

Seagate Hard Drive Parameters (continued)								
Model	Heads	Cyl	Sect	WPC	Cap	AT	Proc	Port
ST 351A	6	820	17		42	28	RLL	IDE
ST 3600 A					525	11	ZBR	IDE
ST 4026	4	615	17	300	20		MFM	ST 506
ST 4038	5	733	17	300	30	40	MFM	ST 506
ST 4038M	5	733	17	-	30	40	MFM	ST 506
ST 4051	5	977	17	-	41	40	MFM	ST 506
ST 4053	5	1024	17	-	42	28	MFM	ST 506
ST 4077R	5	1024	26	-	65	28	RLL	ST 506
ST 4096	9	1024	17	-	77	28	MFM	ST 506
ST 412	4	306	17	128	10		MFM	ST 506
ST 41200N	15	1931	68		1000	16	ZBR	SCSI
ST 4144R	9	1024	26	-	117	28	RLL	SCSI
ST 41601N					1340	11	ZBR	SCSI
ST 41650N	15	2107	98		1600	15		SCSI
ST 43400N					1900	13	ZBR	SCSI
ST 43401N					2800	11	ZBR	SCSI
ST 4385N	16	1024	40		338	11	ZBR	SCSI
ST 4442E					380	16	RLL	ESDI
ST 4702N					613	17	RLL	SCSI
ST 4766E	15	1632	54		663	15	RLL	ESDI
ST 4766N	15	1632	54		663	15		SCSI
ST 4767E					676	12	RLL	ESDI
ST 4767N	15	1356	64		701	11		SCSI
ST 4769E					691	13	RLL	ESDI
ST 9096A					80	16	RLL	IDE
ST 9096N					80	16	RLL	SCSI
ST 9144A	14	1024	17		120	16	RLL	IDE
ST 9144N					120	16	RLL	SCSI

Appendix B

Storage Dimensions Hard Drive Parameters								
Model	Heads	Cyl	Sect	WPC	Cap	AT	Proc	Port
175i					175	18		SCSI"
345i					345	14		SCSI
45i					45	29		SCSI
650i					650	17		SCSI"
90i					90	29		SCSI
AT-100R	8	1024	26		107		RLL	ST 506
AT-120	16	918	17		120	26	MFM	ST 506
AT-133	15	1024	17		130		MFM	ST 506
AT-140	8	1024	34		138		RLL	
AT-155E	7	969	36		150			SCSI
AT-160	16	1224	17		160	28	MFM	ST 506'
AT-160	15	1224	17		155		MFM	ST 506
AT-200R	15	1024	26		200		RLL	ST 506
AT-320	15	1224	35		320			
AT-335E	15	1224	36		330			ESDI
AT-40	5	1024	17		41		MFM	ST 506
AT-650E	15	1632	52		650			ESDI
AT-70	8	1024	17		70	27	MFM	ST 506
HCV 345					345	14		SCSI'
HCV 650					650	17		SCSI
ZFP 175					175	18		SCSI
ZFP 45					44	29		SCSI
ZFP 90					90	29		SCSII

Hard Drive Parameters

Appendix B

SyQuest Hard Drive Parameters								
Model	Heads	Cyl	Sect	WPC	Cap	AT	Proc	Port
SQ306RD	2	306	17		5			SCSI
SQ312RD	2	612	17		11			
SQ325F	4	612	17		22			IDE
SQ338F	6	612	17		33			SCSI
SQ555	2	1275			44		RLL	SCSI

Teac Hard Drive Parameters								
Model	Heads	Cyl	Sect	WPC	Cap	AT	Proc	Port
SD-3105-00					105	19	RLL	SCSI
SD-3105-30					105	19	RLL	IDE
SD-3210-00					210	17	RLL	SCSI
SD-3210-30					210	17	RLL	IDE

Toshiba Hard Drive Parameters								
Model	Heads	Cyl	Sect	WPC	Cap	AT	Proc	Port
MK134F	7	733	26		66	26	RLL	ST 506
MK134FA	7	733	17		42	25	MFM	ST 506
MK156FA	10	830			143	23	RLL	ESDI
MK156FB	10	830			150	23	RLL	SCSI
MK2024FC					86	19		IDE
MK2124FC					130	17		IDE
MK234FB	7	856			106	20	RLL	SCSI
MK234FC	8	776	33		100	20	RLL	IDE
MK53	5	830	17	512	35		MFM	ST 506
MK54	7	830	17	512	50		MFM	ST 506
MK56FA	10	830	17	512	71		MFM	ST 506
MK56FB	10	830	26		107	24	RLL	ST 506
MK58FA	10	830	17	512	71		MFM	ST 506

Hard Drive Parameters

Appendix B

Tulin Hard Drive Parameters								
Model	Heads	Cyl	Sect	WPC	Cap	AT	Proc	Port
TL226	4	640	17		20		MFM	ST 506
TL238	4	640	17		20		MFM	ST 506
TL240	6	640	17		31		MFM	ST 506
TL258	6	640	26		50		RLL	ST 506
TL326	4	640	17		20		MFM	ST 506
TL338	6	640	17		31		MFM	ST 506
TL340	6	640	17		31		MFM	ST 506

Western Digital Hard Drive Parameters								
Model	Heads	Cyl	Sect	WPC	Cap	AT	Proc	Port
93044A	5	977	17	0	40			IDE
AC140	5	977	17	0	40			IDE
AC2120	8	872	35	0	125	16		IDE
AC280	10	980	17	0	85			IDE
AC4200	12	987	35	0	212	14		IDE
AP4200	12	987	35		212	16		IDE

Appendix C
Pin Connections

Power supply pin connections

PIN	Function
1	220V AC
2	220V AC
3	Ground

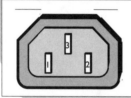

3-plug power supply connector

Motherboard power supply pin layout P8, P9

Pin	Color	Function
1	Orange	Power Good
2	Red	+ 5V DC
3	Yellow	+ 12V DC
4	Blue	- 12V DC
5	Black	Ground
6	Black	Ground
7	Black	Ground
8	Black	Ground
9	White	- 5V DC
10	Red	+ 5V DC
11	Red	+ 5V DC
12	Red	+ 5V DC

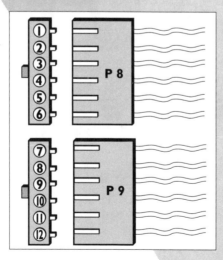

Pin Connections

5.25-inch power supply pin layout

Pin	Color	Function
1	Yellow	+ 12V DC
2	Black	Ground
3	Black	Ground
4	Red	+ 5V DC

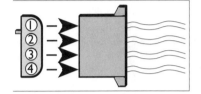

3.5-inch power supply pin layout

Pin	Color	Function
1	Yellow	+ 12V DC
2	Black	Ground
3	Black	Ground
4	Red	+ 5V DC

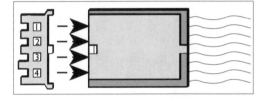

AT keyboard jack pin layout

Pin	Function
1	Clock
2	Data
3	Reset
4	Ground
5	+ 5V DC

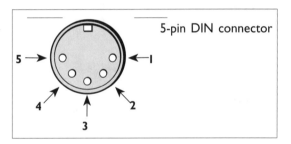

5-pin DIN connector

Battery connector pin layout

Pin	Color	Function
1	+ 6V DC	Red
2	Unused	
4	Ground	
3	Ground	Black

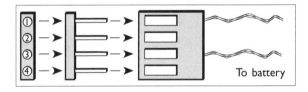

To battery

678

LED keylock connector strip pin layout

Pin	Function
I	Power LED anode
2	Unused
3	Ground
4	Keyboard lock
5	Ground

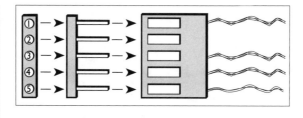

Loudspeaker connector pin layout

Pin	Function
I	Signal
2	Unused
3	Ground
4	+5V DC

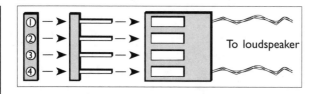

To loudspeaker

679

Pin Connections

Port Pin Layouts

Parallel port pin layout

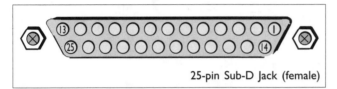

25-pin Sub-D Jack (female)

Pin	Function	Pin	Function	Pin	Function	Pin	Function
1	Strobe	8	Bit 7	14	Autofeed	20	Ground
2	Bit 1	9	Bit 8	15	Error	21	Ground
3	Bit 2	10	Acknowledge	16	Printer Reset	22	Ground
4	Bit 3	11	Busy	17	Select in	23	Ground
5	Bit 4	12	Paper out	18	Ground	24	Ground
6	Bit 5	13	Select out	19	Ground	25	Ground
7	Bit 6						

Pin Connections

Serial port pin layout

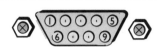

9-pin Sub-D Plug (male)

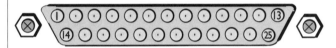

25-pin Sub-D Plug (male)

25-Pin		9-Pin	
Pin	Function	Pin	Function
I	Ground	I	Carrier detect
2	Transmit Data	2	Receive Data
3	Receive Data	3	Transmit data
4	Request to send	4	Data terminal ready
5	Clear to send	5	Ground
6	Data set ready	6	Data set ready
7	Ground	7	Request to send
8	Carrier detect	8	Clear to send
9	Check modem	9	Ring indication
20	Data terminal ready		
22	Ring indication		

Appendix

C

Section

4

Pin Connections

Gameport pin layout

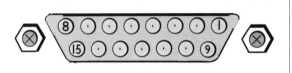

15 Sub-D jack (Female)

Pin	Function
1	+ 5V DC
2	Joystick 1, first button
3	Joystick 1, X-Position
4	Ground
5	Ground
6	Joystick 1, Y-Position
7	Joystick 1, second button
8	+ 5V DC
9	+ 5V DC
10	Joystick 2, first button
11	Joystick 2, X-Position
12	Ground
13	Joystick 2, Y-Position
14	Joystick 2, second button
15	+ 5V DC

External floppy connector pin layout

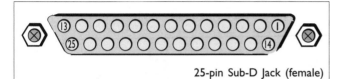

25-pin Sub-D Jack (female)

Pin	Function
1	Index
2	Motor on, Drive 4
3	Drive select, Drive 3
4	Drive select, Drive 4
5	Motor on, Drive 3
6	Direction
7	Step
8	Write data
9	Write gate
10	Track 0
11	Write protect
12	Read data
13	Side 1 protect

Pin	Function
14	+ 5V DC
15	+5V DC
16	+ 5V DC
17	Unused
18	Power on
19	Ground
20	Ground
21	Ground
22	Ground
23	Ground
24	Disk change
25	High density

Appendix

C

Section

4

683

Pin Connections

SCREEN ADAPTER PIN CONNECTIONS

Composite jack pin layout

Pin	Function
1	Ground
2	Signal

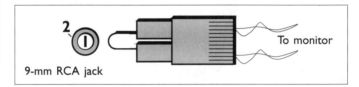

9-mm RCA jack   To monitor

MDA/Hercules adapter pin layout

Pin	Function
1	Ground
2	Unused
3	Unused
4	Unused
5	Unused
6	Intensity
7	Video signal
8	Horizontal synch
9	Vertical synch

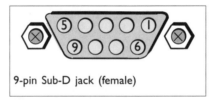

9-pin Sub-D jack (female)

CGA card pin layout

Pin	Function
1	Ground
2	Unused
3	Red
4	Green
5	Blue
6	Intensity
7	Unused
8	Horizontal synch
9	Vertical synch

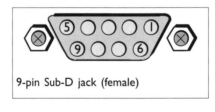

9-pin Sub-D jack (female)

EGA card pin layout

Pin	Function
1	Ground
2	2. Red
3	Red
4	Green
5	Blue
6	2. Green
7	2. Blue
8	Horizontal synch
9	Vertical synch

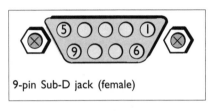

9-pin Sub-D jack (female)

VGA card pin layout (9-pin)

Pin	Function
1	Ground
2	2. Red
3	Red
4	Green
5	Blue
6	2. Green
7	2. Blue
8	Horizontal synch
9	Vertical synch

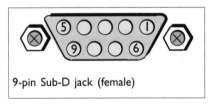

9-pin Sub-D jack (female)

Appendix

C

Section

4

Pin Connections

VGA card pin layout (15-pin)

Pin	Function
1	Red
2	Green
3	Blue
4	Monitor ID 2
5	Unused
6	Ground
7	Ground
8	Ground
9	Unused
10	Ground
11	Monitor ID 0
12	Monitor ID 1
13	Horizontal sync
14	Vertical synch
15	Unused

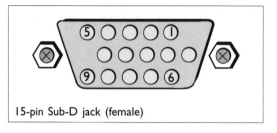

15-pin Sub-D jack (female)

CONTROLLER PIN CONNECTIONS

Floppy disk drive connector pin layout

34-pin Post connector

Pin	Function	Pin	Function	Pin	Function
1	Ground	13	Ground	25	Ground
2	HL	14	Drive Select 2	26	Track 0
3	Unused	15	Ground	27	Ground
4	In use	16	Motor on	28	Write protect
5	Ground	17	Ground	29	Ground
6	Drive Select 3	18	Direction	30	Read Data
7	Ground	19	Ground	31	Ground
8	Index	20	Step	32	Side select
9	Ground	21	Ground	33	Ground
10	Drive Select 0	22	Write Data	34	Disk change
11	Ground	23	Ground		
12	Drive Select 1	24	Write Gate		

Pin Connections

IDE-Interface pin layout

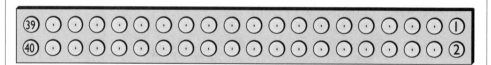

40-pin Post connector

Pin	Function	Pin	Function	Pin	Function
1	Reset	15	D1	29	Unused
2	Ground	16	D14	30	Ground
3	D7	17	D0	31	IRQ14
4	D8	18	D15	32	IO16
5	D6	19	Ground	33	A1
6	D9	20	Locked	34	A0
7	D5	21	IOCHRDY	35	A2
8	D10	22	Ground	36	PDIAG
9	D4	23	IOWR	37	CS0
10	D11	24	Ground	38	CS1
11	D3	25	IORD	39	HD-LED active
12	D12	26	Ground	40	Ground
13	D2	27	IOCHRDY		
14	D13	28	ALE		

Standard Measurements

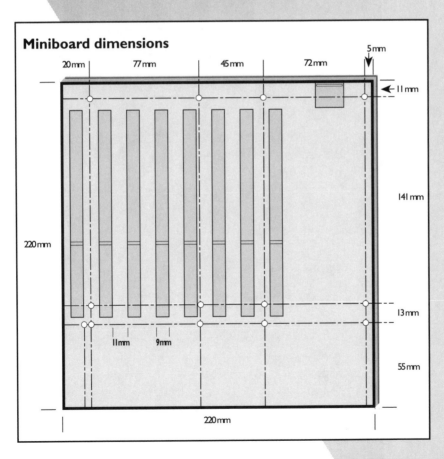

Miniboard dimensions

20mm · 77mm · 45mm · 72mm · 5mm

11mm

141mm

220mm

13mm

11mm · 9mm

55mm

220mm

Standard Measurements

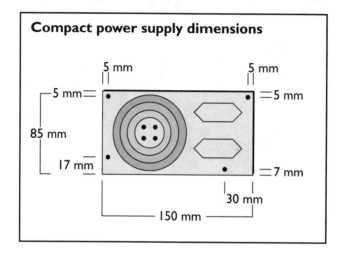

Compact power supply dimensions

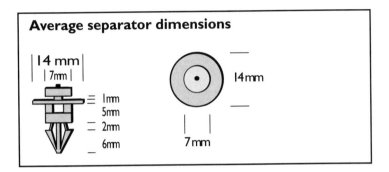

Average separator dimensions

Standard Measurements

Appendix D

Motherboard dimensions

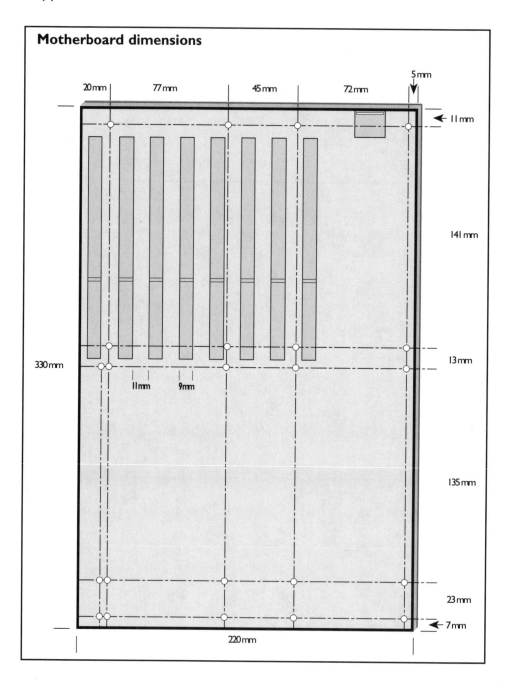

Standard Measurements

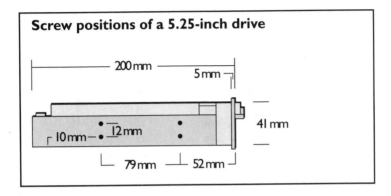

Screw positions of a 5.25-inch drive

Standard Measurements

Appendix D

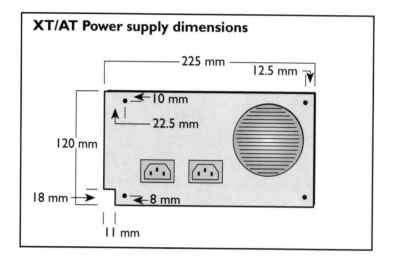

Screw positions of a 3.5-inch drive

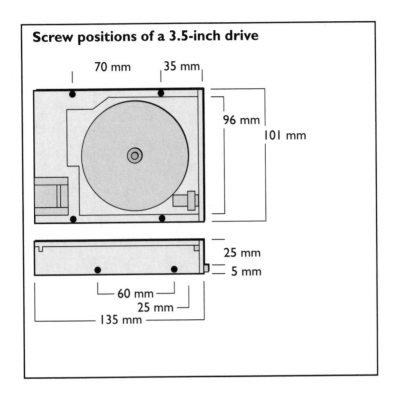

70 mm 35 mm

96 mm 101 mm

25 mm
5 mm

60 mm
25 mm
135 mm

Standard Measurements

Appendix D

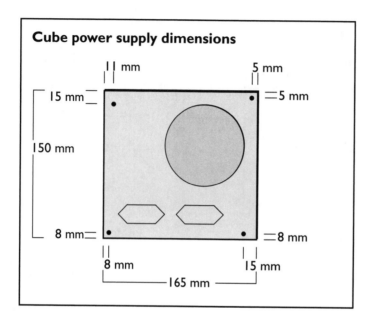

Cube power supply dimensions

Appendix E

Glossary

Appendix E is a glossary of computer and electronic terms and acronyms that are used in this book or that you'll meet with in your upgrading or repairing work. As you can see, this is a fairly comprehensive glossary on the subject matter of upgrading and repairing PCs. We've also tried to make it as up-to-date as possible by explaining the terms corresponding to today's latest technology.

You've already noticed that the PC world is full of acronyms. Therefore, we've listed the definition of a term under its more commonly used acronym. Power On Self Test, for example, is listed under POST and Basic Input Output System is listed as BIOS.

3.5-inch diskette

A specific size of a storage device. They have more storage capacity and are more rugged and portable than 5.25-inch disks. See also Diskette.

5.25-inch diskette

A specific size of a storage device. This type of disk can store up to 1.2 Meg of data or approximately 1,200,000 characters of text. See also Diskette.

8086 processor

An Intel microprocessor developed in 1978. It features a full 16-bit data bus and can address 1 Meg of memory.

8087 coprocessor

An Intel math coprocessor designed to work with the 8086 and 8088 processors. It added 50 new instructions to those processors and performed floating point math faster and more accurately than the main processors.

Glossary

8088 processor

An Intel microprocessor developed in 1978. It features an 8-bit external data bus (for disk drives, etc.) and an internal 16-bit data bus. It was used in the original IBM-PC computers and can address 1 Meg of RAM.

80286 processor

Also called a "286". An Intel microprocessor developed in 1984. It features 16-bit registers and a 16-bit data bus. The 286 processor can address 16 Meg of RAM (in Protected mode).

80287 math coprocessor

An Intel math coprocessor that adds over 50 new instructions to the CPU. It performs floating-point math much faster and more accurately than the main CPU. Designed for most 286-based and some 286DX-based systems.

80386 processor

Also called a "386". An Intel microprocessor that features 32-bit registers, a 16-bit data bus, and a 24-bit address bus.

80387DX math coprocessor

An Intel math coprocessor that adds over 50 new instructions to the CPU. It performs floating-point math much faster and more accurately than the main CPU. Designed for most 386DX-based systems.

80387SX math coprocessor

An Intel math coprocessor that adds over 50 new instructions to the CPU. It performs floating-point math much faster and more accurately than the main CPU. Designed for most 386SX-based systems.

80486 processor

Also called a "486". An Intel microprocessor that features 32-bit registers, a 32-bit data bus, and a 32-bit address bus. The 486 can operate in Real, Protected Virtual, and Virtual Real modes. Includes a built-in cache memory. Also includes a built-in math coprocessor similar to a 80387SX.

80486SX processor

An Intel microprocessor that features 32-bit registers, a 32-bit data bus, and a 32-bit address bus. The 80486SX is similar to the 80486 except it doesn't include a math coprocessor.

8087 math coprocessor

An Intel math coprocessor that performs floating-point math much faster and more accurately than the main CPU. Designed for most 8086- and 8088-based systems.

8514/A

An analog video display card for the PS/2 computer. It provides a high resolution of 1024x768 pixels and 256 colors or 64 shades of gray.

Accelerator board

A board that contains a microprocessor that's faster or more powerful than the one originally installed in your computer.

Access time

The time that elapses from the moment the information is requested to the point that the task is completed. This is normally described in nanoseconds for memory chips. The IBM PC requires 200 nanosecond memory chips and the AT requires 150 nanosecond chips.

Adapter

This is a device that serves as an interface between the system and other devices connected to it. Adapters are more commonly called cards, for example, video cards, graphics cards, etc.

ADC

An acronym representing Analog to Digital Converter, which transforms analog signals to digital samples.

Address

The area in your PC where a specific bit or piece of data is found. Also refers to the location of a set of instructions.

Address bus

A line connecting the CPU with ROM and RAM memory. When the CPU addresses a memory location, it must first place its address on the address bus in order to set the "switches" for access to this memory location.

Addressability (pixel addressability)

Refers to the number of pixels that a video controller can display. It's listed as the number of horizontal pixels by the number of vertical pixels. Common PC pixel addressabilities include: 320x200, 640x480, 800x600, 1024x768, 1280x1024 and 1600x1200, etc.

Glossary

API

An acronym representing Application Program Interface. This is a routine that gives users access to the services provided by the operating system.

Application

A program designed for a specific purpose. Examples of PC applications include word processors, spreadsheets and databases.

Archive bit

A bit in a file's attribute byte that sets the archive attribute. This lets you know whether the file has been changed since the last backup.

ASCII

An acronym representing American Standard Code for Information Interchange. ASCII is the standard for keyboard character codes. The ASCII standard covers key codes 0 to 127; individual computer manufacturers assign their own character to codes 128 to 255.

AT

An acronym representing Advanced Technology. The AT is essentially the "big brother" of the PC. It has a more powerful microprocessor, a higher processing speed in most cases, larger memory capacity beyond the 640K limit set by the old PC configuration, and higher disk storage capacity.

AT bus

An acronym representing Advanced Technology bus. The standard PC compatible peripheral bus to which video cards, I/O cards, internal modem cards and sound cards are added. Also called the ISA bus, it runs at a maximum of 8.33 MHz and has a 16-bit wide data path.

Attribute byte

This is a byte of information that describes various attributes of the file. This is stored in the directory of any file and indicates whether or not it's read-only or whether it has been backed up since it was last changed.

AUTOEXEC.BAT

Abbreviation for AUTOEXECute BATch file. This is a text file containing a series of commands stored in a group. After you switch on the PC, it searches for an AUTOEXEC.BAT file. If one exists, the commands execute automatically. AUTOEXEC.BAT can also be called and executed directly from the system prompt.

700

Average access time

The average time required for a disk drive to begin reading data placed anywhere on the drive. Average seek time is part of the average access time. Latency is also part of the average access time. See also *Average seek time* and *Latency*.

Average latency

The average time required for any byte of data stored on a disk to rotate under the disk drive's read/write head. Equal to one-half the time required for a single rotation of a platter. See also *Latency*.

Average seek time

The average time required for a disk drive's read/write heads to move from one random cylinder location to another location.

Backup copy

Duplicate of an original disk or file. Making backup copies is a good habit to develop. Data on a disk can easily and accidentally be destroyed.

Bad sector

A sector on the hard drive or floppy diskette that is not able to store data because it is damaged or cannot be formatted properly.

Bad track table

Very few hard drives are available without certain defective tracks. Most manufacturers enclose a data sheet ("table") listing the defective sectors or other areas of the hard drive. See also *Low-level format*.

Bandwidth

Also called "video bandwidth." The measure of the range of frequencies within a radiation band required to transmit a certain signal. The bandwidth of a monitor is a measure of the rate that a monitor can handle information from the display adapter.

Bank

A bank refers to a group of memory chips that make up a block or memory readable by the processor in a single bus cycle. This block must be at least as large as the data bus of the CPU (8, 16, 32 or 64 bits). There's also an optional parity bit for each 8 bits, which results in a total of 9, 19, 36 or 72 bits (respectively) for each bank.

Appendix

E

Section

4

701

Glossary

Bank switching

A method of expanding memory beyond the normal memory limits by quickly switching between two banks of memory chips.

Base memory

The first, or lower, 640K of the first megabyte of memory.

Batch file

A file containing a collection of commands. MS-DOS executes these commands in sequence when the user enters the name of the file. Other terms are batch processing or batch job. The .BAT extension must be included with any batch filename.

Baud

The unit used to measure the rate of data transmission. A baud is approximately 1 bit per second. The term baud comes from the French pioneer in telegraphy, J.M.E. Baudot (1845-1903).

Baud rate

The number of signal events (the signal for a 1 bit and the signal for a 0 bit are both "events") that take place on a communications line each second. Standard baud rates include 9600 baud, 14400 baud, 28800 baud, etc.

Bay

An opening in a PC case to hold disk drives or CD-ROM drives.

Beep code

A sequence of short or long beeps made by your PC during the Power-On Self-Test to indicate a problem.

Bernoulli box

A type of mass storage device featuring removable cartridges that contain a rapidly spinning diskette similar to a floppy diskette. The high speed of rotation and the small distance between the head and the disk make a high recording density possible and give the Bernoulli disk a memory capacity comparable to a hard drive.

Binary

A number system consisting of only two numbers (0,1), sometimes called bits. Unlike the decimal number system with its 10 numbers (0-9), the binary number system is better suited to the internal structure of a computer. Both number systems rely on the positional value of numbers. In the binary system the column value increases as follows: 0, 2, 4, 8, 16, 32, etc.

BIOS

An acronym representing **B**asic **I**nput **O**utput **S**ystem. BIOS is a program permanently stored in the memory of the computer and is available without an operating system disk. For example, it performs the internal self test of the computer and searches for the operating system (MS-DOS) on the disk in the drive.

Bit

The smallest unit in the binary number system. It can only assume two states (0,1) and therefore store only two different pieces of information. To store a character, several bits must be combined into a byte.

Bit planes

The number of bits available to store color information for each pixel displayed. The number of colors that can be displayed is calculated as two to the exponent 'n', where n is the number of bit planes. For example, 4 bit equals 16 colors, 8 bit equals 256 colors and 24 bit equals 16.7 million colors.

Block

A string of records, words, or characters formed for technical or logical reasons and is treated as a whole.

Block diagram

A graphic representation of the logical layout or structure of a system.

Boolean operation

Any operation in which each of the operands and the result take one of two values.

Boot/Reboot

The loading process that places the operating system in memory. A disk used for booting a PC must have two "hidden" files available for telling the PC to boot, as well as the COMMAND.COM file.

Bootable

A disk that can be used for booting.

BPS

An acronym for **B**its **P**er **S**econd. The number of binary digits or bits that's transmitted per second.

Buffer

A block of memory used to store data temporarily. All data moving between the peripheral and the computer passes through the buffer. A buffer enables the data to be read from or written to the peripheral in larger chunks.

Glossary

Bug

A persistent error or defect in a program. The term was coined in 1940s when a moth was found squashed between the points of an electromechanical relay in the old Mark I computer.

Compare with *Glitch*.

Bus

A common pathway between hardware peripherals. A bus can be internal between components in your PC or it can be external between workstations. The processor(s), memory banks and peripheral control units are all interconnected through the bus in the PC bus architecture. The bus has two channels. The address bus selects where data is located and the data bus transfers the data. You're connecting into the bus when you insert a card into an expansion slot in your PC.

Byte

A group of eight bits. While a bit can only assume two states, 0 and 1, a byte can store from 0 to 255 conditions. The standard ASCII character set consists of 128 characters; the additional characters generally used in PC software increase the total number of characters to 255.

Cache memory

A special area of RAM to store the most frequently accessed information in RAM. You can significantly improve the speed of your system by using cache memory because it "optimizes" the cooperation among the different components of your system.

Card-edge connector

Part of the card with metal "fingers" which match the expansion slot connector.

Carpal tunnel syndrome

Many computer users suffer this painful hand injury. It's a result of pressure that causes the tendons in the hands to swell and compress the median nerve.

The name comes from the narrow tunnel in the wrist that connects ligaments and bone.

Symptoms of carpal tunnel syndrome include numbness, weakness, burning or tingling in the fingers and hands.

Cartridge system

A removable module, or cartridge, containing a magnetic tape or diskette and used as a storage device.

Cathode Ray Tube (CRT)

A device that generates a screen display with the help of an electron beam that sends electrical impulses to a glass screen at the end of the CRT.

CAV mode

An acronym representing Constant Angular Velocity. It's a disk technique that spins the disk at a constant speed. The number of bits in each track is the same but their density varies because the inner tracks have smaller circumferences that the outer tracks. Contrast with *CLV*.

CD-DA

Also called the Red Book It describes the standards for digital audio CDs. The maximum music capacity of a CD-DA is either 63 or 74 minutes.

CD-R

Refers to a CD-ROM that can be recorded once with a CD Writer and then read in any CD-ROM drive like a normal CD-ROM. These are also called CD-WOs

CD-ROM

An acronym for **C**ompact **D**isc **R**ead-**O**nly **M**emory. A CD-ROM includes extremely high data density and storage capacity of approximately 680 Meg per disk.

CD-ROM drive

A storage device that uses CD-ROMs to store data. CD-ROM drives are much slower than hard drives and most are connected to a PC using the SCSI (Small Computer Systems Interface) bus.

CD-WORM drive

A storage device based on further development of CD-ROM disk drives. It's an acronym for "Write Once Read Many". These disk drives can write on the CD only once but read it as often as required.

Centronics

Standard connection between the PC and a printer. The connection of other devices to the PC occurs through interfaces. There are serial interfaces, in which data is sent as individual bits, and parallel interfaces, in which a byte can be transmitted simultaneously.

Glossary

CGA

An acronym representing **C**olor **G**raphics **A**dapter. A bit-mapped graphics card that can display several colors at the same time (the amount depends on the CGA monitor you're using). The CGA card has three possible graphics modes.

Channel

A path along which signals are sent.

Chip

Complicated electronic circuitry built into a small space. The early days of electronics required huge circuits. Chips compressed this same circuitry into a single silicon chip, and made it possible to develop small computers for the home. The most important chip in the PC is the microprocessor, which does most of the basic tasks needed in a computer.

CHKDSK

Abbreviation for CHecKDiSK. A transient command (read from the DOS disk). CHKDSK A: tests the disk in drive A:, then displays the volume name of the disk and the date and time the disk was formatted. In addition, the total capacity and the overview of the file types and number of files are displayed. CHKDSK also tells the user of any errors on the disk and asks the user if those errors should be corrected. The remaining space on the disk is also indicated. At the end of the display, two lines indicate the total memory available in the PC and how much memory space is still available to the user.

CISC

An acronym representing **C**omplex **I**nstruction-**S**et **C**omputer. This refers to computers that operate with large sets of processor instructions.

Clock frequency

The speed of the processor is measured with the clock frequency. Unlike people, the processor consistently works internally at the same clock frequency. The IBM PC has a clock frequency of 4.77 MHz (Megahertz). Compatibles sometimes use higher frequencies, but higher speeds may create compatibility problems.

Clone

Another word to describe an IBM compatible computer.

Clusters

A group of sectors that forms a unit of storage to the operating system. The size is determined by DOS when the disk is formatted. Also called allocation unit.

CLV mode

An acronym representing Constant Linear Velocity. Disk technique that spins a disk at different speeds. By varying the speed depending on which track is being accessed, the physical density of bits in each track can be the same, This allows the outer tracks to hold more data than the inside tracks. Compare with *CAV*.

CMOS

A Complementary Metal-Oxide Semiconductor that pretends to duplicate the functions of memory chips or other processors. CMOS chips are used primarily in portable PCs, which receive their power from batteries.

Cold start

Switching the computer off and on. Unlike the warm start, the cold start involves completely switching the computer off and then switching it on again. The cold start is the last chance to have the computer start completely new. Since switching the computer off and on puts much stress on the electronic components, use the warm start (Ctrl + Alt + Del) whenever possible.

Color depth

Refers to the amount of memory (and therefore number of simultaneously displayable colors) available to store color information for each pixel.

COMMAND.COM

An operating system file that's loaded last when the computer is booted. This is the command interpreter or user interface of DOS.

Compatible/Compatibility

Hardware and software that work together. A computer that is fully IBM compatible should be able to execute all programs that exist for the IBM PC.

CONFIG.SYS

A file that's created to inform DOS how to configure itself when the machine is started.

Configuration

The collection of devices that comprise the complete computer system (see Hardware). Configuration may also refer to the software integration of the devices. For example, the software configuration for serial interface operation of a printer includes the preparation of software drivers, which instruct the computer to use this configuration.

Controller card

A card (adapter) that connects the disk drive(s) to the computer.

707

Glossary

Coprocessor

Name for electronic components (see Chip) that relieve the microprocessor of some important tasks. Increased performance can often be achieved through the use of coprocessors. For example, a math coprocessor often performs many of the math functions that can slow down the microprocessor during complicated graphic computations.

CPU

Abbreviation for Central Processing Unit. This is the main microprocessor of the PC; sometimes it's also used to describe the PC's case.

Current directory

To access a file or a directory, DOS uses the current directory. A directory can be made into the current directory by indicating the position relative to the current directory or giving the complete pathname. In the first case, use the CD .. and CD NAME commands. In the second case, first the drive (letter and colon) and then the path through the subdirectories must be indicated, separated by the backslash.

Current drive

The standard drive or current drive is the drive to which all disk commands of the computer apply. Usually, and especially for systems with only one drive, this is drive A:. If two drives are available, the second drive can be selected with B:. This command can be reversed with A:. The hard drive can be selected with C:. The standard drive is displayed in the system prompt (see Prompt).

Cursor

A small, rectangular, blinking spot of light on the screen that marks the spot where a character can be placed from the keyboard. The arrow keys (also called cursor keys) move the cursor back and forth.

DAC

An acronym representing **D**igital to **A**nalog **C**onverter. A device used to convert digital numbers to continuous analog signals. See also *Digitize*.

Daisychain

Arrangement of devices connected in series, one after the other. Transmitted signals go to the first device, then are sent from the first device to the second and from the second device to the third and so on.

Daisywheel printer

Daisywheel printers use a typewriter-like wheel. Individual letters press a character on the paper, instead of composing the character from a matrix of dots like the matrix printers. The quality of the printing is comparable to that of a typewriter.

Databases

Application programs that enable you to access data quickly. Many database programs allow different sets of data to be combined into one package, which permits access to the different data sets simultaneously.

Databus

A line used to transmit data between the CPU and RAM or ROM memory.

Data transfer rate

The rate that data is transferred from a computer to a disk drive or from one computer to another computer.

Dedicated line

A telephone line that connects several computers within a limited area. The "line" is usually a cable and not a public access telephone line.

Default

Any setting assumed at start-up or reset by the computer's software and devices. This setting is used until it's changed by the user.

Defragment

To reorganize the hard drive by putting files back into a contiguous order.

Degauss

Magnetic interference caused by a change in the position of a monitor relative to the earth's magnetic field. An artificial magnetic field can also cause discoloration.

To correct this, all color monitors automatically degauss at power-on. Some monitors also have a manual degaussing button.

This allows the monitor to compensate for the change in the magnetic field by realigning the electron guns. Some low cost monitors that do not have degauss buttons require the power to be switched off for at least 20 minutes to get maximum degaussing.

Device driver

A subprogram to control communications between the computer and a peripheral.

Glossary

Dhrystone

A benchmark program used to measure and compare the performance of computers in areas other than floating-point math operations.

Digitize

To convert an image or signal into digital code the PC can understand. You can digitize images using a scanner, digital camera, digitizing tablet, etc.

Digitizing tablets

An input device that converts graphic and pictorial data into binary inputs.

DIP switch

A series of small switches used by computers and peripherals to configure the equipment.

DIR

A DOS command used to display the directory of the current drive.

Directory

Part of a storage medium. Before the hard drive was commonly used, all files were stored in one directory called the root directory.

Because of the capacity of the hard drive, it had to be divided into various directories. These directories are arranged in a tree structure where the root directory can contain files and subdirectories. Every subdirectory in turn can contain files and subdirectories. Most DOS commands act only on the current directory, which can be indicated with CD.

Disk drive

Disk drives are devices that permit the PC to work on the data stored on the disk. The two types of disk drives used today are for 5.25-inch diskettes and for 3.5-inch diskettes.

If the PC wants to read in the MS-DOS operating system, first it accesses the upper or left drive, depending on the construction of the PC. This is the main drive. Its designation is A:. The other drive is then drive B:. If there is a hard drive, it has the designation drive C:.

Only one drive can be active. Its drive letter appears in front of the system prompt on the screen and is constantly displayed on the screen.

Diskette

Removable data storage media. A PC can use two sizes of diskettes although 3.5-inch diskettes are far more popular. Make certain to use double-sided and double-density diskettes. Double sided means that the PC can write on both sides. Double density refers to the density of the magnetic material coating.

710

DMA

An acronym representing Direct Memory Access. A circuit that permits a high-speed transfer of data between a device and system memory.

Dot-matrix printer

Printer that produces characters on paper by driving a set of pins onto a ribbon, which leaves an impression of a character on paper.

Dot clock

This usually refers to the digital clock signal that transfers data into the video card's digital to analog converter. However, it has also become a measure of the maximum gross data throughput of a monitor. Dot clock is measured in MHz and indirectly determines the maximum pixel addressability and vertical refresh rate that a monitor can handle.

Dot pitch

The distance between a phosphor dot of one phosphor triad to its closest diagonal neighbor of the same color on a monitor. Dot pitch is expressed in mm, for example, a .28 dot pitch means .28 mm between triads. A smaller value indicates that the phosphor dots are more closely spaced. This results in a much crisper image.

Double-density diskette

These diskettes have twice as much magnetic material for recording as a single density disk. You should use only double-density diskettes.

Double-sided diskettes

These diskettes can record data on both sides. You should use only double-sided diskettes.

DRAM

An acronym representing **D**ynamic **RAM** chips. A common type of computer memory. It usually uses one transistor and one capacitor to represent a bit. The capacitors are energized several hundred times per second to maintain the charge. DRAM lose their content when the power is switched off.

Compare with *SRAM* (Static RAM chips).

Driver

Also called a device driver. This is a routine that links a peripheral device or internal function to the operating system. Basic drivers are included with the operating system and drivers are added when new peripheral devices are installed (such as mouse, printer, etc.).

Glossary

E-mail

Abbreviation for Electronic mail. It's the transmission of memos, letters, messages and files over a network. Users can send mail to a single recipient or broadcast it to multiple users on the network.

EGA

An acronym representing Enhanced Graphics Adapter. A high resolution graphics card that has a superior resolution compared to the CGA standard. The EGA combined the operating modes of the MDA and the CGA. The EGA is capable of displaying all 16 colors in text mode with a resolution of 640 x 350 pixels.

EISA

An acronym representing Extended Industry Standard Architecture (an extension of the (ISA) Industry Standard Architecture). This is a bus standard that extends the AT bus architecture to 32-bits and allows more than one CPU to share the bus.

Electrostatic discharge

Static electricity that can cause integrated circuit damage or failure. Make sure you are grounded before touching any computer components.

Empty directory

A directory that doesn't contain either files or subdirectories.

EMS

An acronym representing Expanded Memory Specification. This provides a way for microcomputers running under DOS to access additional memory.

EPROM chips

An acronym representing Erasable Programmable Read Only Memory. This is a ROM chip that can be erased and reprogrammed many times. These chips are erased by ultraviolet light and should not be exposed to direct sunlight.

Ergonomics

Science of the relationship between people and machines. A product that is ergonomically designed suggests the device blends smoothly with the user's body or actions.

Error message

A word, combination of words or a dialog box that indicates an error in a program or application.

ESDI

An acronym representing Enhanced System Device Interface. Hard drives using this standard transfer data 2.5 times faster than the earlier ST506 standard.

Expanded memory

Memory above the 640K limit for DOS Version 3.3 (and earlier versions) that can be used for programs requiring large amounts of memory. Remember that this area of memory requires special drivers and works only with software written for it.

Expansion card

A printed circuit card that you can install to add new features and expand the current capabilities of your system.

Expansion slots

Slots or spaces inside the case for connecting cards to the motherboard. Most PCs have these slots so it's easy to upgrade the system.

Extended DOS partition

These are non-bootable partitions that define other logical drives in your system.

Extended memory

Area of memory above 1 Meg that can be accessed by a computer using a 286, 386, or 486 processor.

External hard drive

A hard drive that isn't located inside the case of the PC. Instead, it's outside of the case and connected by cables.

Extra-high density (ED)

The storage capacity of a floppy drive or diskette, in which 36 sectors per track are recorded using a vertical recording technique with MFM encoding.

FAT

An acronym representing File Allocation Table. A portion of all DOS formatted diskettes that contains information on the number and location of files and available storage space.

File

Data stored under a name assigned by the user or manufacturer. Data files (e.g., programs, text, graphics, etc.) appear in the directory of a diskette or hard drive as an entry containing the name, extension, size, and date of storage.

713

Glossary

File attribute

Information stored in the file's attribute byte.

File management

Working with data. Related information is stored in a data set and these are presented in sorted format. An address file is a simple form of file management.

Filename

Name assigned by the user or program to identify a file

File structures

The type and method of storing files on a medium. The root directory can contain both files and subdirectories, and any subdirectory can also contain files and subdirectories.

Filename

A group of letters and numbers identifying a specific file in a directory. A filename can be up to eight characters long (DOS and Windows 3.x) or 255 characters (Windows 95). Filenames can also include a 3 character extension. Spaces aren't allowed in filenames and result in error messages.

Flicker

Fluctuating image on the monitor.

Floppy diskette

A removable storage medium. It is a round disk of flexible material that's housed in a square envelope or cartridge. Early disks were 8 inches square and inflexible. When the first 5.25-inch disks appeared on the market, people referred to them as "floppy disks."

Floppy disk controller

The card or chip that controls the floppy disk drive.

FORMAT

DOS command to perform either a low-level or high-level format on a floppy diskette or a high-level format on a hard drive.

Formatted capacity

The amount of available storage space remaining on the diskette after formatting. It's always less than the capacity before formatting.

Formatting

Preparing a floppy diskette or the hard drive so the PC can read from it or write to it.

FTP

Acronym representing **File Transfer Protocol**. A protocol used to log onto a network, list directories and copy files.

Full-height drive

A drive unit that is 3.25 inches high, 5.75 inches wide and 8-inches deep.

Function keys

Set of keys used to command the computer (called [F1], [F2], [F3], etc.). [F1] is usually the Help key in most programs and applications. Function keys are also used with the [Shift], [Alt] and [Ctrl] keys allowing 40 functions to be performed with the 10 or 12 function keys.

General error

The error message displayed by the PC when it cannot access a disk drive:

The error can be caused by the following: Failure to insert a disk into the drive; the drive is not closed or locked; or, the disk that was inserted isn't formatted. The best remedy is to insert a formatted disk, lock the drive, and press [A] (Abort). The normal system prompt should appear.

Gigabyte (Gb)

A unit of measure equal to 1024 Meg.

Glitch

A temporary or random hardware problem.

Graphics accelerator

This is a highly misused and now almost meaningless term. A graphics accelerator is a coprocessor capable of specific graphics operation, independent of the main system CPU.

Graphics coprocessor

A secondary processor dedicated to performing video display tasks.

Green Book

Defined the standards for CD-I (CD-Interactive). This format is based on the Yellow Book but defines 8 bytes for a CD-I subheader. This standard also defines coding processes for different user data such as graphics, audio, etc.

Ground

To make an electrical current connection to the earth or a conductor of equivalent effect.

GUI

An acronym representing **G**raphical **U**ser Interface. In contrast to text-based interfaces like DOS or UNIX, GUI's provide more flexibility in terms of color, pixel addressability and types of objects that can be displayed. Examples of GUI's Windows 3.1, Windows 95 and OS/2.

Glossary

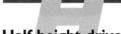

Half-height drive

A drive unit that's 1.625 inches high and either 5.75 or 4 inches wide and 4 or 8 inches deep.

Hard drives

The most widely used means for storing data on a PC. Hard drives have much higher storage capacities than floppy diskettes. A common capacity today is 1.2 Gigabyte but higher capacities are possible.

Hard drives are usually built into the PC case and are usually very sensitive to shock and vibrations. They must be treated with care. If the disk and head come into contact, data can be lost due to a head crash.

Hardcopy

Creating a printout of the current contents of the screen by pressing the Shift Print keys. Following the printout, normal work can continue on the screen.

Hardware

Hardware consists of the computer itself and everything that pertains to it (processor, keyboard, monitor, disk drives, hard drive). Contrast with *Software*.

Head

See *Read/write head*.

Head crash

Damage of the hard drive and possible loss of data through the contact between the medium and the read/write head on the hard drive. This can be caused by dropping or moving your computer while the hard drive is operating.

Head seek

The movement of a drive's read/write heads to a specific location.

Heat sink

A piece of metal connected to a chip carrier or socket to dissipate heat.

Hercules Graphics Card (HCG)

A graphics card that featured a text mode of MDA and a graphics mode with a resolution of 720 x 348 one color (monochrome) pixels.

Hexadecimal

This is a numbering system that uses 16 digits, which includes the letters A through Z, as well as the numerals 0 through 9.

High-density

The storage capacity of a floppy disk or drive in which 15 or 18 sectors per track are recorded using MFM encoding.

High-level format

A DOS formatting operation to include important sections, such as the FAT, the boot record, free tracks, and others on the hard drive.

Horizontal scan rate (horizontal frequency)

The frequency, expressed in KHz (thousands of times per second), at which the horizontal deflection circuit operates. This roughly translates to the number of scanlines displayed on a monitor in one second.

HTML

An acronym representing Hypertext Markup Language.

HTTP

An acronym representing Hypertext Transfer Protocol.

Hz

Abbreviation for Hertz. A unit of measure that's equal to a frequency of one cycle per second.

I/O

Abbreviation for Input/Output. Transferring data between a PC and its peripherals. Every transfer is an output from one device and input into another.

IBM compatible

Clones of the IBM PC/XT/AT computers, which follow the IBM "industry standard." If programs and hardware configurations follow the IBM standard, software can work with any computer. There are many IBM compatible computers that are more efficient than the original IBM computer. However, this efficiency may mean that only 95% of the software written for IBM will work on an IBM compatible computer.

IDE

An acronym representing Integrated DriveElectronics. This describes a hard drive with the disk controller circuitry integrated within it.

Glossary

Inkjet printer

A printer that sprays one or more colors of ink on the paper. Its quality is close to that of a lower cost laser printer.

Interface

Connection between a PC and the outside world. The PC and other devices can exchange data through this connection. Two types of interfaces are used: Parallel interfaces (see Centronics) and serial interfaces (see RS-232 interface).

Interlaced

Standard NTSC television signals are interlaced. This means that each video frame is divided into two separate fields of alternating scanlines.

The resulting fields are displayed sequentially. Then, for example, a 30 frame per second (fps) refresh becomes 60 Hz at half the vertical pixel addressability. Thin horizontal lines will appear to flicker on an interlaced display since their effective refresh rate is only 30 Hz.

Compare with *Non-interlaced*.

Initialization

Another term for the process of formatting a diskette or hard drive so that it can be used.

Install

A process of attaching cards or other devices to the appropriate connectors or sockets.

Integrated circuit (IC)

A complex electronic circuit with multiple transistors and other electrical components on a single piece of material.

Interleave ratio

Also called interleave setting. This is the ratio between the physical sectors of a hard drive that are skipped for every sector used. For example, if the hard drive has an interleave ratio of 3:1, the disk writes to one sector, skips three sectors, writes to one sector, etc.

Internet

A computer network that combines government, educational and private computers together over telephone lines. It began in the 1960s as a research project of the US Defense Department. The network quickly grew to include scientists and researchers all over the US.

The Internet, sometimes called the Net or Information Highway or Cyberspace, is the largest computer network in the world. It consists of thousands of connected networks around the world. A network is several computers that are connected to share information. Most of the information on the Internet is free.

See also *Network*.

IRQ

An acronym representing Interrupt ReQuest. This is a connection between external hardware devices and the interrupt controller.

ISA

An acronym representing Industry **S**tandard **A**rchitecture. This is a 16-bit bus standard which runs at speeds of up to 8.33 MHz. Most modems, sound cards, CD-ROM interfaces and other low-bandwidth applications are still ISA based. VLB and PCI provide higher bandwidth for video and disk I/O operations.

ISDN

An acronym representing Integrated **S**ervices **D**igital **N**etwork. An international telecommunications standard that enables a communications channel to carry digital data simultaneously with voice and video information.

Jumper

Electrical connectors that allow you to customize a circuit board. It's a small piece of rectangular plastic with up to three receptacles.

K

Abbreviation for Kilobyte. It refers to 1,024 bytes and usually abbreviated simply as K, for example, 512K.

Keyboard

The most widely used device for data input.

LABEL

The LABEL command permits the user to add an 11-character volume label name to the disk currently in the drive. Unlike filenames, volume names can include spaces. LABEL must be loaded from a DOS disk because it's a transient command.

Glossary

Laser printer

Printer that creates characters on paper with a special printing process that uses an industrial laser. Laser printers are still expensive, however they're extremely quiet and have excellent print quality.

LCD

An acronym for Liquid Crystal Display. This display uses liquid crystal sealed between two pieces of polarized glass.

LED

An acronym for Light-Emitting Diode. This is a semiconductor diode that emits light when a current is passed through it.

LIM/EMS Standard

A standard, introduced by Lotus, Intel, and Microsoft, that enables software to work with expanded memory above the normal 640K of RAM. Remember that software must be designed to run under the LIM/EMS standard in order to work with expanded memory.

Logical drive

A subdivision of a hard drive indicated by a specific letter. The first subdivision is usually designated as D because the primary partition is designated as C. Any other partitions can contain any number of logical drives designated by a different letter. Use the FDISK command to create partitions and logical drives. See also Partition.

Look-up Table (LUT)

At higher pixel addressabilites, most graphics controllers can not simultaneously display as many colors as they are capable of generating. Because of video card memory limitations, only a subset of all possible colors can be displayed at one time. A look-up table stores the mapping information which determines which subset of all possible colors are available at any given time.

Low-level format

Also called physical format. This is the physical pattern of tracks and sectors created on a disk during formatting.

Math coprocessor

A microprocessor that increases the speed of the main processor by performing mathematical operations.

MCA

An acronym representing Micro Channel Architecture. This includes a 16 or 32-bit bus width and multiple master control.

MCGA

An acronym representing **M**ulti**C**olor **G**raphics **A**rray. A type of video display circuit that supports text and graphics.

MDA

An acronym for **M**onochrome **D**isplay **A**dapter. A type of video display adapter that supports only text.

Meg

Abbreviation for megabyte (1,024K). Also sometimes shown as Mb.

Megahertz (MHz)

A unit of measure that equals a frequency of 1 million cycles per second.

Memory caching

The capability of storing data the computer has recently used. This helps increase the operating speed of the computer.

The two types of memory cache are Internal cache and External cache.

Memory resident program

A program that remains in memory after it has been loaded.

MFM recording method

An acronym representing **M**odified **F**requency **M**odulation procedure. A specific method of storing digital information onto a diskette one bit at a time. It's the least expensive but most inefficient method of storing information.

Compare with *RLL* (Run-length Limited).

Microprocessor

Another word for chip. When used in computer science, the term chip usually refers to the main microprocessor of the computer, which controls the basic functions.

MIPS

An acronym representing **M**illion **I**nstructions **P**er **S**econd. The average number of machine language instructions a PC can perform or execute in one second.

M-O drives

An acronym representing **M**agneto-**O**ptical recording. An erasable optical disk recording technique that uses a laser beam to heat pits on the disk surface to the point at which a magnet can make flux changes.

Appendix

E

Section

4

721

Glossary

Modem

An abbreviation for MOdulate/DEModulate. A modem translates computer information into a form that can be sent over a telephone line (modulates). This allows different computers to share information and data. The receiving modem translates the information it receives back into a form the computer can understand (demodulates).

Motherboards

The large printed circuit board containing the CPU, support chips, RAM and expansion slots. A PC cannot function without the motherboard.

Mouse

Controls the cursor. The mouse is a small box with two or three buttons on top and a ball poking out the bottom. When you move the mouse across a flat surface, the cursor moves in the same direction on the screen.

The mouse is virtually required for today's operating systems like Windows 3.x and Windows 95 and OS/2.

MS-DOS

The standard operating system that was developed by the Microsoft Corporation for IBM compatible PCs. Your PC is usable only after the MS-DOS operating system has been loaded. It consists of several resident and transient commands that can be accessed as needed.

Nanosecond

A unit of time equal to one billionth of a second. It's abbreviated as ns.

NLQ

Acronym representing Near Letter Quality. Higher print quality offered by dot-matrix printers. The printer prints a line, then reprints the same line after slightly shifting the position of the printhead. NLQ mode reduces print speed considerably.

Non-interlaced mode

This means that an entire frame is displayed with each screen refresh. Non-interlaced displays produce a more pleasing screen image since thin horizontal lines don't flicker with each screen refresh.

Compare with *Interlaced*

OEM

An acronym representing **O**riginal **E**quipment **M**anufacturer. Many manufacturers produce versions of their products in large quantities for other companies who either use their name on them or use them as components for their systems. OEM products often make it to the retail sales arena where they are sold at lower prices. An OEM version of a card "may not" be the same as the retail version.

Operating system

The program that enables the computer to perform basic memory and disk management tasks. It permits the user to communicate with the computer through the keyboard. The operating system can be loaded from a disk (MS-DOS) or it can be stored permanently in the computer.

Orange Book

Contains the specifications for recordable CD-ROMs.

OS/2

An operating system developed by IBM and Microsoft Corporation. OS/2 is the successor to DOS and uses the Protected mode operation of the processor to expand memory and to support multitasking.

OverDrive processors

An Intel trademark name for its series of upgrade processors.

PAL

An acronym representing **P**rogrammable **A**rray **L**ogic. A type of chip that has logic gates specified by a device programmer.

Parallel interface

Centronics interface, usually leading to a printer (see also Centronics). Parallel interfaces exchange data 8 bits at a time. LPT1: is the device designation for the first parallel interface. Additional parallel interfaces (if present) are accessed as LPT2: and LPT3:.

Glossary

Parameter

Command elements of a DOS command separated from the command name by a space. The command COPY CON FILENAME uses the command name COPY and the two parameters CON and FILENAME.

Partition

See Primary DOS partition or Extended DOS partition.

PATH

The PATH command indicates the directory in which DOS should search for the resident DOS commands. Without such a path, the search is limited to the current directory. PATH without a parameter displays the path that has been set.

Pathname

Indicates the location of a file or a directory on a volume. It consists of the drive specifier and subdirectories separated by a backslash. For example, a valid pathname for a file named TEXT.TXT could be:

```
A:\text\private\Text.txt
```

PC

Abbreviation for Personal Computer;, which was originally an IBM product introduced in 1981. Its name indicated that it was designed to be used by individuals. This was quite a change from the business systems of the time, which were large multiple user systems.

From this brand name came the generic description PC. It refers to all computers that are IBM compatible (able to use programs written for IBM computers). The introduction of the IBM PC/AT product line with an 80286 microprocessor was based on the concept of sharing system resources through a local area network (LAN). One AT would act as the "file server" for several PCs. The rapid drop in hardware prices and the failure of software producers to provide viable LANs makes these new and faster computers still a personal computer.

PCI

Acronym representing **P**eripheral **C**omponents **I**nterconnect. This is basically the Pentium equivalent to the VLB, but with improvements. It is a 64-bit standard, but is currently only implemented as 32 bits - look for 64 bit PCI in the future. It performs asynchronously to the main CPU, meaning that the PCI bus operates at 33 MHz regardless of the CPU clock. It also allows more than two devices on the bus, unlike VLB.

PCMCIA cards

Acronym representing **P**ersonal **C**omputer **M**emory **C**ard **I**nternational **A**ssociation. These cards add a new capability, such as sound or additional memory, to a computer. Some

PCMCIA cards have multiple functions. These cards can provide, for example, both networking and modem capabilities. PCMCIA cards are also called PC cards.

Pentium Pro processor

A version of the Pentium processor from Intel that is designed for powerful operating systems like Unix or Windows NT.

Pentium processors

An Intel processor with 32-bit registers, a 64-bit data bus and a 32-bit address bus. Like all Intel processors, the Pentium is backwards compatible.

It's an ideal processor for running Windows 3.x or Windows 95 or OS/2. Don't consider buying a new PC that doesn't have a Pentium class processor.

Phosphor triad (dot triad)

This is the smallest dot that can theoretically be resolved on a color monitor and consists of three phosphor dots - one each of red, green and blue. When struck with the electron beam, these dots glow producing a bright spot on the screen.

Practically, 1.2 or more dot triads comprise each pixel on the screen, although the pixel addressability of some monitors is greater than their resolution, and in this case a pixel can be smaller than a dot triad. The result in this case is that small objects may not be resolvable.

Photo CD

Contains digitized color negative and positive films that can be edited with the proper software and hardware. Developed by Eastman Kodak

Pixel

This is the smallest addressable display unit available at a given video addressability. There is no physical thing on a display that can be called a pixel. Pixels exist only in the graphics controller bitmap.

The screen image in the bitmap is composed of an array of pixels, arranged in a rectilinear fashion, with the X axis running horizontally, perpendicular to the Y axis. A pixel consists of intensity only (in grayscale monitors) or color and intensity information (red, green & blue in color).

While a pixel usually corresponds to a square or rectangular area, it is displayed as a number of spots on a CRT. One pixel usually consists of 1.2 or more dot triads. Flat panel displays are a special case where individual pixels correspond directly to a picture element on the display.

Pixel addressability

See *Addressability*.

Glossary

Plug and Play (PnP)

A hardware/software specification developed by Intel that allows a PnP system and PnP cards (such as video cards or sound cards) to configure themselves automatically.

Port address

One of the system's addresses used by the computer to access devices, such as disk drives or printer ports.

POST

An acronym representing Power-On Self-Test. It's a series of diagnostic tests automatically performed by the computer when you switch it on or restart it.

Power supply

An electrical component of the computer that prepares the electrical current for use by the circuitry of the computer. The size and quality of the power supply determines how many enhancements can be added to the computer, since most of them must be connected to the power supply. For example, a small capacity power supply may be able to handle only the computer and two disk drives, but not a hard drive.

Primary DOS partition

The main and bootable part of the hard drive. You must create the primary DOS partition for the hard drive.

Printer

Device that creates a hardcopy of computer data. Everything displayed on the screen is printed on paper. Printer types include: Daisywheel, dot-matrix, and laser. A printer can be addressed through either the serial or parallel interface of the computer. The parallel (Centronics) interface is designated by MS-DOS as LPT1: or PRN:. The serial (RS-232) interface is designated by MS-DOS as COM1:.

Processors

Abbreviation for microprocessor. Most references to a microprocessor in computing refer to the main microprocessor of the computer, (the central processing unit), which controls the computer's internal tasks (e.g., math, data movement).

Protected mode

Advanced feature of the 286 and 386 processors where memory is protected and allocated for specific programs and extended memory.

Rails

Plastic strips on either side of disk drives mounted in IBM ATs and compatibles. Rails allow the drives to slide into place properly.

RAM

An acronym representing Random Access Memory. This is memory in which data can be stored temporarily. Unlike ROM, RAM can be written to and read from. The contents of RAM disappear when the computer is switched off. See also ROM.

RAM disk

Pseudo disk drive created in the computer's RAM with the help of a program on the DOS disk. Because it is not a mechanical device, the RAM disk allows very fast file access, but loses all data when the computer is switched off.

The RAM disk is extremely important to PC users that have only one disk drive. Anything can be kept in a RAM disk, if the files don't exceed the memory limits set for the RAM disk.

Read

The process of retrieving data, usually from a storage device like a hard drive or CD-ROM drive.

Read/write head

Device that reads and writes data on a hard drive or floppy drive. For writing, the surface of the disk is moved past the read/write head. By discharging electrical impulses at the right times, bits are recorded as small magnetized spots or negative or positive polarity,

For reading, the surface is moved past the read/write head, and the bits that are present induce an electrical current across the gap.

Real mode

An operating mode where specific memory locations are given to programs and peripherals.

Red Book

Defines the standards for audio CDs. A sector contains 2352 bytes of useful data. Also, 784 bytes are required for error identification and 98 bytes are needed for management.

Glossary

Refresh

The process of repeating the storage of data to keep it from fading or becoming lost. DRAM must be constantly refreshed.

Refresh rate

When referring to monitors, the number of times that the video card refreshes the entire screen in one second. Expressed in Hz (Hertz).

Resolution

The most common misinterpretation of this term is that it is the same as pixel addressability. In fact, resolution is more closely related to dot pitch, since it is a limitation of the monitor rather than of the graphics controller. The resolution limits how small an object a monitor is able to display.

Refresh rate

When referring to monitors, the number of times that the video card refreshes the entire screen in one second. Expressed in Hz (Hertz).

Removable storage systems

A secondary, usually high capacity, storage device. The diskette or tape is inside a cartridge or cassette that can be removed from the drive for safekeeping. Examples include Bernoulli boxes.

Resolution

A measurement expressed in horizontal and vertical dots for printers and pixels for monitors. The larger the resolution, the sharper and better the image.

The most common misinterpretation of this term is that it is the same as pixel addressability. In fact, resolution is more closely related to dot pitch, since it is a limitation of the monitor rather than of the graphics controller. The resolution limits how small an object a monitor is able to display.

RGB

An acronym representing **R**ed, **G**reen and **B**lue. By varying the intensity of each of these colors in a single pixel, the human eye can be fooled into seeing a wide range of colors.

For example, a combination of red and green appears as yellow, even though no light with a yellow wavelength is emanating from the screen.

This works because the optical system integrates the photons striking a region on the retina, and the combined impulses from green and red sensitive cones are seen as yellow.

RLL procedure

An acronym representing **R**un **L**ength **L**imited procedure. A specific method of storing digital information onto a diskette in a tight format. It stores almost twice as much data as the MFM procedure.

Although more expensive, it's also a more efficient method of storing information compared to the MFM (Modified Frequency Modulation) procedure.

See also *MFM*.

ROM

An acronym representing **R**ead **O**nly **M**emory. ROM consists of information permanently stored on a chip (see Chip), which remains intact after the computer is switched on. When the user switches on the computer, it reads the information from this ROM as needed. Unlike RAM, the user cannot write to ROM (hence the name).

ROM BIOS

The two ROM chips that contain BIOS code (Basic Input Output System) and system configuration information. See also *BIOS*.

Root directory

The main directory on either a floppy disk or a hard drive. It's the highest level directory.

RS-232 interface

Standard serial interface. With serial transfer, data is transferred one bit at a time.

Scanline

The movement of a monitor's electron gun from one side of the screen to the other results in the appearance of a horizontal line of varying intensity and color. Typically, 200 to 1200 horizontal scan lines (lined-up vertically on top of each other) make-up the image you see on your display.

Scratch disk

A disk that contains no useful information but is instead used for testing purposes only.

SCSI

An acronym for **S**mall **C**omputer **S**ystem **I**nterface. Uses a 50-pin connector and allows multiple devices to be connected in daisy-chain fashion.

Sector

A small portion of the track on a disk. It's the area the computer uses to store data at specific locations on the disk for retrieval. Normal PC sectors contain 512K of usable area.

Glossary

Seek time

The amount of time required for a disk drive to move the heads across one-third of the total number or cylinders. Seek time is a part of the average access time for a drive.

Serial interface

See RS-232 interface.

Session

A feature of CD-ROM drives that makes it possible to read CD-Rs that have been recorded in more than one pass (session).

Several older CD-ROM drives are single session drives because they can only access data from the firs session, that is, data stored in the first recording session.

Shadow mask

This is usually a mask which acts to block the electron beam from striking the wrong phosphors in a CRT. The beam passes through holes in the mask to strike the correct phosphor while shadowing neighboring phosphor. In other words, it prevents a beam intended to strike a red phosphor from striking a neighboring green phosphor by causing an electron shadow over the green dot.

SIMM

An acronym representing Single Inline Memory Module. These are memory modules plugged into the motherboard or memory expansion boards. They usually store data 9-bits wide and add 256K or 1 Meg of RAM.

Single density

A diskette type with a very limited amount of magnetic media. Most inexpensive diskettes are single density. Avoid using single density diskettes on your PC, use only double density diskettes.

Single sided

A diskette that is single sided can record on only the "top" side. Most inexpensive diskettes are single sided. Avoid using single sided diskettes on your PC, use double sided diskettes only.

SIP modules

An acronym representing Single In-linePackages. A DIP-like package with only one row of leads.

Slot

Name for a connector inside the PC where additional circuit cards can be inserted to enhance the capabilities of the computer. Some PCs don't have these slots, so they cannot be enhanced easily.

Software

Computer programs, including the operating system and any drivers for peripheral devices.

SRAM

An acronym representing **S**tatic **R**andom **A**ccess **M**emory.

This is a memory chip that requires power to maintain its current. SRAM chips don't require refresh circuitry like DRAM chips. They do, however, require more space and more power.

Storage capacity

The quantity of data the computer can store and access internally. The PC generally has from about 256,000 up to 1,000,000 characters (256K to 1 Meg=1000 kilobytes) of memory capacity.

Storage media

The various devices used to store the contents of the PC's memory outside the computer. Generally these include disk drives, hard drives, and tape drives.

Subdirectory

Refers to a directory stored within another directory.

System prompt

Characters displayed on the screen, indicating that the computer is ready to receive input from the user.

Target disk

Also called the destination disk. It's the disk that will receive data during the backup procedure. When copying data from one disk to another, the disk being copied is the source disk and the disk receiving data is the target disk.

TCP/IP

Acronym representing **T**ransfer **C**ontrol **P**rotocol/**I**nternet **P**rotocol. The language that computers on the Internet use to communicate with each other.

Track

One of several concentric rings encoded on a disk during the low-level format. The tracks allow the computer to store data at specific locations on the disk. See also Sector.

TSR

An acronym for Terminate-and-Stay-Resident. A program that remains in memory after being loaded.

Glossary

TTL

An acronym for Transistor-to-TransistorLogic. TTL is a digital circuit in which the output is derived from two transistors.

UART

An acronym for Universal Asynchronous Receiver Transmitter. A chip that controls the RS-232 serial port.

Utilities

Programs that either help the programmer program more efficiently, or act as tools for helping the user with disk and file management. For example, some utilities optimize the performance of a hard drive, while others help the user recover deleted or destroyed files.

Vertical refresh rate (vertical scan rate)

The number of fields (on an interlaced display) or frames (on a non-interlaced display) that are displayed in one second. A field or frame covers the entire screen area. This is measured in Hz (cycles per second). It is limited by the monitor and video card (pixel addressabilities and color depths). Modern monitors and video cards provide refresh rates of 60Hz+.

VESA

An acronym representing Video Electronics Standards Association. This group has produced standards for the VLB (Vesa Local Bus), VESA SVGA video modes and standards for minimum screen refresh rates at various pixel addressabilities.

VGA

An acronym representing Video Graphics Array. Supports pixel addressabilities of up to 640x480x16. This is the defacto video standard and consists of a number of video modes. It is still heavily supported by DOS-based applications and games.

Video card

A dedicated piece of hardware which performs graphics operations. Also called a display adapter. Consists of microchips and other electronic components mounted on a PC-board which connects into a slot (ISA, EISA, MCA, VLB or PCI) on the motherboard.

Viewable area

Typically monitors are advertised by the diagonal size of the picture tube in inches. Common sizes are 14", 15", 17", 20"+. However, the amount of the screen that can be seen is usually less. For example, most 17-inch monitors have only a 15.5-inch diagonal area used for display, in part because the actual phosphor area is only about 16-inch due to the glass thickness.

This is partially due to the fact that the monitor's case covers the edge of the tube, and partially because monitor manufacturers want to make you think you're getting a larger display than you are.

Virtual memory

This is a technique that simulates more memory than actually exists and allows the computer to run several programs simultaneously.

VLB

An acronym representing **V**ESA **L**ocal **B**us. This 32 bit bus was originally designed to provide higher bandwidth for video cards than is available with the ISA bus. It is optimized for the 486 CPU and can run at speeds up to 40 MHz with one card on the bus, or up to 33 MHz with two cards on the bus.

The speed of the VLB is dependent, and runs synchronously with, the main system CPU. Some VLB cards are not designed to run faster than 33 MHz, though some mother-boards will clock the bus at up to 50 MHz!

VLB 2.0 has been written, but has not been implemented on many 486 motherboards.

VRAM

An acronym representing Video Random Access Memory. A specialized type of DRAM, VRAM is dual-ported, meaning it can be read from and written to at the same time.

Warm start

The easiest way to return the PC to its original condition is to switch off the power (see Cold start). However, the warm start deletes the contents of memory and restarts the system without reloading the BIOS. This means that the computer doesn't count up its memory capacity, test peripherals, etc. Pressing [Ctrl]+[Alt]+[Del] warm starts the computer.

Whetstone

A benchmark program developed and designed to simulate arithmetic-intensive programs used in scientific computing. The speed at which a system performs floating-point operations often is measured in units of Whetstones.

Write

The process of storing data, usually onto a hard drive or floppy disk drive.

Write protect

Protects disks from accidental formatting or file deletion. Disks can be write-protected by covering the square slot on the left side with a paper sticker (5.25-inch diskettes) or by moving the write protect slider (3.5-inch diskettes). Data can be read from this disk into the memory of the PC, but changes cannot be made on the disk. The disk and its data are protected.

XT

Designation of a PC with a hard drive or a PC capable of running a hard drive.

Y-connector

A Y-shaped splitter cable that divides a source input into two output signals.

Yellow Book

A Y-shaped splitter cable that divides a source input into two output signals.

Appendix F

Timeline

This appendix contains an overview of the important events in the history of the PC.

1971

The 4004 debuts as the first microprocessor. This 4-bit processor, developed by INTEL, contained over 2000 transistors. With a clock frequency of up to 1 MHz, it could perform 60,000 instructions per second.

1972

An 8-bit version, called the 8008, follows the 4004.

1974

The successor to previous microprocessors, called the 8080, is widely used.

1975

Digital Research introduces CP/M, an operating system developed for the 8080. Together with the 8080, this operating system will be the standard for 8-bit computers for many years.

Timeline

1976

The improved 8085 makes its debut. At the same time, the Zilog company introduces the Z80, a processor based on the 8080 that's available at a much lower price.

1977

The Apple II and the Commodore PET lay the foundation for the development of the PC, or home computer. These two computers included the Zilog Z80 or the 6502 from MOS, which was also developed from the 8080.

1978

Intel introduces a 16-bit processor called the 8086 and a numeric processor called the 8087. The high cost of these two products, along with the high cost of 16-bit peripherals, discouraged potential buyers.

1979

Intel introduces the less expensive 8088, which has only an 8-bit data bus, but is compatible to the 8086 in every other respect. At the same time, in an attempt to establish 16-bit technology, Motorola introduces the 68000. Although this processor has a 32-bit register, it is a 16-bit processor in every other way. This processor and its successors were very important in computers manufactured by Apple, Atari and Next.

1981

The IBM PC is born. It's equipped with a 4.7 MHz 8088 processor and 64K RAM. The PC includes MS-DOS 1.0, which consists of three files and some utilities. The operating system must be loaded from a diskette, or it can be booted from ROM-BASIC. The PC has an excellent keyboard and a green monochrome screen that cannot display graphics.

1982

Intel completes development of the 80286. This 16-bit processor, which contains almost 150,000 transistors, can address 16 Meg of RAM with its 24-bit wide address bus. The 80286 is fully compatible to 8088s and has Protected mode, which makes hardware multitasking and even multi-user operation possible.

MS-DOS Version 1.1 now supports double-sided diskettes with a capacity of 360K. Errors in the Basic interpreter have been eliminated.

1983

IBM introduces the XT, which has a 10 Meg hard drive.

MS-DOS 2.0 appears at the same time, with hard drive support and a treelike directory structure. Version 2.11 follows later in the year and is able to display national character sets.

1984

The IBM AT is the first computer to include an 80286 CPU. The AT is a 6 MHz computer with a 20 Meg hard drive and a high density drive with 1.2 Meg capacity.

MS-DOS 3.0, which was introduced at the same time, supports all of these new functions.

1985

MS-DOS Version 3.2 is network capable and now supports 720K 3.5-inch diskettes, even though IBM doesn't yet offer this kind of disk drive.

Appendix

F

Section

4

Timeline

1986

The Intel 80386 is introduced. This new processor has a 32-bit address and data bus, expanded multitasking capacities, and Virtual Real mode, which makes simulation of several (virtual) XTs possible. In the same year, Compaq introduces the first computer with the new CPU, Deskpro 386. However, software products capable of utilizing the features of the 386 aren't available yet.

1987

MS-DOS 3.3 allows the operation of 1.44 Meg 3.5-inch disk drives. By creating an extended partition, you can also run hard drives that are larger than 32 Meg.

1988

IBM departs from the standard created by its own computers and introduces the PS/2 series. Because of the altered bus system, Microchannel, it's no longer possible to use cards for the ISA bus. However, IBM equipped the new computers with a 3.5-inch disk drive at 1.44 Meg capacity. It also set a new standard for graphics cards with the VGA adapter, which is capable of displaying 256 colors simultaneously. This standard is still valid. The top model of the PS/2 series, Model 80, was the first IBM computer to use the 80386 processor.

A new operating system, developed by Microsoft, appears at the same time as the PS/2 series. This operating system is called OS/2, which stands for Operating System 2. It utilizes the capacities of the 286 in Protected mode, enabling genuine multitasking for the first time with full MS-DOS compatibility.

Microsoft introduces MS-DOS Version 4.0, a graphical user interface. MS-DOS 4.0 also supports the creation of DOS partitions larger than 32 Meg, as well as linking expanded memory to 386 systems.

In response to Microchannel, the leading computer manufacturers of the world came out with the EISA bus, a 32-bit slot system compatible to the ISA bus. This system makes it possible to continue using all the old cards.

1989

The Intel 80486 is introduced. This highly integrated processor contains a 386, a 387, and an internal cache controller with 2x4K cache memory. As a result of a fundamental revision of the internal communication structure, the 486 has about 2.5 times the performance of a 386 with a coprocessor.

MS-DOS Version 4.01 has fewer defects than previous versions, but still uses a tremendous amount of memory.

1991

After large-scale testing, MS-DOS 5.0 is introduced. This new version allows swapping of operating system parts and device drivers to extended memory, which frees up as much as 630K of main memory for DOS applications. The significantly improved DOS Shell allows limited multitasking or task switching. The operating system supports 2.88 Meg 3.5-inch disk drives as well as a wide variety of accessory programs, such as a program for recovering accidentally deleted files.

1992

Intel has the i586 processor in development. The new processor is supposed to have genuine RISC architecture and about 2.5 times the performance of the 486. Marketers are trying to make the 486 the standard.

IBM is trying to go its own way on the operating system sector with Version 2.0 of OS/2. This operating system has all the advantages of a real 32 bit operating system for an extremely low price. It also contains a complete DOS and a complete Windows.

1993

Microsoft releases a new Version 6 of DOS. MS-DOS 6 has a powerful help system, offers improved data security, with programs for virus detection, backups and recovery of deleted files.

Timeline

Additional features include automatic data compression, a defragmentation program to reorganize your hard drive and an automatic main memory optimizer. A new hard drive cache (SMARTDRV.EXE) offers improved performance with Windows and compressed hard drives.

IBM also releases OS/2 2.1. Intel announces the DX4 clock tripling processors. In addition, IBM has announced their versions of these 486 processors.

Intel introduces the next generation chip called the Pentium. The Pentium has more functions than previous processors. The 486 chip contains the equivalent of 1.2 million transistors. A Pentium has more than 3 million transistors on board.

Today, everybody's talking about multimedia. Although not a new term, multimedia now involves integrating different applications of entertainment electronics such as video, sound, and graphics.

Many articles and books are currently being written about this subject. After a slow start, PCs (both DOS and Windows) are now "multimedia capable." Previously, only a few complex applications were multimedia capable.

The components deliver information in a variety of ways, but achieve their greatest effectiveness through their interaction. Information, images and sounds are technically and aesthetically integrated, then focused on a single product.

1994

Intel shops two new 100 MHz processors: the Pentium and 486DX4100.

COMPAQ Computer Corporation becomes largest producer of PC computers.

IBM and Eastman Kodak announce agreement to include Kodak Photo CD imaging technology in IBM's new 'personal' OS/2 Warp operating system.

Novell Corporation purchases WordPerfect Corporation.

Microsoft settles 3 year old FTC investigation into unfair trade practices.

Microsoft announces the 1994 debut of Windows 4, code-named Chicago, will ship early 1995.

740

1995

Microsoft announces 'Chicago' is now *Windows 95* and further delays releasing it until August, 1995.

IBM announces it has shipped over 1 million OS/2 Warp V3 operating systems.

Microsoft acquires Intuit, makers of Quicken financial software.

The *Internet* emerges as the hottest topic to date for computer users and non-computer users worldwide. The computer book and software markets bulge with dozens of Internet related products.

PC's continue to drop in price and rise in power. IBM, COMPAQ, DELL, GATEWAY, PACKARD-BELL offer multimedia PCs with a variety of sound cards, CD-ROM drives.

Hard drives continue to drop in price.

CD-ROM drives become available in quadspeed versions; and even portable for PCs.

CompuServe purchases Spry, the producer of Mosaic (a Web Browser). CompuServe opens their Internet gateway for over 2.5 million subscribers.

The Internet continues to grow. World Wide Web (WWW) sites grow by the hundreds each week. Corporations are beginning to use the Internet for commercial purposes. It is estimated that over 30 million users are accessing the "Net".

Several manufacturers begin shipping 6x speed CD-ROM drives. 2x and 4x CD-ROM drive prices plummet.

IBM purchases LOTUS (maker of 1-2-3) for $3.5 Billion dollars.

U.S. Anti-Trust lawyers block Microsoft's purchase of Intuit (maker of Quicken).

Microsoft releases Windows 95, Microsoft Office 95, Windows 95 Plus! August 24 with tremendous fanfare worldwide.

Timeline

1996

8x and 10x and 12x CD-ROM drives become available.

Internet multiplayer games become available.

Apple buys Next but continues to lose market share.

Communication Decency Act passed in the US.

MMX announced

RAM prices continue to plummet.

DVD announced.

All areas of the Web continue to expand.

Index

Index

Index

747

Index

749

Index

Index

Index

Index

Index

Index

Index

PC catalog

Order Toll Free 1-800-451-4319
Books and Software

**Includes CD-ROM
with Sample Programs**

Abacus

Nets and Intranets With Win95
Getting Connected

Windows 95 has a surprisingly rich set of networking capabilities. Built-in networking delivers an affordable and easy way to connect with others and benefit by sharing resources—files, printers, and peripherals. Network sharing saves you and your organization time and money and adds convenience.

Another great benefit of Windows 95 Networking is its ability to let you run an Intranet. This book and companion CD-ROM has all the pieces that you'll need to set up your own internal World Wide Web server (Intranet) without the expense of using an outside Internet Service Provider.

**CD-ROM
Included**

- A practical hands-on guide for setting up a small network or Intranet using Win95 or Windows for Workgroups 3.11.

- Take advantage of Windows 95's built in options so you can immediately use its networking features—

  - Shared printers
  - Easy-to-use groupware
  - E-mail and faxes
  - Additional hard drive capacity
  - Centralized backups
  - TCP/IP

- Step-by-step guide to getting and staying connected whether you're in a small office, part of a workgroup, or connecting from home.

- Perfect for the company wanting to get connected and share information with employees inexpensively

Author: H.D. Radke
Item #: B311
ISBN: 1-55755-31-4
SRP: $39.95 US/54.95 CAN
     with CD-ROM

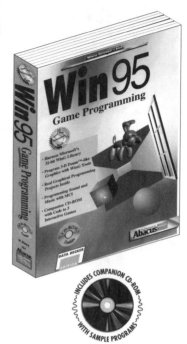

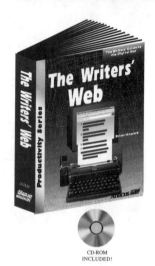

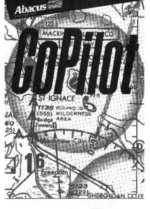

SOFTWARE

Airport & Scenery Designer

Until now, airport and scenery design has been strictly for technical types, who were able to understand the cryptic codes and internal structure of Flight Simulator. *Airport & Scenery Designer*'s unique visual approach hides the complexities and lets users create new places to fly - easily and quickly. The *ASD Wizard* component lets beginners (or even old hands) pop out new scenery designs in a flash. *Want a new airport?* Just click to load a map and point to the place where you'll break ground. ASD asks for the length and orientation and *zap*, the runway is there!
Need lighting and taxiways? A few clicks and you have your choice of types and styles. *How about a few buildings?* No problem; just drag and drop.

These features make *ASD* a standout Flight Sim add-on:
* Creates scenery for FS5.1 and FS6.0 (FS95).
* *ASD Wizard* lets you create "instant", customizable sceneries in only 4 mouse clicks!
* Complete airport design package - easily add runways, lighting, ILS and markers, taxiways and buildings.
* Extensive set of U.S. maps including roads, highways, rivers, lakes, cities and names - let
  you pinpoint any geographic area in which you wish to work.
* Set of detailed global coastline maps let you build scenery around the world.
* Include or exclude any of the original FS airports and navigation aids in new designs.
* Instantly create new navigation aids - VORs and NDBs.
* Design large scenery areas by visually selecting and placing synthetic tiles.
* Easily add authentic mountains and realistic lakes to your scenery.
* Adjust scenery textures for different seasons.
* Choose from a large library of pre-designed objects - ships, storage tanks, water towers.

**CD-ROM
INCLUDED!**

Whether you want to duplicate the exacting landmarks of your home town or create your own new flyer's fantasy land, *Airport & Scenery Designer* will get you there.

Publisher: Abacus
Order Item #B331
ISBN: 1-55755-331-9

Suggested Retail Price
$49.95 US/$54.95 CAN
CD-ROM Included

To order direct call Toll Free 1-800-451-4319

In US & Canada Add $5.00 Shipping and Handling
Foreign Orders Add $13.00 per item. Michigan residents add 6% sales tax.

Visit our website at www.abacuspub.com

Windows 3.11 and Windows for Workgroups 3.11

Windows users type:

MENU `Enter`

Windows 95

The CD-ROM will automatically run for Windows 95 users when the 'autorun' option is on. Alternatively, you can just run the MENU program mentioned above.

Many of the programs included on the companion CD-ROM are fully functioning 'shareware evaluation versions' of the best programs available today. The shareware concept allows small software companies and program authors to introduce the application programs they have developed to a wider audience.

See Chapter 1 and Chapter 16 for complete information on installing and using the companion CD-ROM

A SPECIAL NOTE ON SHAREWARE, FREEWARE AND PUBLIC DOMAIN SOFTWARE

Because shareware is copyrighted, the authors ask for payment if you use their program(s). You may try out the program for a limited time, typically 10 to 30 days, and then decide whether you want to keep it. If you continue to use it, you're requested to send the author a nominal fee. Registration involves paying registration fees, which make you a licensed user of the program.

Check the documentation or the program itself for the amount of registration fee and the address where you send the registration form. Shareware benefits both the user and the author as it allows prices to remain low by avoiding distribution, packaging, and advertising costs.

You'll find program instructions as well as notes on registration for the shareware programs in special text files located in the program directory of each program. You can also see a more complete description in Chapter 15.

Thanks again from the Abacus Editorial and Technical Review Staffs

Windows 95 is a trademark of Microsoft Corp.

The Companion CD-ROM

Thank you for purchasing *Upgrading & Maintaining Your PC*. We hope this book will be an indispensable reference guide to upgrading your PC. The companion CD-ROM contains dozens of practical utilities for checking system info, determining cache benchmarks, finding files and much more.

The following table lists the files you'll find on the Companion CD-ROM root directory:

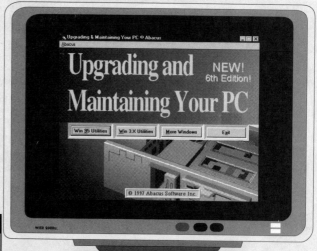

File name	Explanation
ACROREAD EXE	Adobe's Award Winning Portable Document Reader.
BOOKFILE PDF	Requires AcroRead-Load this file to view book.
CD_DIR TXT	Complete text file describing the programs
MAINFILE PDF	The main file for viewing the contents of book.
README TXT	This file.
THREED VBX	Required file.
VBRUN300 DLL	Required file.
WRKSHEET PDF	Print these worksheets using Acrobat Reader.

See Chapter 1 and Chapter 16 for complete information on installing and using the companion CD-ROM

Why use these programs? Perhaps you're uncertain what type of equipment your computer contains. Maybe a friend just bought a computer and they have no idea what the new PC has "under the hood." You can experiment with using the various utilities and diagnostic programs. You can install them from the companion CD-ROM or copy them to a new directory on your hard drive and then run them. The programs are shareware or evaluation programs (or both) written and copyrighted by the authors and companies. Please register the programs you use with the respective author.

The companion CD-ROM can be installed using DOS, Windows 3.11 and Windows for Workgroups 3.11 or Windows 95. See Chapter 1 and Chapter 16 for complete installation instructions. The directories included on the companion CD-ROM are in the file called CD_DIR.TXT. You can print or view this file.